THE VOLKSBÜHNE MOVEMENT

Contemporary Theatre Studies
A series of books edited by Franc Chamberlain, Nene University College
Northampton, UK

Please see the back of this book for other titles in the Contemporary Theatre
Studies series

THE VOLKSBÜHNE MOVEMENT

A History

Cecil Davies

harwood academic publishers
Australia • Canada • France • Germany • India
Japan • Luxembourg • Malaysia • The Netherlands
Russia • Singapore • Switzerland

First published by Manchester University Press and University of Texas Press in 1977 under the title *Theatre for the People*.
Second edition copyright © 2000 by OPA (Overseas Publishers Association) N. V. Published by license under the Harwood Academic Publishers imprint, part of The Gordon and Breach Publishing Group.

Amsteldijk 166
1st Floor
1079 LH Amsterdam
The Netherlands

British Library Cataloguing in Publication Data

Davies, Cecil W. (Cecil William), 1918 –
    The Volksbühne Movement: a history. – 2nd ed. –
    (Contemporary theatre studies; v. 33)
    1. Theatre – Germany – History   2. Theatre and society – Germany
    I. Title   II. Theatre for the people
    792′.0943

    ISBN 90-5755-089-X

Cover illustration: Exterior of the Volksbühne on the Luxemburgplatz in 1975.
Photo: Cecil Davies.

CONTENTS

INTRODUCTION TO THE SERIES

Contemporary Theatre Studies is a book series of special interest to everyone involved in theatre. It consists of monographs on influential figures, studies of movements and ideas in theatre, as well as primary material consisting of theatre-related documents, performing editions of plays in English, and English translations of plays from various vital theatre traditions worldwide

Franc Chamberlain

ACKNOWLEDGEMENTS

This book could not have been written or brought up to date without the active help of many individuals and institutions. To all I wish to extend my thanks, and in particular to: Professor George Wedell, who originally proposed the subject to me; the late Gerhard Schmid, Geschäftsführer of the Bund der deutschen Volksbühnen-Vereine, who guided me through the intricacies of the movement and enabled me to make contact with countless officials and members of Volksbühne Associations; the late Professor Walther G. Oschilewski; the late Professor D.Phil. Jürgen-Dieter Waidelich; Herr Franz-Heinz Köhler, Vorsitzender des Bundes deutscher Volksbühnen e.V. (1994–6); Frau Erika Müller-Scheffler, Bundesverband der deutschen Volksbühnen-Vereine; Herr Wolfgang Meisen; Dr Ruth Freydank, Vorsitzende, Freie Volksbühne Berlin; Dr Dieter Hadamczik; Dr Gotthard Welzel, Bund der Theatergemeinde; Frau Roswitha Kleinwächter, Bund der Theatergemeinde; the Senatsverwaltung für Kulturelle Angelegenheiten, Berlin; all the officers of Volksbühne Associations who answered my questionnaire of 1994; the library staff of the Goethe Institute, Manchester; the library staff of the John Rylands Library of the University of Manchester; my ever-helpful editors at Harwood Academic Publishers; and my wife, Marian, for her support, especially during the preparation of this new edition.

I am grateful to Stapp Verlag, Berlin, for allowing me to reproduce illustrations from their publication *Freie Volksbühne Berlin*, 1965.

LIST OF PLATES

Even if he is not very observant, the traveller who comes from the east and enters Berlin at night sees a strange picture. The weary engine moves painfully over the railway track which ploughs like a furrow through the midst of the mighty city, and somewhere, far outside, comes to an end on lifeless lines. The cosmopolis hammers at the stranger with merciless blows. First it destroys an illusion – on this short journey it does not shine in its Sunday best: it lays all its features bare: floods of light alternate with murky terraced streets; interminably empty black walls lead to the overhead railway; the eye takes a long, endless, sobering look at eternally identical rows of windows, yards, alleys and dark canyon-like streets. Thus the monster, Berlin, offers its visiting card: impersonal, factual, busy, almost cynical and brutal. But suddenly a sharp gap opens to the observer for a few seconds in the black walls; in huge illuminated letters a word shines out like magic, only to sink again into the grey of the grey walls. What was it? – Volksbühne? – Yes. Somewhere the great building of the Theatre on the Bülowplatz breaks into a scarcely cheerful row of houses in the busiest part of the capital. In flaming letters of light it stamps one word upon the dark night of its surroundings, the word that, over the years one might say was transformed from a proper noun to the concept of Culture.

When this shining beacon in 'Berlin C' is extinguished and the bright day dawns, the other inscription on that great building becomes visible, like an answer. It reads: Art for the People.

Albert Brodbeck, 1930 [1]

PREFACE

The Volksbühne movement is Germany's unique contribution to the history of the theatre and its audience. It is arguable that it could not have arisen in any other country, and certainly attempts to transplant it have never met with more than partial success. The tradition of theatre as a moral institution with an educational function, running from Lessing through Schiller and Hauptmann to Brecht, is its foundation. Because of this tradition nineteenth-century German working-class movements could naturally and unselfconsciously use drama as a medium for social education and propaganda, and could regard the Naturalism of Ibsen and Hauptmann as organically related to the aims of social revolution. A comparable movement in England led to the founding of the Workers' Educational Association: evening classes were an appropriate expression of working-class aspirations; theatre was not.

The Volksbühne could also only grow in a country where regular rather than occasional theatre attendance was regarded as normal. In England the nearest parallel is perhaps the regular cinema-going of the 1920s and 1930s; but a German movement that offered its members not only the most significant plays, but offered them on a regular monthly basis, could gain thousands of members in pre-1914 Berlin, and develop into a mass movement in the politically more favourable climate of the Weimar Republic.

Such a movement is bound to be the object of attacks, and the Volksbühne has been attacked throughout its existence – from the right, because of its Social Democratic associations; from the left, because it has never subordinated the human values of art to party political aims; from theatre directors who have believed that the Volksbühne inhibits experiment and from dissatisfied members who thought it offered too many serious or experimental plays. It has been attacked by commercial interests who saw it as a competitor, and by politicians and taxpayers who have resented subsidies its theatres have received. Some accuse it of being a mere cheap ticket organisation, a theatrical soup-kitchen; others of diverting the theatre to political ends. The Nazis dissolved it and burnt most of its records; the Communists of East Germany tried to bend it to their purposes – and eventually also dissolved it.

When *Theatre for the People*, then sub-titled *The Story of the Volksbühne*, was published by Manchester University Press and the University of Texas Press in 1977, the publishers required on economic grounds that the book should concentrate on the Volksbühne in Berlin and that the development of the movement outside that city should be outlined only very briefly. Happily

xiv

the publishers of this new edition, now more appropriately titled *The Volksbühne Movement: A History*, have asked for a full treatment of the subject. A section has therefore been added on the nationwide development of the movement in the Weimar Republic, flesh has been added to the sometimes skeletal material of the earlier edition, and the history has been continued up to 1998. As a result the new edition gives a much truer picture of the movement as a whole than did that of 1977.

1. Dr Bruno Wille (1860–1928), founder of the Volksbühne movement.

PROLOGUE

BEFORE 1890:
THE PREHISTORY OF THE VOLKSBÜHNE

Founded in 1890, the Freie Volksbühne was the first of the audience organisations that have been a characteristic feature of German theatre-going. It was a child of its time, born of a marriage between political and artistic movements, socialism and naturalism.

Bruno Wille's announcement and appeal for support for the new body, published in Berlin on 23 March 1890, began:

> The Theatre should he a source of high artistic gratification, moral uplift and a powerful stimulus to thinking about the great topics of the day. But it is debased to the level of drawing-room wit, society small-talk and penny-dreadfuls, the circus and comic papers. The stage is subjugated to capitalism, and the taste of the masses of all ranks of society has been corrupted primarily by certain economic conditions.
>
> Nevertheless, under the influence of sincerely struggling poets, journalists and speakers, a section of our people has freed itself from this corruption. Writers like Tolstoy and Dostoyevsky, Zola, Ibsen and Kielland as well as a number of German 'Realists' have found a sounding-board in the working people of Berlin. [2]

To understand how Wille's appeal came to be couched in such terms, and why it met with an enthusiastic response one must try to appreciate the political, social and cultural context in which it was written and read.

In the mid nineteenth century over two-thirds of the population of Germany was rural. In the following sixty years (to 1910), while the population as a whole did not quite double itself, the urban population quadrupled. The Silesian weavers whose abortive revolt in 1844 was the subject of Hauptmann's *Die Weber* (*The Weavers*), were handloom workers in a cottage industry; by the time the play was written (1891) there were over 150,000 factory workers in Berlin alone. During the same period Germany was transformed from a politically impotent group of states to a powerful Empire dominated by Bismarck under the hegemony of Prussia. But this 'united' Germany was socially divided, and the rapidly expanding urban proletariat developed into a political and social power that even Bismarck was unable to check.

1

The political and economic aspirations of the new working classs were expressed through the movement known as Social Democracy. Before 1848 it was extremely difficult for the workers to achieve any political organisation at all. Nevertheless, even as early as 1834 German emigrés founded in Paris a 'League of Outlaws' (Bund der Geächteten). Four years later came a similar body, more firmly grounded in the working class, the 'League of the Just' (Bund der Gerechten). At the beginning of 1846, Marx and Engels founded a 'Communist Correspondence Committee' (Kommunistische Korrespondenzkomitee) in Brussels; then, prompted by the London section of the League of the Just, they founded in 1847 the League of Communists (Bund der Kommunisten), the first revolutionary workers' party, and in February 1848 issued the Communist Manifesto.

The principal founder of the German Social Democratic Movement in Germany itself, however, was not Marx or Engels – exiles in England, whose names were known to comparatively few German workers – but Ferdinand Lassalle, a child prodigy, son of a Jewish silk merchant. Born in Breslau in 1825, Lassalle was intended for commerce but after a year at the Trade School in Leipzig (1840-41) he changed course, studying in Breslau and Berlin, visiting Paris and becoming a convinced Hegelian. He published a number of books and pamphlets of which the most important and scholarly, the *System of Acquired Rights* (1861), anticipated some of the basic ideas of Marx's *Capital* (1867). In 1862 he became a political agitator among the German workers, advocating a system of state socialism in his working-class programme. In May 1863 in Leipzig he founded the General German Workers' Association (Allgemeiner Deutscher Arbeiterverein: ADAV) which he led dictatorially, a fact which naturally had a detrimental effect on its politics and internal democracy. Lassalle was killed in a duel in Switzerland on the last day of August 1864. Almost religiously honoured by his followers, a *bon vivant* of social democracy, he was an opportunist who had gone so far as to offer Bismarck his support in smashing the Prussian Constitution if Bismarck in return curbed the power of the capitalists and provided measures of social security: Bismarck was not impressed, remarking, 'What could the wretched man offer me?'

Lassalle's ADAV had a wide basis upon which to work. In the late fifties, especially after the economic crisis of 1857, workers' associations multiplied rapidly and by 1860 there were over eight hundred workers' associations and workers' educational associations in Germany. In fact a majority of these held aloof from the ADAV and formed themselves a few weeks after its foundation into the Union of German Workers' Associations (Verband – originally Vereinstag – der deutschen Arbeitervereine: VDAV) under liberal middle-class leadership. In 1868 the middle-class elements were forced into resignation and in 1869 at Eisenach the remaining members and member bodies joined with opposition members of the ADAV and the German section of the International Working Men's Association (Internationale Arbeiterassoziation), led by Marx and Engels, to form the Social Democratic Workers' Party (Sozialdemokratische Arbeiterpartei), which thus became the first revolutionary and primarily Marxist party in Germany.

In article II, paragraph 6 of its constitution the new party declared:

> Taking into consideration that the liberation of labour is neither a local nor a national but a social problem, which comprehends all countries in which modern Society exists, the Social Democratic Workers' Party regards itself, as far as the laws covering associations permit, as a branch of the International Working Men's Association [First International] identifying itself with its endeavours. [3]

In thus declaring an international loyalty to class before loyalty to State the party was challenging conservative and national forces. [4] Its programme, too, was likely to disturb Bismarck. It included demands for adult male suffrage, direct legislation 'through the people', separation of Church and State, school and Church, compulsory free education. The economic collapse (1873) with widespread unemployment and lowering of wages that followed the temporary war boom of 1870-71 seemed to confirm Marxist theory in practice. The party grew. It was indeed the first German political party to develop a real party organisation, and towards the end of the seventies its membership had reached half a million. Bismarck, who understood no policy in such a situation except suppression, brought his proposed anti-socialist legislation before the Reichstag in May 1878. It was thrown out; but after the July elections in which the Conservatives gained seats, the anti-socialist law (Sozialistengesetz) was passed in September. The passing of this law (which was renewed until 1890) was the most important event in the development of German Social Democracy. Theoretically it should have resulted in the elimination of the Social Democratic Party, which it declared illegal. This celebrated – or notorious – law was actually called:

> Law against activities of social-democracy which constitute a public danger.

Its first clause – which was the keynote of the whole law – reads:

> §1. Associations which aim to overturn the existing order of the State or society through social-democratic, socialist or communist activities, are prohibited.
>
> This also applies to associations in which social-democratic, socialist or communist activities come to light which are aimed at

overturning the existing order of the State or society in a manner
which endangers public peace, especially harmony between the
classes of the population.

Societies of every kind are regarded as "Associations".

Many leading social democrats were expelled from the capital, party
property was seized and its press suppressed. Yet,

> Bismarck treated the Social Democrats in a curiously old-fashioned,
> high-principled way. Men are bound by their generation, and
> Bismarck, despite his Realpolitlk, had much more resemblance to
> Gladstone than to Hitler ... this persecution bore the unmistakable
> stamp of the liberal era; Social Democrats were still allowed to be
> candidates at the elections and to sit in the Reichstag; the number of
> members of the party increased steadily, and in all about 1,500
> persons were imprisoned (an average of a little over a hundred a
> year). [5]

In fact, there was just enough persecution to stimulate growth and the
development of a good, tight, organisation; the Social Democratic vote
doubled in twelve years. By 1890 the Social Democratic Party was the
strongest in Berlin. Far from weakening its stance during the period of
illegality the party had adopted a more distinctly Marxist position.

To evade the anti-socialist law, and at the same time to collect money to
help those suffering under it, many societies whose true intentions were
kept secret were founded upon various pretexts. They multiplied
particularly in the last years of the anti-socialist law. Their names were
harmless-sounding, often absurd. The Camel Club, Goblin's Grotto, Miller
and Mayor, Sowtooth, Blue Onion, Old Aunt. Many were, or claimed to be,
literary or debating societies. Some indeed, changed in character, and the
interest in literature which had been a mask became a reality, for the
legislation that prevented the workers from organising themselves
politically also prevented their cultural and educational development. The
motives that led the workers to want culture and education were mixed.
On the one hand culture was seen as bourgeois privilege of which the worker
was deprived; on the other hand education was seen as an instrument for
promoting the idea of socialism. In any case, the cultural and educational
aspects were as old as the movement itself. As we have already seen, many
of the workers' associations that went to form the Social Democratic Party
were themselves educational. The importance of drama, too, had been
recognised from the very beginning. Engels himself hastily wrote a one-act
play (now lost) for a festival of the Brussels German Workers' Association
(Brüsseler Deutscher Arbeiterverein) in 1847. Its subject was malad-
ministration in a small German State and the downfall of the prince through

a popular revolution. It was rehearsed in a few days and performed by members of the Workers' Association and their supporters. Lassalle too, in 1856-58, wrote a tragedy, *Franz von Sickingen*. Its subject was the Peasants' Revolt – for Lassalle, in common with many others, saw parallels between its failure and that of the March Revolution. Lassalle saw in each a 'tragic collision' between the 'Idea' and the 'necessity for compromise', between 'revolutionary ends' and 'diplomatic means'. He considered that false revolutionary tactics had brought about failure, both in the Peasants' Revolt and in 1848-49. After its publication in 1859 Lassalle sent copies with long covering letters explaining his tragic idea to Marx and Engels, both of whom answered him at length with keen but friendly criticism. It is true that when Lassalle wrote again to Marx countering his criticisms, Marx's only reaction was in a short letter to Engels: 'Incredible, that a man at this time and in these circumstances of world history not only finds time to write such stuff, but demands our time to read it.' [6] But the fact remains that for Lassalle, Marx and Engels a play could be relevant to the political struggle in which they were engaged.

An historical play such as *Franz von Sickingen* was, however, not typical of the drama of the social democratic movement. The plays performed by the workers' groups on small, often improvised stages were not plays, like Goethe's *Götz von Berlichingen* and Schiller's *Die Räuber* (*The Robbers*), in which exceptional individuals help the poor from outside. The great individual had no place in them. The new Socialist hero grew out of the collective idea; the message was the power of solidarity; and the joy of acting was inseparable from the will to reveal the class struggle. The plays took many forms and included much comedy and satire. During the sixties there were all kinds of one-act agitation pieces, election farces, festival items, *tableaux vivants*, and full-length plays, especially strike-plays. Whatever the form and however amateur the players, the workers' theatre dealt with the great social and national questions whose solution was necessary to the workers' well-being. Had the middle and upper classes known what was going on in the workers' clubs the opposition would have been as strong as it later was to Hauptmann's *Die Weber*. And in some ways the performances in these clubs anticipated the naturalist movement.

Just as the workers' clubs themselves had to hide under innocuous names under the anti-socialist law (1878-90) so too the revolutionary plays had to be disguised. No longer was the hero's name Roth (Red), Fels (Rock), Stein (Stone), or Frei (Free). During these twelve years historical subjects in which, as in Lassalle's play, parallels could be seen with contemporary events, but which at the same time might avoid the attentions of the police did become typical. [7] Nor did the socialist amateurs confine themselves to propagandist plays. A few of the groups, if they were good enough, played classics, but on the whole the rest of the material was 'harmless rubbish'. It is a great mistake to idealise the nineteenth-century German workers. On the whole they preferred popular farces to Ibsen and Zola.

The German stage generally was suffering in the eighties from a feeling of stagnation, and the most lively and progressive movements in production and in dramatic writing were failing to penetrate the official theatres. Yet in this period, before cinema and radio existed and before sport had become mass entertainment, the theatre was at the centre of interest in matters of entertainment and 'improvement'. In the seventies there had been considerable theatrical success, and the opening of the Bayreuth Opera in 1876 had induced a feeling that a new era was about to begin. Therefore there was in the late seventies and the eighties a multiplication of theatrical enterprises in the capital. Alongside the two 'Royal' theatres a whole circle of others competed for the public. The reputation of the Deutsches Theater founded by Adolf L'Arronge in 1883 was very high, perhaps even higher than that of the Royal Theatres. In 1888 Oscar Blumenthal founded the Lessing Theater and in 1889 Ludwig Barnay created the Berliner Theater out of an operetta-house. It was thought of as a People's Theatre when founded and its prices were somewhat lower than most, though its audience was still middle-class, not working-class. There were also the Wallner Theater, the Residenz Theater, the Belle-Alliance Theater, the Zentral Theater and the Ostend Theater. But still a lack of life was felt. To the political censorship, which banned plays dealing with social problems, hunger, poverty and so on, was added the self-censorship of the theatre managements who, in a city of timid critics and a thoughtless public, put business before art in order to assure themselves of a regular audience. The repertoire consisted largely of Scribe, Sardou, Dumas fils, and the endless legion of well-meaning but powerless descendants of Schiller. There was no place for the real modern drama. Problems were avoided and theatres concentrated upon cheap effects, circus-like comic situations and showy settings. A high subsidy granted to the Königliches Schauspielhaus specifically for productions involving financial risk was used for productions involving none. Bruno Wille's castigation of the theatre as 'debased to the level of drawing-room wit, society small-talk and penny dreadfuls' and at the same time enslaved to economic conditions was fully justified. Even this theatre, for what it was worth as entertainment, was largely inaccessible to the working classes. The ten-hour working day was normal, and the battle against the twelve-hour day not completely won, but the theatre performances started at 7.30 p.m. or even earlier. The prices of most seats were beyond the means of men earning an average wage of 20 to 25 Marks per week. Though most theatres had a gallery at 1 Mark or 75 Pfennigs per seat, even this was high to working men, many of whom also felt humiliated at being segregated at a separate entrance from the well-heeled majority in the theatre.

Thus the deep divisions in German society were reflected in the theatre. Schiller had said, 'Wir Deutsche sind noch keine Nation' (We Germans are still not a nation) and the English historian Buckle said in his *History of Civilisation in England* (1857-61): 'There is no nation in Europe in which there is so great a distance between the highest and lowest minds' (*sc.* as in Germany). These divisions remained after the founding of the Empire in 1871 and were still there in 1890. In the theatre their existence was partly the cause and partly the effect of the non-existence of a national theatre and because there was no national theatre attempts were made throughout the nineteenth century to introduce the working class into the theatre. Such plans for reform were always linked with a political party, a profession or a specific world-view, and the distinction was always drawn between theatre as entertainment and theatre as education. Naturally, in the first half of the nineteenth century the phrase 'working class' only meant the lower middle classes (die kleinen Bürger), the so-called Third Estate, not the true proletariat, the Fourth Estate, which developed in the second half of the century.

Das vierte Stand was rootless and totally without traditions. Whereas even the poorest farm-labourer felt the security of long-established customs and the centuries-old validity of the ecclestiastical year, the proletariat lived in a world of perpetual change, somewhere between the peasants and the bourgeoisie. Even their places of work, their dwellings, their neighbours, were constantly changing.

In 1848 Landenberg, a government minister, introduced a National Theatre Law with the support of the Ministry of Culture. This led to many ideas for 'underprivileged' and 'educational' theatre. But Landenberg died and the idea was lost. In 1859 a petition was presented in Berlin for concessionary cheap seats for workers. 'For a really small admission charge, to present carefully rehearsed classical and improving dramas, and thus to counteract the trivial-obscene tendency in the people'. [8] The petition was refused. The Oberpräsidium thought the people did not need theatre, and the Minister of the Interior, Count Schwerin, thought it wrong to encourage the workers' 'passion for pleasure' (*Vergnügungssucht*). Yet Schwerin himself authorised three new 'Possentheater' !

As the working-class movement grew some conservatives saw that theatre-going was part of the workers' standard of living. Theatre then became a factor in social politics. It was thought that access to the theatre would stop the workers thinking about socialism – a secular 'opium of the people'. Let the workers be given a share in the culture of the higher classes and they will seek to alter but not to destroy it. From interested motives some theatre managers hoped to improve the state of the theatre by getting the poor as additional audience.

Other reformers were disinterested. Some idealists wanted a revival of the ancients as a 'sublime example'; they wanted large theatres, cheap seats and material suitable to the mass of the people, so as to re-establish the ancient ideal of theatre. Even the Church expressed the view that theatre was good for the cultural development of the people, and an anonymous essay of 1890 under the title 'Theatre and Church' claimed that the Church was not opposed to the theatre.

More practical was the action of Botho von Hülsen, Intendant of the Königliches Theater, who in the late seventies halved his prices, partly to get over the bad months of the year, partly to make theatre-going possible to a broader mass of the people. The policy proved to be good business and the theatre was sold out every evening instead of being badly attended. It is a mystery why this experiment did not develop further. Even this wider audience, however, was lower-middle-class, not working-class.

In 1886 a new Director of the Ostend (East End) Theater, Kurz, tried to establish a people's theatre with a 'literary programme'. He gave over a hundred performances of *Das Neue Gebot (The New Commandment)* by Ernst von Wildenbruch. [9] It is difficult today to understand why this wordy, rhetorical polemic against celibacy by an author whose patriotism was to him a religion and whose historical dramas had only superficial parallels with contemporary Germany should have been chosen for this, as it proved, unsuccessful experiment. The audience for the literary programme came to the Ostend Theater from Berlin's West End. Like the workers, they preferred new plays to classics. Under a new director the theatre went in for spectacular 'Possen' with song and dance, and then the audience came once more from the working-class districts. In 1888 Witte-Wild tried a similar experiment in the same theatre, but could not hold out for long. He was also involved in the following year with the schemes of Baron von Malzahn. In May 1889 Baron von Malzahn delivered a speech in Berlin, 'The Founding of a German People's Theatre, a national task', which was also published as a pamphlet. Though much of it was platitude the speech contained definite proposals for an experiment that involved constructing theatres using, for cheapness, iron, not stone, as building material. The first theatre was to be in Berlin. On the basis of this speech an attempt was made to found an Association for the Founding of People's Theatres (Verein zur Begründung von Volksbühnen). The matter was discussed with Ludwig Barnay, Director of the Berliner Theater and a General Meeting was held in October 1889 at which plans for a theatre seating three thousand were advanced. But nothing came of it. The plan failed partly through lack of resources, partly through the lack of any inherent *idea* that might have interested wider circles and attracted a membership.

In March 1890 an economist, Georg Adler, published an article, later reprinted in the *Berliner Neueste Nachricht*, opposing the building of People's Theatres as impracticable. They would need too much subsidy to raise through collections, and State help was unlikely. He proposed instead that the 'Court' theatres should, as a condition of their subsidy, have to put on a workers' performance once every eight days at which seats in the stalls would cost 50 Pfennigs, the circle less. Tickets were to be sold through the Workmen's Sick Pay Office and the plays were to be taken from the existing repertoire. There was little response: from the Kaiser, none. [10]

All these schemes failed because their founders did not themselves belong to the working people. As Otto Neumann-Hofer wrote in September 1890:

> Are educated people in a position to create a workers' theatre? They may try. They will raise the money – no worker will go to the theatre.... The 'People' has confidence only in its own creation. [11]

The people would not be patronised, he went on. It must not be a question of 'spreading education' or 'teaching the ability to appreciate', but of sharing one's own artistic life. The attempt to found a people's theatre must come from the people themselves. In the end it did so, but in a very particular way.

The most important movements in the European theatre and drama of the eighties were those which are usually grouped under the broad heading of Naturalism. The seventies saw a great development in the German-speaking theatre of a meticulous historical accuracy in externals derived from Charles Kean's productions at the Princess Theatre, London, adopted by German directors. From our point of view this fashion would not have been of particular importance – and was in fact attacked by many young Naturalists - had it not also been associated with the Meiningen Court Theatre (Herzoglich-Meiningensches Hoftheater), the creation of the Duke George II of Saxe-Meiningen, his actress wife and his Director Ludwig Chronegk which through its tours between 1874 and 1890, extending from New York to Moscow, exercised an extraordinary influence upon theatrical production. The repertoire of the company was primarily serious and classical. As contemporary plays Ibsen's *The Pretenders* and *Ghosts* were exceptions and their most popular productions were *Julius Caesar* and *The Winter's Tale*, with German classics such as Schiller and Kleist. But the style of the Meiningen company, with its attention to detail and its use of ensemble playing instead of star acting, provided the ideal medium for the production of the new naturalist drama in which ordinary men and women are often represented as products of their environment and whose actions are both interdependent and dependent upon external and social forces. In France, André Antoine, who founded the Théâtre Libre in 1887 for the performance of naturalistic drama, was partly influenced in his style by the Meiningen Players. In Germany it was Otto Brahm who applied what he learnt from Chronegk to the production of the new naturalistic drama.

1878, the year of the anti-socialist law, may also be regarded as the birth year of the naturalistic movement in German literature. [12] In that year

Ibsen's *Pillars of Society* was given its first performance in Germany, and, coincidentally, the first of many journals associated with the brothers Heinrich and Julius Hart, the *Deutsche Monatsblätter*, appeared. Ibsen did not immediately have a striking influence upon the German Naturalists, whose model at first was Zola, and it was nearly a decade later, in 1887, that the performance of *Ghosts* in Germany firmly established his supremacy. Meanwhile many of the greatest European plays of the naturalist movement were written: Ibsen's *A Doll's House* (*Nora* in Germany), *Ghosts*, *An Enemy of the People*, *The Wild Duck* and *Rosmersholme*; Strindberg's *The Father*; Tolstoy's *Power of Darkness*. Of these only *Nora* had a German production (1880) during that period though at the same time the most influential critics, first the Hart brothers, later and even more importantly Otto Brahm, were declaring these to be the most significant contemporary plays.

Brahm and his friend Paul Schlenther together saw the 1878 production of *Pillars of Society*. In retrospect this seemed to Brahm to mark the beginning of his enthusiasm for Ibsen. Writing in 1904, he said:

> The first powerful theatrical impression which I experienced when I began to look at the world, the world of the theatre, with my own eyes, and which passionately involved my interest, – the first powerful impression of the production of a living dramatist came to me through Henrik Ibsen . . . [after a reference to 1878] . . . . From that hour we adhered to the new naturalistic art, and our aesthetic life had welcomed its content. [13]

Schlenther's recollection was different:

> When we first saw the *Pillars of Society* in Berlin in 1878, Brahm saw in this pioneering work not much more than in Björnson's *Bankruptcy*. When afterwards we discussed the performance we had experienced together, while I stressed the novelty of the piece, Brahm criticised its weakness, which today, spoilt by Ibsen himself, everyone sees.

In an unpleasantly snobbish reference to Brahm's early career in a bank, he added: 'To the man who had escaped from being a counter-clerk, a knight's boot was still considered more poetic than a cheque book'. [14] Even concerning *A Doll's House* in 1883, says Schlenther, Brahm expressed himself with reservations. Whichever memory is correct concerning *Pillars of Society* and *A Doll's House*, from the time that Brahm read *Ghosts* in 1884 he became the German apostle of Ibsen, and in the following years campaigned for him to be performed. His work was eventually rewarded. In 1886 there were two private performances of *Ghosts*, one in Augsburg on 14 April, described because of censorship problems as a 'dress rehearsal in camera for invited guests', and one on 22 December at the Meiningen Court Theatre. Then, less than a month later on 9 January 1887, the police permitted a single performance of the play at the Residenz Theater, Berlin. Brahm wrote this up enthusiastically in the *Frankfurter Zeitung*, and in *Die Nation*, perceptively comparing its effect with that of Sophocles' *Oedipus Rex*. He also used the occasion to announce an aesthetic creed:

> In the whole wide world, among people and things, I see nothing, absolutely nothing, which cannot be submitted to artistic treatment: Everything lies there, openly and freely, the poet has only to lay hold upon it, unhindered by any barrier of theory. It is not the 'what' that is decisive but only the 'how'. [15]

This is very far from the counter-clerk's scorn of the cheque book. The 1887 Ibsen performance was followed by others; *An Enemy of the People* and *Rosmersholme* (1887); *The Wild Duck, Lady Inger* and *A Doll's House* (1888); *The Lady from the Sea, Pillars of Society* and *Ghosts* (again only one performance) (1889). A Berlin Ibsen Society was formed which provided an enthusiastic nucleus of the audiences. The time was ripe for the establishment of Brahm's own theatre society: the Freie Bühne.

Although the dramatic groups within the Social Democratic party did not perform the plays of the naturalistic school, the position was different within the reading and discussion clubs. Here the works of the Naturalists were read and discussed avidly. The members were excited by the expressions of Darwinism and Determinism in works of art. In this art they saw a genuine attempt to show life 'as it really is' both in matter and in manner. They saw this new 'real' art as something set against the unreality of bourgeois art. Its themes, if not socialist, were strongly social and were closely related to the theories of the influence of environment and of historical materialism which were the mode of thought of the Marxist left. Ignoring, or simply not perceiving, Tolstoy's religion and Ibsen's individualism (which Brahm saw and underlined), the workers claimed Naturalism as *their* art, as the new *Weltanschauung*. In this light such widely different works as *Crime and Punishment* and *A Doll's House* were read and fully discussed in the social democrat clubs. Of course, the men who formed these reading and discussion groups were themselves an élite within the working-class movement, but an intellectual élite which wanted to see the new poetic art become the art of the whole 'Fourth Estate': 'The old poetic art is dead, a new one is in embryo! May it find entrance into the heart of the proletariat!' [16] The principal practical step towards realising this ideal was the founding of the Freie Volksbühne.

ACT I

1890–1914

FROM BRAUHAUS TO BÜLOWPLATZ

Scene I

THE FIRST DECADE

Otto Brahm and the Freie Bühne

Otto Brahm, the son of a small merchant called Abrahamsohn, was born in Hamburg on 5 February 1856. After leaving school he spent those three years in the bank to which Schlenther later made wry reference, experience that taught him a business sense that was later very valuable to him as a man of the theatre. The life of a student followed, in Berlin, Heidelberg, Berlin again, Strassburg and Jena. At Strassburg he formed his lifelong friendship with Professor Erich Schmidt, and at Jena in 1879 he gained his doctorate with a dissertation on a specialised aspect of eighteenth-century German drama. The firm literary foundation of his later theatrical career was laid. Returning to Berlin he dedicated himself to writing, especially on theatre, and became critic on the *National-Zeitung* and the *Augsburger Allgemeine Zeitung*. Because of the current antisemitism Abrahamsohn wrote at first under the pen-name Otto Anders but later altered his name to Otto Brahm. Soon after, he became critic for private theatres on the *Vossische Zeitung*. The paper's critic for the 'Royal' theatres was Theodor Fontane, and the two critics became friends. Finally he became critic of the free-thinking weekly, *Die Nation*, remaining with it until 1889.

In a decade he became Berlin's greatest theatre critic. As such he 'learnt to see and feel theatrically', and later as a theatre leader he fulfilled what as a critic he had demanded. His stance was on behalf of contemporary dramatists, at first Ernst von Wildenbruch, Paul Heyse and Otto Ludwig, later Anzengruber, Björnson and, above all, Ibsen. But as well as championing contemporary dramatists, and severely criticising the Deutsches Theater for excluding these and playing only safe classics, Brahm as critic also prepared the way for a new art of acting. Impressed and influenced though he was by Chronegk, he stressed also the importance of the actor's being wholly and continually absorbed and submerged in his role. He criticised many actors for 'playing cat and mouse' with the parts they acted, moving in and out of character according to whether they were active in a scene or not. But he emphasised that the individual actor must play within the framework of the production as a whole. In the same article in which he criticised the Deutsches Theater for its timorous repertoire during its first two seasons, he praised its Chronegk-influenced style:

Seldom has the most important problem of the actor's art been so happily solved as here: the problem of perceiving the spirit of a work of imagination and expressing it in the performance, the individual tone and mood which this work and no other has by nature....
Whoever wishes to raise a poet's creation to life on stage must be capable of perceiving the fundamental notes which give the work its mood and make them reverberate in the listener through the medium of his performers. [1]

Four years later, when he had founded the Freie Bühne, he declared:

I have a pugnacious disposition and I work happily to carry through the new forms of poetic art in order to win back for the theatre, which threatens to lose touch with modern German life, its full significance for our intellectual life. [2]

It used to be said that Brahm's Freie Bühne was modelled upon Antoine's Théâtre Libre, but this is not wholly true; the Freie Bühne was no mere imitation of the Théâtre Libre. Nor did Antoine's company visit Berlin in 1887 as was formerly thought. Its first foreign tour was to Brussels in 1888, and the 1887 production of *Ghosts* in Berlin was not, as was believed, by Antoine's theatre. The starting point of the Berlin company was very different from that of the Parisian one. Antoine did not have to cope with censorship problems – a major reason for the need for a private, independent theatre in Germany. He established a private theatre so as not to compete with the commercial ones, to avoid making enemies and to get kinder critiques. His plays were deliberately chosen from those not performed elsewhere in Paris. As these were largely the naturalistic plays it has even been suggested that the Théâtre Libre became the home of naturalistic drama more by accident than by design. Brahm, on the contrary, was the conscious champion of Naturalism and required a private theatre club in order to perform naturalistic plays which the censor would not pass.

The founding of the Freie Bühne was planned at a meeting held in the Weinstube bei Kempinski on 5 March 1889. The actual invitation was issued by Theodor Wolff and Maximilian Harden, but from the very start Brahm was the leader of the discussion. Also present was Brahm's friend Paul Schlenther, the inevitable Hart brothers and another writer, Julius Stettenheim. Very sensibly the initiators had also brought in a sympathetic publisher, Samuel Fischer, a lawyer, Paul Jonas, and a theatre agent called Stockhausen. [3] One month later, on 5 April 1889, the Theaterverein 'Freie Bühne' was founded. The constitution provided for two categories of membership, active and passive. The active membership consisted only of the ten founders; the passive, all the rest. There was no pretence of democracy. The ten had control of the society and were free to carry out their aim of leading the theatre in a new direction. Even ten was too large a committee for practical day-to-day purposes and a smaller executive committee (*Vorstand*) was created consisting of Brahm himself as Chairman, Paul Jonas as vice-chairman and legal adviser, and Samuel Fischer as treasurer. Within even this smaller committee Brahm had almost dictatorial powers, including those of choosing both the plays and the actors. He valued Fischer's artistic judgements, and, of course, Fischer Verlag could publish the plays. It was a good executive, and though the other seven did unselfish work, it is noteworthy that of the founders only these three were still members at the time of the society's last production in 1909.

The Freie Bühne was not created in order to produce plays at regular intervals or as a resident company. It did not need to have its own theatre and required little capital. Its aim was simply to hire a theatre from time to time and organise there a production of a specific play belonging to the new, naturalistic trend. In order to avoid the censorship this production always had to have the character of an event arranged for a closed circle of people. Ten such performances a year were anticipated.

In the first instance all members paid an annual subscription to cover the ten proposed performances. This assured the society of its financial security in advance – again in contrast with Antoine, who lacked this. In fact it was only in the first year that the full ten performances were given. The growth of passive membership was quite rapid. By June 1889 there were 354 members, by the end of 1889 there were over nine hundred, and by June 1890 there were over a thousand. By then the subscriptions had brought in as much as 25,000 Marks. (The average price of a seat at the beginning was 3.50 Marks, plus a subscription of 1 Mark.) The Freie Bühne quickly came to be regarded as the most interesting association in the city and its members soon included many theatre directors, writers, actors and actresses, critics, and an array of professional people – professors, lawyers, doctors, high-ranking civil servants and so on. Their names had drawing power and no doubt some people joined later out of snobbery.

During the first months of its existence the new society had to cope with its own growing pains and internal frictions, to choose a repertoire and to find a host theatre. Over disagreements as to actual plays to be produced three active members soon resigned, Harden completely, Wolff and Stockhausen to become ordinary members, and later enemies of the Freie Bühne. They were replaced by the writers Ludwig Fulda, Fritz Mauthner and, most importantly, Gerhart Hauptmann, then still completely unknown to the public, changes which strengthened still more the literary basis of the group. In June 1889 Fischer complained that Brahm in some matter or other had gone over his head as treasurer. Brahm apologised. Later, when Brahm edited the society's periodical, Fischer objected to Brahm's receiving an honorarium for this work. Brahm gave up the editorship. Later, too, Stettenheim left and Mauthner became estranged because of Brahm's arbitrariness and inability to compromise. It is hardly surprising that frictions should have arisen quite soon between Brahm and the Hart brothers. Their concept of Naturalism was far more idealist than Brahm's, and their use of the word was broad enough to include Goethe. Heinrich Hart claimed later that he actually opposed the appointment of Brahm as the society's virtual director in 1889, on the grounds that Brahm was insufficiently an idealist. The Harts were very critical of Brahm as a person, saying he was cold and uninspiring; they tried to alter the constitution to give the passive members more power; they were annoyed when Julius Hart's play *Der Sumpf* (*The Swamp*), which was originally on the list of proposed productions, was turned down by Brahm. In 1890 they were involved in the founding of the Deutsche Bühne, on the same principle of ten performances a year – but of plays by German authors only. They attacked the Freie Bühne publicly, and Brahm replied with fierce irony. Thus in the very first year they were both estranged, but did not officially resign until 14 April 1897.

Meanwhile, despite frictions, the work proceeded. All active members chose plays to submit to Brahm – and Hauptmann of course, was actually writing. Schlenther helped in due course with the selection of artists; all did routine chores. Fontane, though only a 'passive' member, was a valuable promoter of the Freie Bühne in his writings. The problem of a host theatre seemed to be solved in June when an arrangement was almost concluded with Lautenberg at the Residenz Theater, but it fell through, and in July a contract was signed with Blumenthal at the Lessing Theater which, in spite of frictions, gave the society a home for its first season. Nor was it perfectly simple for the Freie Bühne to obtain its actors. Other theatres feared its rivalry, even though it was merely a Sunday afternoon society; they thought its founders were seeking private profit and that they were corruptible. So many of the best players were banned by their managements from playing for the Freie Bühne and for the first production some of the leading actors had to be brought from Breslau and Vienna. There were other problems, too. Many of the passive members had no real interest, and there was anxiety as to how large the actual audience would be. Inevitably many an unacknowledged genius brought his ancient manuscript and became the Society's enemy when it was turned down, or when, having been praised by the Freie Bühne it was turned down by other managements. But Brahm and his colleagues were not to be discouraged. 'Freie Bahn der Freien Bühne!' (Free way for the free theatre!) Brahm concluded his article in *Die Nation* (5 October 1889) immediately after the opening production.

That production was, of course, of Ibsen's *Ghosts*. It was nominally directed by Hans Meery, but in fact Brahm gave such detailed directions and supervised so closely that in effect he himself directed – no wonder that in the *Nation* article he said it would be unbecoming for him to enter upon a proper critique of it! To attempt to recapture the quality of the performance we are dependent upon the critics partly because of all prompt copies and the like from the entire output of the Freie Bühne, only one production copy, two stage managers' books and one actor's copy survive, together with some stage plans and some letters. We know that the play was neither cut nor altered – which was remarkable enough at that time. Fontane approved its choice, but Landau did not feel it to be the real start of the activity of the new society, more the epigraph to the book. But he praised the production highly and compared it with the Meiningen players, referring to the unity of style. This unity was evidently a characteristic of the production, every aspect of which was consistently real, whether the dark, shadowy setting or the manner of acting. In all things there was plainness and simplicity, an avoidance of non-essentials and of exaggeration. Silent expressiveness was a noteworthy feature. Frenzel noted the *Kunstpausen* (artistic pauses) though he thought them too long. But these pauses were one of the keys to a new stage style and allowed time for the psychological effect of word and action to communicate itself fully. This was nine years before Stanislavsky's historic production of Chekhov's *Seagull* in 1898 which is often popularly regarded as having introduced 'the pause' into European acting. Naturally the critics tended to compare the individual performances with those in the production of 1887. Oswald, played by Emmerich Robert from the Vienna Burgtheater, was the most highly praised. Fontane compared him with Franz Wallner, the Oswald of 1887, saying that whereas Wallner had merely presented an unfortunate, Robert gave a character and a psychological study of neurosis. He evoked the audience's sympathy not simply with a 'sick man' but with a *person* (*Mensch*). The *person* once more became the central point of the stage. At the end, 'The applause of the audience was strong and loud, despite hisses from opponents of Ibsen.' [4]

In this same review article Brahm took the opportunity of giving further publicity to the proposed programme of the Freie Bühne, which was to include, after *Ghosts*:

Gerhart Hauptmann: *Vor Sonnenaufgang* (*Before Sunrise*)
Edmond and Jules de Goncourt: *Henriette Maréchal* (1865)
Tolstoy: *The Power of Darkness* (1886)
Anzengruber: *Das vierte Gebot* (*The Fourth Commandment*)
Björnson: *The Glove* (1883)
Arthur Fitger: *Von Gottes Gnaden* (*By the Grace of God*)
Strindberg: *The Father*

Although three German authors were listed, Brahm had to defend himself immediately against accusations of a predilection for foreign wretchedness. All these plays were in fact performed in the first thirteen months of the society's existence, with the addition of:

> Holz and Schlaf: *Die Familie Selicke* (*The Selicke Family*)
> Alexander Kielland: *On the Way Home* (these two as a double bill)
> Hauptmann: *Das Friedenfest* (*The Feast of Reconcillation*)

There was some justification for Landau's feeling that the production of *Ghosts* was more an announcement of policy than a true beginning, for it was the second production, on 28 October, of Hauptmann's *Vor Sonnenaufgang* that Brahm himself felt to be a real 'new beginning'.

Gerhart Hauptmann was not only the central figure of German Naturalism, but is also a key figure in the history of the Freie Bühne and the Freie Volksbühne. He was associated with a Berlin literary society called *Durch* (*Through*), among whose members were Bruno Wille and some of his friends. *Vor Sonnenaufgang*, his first play, had already been published in the summer by C.F. Conrad, and controversy had raged. Brahm wrote about it in *Die Nation*. He was impressed by 'the audacity and originality of the observation, the complete aliveness of the characters, and the fearless consistency in the shaping of gruesome and distressing material'. [5] The actual performance was therefore eagerly awaited both by supporters and opponents of the new Naturalism. In advance, the actors were harried and threatened in anonymous letters. At the performance the hostile first-nighters, their indignation fully roused through the weeks of lively controversy, used all the well-known tricks of their kind, whistling and jeering, to try to put the actors off their parts. The first act, in its quite austere and simple naturalistic setting, passed off quietly enough, but the setting of the second gave the cue for mounting noise. The farmyard scene with its dwelling house, servants' quarters, fields, the archway between the cattle stall and the hay-loft, the village inn, vegetable garden, dove-cote, green fence with white points, oak tree with surrounding bench led the critic Frenzel to comment sarcastically that 'they forgot the dunghill with the crowing cock on it'. [6]

> ... and as fanatical admirers advanced against fanatical opponents,
> a battle developed of lungs and hands, of hissing and clapping,
> which was pursued with quite unusual violence and fluctuated
> inconclusively from one side to the other, until a great love scene
> in the fourth act made even the opposition applaud. [7]

The opposition was evidently awaiting the fifth act when, as they knew from their reading, Marthe is in labour off stage, and Dr Schimmelpfennig constantly having to go off to attend to her; so, although Brahm tactfully eliminated the off-stage 'cry of a woman in childbirth' which Hauptmann prescribed in the stage directions, a certain Dr Isidor Kastan, possibly pretending impatience at the birth's delay, stood up in his seat, waving over his head a pair of obstetric forceps, as if he intended to hurl them on stage, and shouted, 'Are we in a brothel, then?' [8]

Kastan's moral objection was voiced more deliberately in Frenzel's critique, where the play was described as 'an offence against morals, sentiment and taste'. [9]

The great breakthrough of Naturalism into the German theatre had taken place.

The Founding of the Volksbühne

The programme of the Freie Bühne continued through the winter as planned, and aroused the greatest interest even among non-members. In particular the productions were discussed in a workers' debating society founded during the period of the anti-socialist laws and given the innocuous, rather absurd name, of *Alte Tante* (*Old Aunt*). Unable to afford individual membership of the Freie Bühne, the club conceived the idea of applying for corporate membership. One or two members would attend the show and report upon it to the other fifteen or twenty members. Apparently hestitating to make an official approach to Brahm himself, they decided to send a delegation to an individual member – not indeed, one of the ten 'active' members – whom they could trust, to ask him to act for them. They chose a monumental mason, Schleupner, and a bookbinder, Willi Wach, to visit Dr Bruno Wille.

Bruno Wille, the son of an insurance inspector, was born in 1860 in Magdeburg. As a student in Bonn and Berlin, he first studied theology, but finding this inconsistent with his philosophy of life, he changed his studies, devoting himself to philosophy, with history, mathematics, science and economics. But he never lost some of the attitudes engendered by his theological beginnings; his mind always moved in 'higher' regions, the world of ideas and dogma; he never fought for anything in which he did not really believe; and he was ready to turn against himself when convinced that a new course was right and honourable. He had a strongly developed personality, many-sided, rich in talents, imagination and fire, verging on the eccentric. Even as a student he felt the injustice of his intellectual and artistic privileges and came to see later that the workers' need for intellectual and artistic things was as important as their physical needs. Writing in 1893, he said:

> I am painfully aware that I personally cannot be free so long as
> human society is not free ... and what has led me on to the side of the
> materially deprived masses is not the sensual pleasure of tasting
> good food, of a full belly and idle body, but the recognition that the
> liberation of the people from political control and economic
> exploitation would bring immeasurable spiritual advantages. [10]

His socialism was never orthodox, therefore, and in some sense not deeply rooted. He and his friends moved in the same circle of ideas as the socialists (equality of women, environmental theory and so on) which were also the themes that the Naturalists took up in writing. His sympathy was with individuals rather than with the workers as a body and he wanted to see the individualisation of the masses rather than the stereotyping of individuals in a monolithic party. His aristocratic nature could not stand party discipline for long: he had to follow his own convictions and made no secret of his undemocratic sentiments even in the political field. In 1890 he and his friends were thinking and acting socialistically: later on, socialism was replaced for him by other interests – Zola and Ibsen made a deeper impression upon him than Marx.

Intended by his parents to be a teacher, he became for a short time a private tutor in Bucharest, but his dislike of teaching led him to take the risk of earning his living as a freelance writer and lecturer – a hard life. His articles were printed, however, and through his lectures to workers' clubs he became known and liked by the working-class people. Soon after having completed his studies he joined the circle *Durch* where he met Leo Berg, the Harts, Arno Holz, Wilhelm Bölsche, Gerhart Hauptmann and his brother Carl. He was the ideal person to form the bridge between the literary and political movements of his day.

More is known of 'Durch' than of most similar literary circles of that period as some of its principal records survive, particularly the *Bundesbuch* (1886-7) and the *Protokollbuch* (Minute Book for 1887). Although in its beginnings it was a bit 'undergraduate' – one of its founders, Konrad Küsher, a doctor, had tried to reform the notoriously conservative student fraternities or *Burschenschaften* – it soon became more serious and was particularly interested in questions of literary theory. Its *Ten Theses* (see Appendix A) summarise the views generally held by, but not binding upon its members.

Taking with them another bookbinder, the young Heinrich Wibker, Schleupner and Wach visited Bruno Wille on a Sunday. Together with his friend and fellow-lodger Wilhelm Bölsche and a few other friends they walked with him to Friedrichshagen and strolled on past the Müggelsee to Wilhelmshagen, while the three workmen explained their proposals to Wille. Wille thought the idea of corporate membership of the Freie Bühne to be impracticable, but he promised to think the matter over: he said that a way must be found to give the workers and the poor *entrée* to the theatre, and especially to a theatre producing the works of the young dramatists. Wille's mind moved quickly. Naturally enough Brahm's society offered itself as a prototype, and he conceived the idea of setting up a Freie *Volks*bühne, alongside the Freie Bühne. One evening in a *Lokal* on the Alexanderplatz he asked his friend Julius Türk, 'Do you think one could found a *Freie Bühne* for the workers?' Soon after the Sunday afternoon walk, the

BerlinerVolksblatt, the organ of the Berlin social democrats, published, on 23 March 1890, Wille's *Aufruf zur Gründung einer Freien Volks-Bühne (Appeal for the founding of an Independent People's Theatre)*. The appeal began as we have seen with a triple declaration of faith as to the true nature of theatre: it should be 'a source of high artistic gratification', a source of 'moral uplift' *and* 'a powerful stimulus to thinking about the great topics of the day'. It is a declaration that has remained the fundamental ideal and Credo of the movement from that day to this, but it contained in embryo all the major internal conflicts in the future history of the Volksbühne – conflicts between art and politics, conflicts between propaganda and the improvement of the individual. Wille then unequivocally laid the blame for the trivialisation of contemporary theatre at the door of capitalism, which he blamed not only for the commercialisation of the theatre itself but primarily for the corruption of public taste. The appeal continued with a reference to writers – and not only dramatists – who had freed themselves from this corruption and 'found a sounding-board in the working people of Berlin'. The list of examples is limited neither to writers of the left nor to Naturalists in any doctrinaire sense: Tolstoy and Dostoyevsky, Émile Zola, Ibsen and Ibsen's younger fellow-countryman Alexander Kielland (1849-1906), and a general reference to 'several German "realists"'. Wille went on:

> This section of the population which has been converted to good taste needs not only to read the plays of their choice but also to see them produced. But public performances of plays in which the revolutionary spirit lives are frustrated either by capitalism, for which they do not prove to be good box-office, or by police censorship.

These difficulties could be evaded in club performances:

> These obstacles do not exist for a closed society. It is therefore possible for the Freie Bühne to arrange the production of plays having the tendencies referred to.

But membership of the Freie Bühne was too expensive for working people: '.... therefore the founding of a Freie *Volks*-Bühne seems to me to be appropriate.' There followed Wille's practical proposals, which were extremely well thought out. Whatever later changes occurred, he was undoubtedly on the right lines:

1. Following the example of the Freie Bühne, the new association would consist of a 'leading group' and of its 'members'.
2. The leaders would choose the plays and the players.
3. For a quarterly subscription members would get seats for three performances.

4.   One performance would take place each month, on a Sunday.
5.   The subscriptions would aim to cover only the rent of the theatre and honoraria for the players.
6.   The subscriptions would be as low as possible. It was hoped that the cheap seats would be obtained for 1.50 Marks quarterly – that is for three performances at 50 Pfennigs each.

Those interested were invited, without commitment, to send their names and addresses on postcards to Wille, with a note of the subscription they thought they could afford. From the response the founders would know roughly how many members they could count upon and therefore know how low the subscription could be. 'If sufficient addresses arrive an undertaking is assured that can contribute something to the intellectual uplift of the people.'[11] In conclusion Wille promised that the outcome of the appeal would be published, through newspapers, and associations.

There was in fact a very good response. Young enthusiasts collected signatures (several could be put on one postcard) and soon Wille had several hundred names. Altogether about a thousand responded. The appeal had been well formulated. While making clear that the new organisation would consist of supporters of Naturalism and of socialism, neither of these was narrowly defined, and all party-political reference avoided. While this may have been partly in view of the still valid anti-socialist laws and a wish to avoid initial conflict with authority, the appeal was also an expression of Wille's own beliefs. He asserted a couple of years later that he had not published the appeal

> in order to advance sociopolitical propaganda and to subordinate art to such 'agitational' ends, but to bring together two things dear to his heart, people and art, so that they might mutually ennoble each other. [12]

He saw the proletariat as being educated by an élite of its own number, which the Freie Volksbühne would serve.

Before calling a public meeting, Wille gathered a group of colleagues for the enterprise. One, of course, was Wilhelm Bölsche. Bölsche was Wille's age; he had published two novels, but had made no money, though he was better off than Wille and remained dependent upon his father, editor of the *Kölnische Zeitung*. Like Wille he was not a party man. Another was Julius Türk, also a friend and fellow-lodger. Born in 1865 at Lautenburg, Türk moved with his parents to Berlin at the age of six and attended the Gymnasium zum Grauen Kloster. But just before he entered the fifth form, the second from the top, he ran away to become an actor. He joined a travelling troupe and finally got an engagement at Sonnenburg; but the theatre closed down, and he was forced to return to Berlin, where, through the influence of his brother, later Professor Dr Moritz Türk, he became a book-keeper in a well-known wholesale business. He still read and wrote plays. He became a social democratic agitator and speaker, lecturing on art, drama and the theatre as well as on the French Revolution, Siberia and social and political questions. A far more deeply convinced socialist than Wille, he became after the lapse of the anti-socialist law an enthusiastic member of the legal Social Democratic Party. Türk was a hearty, fundamentally good-natured man, though he easily sulked. He was a man of many parts, though of one ambition – to succeed in the theatre. Perhaps, however, he was too many-sided to excel in any one thing, and it was his fate always to be in close contact with the great men of the naturalist and the socialist movements, all of whom were considered his superiors in their special ways. Thus a tragic fate seemed to pursue him – until his ultimate suicide. At this time, however, he had his close friendship with Wille: the two gave each other financial help, and spoke together at meetings. Like Bölsche he was an eminently suitable partner for Wille in the new scheme. The third primarily literary colleague whom Wille selected was Julius Hart, a socialist by feeling, always ready to raise the banner of revolt against narrowness, prejudice, darkness and abuse of power. With great determination he had left his Westphalian home in the eighties and had come to Berlin, where he was soon in the forefront of those who declared war on pseudo-archaic lyric poetry (*Butzenscheibenlyrik* - Paul Heyse's ironic word) and turgidity.

To these literary friends, Wille added three more who seemed to him to be leading spokesmen of the workers' movement. Curt Baake at the age of twenty-six had already been for five years editor of the Berlin party paper *Das Volksblatt*. He was clever, a good speaker and exceptional tactician: and he was keen on the theatre. His contemporary Dr Conrad Schmidt edited the *Volkstribüne*, and was an enthusiast for Naturalism. One man represented the manual workers themselves, Carl Wildberger, a master upholsterer. He was 'one on his own', a giant in stature, liked a drink, a daredevil. A good-natured, helpful man, he was body and soul in politics, and a good speaker. It was typical of him that he used to read aloud to his workers in the workshop books that he thought worth while, including plays of the young realists.

One of the most important modifications to Wille's original plan was suggested by another friend of his and Türk's, Paul Richter, a wine merchant. Wille had originally thought of graduated seat prices [13] but the others wanted to abolish distinctions based upon cash. How was it possible to have a single price and yet avoid injustice to those in poorer seats? Richter solved this by proposing that a lottery for seats be held.

On 20 July Wille proposed to his colleagues a series of plays for the new society. They were:

Power of Darkness (Tolstoy)
Pillars of Society (Ibsen)
A Doll's House (Ibsen)
Ghosts (Ibsen)
Dantons Tod (Danton's Death) (Büchner)
Robespierre (Griepenkerl)
Vor Sonnenaufgang (Hauptmann)
Die Familie Selicke (Holz and Schlaf)
Der Sumpf (Julius Hart)
Brot (Bread) (Conrad Alberti)

Six of these had already been performed by the Freie Bühne, but not *Robespierre, Dantons Tod, Der Sumpf* and *Brot.* The list apparently included also a play by Bleibtreu.

Less than a fortnight later, on a hot summer afternoon, 29 July 1890, the inaugural meeting took place in the ballroom of the Böhmisches Brauhaus(Bohemian Brewery) on the Landsberger Allee, a spacious room with a large dance floor surrounded by tables and chairs and having a stage with a small proscenium at one end. Even this hall, designed to hold 2000, proved too small for the meeting and was soon over-filled. In spite of the heat people, both men and women, turned up in droves. The tables had to be removed, people had to stand, and even so the police had to place a limit upon numbers. Yet this vast gathering remained until after midnight, fully attentive and enthusiastically unanimous in support of the meeting's aims – so we are assured by Otto Brahm, who was present and wrote up an account of it in his periodical *Freie Bühne für modernes Leben.*(1,1890, p.713).

Most of those sitting, or standing in the gangways were working-class, but there were also many intellectuals, writers and students who were in sympathy with contemporary drama. As well as Brahm, there was the dramatist Ludwig Fulda, whose Naturalist, Ibsenite play *Das Recht der Frau (The Rights of Women)* had appeared two years before; Otto Erich Hartleben, who had recently thrown up his career in law to come to Berlin and was now a theatre critic; Richard Dehmel the poet – still compelled to earn his living with a Life Insurance Company; and the brothers Julius and Heinrich Hart. There were also many working-class people present who were later to play important roles in the history of the movement: the piano-maker Robert Schmidt; the plumber and instrument-maker Heinrich Neft; the bookbinder Heinrich Wibker; the monumental mason Gustav Winkler; the young composer Albert Weidner.

A group consisting of Julius Türk, Otto Brahm, Büchner (a gardener) and Ottilie Baader, later (1900–1908) to become leader of the German Working-Women's Organisation, was elected by acclamation to conduct the meeting.

Bruno Wille then delivered the opening address, whose keynote slogan *Die Kunst dem Volke* (*Art for the People*) became the 'motto' of the Volksbühne.

Wille said that this demand had excited the best minds of ancient Greece and of the German classical period; that working people were no longer satisfied with the treasures of art that already existed; that the new organisation aimed at improving the life-style of the people. Critical of the existing theatrical situation, and casting scorn on the profit motive, Wille declared that it was not possible to wait until the workers had power, but that organised self-help was needed, now. His detailed proposals followed. He was emphatic, surprisingly, that the choice of plays must be left to the 'judgement, taste and intelligence of the majority of the members', but that most would be plays arising out of the struggle for truth. He named not only naturalist plays and the others in the list of 20 July, but also plays of Goethe and Schiller, as well as Büchner, Tolstoi, Ibsen, Julius Hart's *Sumpf* and Arno Holz' *Familie Selicke*.

He refuted the accusation that this would create a 'Social Democratic Theatre': it would serve no party, and there was no need for its members to adhere to the Social Democratic Party. To this extent the Freie Volksbühne would be no different from the Freie Bühne, with which under some circumstances a joint trust might be formed. Like the Freie Bühne, it would use professional artists. But all seats would be the same price, and the seats would be allocated by a lottery. The minimum charge would be 50 Pfennigs, but anyone who could afford to pay more was expected to do so. For the secure establishment of the society enough members were needed to form two sections, so that there could be two performances of each play. Actors were available. Wille added that one could assume that if the Freie Volksbühne in Berlin were successful, other towns would follow the lead. After pointing out that there would be no profit to the founders and that there was no literary clique behind this, wanting to produce their own works, Wille concluded with an appeal for a large membership as the surest way of confounding the scorn of critics and opponents.

A lively discussion followed which became more emotional and turbulent when the author Conrad Alberti (actually 'Sittenfeld') made a lengthy contribution to the debate. Alberti, a young man of 28 originally from Breslau, worked with Dr Michael Georg Conrad on the latter's monthly periodical *Die Gesellschaft* (*Society*), founded in 1885 as a mouthpiece of naturalism – though its title-page even in 1887, showing an almost naked woman apparently floating in mid-air as she smells a flower on a tall-stemmed plant from which a snake raises its head and forked tongue, showed that at any rate in visual art the editors still had very confused ideas of Naturalism. Similar confusion was manifest in Alberti's speech. He welcomed the founding of a Volksbühne, even though, as he said, he did not belong to the 'circle' from which the idea had come. He attacked commercial theatre, saying that it debased even good plays to mere spectacles. He went out of his way to soft-soap the founders, but only to prepare the ground for the real intention of his exposition, namely, to attack their proposed choice of plays: naturalistic plays must not be put in the foreground. Plays about 'softening of the brain' were no food for 'healthy German workers' – an obvious reference to Ibsen's *Ghosts* – adding, "Naturally nothing like that happens among us!"

Though himself not a socialist he proposed weaning the socialists in the meeting away from Naturalism by reviving Lassalle's historical verse play *Franz von Sickingen* as the opening production. At the same time he suggested that the choice of plays should be made by meetings of the members after hearing introductory talks on the plays.

But he had no luck with his proposals and many spoke against him, most effectively Curt Baake. Rejecting both proposals, he warned the audience that Alberti was 'a wolf in sheep's clothing' who was offering a swindle (*Bauernfängerei*). He attacked Alberti for having, in print, appealed to the Kaiser to give the masses a better understanding of art! Alberti intervened to protest that he had only asked the 'government' to provide public funds to support the pursuit of the arts. But Baake did not ease off and inflicted yet another snub on Alberti. By now Baake had the whole meeting behind him. At one point, Brahm tells us, a workman in his working clothes, having come straight from the factory, rose to speak from the middle of the crowd. His face bore the marks of suffering and he did not find it easy to express himself in words; but it was moving, says Brahm, to hear how this working-man developed a programme to which every one of the Naturalists could have subscribed.

> "We don't want to see lies for ever on the stage," he cried, " we want to learn the truth about life and we'd rather see awful things, vice and illness, than have dust thrown in our eyes by noble lords who chuck hundred-mark notes around, and by titled businessmen."

Brahm's article concluded:

> And this was the word which sounded through the meeting like a *Leitmotif: Give us the Truth!* "Not classical or romantic works: we want realistic ones in which the thirst for Truth and the sensitive sense of reality of this present time is expressed. We want to see life as it is, not as it is not."

Alberti had not been helped by the fact that he was a very poor public speaker in spite of the fact that, ironically, he had very recently published a book on *The Art of Rhetoric*. He did, however possess the saving grace of a sense of humour and a few days later he sent a copy of his book to Baake, with a dedication.

Two motions were finally carried unanimously. The first was: 'The meeting declares itself in agreement with the speaker's proposals as to the need for a Freie Volksbühne Association, and resolves to found such an association.' [14] The second appointed a commission to draw up a constitution. The commissioners were Bruno Wille, Wilhelm Bölsche, Julius Türk, Curt Baake, Conrad Schmidt, Carl Wildberger and, notably, Otto Brahm. A third motion which was carried with four dissenting votes, agreed to a retiring collection in aid of the Hamburg building workers, who were on strike at the time.

The commission started work at once, though not without conflicts which were focussed primarily on Wille's pronounced individualism and the democratic commitments in the constitution; nor was Wille skilful in leading negotiation.

Only a few days before the public meeting Bruno Wille had published an article in the *Sächsische Arbeiterzeitung* (23 July 1890) in which he said that the anti-socialist laws had 'corrupted' the Social Democratic Party. He did not mean that individuals had been corrupted, nor did he mean bribery – he used the word philosophically or figuratively – but the literal and more derogatory interpretation was possible. In other ways, too, Wille's individualism opposed itself to the party attitudes. He was not appointed secretary of the commission and there was considerable friction. Baake as a friend of Wille's tried to keep the peace by suggesting other leadership, but Wille would not agree. Eventually the members resolved their differences, or rather agreed to ignore them, and set to work. After one good week's effort the constitution was ready. [15] It was well conceived, and though changes, mostly minor, were later made from time to time, it provided an excellent basis for the new association. The twenty-five clauses covered a broad policy statement: method of enrolment; arrangements for general meetings (two a year) and extraordinary general meetings; election of officers; composition and responsibilities of committees, the amount of the entrance fee and monthly subscriptions; details of payment, stamping of cards and so on; responsibilities of the treasurer and auditors; minimum number of performances (one for every member, monthly from October to March); equal opportunities for all sections; the conduct of the lottery by the 'organisers' (*Ordner*); the dates of the association's working year (1 September to 31 August); conditions under which the constitution could be changed; and the method of dissolution.

The officers elected at the August general meeting were to be a chairman, treasurer, secretary, six members of the board of management (*Ausschuss*), the organisers and three auditors. The chairman, treasurer and secretary were to form the executive (*Vorstand*). This executive had wide powers, including choice of producers, actors and lecturers. If the Association's assets were adequate the executive could conclude firm contracts with the acting company. The Board of Management, consisting of the executive plus the six other members, would choose the plays and the subjects of lectures and recitals and decide all questions affecting the Association's literary standards. Bruno Wille disapproved of this more democratic aspect of the constitution, and the elections at general meetings, and he warned the others against this form of organisation. But he was forced against his convictions to yield to the majority, who felt the need to satisfy the workers, and so he lost control from the very beginning; and although Brahm had considerable influence on the 'artistic' paragraphs of the constitution, the Freie Bühne was not the model for the form of the new association.

The machinery through which one acquired membership of the Association and a seat in the performance was described in some detail. Membership cost 1 Mark and lapsed if the monthly subscription was not paid by the seventh of the month. The monthly subscription was 50 Pfennigs (minimum) from October to March and 25 Pfennigs (minimum) for the rest of the year. It was the treasurer's responsibility to set up agency offices in all parts of the city according to need, whose proprietors would receive enrolments and subscriptions. (In practice these agencies were tobacconists' shops and the like.) A membership card, valid only for that member, was to be issued on payment of the enrolment fee, and subsequently monthly subscriptions could be paid at any agency: a receipt was to be gummed on the card opposite the appropriate month. Only the fully paid up member had a right to attend performances or general meetings. At the theatre all arrangements were conducted by the honorary 'organisers' who were to choose from their own number a chairman (*Obmann*) and two committee members (*Beisitzer*). These three put the tickets in the urns in the foyer, and also decided which seats were to be excluded from the lottery if there were too few members to fill them all. The lottery was to begin at least one hour before the performance. Each member, having had the validity of his membership card checked at the entrance, was to go up to the lottery tables on which the urns with the tickets stood, each overseen by an organiser, and draw out a ticket giving the actual number of the seat.

The second public meeting took place on 8 August again in the Böhmisches Brauhaus, and again with about two thousand present. Wille, Wildberger, Baake, Brahm and Hedwig Gröber were called to lead the discussion, while Türk gave the opening report. With regard to plays, he emphasised that the association did not exist simply to produce German plays, nor was it interested in operettas or farces. 'True poetry' must be the watchword. The Commission had considered the original list of plays and now proposed the following opening plays: *Dantons Tod*; *Power of Darkness*; *Thérèse Raquin*; *Vor Sonnenaufgang*; *Ghosts*; *An Enemy of the People*; *Die Familie Selicke*. [16]

Once more there were lively debates and twice the disturbance was so great that the police threatened to close the meeting. The first important point of dispute was on the first clause of the constitution. This read:

The Freie Volksbühne Association sets itself the task of bringing before the people poetry in its modern sense, and particularly to present, read in public and explain through lectures up-to-date works executed with truthfulness. [17]

Some members wanted one word altering so that the clause would refer to poetry in its 'popular' (*volkstümlich*) sense instead of in its modern sense. The amendment, which was defeated, showed that the policy statement was too much weighted on the cultural side, rather than the socio-political, to satisfy everyone. Another more practical amendment, that the closing date for monthly subscriptions should be later than the seventh of the month – the fifteenth or eighteenth – was also defeated. There was also a considerable discussion as to how to attract young people into the association. In the elections that followed, Wille became chairman, Wildberger treasurer and Türk secretary, these three thus constituting the executive committee. There was much opposition to Brahm's being elected to the board of management: he was suspect in the eyes of many of the workers as not being closely enough attached to the left. He was defended by Baake, and eventually both Brahm and Baake were elected, together with Bölsche, Julius Hart, Conrad Schmidt (all 'intellectuals') and one 'worker', Richard Baginski, a shoemaker. The three auditors were workers (the leader of the shop assistants, the organiser of the metal workers and a printer), as were all the honorary organisers. Most of the elections were almost unanimous, at most there were a dozen dissidents. A further collection for the Hamburg strikers was forbidden by the police, so one was made for Freie Volksbühne funds. The new association, with six or seven hundred members, was founded.

The First Two Years

The first two years of the life of the Freie Volksbühne were unique in its history and possessed characteristics which never exactly recurred in later periods. During these years the organisation managed to contain within itself the conflicting personalities and divergent aims which ultimately and, it now seems inevitably, led to the great schism of 1892: and those very conflicts and divergences, though they produced in the end intolerable tensions and tore the movement in two, nevertheless actually enriched the achievement of the young organisation in its initial stages. A body which united – with however much friction – apostles of a literary movement and leaders of a political, and which could contain even for a short time in its executive committee both the despotic idealist Wille and the ambitious maverick Türk, was bound to exhibit more life, though stormy life, than one with a single artistic or political aim and no more than one powerful leading personality.

After the meeting of 8 August the committee wasted no time. First it was necessary to find a theatre. An idea of sharing a regisseur and actors with the Freie Bühne proved impracticable. Indeed, Wille's calculations at this time even seemed to suggest that the whole conception was after all impracticable. As Türk said: 'The Association was founded, but poverty-stricken. It possessed no theatre, no actors, no scenery, no director and no money.' [18] Brahm had believed that many theatres would welcome the new association, but whether through the influence of the press, the fear of socialism, the plays proposed or the money offered, 'they declined, silently and politely. The child must be put into the street.' [19] Eventually the association was reduced to the Ostend Theater. This theatre, seating 1,200, had been opened in 1877 with ambitious plans for a classical programme, but the public had not supported it and its artistic personnel had gradually disbanded. Even an attempt to bring in an audience through a sensational play failed. Then, as we have seen, Kurz in 1886 and Witte-Wild in 1888 had tried unsuccessfully to develop serious programmes. Then Max Samst took over the theatre, with E. Friedrich as his partner. Samst had long defended the existence of this theatre and he now sought, by making big concessions to popular taste, to build up his audience. He put on many local and topical farces, with song and dance, sensational pieces, dramatisations of popular novels and occasional classics. He was an energetic theatre director. Often there were (after the coming of the Freie Volksbühne) three performances on a Sunday of three different plays – sometimes all directed by him. The executive saw some productions there and were not impressed. Beggars, however, could not be choosers, so on 1 September 1890, hardly more than three weeks after the founding, an agreement with Samst was signed. According to its terms the association hired the theatre, with lighting and personnel for certain Sunday afternoons at 350 Marks a performance, but it retained the right to bring in its own director and to use outside artists for important parts, at its own cost. The director was Cord Hachmann, who also worked for Brahm's Freie Bühne. In him the Freie Volksbühne gained a man who, in the service of the new drama, endeavoured to achieve a style of performance which drew the actors away from declamatory emotionalism and towards a style of speech and movement which imitated actual life. He remained the Freie Volksbühne director until the autumn of 1891, when he went to America. Samst, of course, could only gain by the arrangement and hoped that the new Sunday afternoon audience would also come on Sunday evenings.

Even the six weeks or so that had to elapse between the signing of the agreement and the first actual production, were not wasted. Apart from the practical work of establishing agencies (nineteen at first, later twenty-six), printing membership cards and so on, a recital of 'freedom poems' was given at the Sans Souci Concert Hall on 17 September before an audience of two thousand and a week later there was a lecture by Dr Conrad Schmidt (repeated on 3 October), 'Naturalism and the worker'. Two days before the first performance, Wilhelm Bölsche delivered an introductory lecture on the play to be performed and the next day (18 October) an important article by Wille appeared in the *Magazin für Literatur*, in which he described how the Freie Volksbühne had arisen out of the struggle to awaken the intellectual hunger of the workers, and how the Freie Bühne had provided the model and inspiration for the new body.

The first Freie Volksbühne performance began three quarters of an hour late, in an unheated Ostend Theater on Sunday afternoon, 19 October 1890, the play being Ibsen's *Pillars of Society*. It was obviously an excellent choice of play for the occasion. Being one of Ibsen's realistic dramas it pleased the supporters of the naturalistic movement, and being his simplest, most transparent piece of social criticism it pleased the socialists and was easily comprehensible to an audience unaccustomed to theatre-going and so naïvely delighted by the occasion that there were no complaints even about the cold or the delay. The play was preceded by a Prologue in verse, written and spoken by the poet Richard Dehmel, then a young man of twenty-seven.

The thousand or so original members of the Freie Volksbühne heard the play with 'devout seriousness', with 'intense, intelligent attention'. Otto Erich Hartleben, who made these comments, also said that they had understood Ibsen in their hearts, that they were able to surrender themselves to him because they 'brought their own revolutionary seriousness to meet the seriousness of the revolutionary poet'. [20]

The second production, less than a month later (9 November) revealed other aspects of this new theatre audience. The play was *Vor Sonnenaufgang*. For some reason or other, although Dehmel gave a recital on 7 November, two days before the performance, the 'introductory' lecture by Wille was not given until 14 November, five days after it, so that the audience came to the play without special preparation, and knowing only what they had heard and read previously. The play as a whole was vigorously applauded, but Hartleben was somewhat disillusioned by certain specific reactions. Often, he wrote, there was laughter in the wrong places; the tendencious tirades of Loth, made more conspicuous by the very poor actor who took the part, filled the audience with enthusiasm, while they did not react at all to poetic subtleties, and broke into 'unseemly merriment' at the sight of

Krause, the drunken peasant. The *Volkstribüne* disagreed with Hartleben editorially, saying that not all the positive reactions arose from the tirades, that indeed not one of these had been followed by a burst of applause, and that the reaction to the drunk could be explained psychologically. Not that the paper was wholly satisfied with the behaviour of the audience: 'a certain tense feeling of apprehension was lacking'. Two members of the Association also wrote letters which were published. They said that Hartleben was right in part – some of the audience had behaved as he described; but they insisted that the majority possessed the kind of understanding needed to appreciate this kind of play. These were clear, logical letters that can probably be accepted as giving a balanced view.

Between this production and the next there were arranged, apart from a further recital by Dehmel, three lectures on the Berlin working class and the Freie Volksbühne, given by Bölsche, Türk and Dr Franz Lüttgenau, and on Saturday 13 December Wille gave an introductory lecture on Ibsen's *Enemy of the People*, which was performed the next day. Membership, through energetic recruitment, had now risen to about sixteen hundred and a second section had been formed. In mid-January, because the fees had been lowered, the membership stood at about eighteen hundred. This month Otto Brahm gave two introductory lectures on Schiller's *Kabale und Liebe* (*Intrigue and Love*), which was then given two performances, one for each section.

On 8 February at the invitation of Oscar Blumenthal, the first section was enabled to see a special performance of Sudermann's *Die Ehre* (*Honour*) at the Lessing Theater. It was evidently this performance to which Sudermann also invited Ibsen. Ibsen was deeply impressed by the attentiveness and responsiveness of the Freie Volksbühne audience and kept repeating 'Das sind Hörer! Das sind Hörer!' (What an audience!)

Franz Mehring, commenting on Sudermann's portrayal of the 'Lumpenproletariat' in this play, wrote:

> People of this kind run around in thousands in the Lumpen-
> proletariat of today's society. To portray them photographically
> true to nature was perhaps not so difficult, but to embody them
> vividly as products of the bourgeois economy, that is in its way a
> significant achievement in which the dramatist was to a great
> extent successful. (21)

In 1891 Oskar Blumenthal put on this production in the Lessing Theatre for the Volksbühne audience. He wrote that the vast auditorium

> was filled to the last seat with an audience of workers whose
> intelligence, intrepidity and liveliness flamed out of their eyes. And
> how, immediately after curtain-rise all eyes were fixed expectantly
> on the scene, how after the very first words the most intimate contact

developed between players and audience, how every word which found an echo in the convictions of the audience was accompanied by a whisper of agreement ..... until finally, in the last act the words of the passionate scene of reckoning between the bourgeoisie (*Vorderhaus*) and the proletariat (*Hinterhaus*) fell like tongues of fire into every heart and a storm of applause thundered through the theatre.... – that is one of the finest memories which I have carried home from the Lessing Theatre.[22]

O. E. Hartleben quotes and comments on a speech of the young Robert Heinecke:

"We spend our life in hard labour for you, and meanwhile you seduce our daughters and sisters and rob us of our honour, and pay for it afterwards with the money which we have earned for you!" ... The demonstration [i.e. of applause] that followed was certainly something other than an expression of aesthetic satisfaction; for people who had ears to hear a note rang out of it, a frightening note like that of the distant thunder of an ocean that beats against the dykes. [23]

This was the one play (and the performance was offered to the association free) over which the Freie Volksbühne did not exercise its own choice. In one sense the choice in these early days was easy – the whole range of drama was available, because it was being offered to a new audience. Because the performances were private, there was no need to consider possible clashes with other theatres – nor did the association think it necessary to pay full royalties. Nevertheless, lack of money limited the number of able players who could be engaged, educational considerations were always borne in mind, and the leaders had a natural desire to break new ground. In spite of a close sense of kinship with the Freie Bühne, only four of the twenty plays produced in the first two years had previously been produced by that association. [24] Pissemski's *Der Leibeigene* (*The Serf*) had actually been turned down by the Freie Bühne (perhaps Brahm thought it more suitable for a working-class audience) and it became the Freie Volksbühne's first world première. The second was *Kein Hüsung* by Fritz Reuter, adapted by Jahnke and Schirmer. This caused some arguments, as Jahnke added a fourth act which really contradicted the rest of the play. Eventually this was dropped. *Kein Hüsung* was preceded by Fulda's *Das verlorene Paradies* (*Paradise Lost*), the first production to be performed for three sections (March-April, 1891) and was followed by a single performance of Schiller's *Die Räuber* for the second section only. An almost absurd search for a comedy suitable for this earnest association led to the choice of Anzengruber's *Doppelselbstmord* (*Double Suicide*) to end the first playing year.

Meanwhile the introductory lectures had continued regularly with occasional evenings of recitations, while on 1, 2 and 3 May 1891 a special May Festival had been held in the Ostend Theater. This clearly had the character of a socialist junketing. There was a prologue by Karl Henckell, a programme of singing and oratory, and a melodrama by Wille, *Durch Kampf zur Freiheit* (*Through Struggle to Freedom*), of which it is said that it would have been better omitted. Its subject, however, is of interest: it was about the Silesian weavers. At the end all joined in singing the *May Festival Marseillaise* by Wurm.

During that first playing year 3,948 people altogether had been members of the association, but never more than 2,500 at the same time. Indeed at the end of the working year the membership was only 1,873, so that over 50 per cent, some 2,075, must have left during the year: and they left not only towards summer, but even after the second performance. Another 1,774 joined in the second year, throughout which the average membership was something under 3,000, in three sections, and it sank at the end of the playing year to 2,567. So about 30 per cent left during the second year. This large turnover in membership greatly reduced the educational value of the association's productions and lectures.

The agreement with the Ostend Theater did not long stand up to the tests of practicability. Troubles constantly arose over such matters as the availability of the theatre for rehearsal – no doubt Samst with his slapdash approach thought the rehearsal requirements of the association excessive; and in any case rehearsals produced no income. The actors at the Ostend Theater were so badly paid that it seemed a betrayal of the ideals of the Freie Volksbühne to allow them to be so exploited, for salaries of 2 Marks to 5 Marks per day. The Freie Volksbühne itself therefore paid the actors an extra gratuity. This seems to have averaged about 5 Marks per performance for each actor – but only the total expenditure is known, and the size of the part may have been taken into account. Three of the best actors of the Ostend Theater were not on permanent contracts, and these had to be taken on individually and paid special honoraria. In the spring of 1891 Samst offered to reduce the rent to 200 Marks per performance, provided that productions continued throughout the summer. The Freie Volksbühne offered 150 Marks – the additional 50 Marks being for the benefit of the actors. The matter was apparently concluded and the association committed, when the theatre management declared there had been a 'misunderstanding', and asked for the original rent of 350 Marks. Wildberger as Treasurer was furious and there were polemical exchanges in the press. The upshot was that in July, at the end of the season, the Freie Volksbühne left the Ostend Theater – though it returned on 6 September for a single anniversary performance of *Vor Sonnenaufgang*.

During the theatrical close season an Open Air Festival (*Waldfest*) was held on Sunday 9 August at the Müggelschlösschen at Friedsrichshagen. The plans included a concert at 11.00 a.m. by the Friedsrichshagen Kurkapelle, and in the afternoon competitions for women and children, a Punch and Judy show, *Moritat* singing, a men-only show, surprise-theatre, and book raffle. In the evening there was to be a torchlight procession and firework display, also a *Wasserapotheose* and community singing of the *Workers' Marseillaise* and other songs. In the event it rained that day until 4 p.m.; but after that it cleared up and so many people streamed out of the city that there was a shortage of tables and chairs. Altogether some eight thousand or ten thousand people were attracted to the festival, and the atmosphere was good: people took home a very good impression. The *Wasserapotheose* was poetically described in the *Volksblatt*:

> Near the shore a skiff moved slowly along in which stood a lady in appropriate costume and pose, holding a great banner in her hand and lit by red Bengal Lights, while the band played appropriate tunes. [25]

When the thousands of working-class people joined in the *Workers' Marseillaise*, other visitors to the Müggelschlösschen struck up *Die Wacht am Rhein*, but this caused only merriment and no bad feeling.

For the second season the Freie Volksbühne moved to the Belle-Alliance Theatre in the south of the city. It was a larger theatre than the Ostend, seating 1,400, and more expensive to hire. It was not a leading theatre, but of better reputation than the Ostend, and its actors were paid four or five times as much. There were difficulties, but there were fewer guest artists to pay. Hachmann at this time going to America, George Stollberg was appointed as his successor. Stollberg was a competent director, but of no great originality. Once more an Ibsen play, *The League of Youth*, was selected to strike the right note at the start of the season, which also included *Ghosts*, *A Doll's House* and Zola's *Thérèse Raquin*. Contemporary social drama was represented by Ludwig Fulda's *Die Sklavin* (*The Slavegirl*) and the world première of Max Halbe's *Der Eisgang* (*The Ice-breaking*). Anzengruber's *Der Pfarrer von Kirchfeld* (*The Pastor of Kirchfeld*) was no doubt included so that this serious play could build on the success of *Doppelselbstmord*. The older plays were Gogol's *Government Inspector*, Otto Ludwig's *Der Erbforster* (*The Hereditary Forester*, 1849) and Hebbel's domestic tragedy *Maria Magdalena* (1844). After the end of the season a second *Waldfest* was held (14 August) at the Müggelschlösschen. A prize of 100 Marks had been offered for a suitable play to be performed at this, but there were no entries. Instead there was a morning concert, songs, Punch and Judy, games for adults and children, swimming races, a comic regatta, a water-farce, bowls and gymnastics, a fortune-teller, raree show, gypsies, living pictures with Bengal Lights, torch-light procession, fireworks display and a book raffle. Wille produced a special *Waldfestnummer* of the periodical *Freie Volksbühne* for the occasion. This periodical had been started early in 1892. At first the *Berliner Volkstribüne* had offered space for printing introductions to plays, but later partly because of the tensions between the association and the Social Democratic Party, the Freie Volksbühne decided to have its own periodical. It sold at 10 Pfennigs for sixteen pages and six numbers were issued under Wille's editorship, with introductions to plays written by himself, Bölsche, Heinrich Hart and others. The periodical reached more members than did the lectures, and in any case the lectures ended with the introduction to *A Doll's House* on 15 January 1892, because of police objections.

From its very inauguration the Freie Volksbühne had to fight a running battle with the authorities, represented by the police. The police had no standing in cultural matters, but they could nevertheless place many difficulties in the way of a society. They came to public meetings and behaved rudely and provocatively. Even at the first meeting of all they had insisted on a limitation of numbers, and at a meeting in November the interference became really ludicrous. The police lieutenant tried to have the gallery cleared. This 'gallery' was only about three feet above floor level, but when the management of the Böhmisches Brauhaus said that although hundreds of gatherings had been held there, the police had never demanded this, the lieutenant said that he did not regard the gallery as part of the hall. This remark caused laughter, and the lieutenant, very formal in his helmet, threatened to dissolve the meeting. So Wille gave way. Later in the meeting the lieutenant insisted on all speakers giving their names and addresses. Then some ingenious sea-lawyer suggested that in fact the meeting was not in session because the policeman had his helmet on. This time it was the lieutenant who gave way. He removed his helmet.

Basically the police had two objections to the Association. The first was that so many socialists were gathered together at its meetings and performances. The second was irritation that the Association was able to avoid the censor. As in Britain until the abolition of the powers of the Lord Chamberlain, only the theatre was actually subject to censorship as such. Article 27 of the Prussian constitution declared that everyone was free 'to express his opinion through word, writing, print and pictorial representation'. The Freie Bühne had been called into being to evade censorship, and the Freie Volksbühne was clear that it could only achieve its ends as an association (*Verein*). Under a law of 1850, all *Vereine* were divided into three categories: (i) inoffensive, simple associations such as smoking clubs, and associations purely for amusement, with no special social aims; (ii) associations that aimed to influence events; (iii) political associations. The ambiguity of these definitions gave the police an open door for creating difficulties. At first they entered the Freie Volksbühne under category (i). In view of the declared policies of the association this was strange. The association was 'a child of the working class movement'. [26] It was natural that it should take up collections for strikers and join in May Day demonstrations; and when eventually the police said that the Freie Volksbühne aimed at 'influencing public affairs', Türk's response was, 'Yes, we do wish to influence public affairs, and we're proud of it.' On another occasion he recalled the opening sentence of Wille's original appeal – the theatre should provide a strong stimulus to thinking about great topical questions. Türk was, indeed, more 'political' than some of the committee and thought the Social Democratic party ought to have more influence in the association. Even so, his notion of 'political theatre' was very unlike later conceptions – Piscator's, for example, – and was probably far nearer that expressed in an article in the *Volkstribüne* in 1890 (unsigned, but probably by Conrad Schmidt) which said that the theatre should 'assist the liberation of mankind', and distinguished between the functions of politics and art, saying that that of politics was 'to fight for the rights of man', and that of art, 'to ennoble feeling and will'.

On 20 April 1891 the police chief demanded from the association certain information, such as lists of members' names and addresses, a demand which by implication put the association in the second category. It was feared that it was only a step from this to the third category. Among other restrictions, women could not be members of associations entered under category (iii), so the fate of the Freie Volksbühne, which had many women members, would have been sealed. On legal advice, the association appealed against the chief of police. The case was heard on 30 June 1891. The police statement gave evidence as to why the Freie Volksbühne was a category (ii) *Verein*: its aim was to change the economic structure of society-Wille's original appeal was cited; Wille in an essay introducing *Vor Sonnenaufgang* had written: 'We live in a time before sunrise; in a transitional age; we still do not see the approaching sun; but we see how dawn begins to glow on the horizon'. He had also criticised society in his introduction to *An Enemy of the People*. Conrad Schmidt and Julius Türk were also quoted, as was the phrase, 'Poetry can inspire great deeds'. Reference was made to the May Festival, to collections taken at meetings in aid of the Social Democratic Party (though this had been without the knowledge of the executive) to the fact that many of the committee were Social Democrat agitators, and to the choice of plays. One could not say this was an 'inoffensive' association, rather it was a disguised political association. In fact they concluded that the association ought to be entered under category (iii)!

For the Freie Volksbühne Dr Wolfgang Heine said that the police had drawn a false conclusion. Popular education, he said, was a public event.

Art aims at educating people. Therefore the Freie Volksbühne which aimed at educating people through art *must* aim at influencing public events, and so be entered under category (ii). He maintained that they did not argue from artistic premises to economic and political conclusions, but looked at artistic questions from a socialist standpoint. Therefore, they were not playing politics. After a two-hour discussion the District Commission decided on lifting the police order. The judgement said that although most members of the association were socialists, socialism was not a party but a philosophy – which could be expressed through art. The Freie Volksbühne cultivated this philosophy in the realm of art. There was a distinction between, for example, giving a lecture on socialism, and handling an artistic theme from a socialist viewpoint. On the other hand, it could be argued that art influences life and that therefore the Freie Volksbühne influenced public affairs through the power of a philosophy.

This judgement did not satisfy the police, but they realised that it was not going to be easy to prove their case. Police President von Richthofen [27] was an honest and certainly not unreasonable man. He genuinely saw the Freie Volksbühne as he said he did - as a dangerous body working directly towards revolution. He appealed to a higher court, saying that for the converted, Social Democratic associations arranged meetings with speakers on politics and economics. For the uncommitted – which included many women and girls – a more indirect approach was needed. They must gradually absorb the party spirit through social cheer and pleasant conversation. To this end, he said, workers' and children's festivals were arranged and associations founded whose declared aims were simply amusement. Recently, in the same way that an attempt had been made to draw together the educational associations by founding a school for workers' education, so too, federations of working-class singing-clubs and working-class social clubs had been formed in order to consolidate their forces and achieve some centralisation. He saw the founding of the Freie Volksbühne association just at this juncture as quite obviously intended directly to further the Social Democrat cause. He asked how such 'propaganda', through 'producing poetry in its modern tendency' could be understood otherwise than as an intention to fill the 'so-called Proletariat' with a particular view of the social order, and to convince them of the necessity of revolution. He did concede that up to the present the plays presented did no more than portray shortcomings in the existing social order through particularly shocking examples. But he firmly maintained that such an education of a particular class of people must have its influence upon public affairs, as it exercised a decisive influence on each individual in relation to the way he fulfilled his civic duties. Therefore, he concluded, an association having these aims and working in this way, does exercise an influence upon public affairs.

Von Richthofen was obviously justified in his opinion that the association did influence public affairs and did intend to do so, at least in so far as it wanted to strengthen its members' class-consciousness. In saying that it was working directly for revolution, he was wrong, though only to the extent that he credited the whole body with the opinions of some of its members. He did not understand the conflict between the 'revolutionary' and 'cultural' wings within the association, but he doubtless did know of the attitude expressed by Bela Balázs: They didn't want to change theatre-styles, but the world. [28]

The court gave judgement in favour of the Police President. The judgement reads fairly enough, though it is so wordy and tortuous that when Wille cited it in a periodical the following May he inserted after the first sentence – of eighty-nine words: 'What a long sentence!' It was followed by a sentence of ninety-nine words. The court said, in effect, that if sober discussions of social questions could spread and confirm Social Democratic views in working-class circles, then imaginative works showing the exploitation of the workers and appealing to imagination and emotions would obviously do so in a far higher degree. It admitted that even the Social Democrat founders might well have seen as their immediate aim only the presentation of naturalistic plays primarily to the working class. But it suggested that perhaps people like Brahm and Hartleben were not quite clear as to the implication of what they were starting. Later, the judgement said, it was hardly credible that the leaders of the association were not aware that they were influencing public affairs or that they did not, at least as a distant aim, wish to do this. The plays were all chosen to show the 'hollowness and untenability' of the present condition of society and to arouse discontent in the working class. The introductory lectures to a number of plays were quoted, to show that the audience had been invited to see them in the light of Social Democratic ideas. The judgement, however, did not go along with the Police President's argument that the association was working directly for 'revolution', and entered it under category (ii). This judgement, given in January 1892, was really all the Freie Volksbühne wanted. It was no longer in danger either of being dissolved, or of being entered under category (iii). To avoid further trouble the lectures were dropped, their place being taken shortly afterwards by the periodical. The association was then left in peace for a long time, and even the political implications of the split later in the year did not arouse the police to action, as it was feared they might.

That fear arose because the split brought into sharp focus the ideological conflicts which underlay it and inevitably made patent the strong political motives of those opposing Wille. In some sense it can be argued [29] that both the Social Democratic Party and the movement that led to thoroughgoing Naturalism originated partly in historical materialism, and that although these are two clearly independent movements, one artistic, the other political, their paths crossed in 1890 and thus provided the unique opportunity for the founding of the Freie Volksbühne. The founders, on both sides, however, saw only the convergence and could not anticipate the almost immediate divergence. Von Richthofen's reference to the recent (1890) founding of the School for Workers' Education (*Arbeiterbildungsschule*) was by no means irrelevant. Although Wilhelm Liebknecht, and with him the Social Democratic leadership, had declared belief not in achieving power and freedom through knowledge but in achieving knowledge and education through power, the demand from the rank and file for immediate education so grew during the period of the anti-socialist laws that it could not be resisted by the leadership. The founding of the School for Workers' Education was one result of this. The struggle for participation in artistic experience was seen as part of the struggle for education.

Three years later (1893), Franz Mehring said that art is so inseparably a part of the life of a complete person that the more the socialist movement developed the workers into complete people, the greater was the demand for art. Thus the party leadership saw art as a means of broadening the workers' education. Into this situation came, from the artistic side, the naturalistic movement, which Dr Conrad Schmidt referred to as 'Our Ally'. So it was not simply theatre, but specifically naturalistic drama, that was seen by the active social democrats as their fellow-fighter. It was therefore appropriate that the working-class Freie Volksbühne should take as its prototype the bourgeois Freie Bühne, itself founded primarily to produce the Naturalist drama. Kautsky, editor of *Die Neue Zeit*, who expressed this opinion, added that if the Freie Volksbühne promoted plays that any other theatre would put on and was distinguished only by its lower prices, if it sank to being a 'dramatic soup-kitchen', it would lose all cultural and historical significance. Nevertheless, it was the party rank and file, not the party leadership, that took part in founding the Freie Volksbühne. Even Franz Mehring showed no interest at this time. The leadership simply remained silent. Some may have hoped for so immediate a coming of the socialist state that they could regard the association as preparing the proletariat for its new status. In any case the anti-socialist laws were in operation until 1 October 1890, so that in July and August Liebknecht dare not have gone to Berlin. Bebel was speaking in Dresden on 10 August, two days after the founding meeting. But even had they been in Berlin, these two men might well not have seen the meeting as important enough to warrant their attending it. Wille's personality had already alienated the party leadership.

Obviously the Freie Volksbühne movement could not have succeeded had the social-democratic leadership been actively opposed to it; and in spite of the silence of the leaders, the central organ of the party in the capital, the *Berliner Volksblatt*, under the editorship of Baake, did support Wille and printed his initial appeal. The importance of Baake's presence in the Freie Volksbühne at the time of its coming into existence cannot be overrated.

Initially the conflict between Wille and the others was not an open one. Although he wanted the spread of education for the development of the individual, while the workers wanted it in preparation for the coming take-over of power, it was easy for the two sides with naturalistic drama as their common ground not to see that they had different aims. When Wille used the phrase 'through education to freedom', his hearers could put a political interpretation upon it. Those with strong political aims for the new movement did not emphasise them, as this could have compromised its beginnings. Nevertheless, some things said at that time make it clear that 'art' was unimportant to some of the political wing. There were those who emphasised the importance of the *content* of plays – they ought to show economic and class conflict. The proletarian membership did not stress artistic qualities: they thought in terms of 'education'. In fact even 'education' does not describe what the ordinary member wanted. He was not interested in Naturalism but wanted the *edification* of seeing his own outlook confirmed on the stage, and in addition simple enjoyment.

The lifting of the anti-socialist law had far-reaching consequences for the new movement. Because the changes that had been hoped for did not come quickly enough many artists lost interest in politics. It was at this time (and in part for this reason) that the naturalist movement began to be more concerned with the individual and less with the mass. It was – though this was not yet obvious – the parting of the ways for the Freie Volksbühne and the Social Democratic Party. Big differences emerged at the party conference held in Erfurt in October 1891. Part of the opposition was turned out, and others, including Wille, left voluntarily. This excluded opposition formed the short-lived League of the Independent Socialists (Verein unabhängiger Sozialisten), forerunner of the Independent Social Democratic Party (Unabhängige Sozialdemokratische Partei: USDP). Wille was a member of this for a time, and then withdrew from politics altogether. After this conference some of the party members tried to collect a hundred signatures in order to call an extraordinary general meeting of the Freie Volksbühne to oust Wille from the chairmanship; but they were unsuccessful.

Meanwhile conflicts had occurred within the committee. The three original members of the executive (Wille, chairman; Carl Wildberger, treasurer; Julius Türk, secretary) should have been complementary to each other; but in fact, frictions developed. Politically Türk was opposed to his two colleagues, and was critical of their competence. Franz Mehring said later that the chief merit had been not in having the idea of the Freie Volksbühne, but in the detailed work that made its realisation possible. Türk did most of this and gave all his strength to the new organisation for a very modest salary. Wille did so little that Baake wanted him to be made 'honorary chairman' and removed from the leadership. Wille, for his own part, could not avoid suspecting that Türk was carrying on intrigues with the aim of becoming the leading figure of the organisation, and in particular of taking charge of the actual productions.

Tension within the executive committee increased and in the spring of 1891 Türk handed in his resignation as secretary. Probably to avoid publicising the internal frictions he gave personal reasons for his resignation. He was replaced by Otto Erich Hartleben, Türk remaining an ordinary committee member. At the Erfurt Conference Türk alone of Wille's circle did not secede with the 'independents', and from that time regarded himself as a representative of the official party on the Freie Volksbühne committee.

As the next annual general meeting approached in the summer of 1892, Türk wished to regain a position on the executive. Carl Wildberger needed a break from the treasurership, which carried an honorarium. Apart from a desire to increase his own influence, Türk also needed the money, so that when some members asked him to accept nomination for the post, he accepted. The general meeting in July 1892 was stormy. Wille and his supporters strongly opposed Türk's nomination, but even in the face of this he was elected treasurer. At the same time, an 'independent', a supporter of Wille, Bernhard Kampffmeyer, was elected secretary; the situation was explosive.

Conflicts concerning theatre and politics, unimportant in themselves, but serious in the context, occurred almost immediately, in August and September. The committee supported Wille, who accused Türk of personal and political agitation against his leadership, saying he would shortly offer proofs. It may be that Türk had already, as Wille believed, plotted a major offensive against him, or he may have decided on one at this point. On 21 September an appeal doubtless initiated by Türk, though his name was not among the twenty-three signatures, appeared in *Vorwärts* attacking Wille on several grounds. Very few of the signatories held, or had held office in the association. At a committee meeting two days later, Wille took Türk to task, but Türk insisted on a general meeting. The full committee then decided to publish a pamphlet explaining the whole position to the membership. Türk, however, refused to put his side of the argument in the pamphlet.

Two thousand members of the Freie Volksbühne met in the Sans Souci on 4 October 1892, for a tumultuous general meeting that lasted until 2 a.m. First, Wille put the case against Türk. Türk responded with a two-hour speech leading to a resolution that the committee should accept his accusations. In the vote on this Türk's supporters were in an obvious majority. Wille tried to speak out of turn. Tumult rose and the meeting was adjourned. When it resumed, a new chairman was elected. Wildberger was called upon to justify his book-keeping, which he did, not without attacking Türk, and he received some support.

Then Paul Dupont, one of the twenty-three signatories, spoke. He demanded the enlargement of the executive, saying that it needed fresh blood and representatives of the proletariat. If the 'literary gentlemen' didn't agree, well, the workers no longer needed them and could undertake the leadership alone. There were loud and general cries of 'Hear! Hear!' The speech was seen by Wille and his friends as highly provocative and it played a large part in later conflicts. The discussion continued, and about one o'clock Wille spoke again. Woe to the association, he declared, if the writers were excluded from it. Then he concentrated upon the need for complete political independence for the association. Türk had endangered this, and were he given a free hand the police would soon declare the association political and threaten its whole existence. At this the noise became so great that Wille could no longer make himself heard and the meeting had to be dissolved.

Although no decision had been reached it was clear that Wille's days in the association were numbered. His opponents, however, had difficulty in finding a suitable successor. Eventually Türk advertised continuation of the adjourned meeting at the Sans Souci, while Wille advertised one for the same day at the Böhmisches Brauhaus. For a moment it seemed as though the split had already happened, but Türk gave way, and on 12 October the meeting was resumed again with almost two thousand members present. Wille continued his former speech with much interruption: one heckler was thrown out. Then, unexpectedly, Türk's supporters moved the closure. Wille protested that Kampffmeyer had as yet had no opportunity to speak. But the closure was carried. It was evident that the majority were determined at all costs to have a change of leadership. Being in a hopeless minority Wille and his friends gave up the fight. Amid loud cheers Wille, Kampffmeyer and most of the association's officials, together with two or three hundred supporters, left the room. Of Wille's friends only a small group around Wildberger remained. Wildberger, who announced triumphantly that a new association would now be formed elsewhere, still wanted to defend himself and attack Türk, and his trump card was that he still held the profits from the last open-air festival, which he refused to hand over. After long and bitter argument, Türk himself conceded that they must look to the present rather than the past. Business then continued. The constitution was altered so as to enlarge the executive to five members – a first and second chairman, a first and second secretary, and the treasurer. The old executive was declared to have resigned, but Türk of course was re-elected as treasurer. Two unremarkable men were elected secretaries. The second chairman was Paul Dupont, a representative of the working classes and leader of the stone-masons' union, but in no way a horny-handed proletarian. Despite his attack on the 'literary gentlemen' he was himself well read, a clever and subtle thinker, a skilful speaker and editor of the stone-masons' journal. For chairman no less a figure than that of Franz Mehring had been found.

After the election of officers it was agreed to raise a loan of two or three thousand marks.

Wildberger had good grounds for declaring that a new Volksbühne would be formed. Wille had already realised that if he were defeated he must found a new association, and now he, with some hundred and fifty or two hundred of those who had left with him, hurried to the Strausberger Strasse, where they crowded excitedly into the Fortuna Festsälen. Far from throwing up the sponge, everyone felt that this was the opportunity to found a body avoiding the mistakes of the first. Wille, Kampffmeyer and Wildberger (who came over after the end of the meeting at the Sans Souci) were asked to prepare a constitution.

When most had gone home, Wille and a close circle of friends, some old, some new, sat until morning in a café, talking things over.

Three days later (15 October), the committee, with co-opted friends, met and formally constituted the Neue Freie Volksbühne. This time there was no one to thwart Willie's undemocratic ideas – ideas which had been strengthened by his experiences in the Freie Volksbühne. The constitution drawn up was non-democratic. For an organisation intended to reflect the broad mass of workers it was extraordinary that the draft showed clearly that its originators detested the very idea of constitutional control. Its ideal was rather that of a free society of equals. It revealed important assumptions about the association's work, and particular evidence of Wille's mind – always bold, full of ideas, spacious but unpractical. While keeping closely to the original formulation of aims, Wille widened the intended field of operations:

> The association proposes to bring before its members elevating and liberating works of art of all kinds, especially theatrical performances, poetry and musical works, also when possible works of painting and sculpture, and to explain these through lectures and articles. [30]

There was to be an annual general meeting, but its powers were remarkably limited: it elected three auditors, and, with a three-quarters majority it could *object* to particular members of the leadership – but it could not elect them! The leadership consisted of twenty 'artistic experts' (five of them musical), and twenty 'technical experts' (corresponding to the *Ordner* of the original Volksbühne, and responsible for practical arrangements, especially the lottery for seats). Who selected the original members of these two groups, or how, is not stated. Evidently they were hand-picked by Wille and his closest associates. Once in being, both bodies were self-perpetuating, having power to fill gaps in their own number, and to co-opt advisers. The artistic experts alone elected the chairman and secretary; the two groups of experts voting together elected the treasurer: chairman, secretary and treasurer constituted the executive. An interesting concession to 'democracy' was that *any member* could sit in on meetings of the technical experts – but not of the artistic, where the real policy-making power lay. The names of the original technical experts can only be guessed at – probably many were *Ordner* who had seceded with Wille and knew the ropes: indeed, we know that these seceding officials took with them the actual urns and other impedimenta of the lottery, thus nearly wrecking the seating arrangements at the first performance of the 'old' Volksbühne – whose committee, presumably, did not discover the loss until the last moment. And whatever theoretical objections may be felt to the undemocratic selection of the artistic experts, the original list is certainly impressive, though many of the newcomers did little but lend their names. [31] For the rest, the practical articles of the new association were much the same as those of the old: registration fee of at least 1 Mark; monthly subscription of at least 50 Pfennigs, the right of the committee to raise these minima; payment through agencies before the 15th of the month, Sunday afternoon performances, ten plays a year; lottery for seats.

Sadly, if inevitably, the split was followed by bitter conflict between the two organisations. The dispute over the festival profits held by Wildberger actually led to legal action, though it never came to court, and the ideological fight was continued by the leaders of both sides in periodicals devoted to literature and social criticism.

Seen in the perspective of the later history of the two associations the differences between them seem perhaps less important than the resemblances. The literary element did not lose all influence in the 'old' association, nor was the leadership of the 'new' wholly cut off from or uninfluenced by its working-class membership. But at the time personal bitterness and political fanaticism emphasised the depth of the rift, which was not formally and completely healed until 1920. Until then the narrative of the vicissitudes and growth of the two so closely related organisations must be pursued along parallel lines, first of all to the next crisis of their history in 1895.

The Freie Volksbühne to 1895

What determined above all the history of the Freie Volksbühne during the three years between the split and the association's temporary dissolution in 1895 was the appointment of Franz Mehring as chairman. The appointment was remarkable, for Mehring had never been seen at any previous assembly of Volksbühne members and had in fact been the association's quite bitter enemy. It is therefore important to try to understand why Wille's opponents chose Mehring as his successor, and why he accepted the office.

Franz Mehring was born on 27 February 1846 in Schlawe, Pomerania. From his north German family and background he inherited a melancholy disposition, combined with great depth, thoroughness and devotion to duty. He had a passionate sense of justice and was not a man for half-measures: both his devotion and his hatred were whole-hearted. At the same time he was excitable, often changing his opinions – though not the profounder principles that underlay them – and because he became emotionally involved in ideas he could not separate people from their opinions. One of the so-called 'socialist academics', Mehring studied philosophy in the Universities of Berlin and Jena. From 1883 he became celebrated as editor of the left-wing middle-class paper, *Berliner Volkszeitung*, through whose pages he waged war on the anti-socialist law, and when he ceased to be its editor he became a regular contributor to (and later joint editor of) the socialist periodical *Die Neue Zeit*. At the time of the founding of the Freie Volksbühne Mehring showed no interest. With other Social Democratic leaders he feared such a body would divert energy from what he saw as the central tasks of the socialist movement and was suspicious of Wille's highly individual brand of socialism. When the split in the association became imminent, Mehring at first declined to be put forward as Wille's successor. It was only when Türk put it to him that the Association must have some literary person on the executive, lest the workers should really appear (as indeed they were later represented in some sections of the press) as enemies of the intellectuals, that Mehring agreed to stand for election.

Türk's argument certainly expressed part of the truth: it was important that the Freie Volksbühne should neither in fact nor in image lose its literary-intellectual aspect. At the same time a leader was wanted whose loyalty to the Social Democratic Party was unquestioned, as only such a leader could command the trust of the majority of the working class and so ensure a maximum growth in membership. One suspects that Mehring was also welcomed by Türk because, as a man whose interest in the theatre was secondary to his socialism, he was unlikely to block Türk's own growing theatrical ambitions. To Wille's opponents in general and Türk in particular, Mehring appeared as the ideal successor. Whether he really was so is another matter, but just as Mehring's life was 'burdened with tensions which, naturally enough, reflected just as much tensions of the times as the tenseness of a receptive and sensitive mind', [32] so, within the Volksbühne movement, his presence and activity expressed the tension between political and artistic aims inherent in the original foundation.

Why he accepted the office is more difficult to see. That he intended simply to lend literary respectability to a primarily working-class organisation cannot be the whole explanation. Perhaps at this point in time he anticipated a new wave of proletarian drama. When the Freie Volksbühne was founded two years earlier with naturalistic plays in the forefront of its programme, many socialists had supported the foundation because they 'had founded upon Naturalism the hope that it would develop into the art of the fourth estate if it were given fruitful soil. And', Heinz Selo goes on, 'it had not so far fulfilled this hope'. [33] In January 1893, within a few months of taking office, Mehring was writing that Naturalism showed the world that was passing away, and he was asking whether it would have the courage to take the second step and show the world that was coming into being. Mehring clearly failed to appreciate the primarily critical function of drama and may have been looking for something like the later 'preaching' Shaw or the products of Russian socialist realism. Fortunately for the theatre the naturalistic writers did not take this road: Ibsen and Hauptmann were already writing subjectively and individualistically. [34] But Mehring may well have expected otherwise and his disappointment in the failure of such a drama to develop may have strengthened his apparent willingness to dissolve the Freie Volksbühne in 1895 and devote himself to other socialist activities. He did in fact say that in the struggle of the working class not to sink into misery and degeneration and to shape the society of the future, *art is a tiny factor* compared with universal voting rights, the value of strong organisation, and the influence of a flourishing Trades Union press.[35] Whatever his motives, it was not in Mehring's nature to do a job less than whole-heartedly and he evidently threw all his energies into his new responsibilities.

The loss of a few hundred members did not appreciably weaken the Freie Volksbühne; indeed, the removal of the non-working-class 'writers' and the chairmanship of Mehring led to a rapid increase in membership.[36]

Although statistics for these earlier periods are scanty and haphazard, a census of occupations of members made in the season 1893/4 shows strikingly that the association was predominantly working-class, with a particular appeal to skilled workmen; [37] it was genuinely and unmistakably a working-class movement. Mehring, who claimed at the time of the split that there was no change in the policy of the Freie Volksbühne, later called it 'a serving member in the great struggle of the working class for emancipation'. It was to play its part in the self-liberation and self-education of the worker; it was not revolutionary; 'to overturn the bourgeois theatre in the bourgeois world' lay wholly outside its power. He emphasised its democratic character, contrasting its members' freedom with Wille's 'adult-educational undertaking'.

The will of the membership made itself strongly felt in many ways, not least in the choice of plays. From the start Mehring's own intention was to emphasise much more strongly the political tendency of the association. He declined an offer from Raphael Löwenfold (1893) to co-operate with the Schiller-Theater, stigmatising it as 'capitalistic' and at first opposed creating a new 'section' which he feared would let in 'bourgeois' elements, interested only in seeing plays cheaply. This did happen. Schutzmann Gerlach, the regular police observer, made a note on 1 June 1893 that many members did not belong to the Social Democratic movement. Like Mehring, he assumed that these members were only interested in cheap tickets. Similarly Mehring hoped for the new naturalist plays that would confirm the workers' image of the new world. When these failed to materialise he was left with a potentially dangerous vacuum. He saw that a 'modern' form did not ensure unexceptionable content and that many 'classics' had a revolutionary content hidden under the dust of ages.

Meanwhile the demands of the membership became more and more diverse. As a compromise it was agreed that there should be more modern plays, if very good, full of teaching and 'revolt' – and also more classics. But in fact the seasons included fewer and fewer untried new plays: Mehring's excuse was that it was easier to experiment with one or two thousand members than with seven or eight thousand, as the risk was much less.

Throughout the period 1892 to 1895 members were offered productions from the repertoire of the Lessing Theatre and productions of the Volksbühne itself at the National, as the Ostend Theater was now called. Although the association had no real control over the plays presented at the Lessing Theater, the high quality of the productions attracted a large membership, and when in the spring of 1895 a proposal was put forward to leave the Lessing Theater and rely entirely on performances at the National, membership growth was checked. [38]

Ironically enough, under Mehring's consciously 'socialist' direction the danger actually increased of the Freie Volksbühne becoming what its enemies in the Social Democratic Party called it – a 'dramatic soup-kitchen' or 'humbug education'.[39] Much of the best energy of the Social Democratic movement went into the Volksbühne and other educational bodies, though many party workers (at another time Mehring might have been of their number) regarded this as unwarrantable dissipation of resources. Mehring defended the Volksbühne's work by saying that the people needed 'recuperation', and by asking where better they could get it than in the theatre? – a sad retreat from the Volksbühne's original position, and indeed from Mehring's own.

In fact the plays actually offered to the members are not unworthy successors of Wille's repertoire from 1890 to 1892. At the Lessing Theater members saw four plays of Anzengruber, three of Sudermann, two of Lessing, and plays by Grillparzer, Kleist, Augier, Björnson and Ibsen. The standard of the productions at the National Theater was so low that apologies were made in the periodicals But the repertoire itself included Goethe, Schiller, Molière and Calderón, and many contemporaries or at least moderns. There was no shame in a programme that included Verga, Augier, Heyse and Hauptmann (*Die Weber*, 1893, *Der Biberpelz* (*The Beaver Coat*), 1894).

The performances of *Die Weber* were the high point of the work of the Freie Volksbühne in this three-year period, as indeed in their own theatres were the performances of it given by the Freie Bühne and the Neue Freie Volksbühne. This is not the place to repeat the history of the writing of this play and the struggle with the censor, nor to attempt any new or deep critical assessment. Yet all these must be touched upon if the importance of the play in the history of the Volksbühne movement, and the importance of the Volksbühne movement in the history of Naturalist drama, are to be understood. Even in its own day *Die Weber* was already a symbol as well as a fact; though a unique and unrepeatable work of art – strictly inimitable – it was regarded as a prototype for a new proletarian art, as well as a high achievement of the naturalist movement. The disputes with the censor and the disputes within the ranks of progressives as to the play's significance epitomise the broader disputes and disagreements of the period.

As early as autumn 1888 in Zürich, Hauptmann had conceived the idea of a play based upon the revolt of the Silesian weavers in 1844. He began working on the material early in 1890, made two journeys to the 'weaver' country, the Eulengebirge, in 1891, and by the end of that year had completed a dialect version of the play (*De Waber*) and about two months later, the High German version (*Die Weber*)–though this too is heavily weighted with Silesian dialect. Both versions were rejected by the censor – the High German version being regarded by the police as even more dangerous than the dialect version, because more intelligible. The play could, of course, have been performed by the Volksbühne, but Hauptmann was anxious for public performances and would not release the play for Volksbühne use while his appeals were proceeding. He did, however, allow a performance in February 1893 by Brahm's Freie Bühne. This association had by now little more than a nominal existence (in 1892 it had presented only one play, Strindberg's *Miss Julie*), but it was revived for the occasion. [40] Permission for public performance, at the Berlin Deutsches Theater only, was given, surprisingly, on 2 October 1893, though the first public performance did not take place there until nearly a year later on 25 September 1894, less than a month after Otto Brahm himself had taken over the direction of the theatre. As soon as the play had been passed for public performance, Hauptmann released it to the Freie Volksbühne and the Neue Freie Volksbühne, and within a fortnight (15 October) the latter presented the play to its members in the Viktoria Theater. The performances arranged by the Freie Volksbühne did not take place until December, at the National Theatre. During that month the play was presented to all five Freie Volksbühne sections, and in January two additional performances were also sold out.

Brahm's production at the Freie Bühne was apparently a muted one. He put the author's interests before those of his society: an explosive production might well have been good for the Freie Bühne and its reputation, but it would almost certainly have made the police even more determined to stifle the play. When Brahm produced the play – at least when Cord Hachmann produced it under his direction (at the Deutsches Theater a year later) – he departed from his normal attitude of respect for the text of a new play. Normally he would not, for the first night with the critics present, allow cuts or alterations in new plays, though to reduce length he would subsequently introduce cuts, usually of whole scenes. This time he simplified the texture of the play, cutting anything that reflected badly on the workers, and anything contributing to Dreissiger's humanity. Brahm's *Weavers* must have been a thinner and poorer thing than Hauptmann's.

The arguments about the play continued stormily throughout 1893. Hauptmann himself in a letter written in August declared that the play was indeed social, but not socialist [41] and Julius Hart wrote about it in these terms in the *Tägliche Rundschau*. Gerhart Hauptmann, he said, is one of the very few in our times 'who bear on their shoulders the wings of the true poet and raise themselves upon them high above the fog and fume of everything party-political'. [42] Mehring responded to this in a piece of characteristic polemic: 'Mr Julius Hart is just as well informed as we are how deeply *Die Weber* is rooted in "the fog and fume of everything party-political".' [43]

In December 1892 the enrolment fee had been lowered to 50 Pfennigs to encourage working-class recruitment. The monthly subscription of 50 Pfennigs was called a 'minimum', but 99 per cent of members paid only the minimum. In 1893 both the enrolment fee and the monthly, subscription (for eleven months per year) had to be raised to 60 Pfennigs. But *Die Weber* was so costly a production – with large cast and five distinct settings – that a special supplementary fee of 30 Pfennigs was required for this play in December; this did not prevent its being a complete success. It was also exceptional in being twice as expensive to stage as most productions at the National Theater. The police reported that at the Freie Volksbühne performance (presumably the first) the applause and cries of 'Bravo!' at the end of the fourth act (when the weavers storm Dreissiger's house) seemed as though they would never end.

What appealed to this audience was the subject-matter, not the style of the dramatist or the skill of the direction or acting. It was not Naturalism as an art form that attracted the working-class audience, and the greatest successes of the first five years – with the exception of *Die Weber* – were not naturalistic plays. In this respect the working-class audience was no different from the middle-class, though the squalor of some naturalistic settings did not offend them as it did the middle classes. Mehring himself came to see that there was a cleavage between the aims of the contemporary playwrights and those of the working classes. Modern art, he thought, was deeply pessimistic; the modern proletariat deeply optimistic. In seeing only pessimism in plays of social criticism Mehring again showed the limitations of his understanding of the nature of drama. He also failed to realise that the working classes were (and usually are) conservative in art even when revolutionary in philosophy. They were more interested in hearing their own views and prejudices emphasised than in seeing an art work presented in a consistent convention. Thus Alfred Loth's two socialist speeches in *Vor Sonnenaufgang* were delivered straight at the audience in a way quite out of key with Naturalism – and gained great applause. Nor did this audience distinguish between the actor and the role: it was the role, not the actor, that was applauded. Bruno Wille understood perfectly well this inability of the audience to appreciate the art of the theatre.

Nevertheless, this audience, which so impressed Ibsen, had many positive qualities as well as other often laughable faults that could not have been predicted by middle-class theatre people. Much stemmed, on the one hand, from their goodwill and on the other from their lack of education as theatre-goers. The Freie Volksbühne was felt to be their own theatre – therefore it was good. They wore their best clothes and thought of the Volksbühne performance as a 'day out'. The performance was for them a symbol of social ideals and aspirations. Thus they applauded heartily whether they liked and understood the show, or not. Such an audience fascinated the critics. It was the unpredictable, apparently unprejudiced audience that some twentieth-century dramatists have claimed to long for. Its members showed their feelings openly, expressed their laughter and fear without inhibition. They would shout out their anger at individuals in the play, loving, hating, anxious and rejoicing, watching the drama breathlessly. They were, as Brahm saw, a naïve audience in the best sense. To a factory worker with no job-satisfaction it was of immense psychological value to give human feelings expression. He knew once more what it was *to be a person – ein Mensch zu sein* (Schiller).

The naïvety and lack of 'theatre-education' brought corresponding shortcomings. Like the middle classes, the audience arrived late – but perhaps for different reasons. The women did not know that they ought to remove their hats (but in the second season the programme asked them to do so); the men used to variety houses, with a bar in the room, took spirits into the auditorium. Not knowing what to do with children, parents tried to bring them to the theatre; later they realised the advantage of husband and wife belonging to different sections and taking turns at baby-sitting.

However presented, certain aspects of life produced stock reactions. Drunks and bad language were something familiar and amusing, even in the context, for example, of *Vor Sonnenaufgang*. The audience was anticlerical and ready to laugh at the celibacy of the parson in Anzengruber's *Der Pfarrer von Kirchfeld* (*The Pastor of Kirchfeld*). Erotic scenes were enjoyed with a smirk. References to class evoked immediate response. In Fulda's *Verlorenes Paradis* a rich idler presses a tip into the hand of a worker on strike.

> One must feel how tensely the audience, more than a thousand strong, waited to see what would happen next. And when the worker thereupon said 'I'm not no beggar'(Keen Bettler bin ich nicht), pent up, spontaneous applause broke out, as if the dramatist had withdrawn a slander. [44]

The audience responded warmly to human love, a sense of justice or a fine deed.

> When in the second act of *Kein Hüsung* (*Homeless*) the senior farm-hand Johann pushes the Baron aside and storms out to rescue the child from the fire, the wild applause throughout the whole house lasted several minutes, holding up the action of the play for a time. It became even louder when the farm-hand came back with the rescued child .....
>
> This mighty storm of applause was surpassed in the third act when Johann throws the Baron, who is molesting Johann's bride-to-be, to the ground and then stabs him in a moment of mindless rage. The unparalleled applause was like a whoop of joy at being released at long last from the fear of oppression. [45]

They became angry at intrigue. They wanted above all to laugh. So they liked inoffensive comedies and often laughed where laughter was really out of place. Even *Die Weber* drew some inappropriate laughter.

The worker in the theatre usually forgot his class-consciousness unless the play itself (helped by the introductory essay in the periodical) reminded him of it. There was always the 'danger', in the eyes of Mehring and others, of the Volksbühne audience becoming 'simply' a 'Sunday afternoon public'. In fact, the relationship of socialism, Naturalism, theatre-going, working-class culture and the Volksbühne movement was far more complex than anyone involved at the time could appreciate. The bifurcation into Freie Volksbühne and Neue Freie Volksbühne at least enabled people who saw the relationship in different terms and with different emphases to continue working with enthusiasm and good conscience right up to the First World War, growing gradually closer to each other until reunion became the natural step. Had the split not occurred, the whole venture would probably have foundered in its first few years, destroyed by internal divisions.

The Neue Freie Volksbühne to 1895

If Mehring's Freie Volksbühne carried on the Social Democratic tradition of the association, Wille's Neue Freie Volksbühne preserved the artistic and educational ideals which he had expressed in his original appeal. And simply *because* it was educational, Wille argued, it could not be fully democratic. The proletariat, he said, could not educate itself; and anyway, the principle of the association was of free agreement. 'No one is obliged to belong to the association against his inclination.' [46] It was, he said at the founding meeting (30 October 1892), to be a society for 'uplift' not for 'amusement', and in a series of articles he tried to convince his members that the value of a work of art does not depend upon the opinions of the artist, but on the artistic form. Like Hart and unlike Mehring, he valued *Die Weber* just because it was not one-sided or party-political, though ironically enough, the programme of the Neue Freie Volksbühne contained more new plays, problem plays and plays of social criticism than that of the 'social democratic' Freie Volksbühne. [47]

Most of the productions in this period were the association's own, and Wille was fortunate in obtaining the services of Emil Lessing as artistic director of the productions. No leading personality, Lessing was artistically serious, industrious and sensitive. Working within the naturalistic framework, he was not doctrinaire. He was able to get together some of the best Berlin players, and though they could not work together continuously he was able to create something like an ensemble. The keynote of high artistic ambition was struck in the first production, Goethe's *Faust, Part I*; and if some of the new plays produced were not of the highest quality, their inclusion was artistically adventurous.

Even so, Wille found experiment within the association difficult. Two attempted 'special performances' led to misfortune. Wille wanted to give two performances of *Meister Oelze* by Johannes Schlaf. To be sure of two houses Wille offered one of them to the Academic Dramatic Association, who guaranteed 750 Marks for it. Schlaf, however, hoped that Brahm might produce his play at the Freie Bühne (he never did), and when rehearsals were well advanced, he sent his friend Arno Holz along to cancel the arrangement. When Wille refused, Holz, very angry, went to the Academic Dramatic Association and persuaded it to withdraw. Wille went ahead; the result was heavy loss. On another occasion Agnes Sorma offered to play Voss's *Eva* for the Neue Freie Volksbühne. This would have been an enormous attraction, and the Zentral Theater was booked for two Sunday afternoons in February 1895. But then her own management, the Deutsches

Theater, insisted that she play for them on those afternoons, so the whole thing came to nothing.

The experience with Schlaf, however, had already shown Wille the difficulties of experiment in the Volksbühne, so he founded in 1894, an experimental theatre specifically to produce plays by young literary talent. A special periodical, *Die Versuchsbühne*, was also produced under Wille's editorship. In the event there were only two productions, before the police shut the venture down. The response to these productions was disappointing and the future of the experimental theatre might well have been in doubt quite apart from the police.

Wille's proud comment that no one need belong to the Neue Freie Volksbühne who didn't want to was answered by the fact that very few did want to. About three hundred people left the meeting with him on 12 October 1892. A call for new members did no more than double this number, and towards the end of the year membership had reached a thousand. As only nine hundred could see a performance at the Belle-Alliance a second section was needed. A recruiting slogan 'Every member a booking office' resulted in several hundred new members and in February 1893 a second section was launched, even though the total membership was only about fifteen hundred. The next season also opened with two half-filled sections, but the release of *Die Weber* to the Volksbühne associations brought in hundreds of new members. Two sections were filled and a third and fourth set up. But membership quickly declined again. The fourth section dropped out; by January 1894 amalgamation of the second and third was threatened. By the end of the season there were under two thousand members, and at the start of the 1894-5 season the second section had only four hundred; so that there were five hundred empty seats at its performances. By the second half of the season one performance was enough for the total membership.

There are no statistics, but probably the members were largely working-class, though in a smaller proportion than in Mehring's association. They applauded during performances and were openly rebellious during Ostrovsky's *The Storm*, evidently having not lost the spontaneity that was one of the original Volksbühne virtues. Antoine, founder of the Paris Théâtre Libre, was present at a Neue Freie Volksbühne performance of *Die Weber*, and was impressed by the audience much as Ibsen had been impressed at the Freie Volksbühne two years before. 'It was worth a journey from Paris to Berlin to see that', was Antoine's comment on the audience.

In the 1893-4 season frictions developed between the technical and artistic organisers, and a group comprising some three-quarters of the technical organisers called a meeting for 30 May 1894. On 15 September 1894 a further protest meeting was held, this time to question the whole relationship of membership and management. The principal speaker, Julius Müller, thought he had produced a trump card in accusing Wille of being well paid for his post on the executive. Into this situation a brief note from Wille burst like a bombshell:

> Weary of the persistent agitation that frustrates my efficiency and that of the Executive and Committee, I am hereby resigning from my post. I wish the beloved association well in every way but I have little hope. [48]

The resignation gave many members second thoughts, and a commission was appointed to meet Wille, who refuted the charges against him and resumed his post. Only a month later, however, at the ordinary general meeting (22 October) strong feeling against Wille was again expressed, especially over the power to assign good seats. Adjourned, the meeting continued eight days later. Wille finally won the battle, insisting that the players must retain the power of giving good complimentary seats. The ringleaders, Hermann Berger and, Julius Müller, however, continued to agitate and were struck off the list of organisers. They then (27 November) called a public meeting on the theme 'The corruption of the Neue Freie Volksbühne'. Only 120 people came, including some of Wille's supporters; but these eventually left and a unanimous vote of no confidence in Wille was then passed, and the meeting decided to found a Third Freie Volksbühne. Berger, Müller and a third, Stehl, were appointed to carry this into effect. They began negotiations with theatres, and misused the name of the Neue Freie Volksbühne. Wille threatened legal action and the whole thing collapsed.

Struggles with the Authorities, 1892–96

The judgement of January 1892 that the Freie Volksbühne was a category (ii) association made possible a degree of police control; but this was not strongly enforced. Early in 1893 an official statement was made that the performances could no longer be said to be really 'private', and it appeared for a time as if both bodies might have to submit to censorship. But in spite of the judgement nothing was done. It seemed as if troubles with the police might be over, but the truce proved to be only temporary. Already the Volksbühne idea had aroused interest outside Berlin, the strongest movement being in Hamburg and the neighbouring Altona. [49] In the autumn of 1894 the Altona police sent to the Berlin police saying that an attempt was being made in Altona to found a Volksbühne on the Berlin model and asking whether the Berlin Volksbühne performances were entirely private or whether, because of the large membership and because apparently anyone could get in by paying enrolment and entrance fees, they were not in fact to be regarded as public. This enquiry seems to have set the ball rolling again. At all events, on 18 April 1895 the Freie Volksbühne, the Neue Freie Volksbühne and the Versuchsbühne all heard from the police that they must now submit all scripts to the censor, fourteen days in advance of the performance. The message reached the chairmen on 19 April and on the 20th the directors of the National Theater (Freie Volksbühne) and Zentral Theater (Neue Freie Volksbühne) refused further performances of uncensored plays.

It was, however, too late to cancel the scheduled first performances of *Einsam* (*Alone*), a dramatisation by Agrell of a novel of Anzengruber, by the Neue Freie Volksbühne at the Zentral Theater on 21 April. The players and the audience both turned up, but the police lieutenant 'stood between them with the flaming sword of the censorship order' [50] and there was no performance. This production may well have been one of those other factors that led to the end of the 'provisional' freedom from censorship. The play was a passionate attack on clerical arrogance and parsonical intolerance. Nevertheless, the police action took the associations completely by surprise; they had been lulled into a sense of false security, and now, overnight, their meaningful existence was threatened. Both arranged general meetings. That of the Freie Volksbühne was immediate (23 April). A resolution was passed instructing the executive to fight the police decision. At the same time the association decided to suspend its operations, rather than continue, even temporarily, under censorship. The periodical was to continue in order to hold the membership together.

The administration of the Neue Freie Volksbühne, although unanimous that they should fight the police in the courts, could not agree on other aspects of policy. Some of them wanted to follow Mehring's example and suspend operations. Wille, characteristically putting theatre before politics, wanted to continue, replacing private performances by public ones. Eventually Wille's views prevailed and they were endorsed by a general meeting held on 17 May. The experimental theatre also decided both to continue its activities and to fight the police. Thus, to begin with, there was a three-pronged legal attack on the police action, but the two smaller bodies soon ran out of money and only the Freie Volksbühne was left in the field; and indeed, only one successful court action was needed for the whole movement.

There were long delays before judgement; even the first court did not meet until the summer. The whole of 1895 passed. The Freie Volksbühne, with a good fighting fund of 1600 Marks, arranged a 'Heine evening' and a concert. The Neue Freie Volksbühne tended to stagnate. There were four 'open' productions of established plays at the Schiller-Theater, but these ended in the autumn, and the general meeting in November 1895 decided to suspend regular performances. Meanwhile plans were afoot to alter the constitution so as to make it acceptable to the police.

While the official associations thus stagnated, the restless, stage-struck Julius Türk saw his opportunity to win his 'theatrical laurels'. Immediately after the suspension of Freie Volksbühne productions he established himself as a private manager and took over the Freie Volksbühne's agreement with the Ostend Theater (National Theater) – though the theatre-director, Max Samst, had to take part of the risk. At Whitsun 1895 he advertised in *Vorwärts*, 'Popular Performances in the National Theater, arranged by Julius Türk'. The first production was Hebbel's *Maria Magdalena*. Tickets were all one price, 75 Pfennigs, but for Freie Volksbühne members they were reduced to 60 Pfennigs. A long list of ticket-agencies was given: precisely that of the Freie Volksbühne. As treasurer of the association Türk obviously had excellent contacts here. After two productions at the National Theater Türk moved to the Alexanderplatz-Theater, and after that took his Volksbühnen-Ensemble on tour to Magdeburg, Halle, Leipzig and Hannover. Although he had some quite respectable actors, he did badly, especially on the tour, which was a complete fiasco. The Freie Volksbühne general meeting in July wanted to stop his activities, but were unable to do so. Nor was he now to be deterred by financial difficulty. He had tasted theatrical blood. In the autumn he offered Sunday afternoon performances at the Belle-Alliance - once more with single price tickets, using the Freie Volksbühne agencies. He just scraped through.

The appeal was laid by the Freie Volksbühne's lawyer, Kauffmann on 26 April 1895. Judgement was not given until January 1896. Meeting on 3 January, the High Court could not reach agreement. It did so on 24 January. Judgement was against the Freie Volksbühne, but a rider clearly hinted that constitutional changes might radically alter the position. The hint went unheeded. Perhaps Mehring welcomed the opportunity to get the Old Man of the Sea off his back. [51] The executive did not wait for the written judgement (which anyway didn't come until months later!) but called a general meeting for 9 March 1896. It was poorly attended, and after a short debate it was agreed to wind the association up. Five liquidators (including Türk!) were appointed. The assets, about a thousand Marks, were divided between the Social Democratic Party, the Workers' Education School and the weavers on strike at Kottbus. 'A burial without pomp and touching speeches of farewell', remarks Nestriepke. The experimental theatre was also dissolved and only Wille's own Neue Freie Volksbühne remained in existence, though dormant, to keep a faint line of unbroken continuity in the history of the movement. The general meeting held on 22 August 1896 formally resolved to seek alterations in the constitution to allow the association to continue. The new constitution, passed on 28 November, was far from ideal and some of the police requirements were very pernickety. It was not an easy rebirth and for many years it must have required a vast amount of faith to keep the association in being with fewer than two thousand members. But the faith was there, the continuity was maintained and the Neue Freie Volksbühne was ready when, early in the new century, the opportunity arose for its unprecedented growth.

Scene II
DEVELOPMENTS OUTSIDE BERLIN

Outside Berlin the Volksbühne idea quickly aroused practical interest. As early as 1892 a Committee for Popular Lectures, founded in Frankfurt am Main in 1890, successfully demanded cheap performances at the municipal theatre. Much later, from 1908, this committee arranged closed performances on Volksbühne lines.

In the same year, 1892, leading personalities of the local Freethinkers' Association in Cologne attempted to set up an organisation on the lines of Wille's in Berlin and called a public meeting to promote the scheme, but they gave it up as hopeless when they found that it was opposed by the most influential Social Democratic leaders.

Later, in 1908, a serious attempt was made to develop Volksbühne Associations in the Rhineland industrial conurbation. At a conference held in May at the Trade Union Building in Düsseldorf of representatives of Trade Unions from many towns in the Rhineland and Westphalia a commission was set up to study the practicability of such a project and to work out a precise plan, but despite the clarity of the discussions both in depth and in detail, the commission found that the scheme would fail except in Cologne and Düsseldorf. Various ways forward were suggested, even co-operation with amateur companies, but in the end the project was never fulfilled.

The first actual Volksbühne to be founded outside Berlin was the Freie Volksbühne Hamburg, whose founding meeting was held in December 1892. This was followed by a public meeting on 31 July 1893 which brought together a large number of people, members of a wide variety of organisations including, as in Cologne, the Freethinkers' Association. Here too the leadership of the Social Democratic party were ill-disposed to the founding of a Volksbühne as they feared it would lead to a split in the working-class movement. Even some colleagues of Adolf Sonn, a prophet of the Volksbühne idea, let him down. Nevertheless, he issued a public appeal, on the lines of Wille's. Several hundred people responded and at the meeting of 31 July, under the leadership of Herr Krause (later, in the 1920s, a Hamburg Senator) an Association was formed and a Commission of eleven was appointed to steer the movement. A leaflet was published and the first function, a lecture evening, with recitations, took place on 30 August. A General Meeting on 30 September discussed the constitution and elected an executive committee. Membership stood at around 500, so a performance was now possible. But in the Hamburg of that time, dominated by the police and the commercial theatre managers, the question of where to put on the production presented serious difficulties. The theatre directors were afraid of losing their monopoly: above all, it was Pollini, Director of the municipal theatre, who was at once a man of the theatre and a business man, who feared that if a Volksbühne were established it would oust his theatrical products from the Hamburg market.

At last the Volksbühne was successful in obtaining the Thalia Theatre, whose Director was Cléri Maurice, for the first performance. Hauptmann's *Vor Sonnenaufgang (Before Sunrise)* was to be presented in the middle of October 1893, but in the very week when the performance was due to take place Pollini, all-powerful as municipal Theatre Director, succeeded in getting Cléri Maurice, who was anxious to avoid conflict with his colleague, to withdraw his undertaking to allow the Thalia Theatre to be used. Instead, the Volksbühne obtained the Carl-Schulze Theatre in St. Pauli. This was an unsatisfactory makeshift, but it did enable the first performance, *Vor Sonnenaufgang*, poorly acted and inadequately directed, to reach the stage on 22 October 1893, its shortcomings overlooked by the enthusiastic friends of the Volksbühne. In the end Pollini succeeded in getting the management of this theatre also to bar the Volksbühne from its stage. Now the Hamburg Police and Pollini mounted a real witch-hunt against the Freie Volksbühne until at last the organisation shook the dust of the inhospitable "Free City" off its feet and migrated to Altona which, though almost a suburb of Hamburg, was under Prussian rule. Here in the Floral Hall of the Große Freiheit, in the Ernst Drucker Theatre and other venues, the Volksbühne presented a repertoire that embraced Hauptmann (*Vor Sonnenaufgang*, *Kollege Crampton*, and *Biberpelz*), Ibsen (*An Enemy of the People, Hedda Gabler, Nora (i.e. A Doll's House)* and *The Lady from the Sea*) as well as major works by Goethe, Shakespeare and Kleist, and plays by Halbe, Wolzogen, Hartleben, Fulda and others.

Unfortunately the Altona Police also allowed themselves to be strongly influenced by Pollini. He had talked them into believing he had sole production rights over Hauptmann's works in Hamburg and Altona and therefore could have the Volksbühne performances of Hauptmann cancelled by the police. He failed in this attempt, as the playwright had separate performing rights in Hamburg and Altona.

The Hamburg Volksbühne, during the whole period of its activity until 1899, had constantly to suffer under the allegation that it was a party-political institution controlled by the Social Democratic Party. To counter this, the Hamburg poet, Gustav Falke (1853-1916, whose basic position was that of middle-class conservatism) was elected as principal Chairman, in which honorary post he wore himself out. Pollini failed to appreciate the importance of the Volksbühne movement to the theatres themselves and piled up difficulties. The Police everywhere harassed the Freie Volksbühne and so finally in August 1899 Pollini and the police achieved their common aim: the first attempt to create a new theatrical culture in Hamburg through the Volksbühne movement was finally buried with a production of Goethe's *Faust*. The Association was wound up and Herr Krause pronounced its epitaph: "The old State [for Hamburg is a city-state] with unheard-of failure to appreciate its own responsibility, has harassed the Freie Volksbühne to death".

Thanks to the efforts of Adolf Sonn, "father" of the Hamburg Freie Volksbühne, an attempt was made in the Spring of 1894 to establish an Association in Kiel. A preparatory committee was formed and on 9 April, a mere six months after the first performance of the Hamburg Volksbühne a Freie Volksbühne for Kiel and its Environs was founded at the Kiel Colosseum. Sonn addressed the meeting and of the 400 people present, 250 joined the new organisation and a provisional committee of five was elected. The first event organised was a lecture on Hauptmann's *Die Weber* illustrated with recitations, after which regular performances, arranged by the Association, began to be given. Great difficulties were encountered. The Association failed to obtain the municipal theatre for its productions and had problems with the proprietor of the Colosseum, who did not keep to his agreements and repeatedly raised the rent originally agreed.

The leadership also gained the support of a number of academics, including Dr Eugen Wolff of Berlin, who had moved to Kiel. This made it possible to set up, alongside the Committee, a 'Literary Commission' consisting half of members of the Freie Volksbühne and half of "specialists". This Commission was charged with arranging the current artistic programme.

The Kiel Freie Volksbühne was so strongly suspected of being a party-political organisation that the Association changed its name to *Freie Bühne für jedermann* (*Independent Theatre for Everyone*). In the 1894-5 season it had a really comprehensive programme of activities including a variety of lectures and about twenty theatre performances (Hauptmann, Ibsen, Anzengruber, Halbe and others). It carried on with this basis until March 1897, when Dr Luppe, later to become Mayor of Nuremberg, was elected to the committee, a prestigious appointment even then.

The police authorities constantly made difficulties. The police chief declared the Volksbühne performances to be liable to censorship, and consequently the choice of plays was very severely limited. The authorities also constantly put difficulties in the way of the theatre proprietor until in the end he refused the Freie Volksbühne the use of the auditorium because he was afraid of police reprisals and feared he might lose the booking for the celebration of the Kaiser's birthday. Consequently an Extraordinary General Meeting on 24 October 1898 found itself obliged,

"in spite of the magnificent idea of the Association, to regard the
preconditions for the continued existence of the Kiel Freie
Volksbühne as no longer existing."

The dissolution was agreed by a large majority on a simple motion.

In the Autumn of 1894 a Volksbühne Hannover-Linden was founded,
apparently out of the local workers' movement. Julius Türk (Berlin) spoke
at one promotional public meeting and Dr Berthold (Chairman of the
Hamburg Association) at a later one. The first production was of Schiller's
Kabale und Liebe in the Great Hall of the Odeon in November. Other
productions followed though in the face of great opposition. Theatre
managements tried to prevent actors from appearing for the Volksbühne,
which responded by using amateurs. Taking up the Berlin example of 1891
the police claimed that the Volksbühne aimed at influencing public affairs.
When the committee could not produce a list of members, prosecution
followed. The police continued to insist that the Association was political,
and it dissolved itself - or at least ceased productions – in 1896.

The only Freie Volksbühne Association outside Berlin founded before
the First World War to survive that war (and, in fact, the Second World War
also) was Bielefeld in Westphalia, founded in 1905. When a municipal
orchestra was established there in 1901, individual trades unions decided
to promote special concerts. In a parallel development in 1902, when Norbert
Berstl took over a Summer Theatre outside the town gates he worked closely
with workers' organisations. In particular a production of *Egmont* for metal-
workers was an unprecedented success and was followed by regular
performances for similar audiences, thus providing the right conditions
for establishing a Freie Volksbühne when the Bielefeld Municipal Theatre
opened in 1904. After some technical preparations the Association was
founded at the beginning of January 1905. Chairman was Carl Severing,
who fulfilled this office for many years. The infant Freie Volksbühne was
subject to all kinds of social uncertainties and problems. During the first
twenty-five years of its existence it operated with only one Section and
with two performances a month, so that when in January 1930 it celebrated
its Silver Jubilee it had filled some 600,000 theatre seats. The Festival Address
was given by Carl Severing, now a Minister of the Reich.

From the start a single price was fixed for all performances and a
considerable proportion of the seats was reserved for the disabled – a
remarkable policy for its period. Until the outbreak of war the enthusiasm
and sacrifice of the active members overcame all difficulties, and after the
war had temporarily interrupted its activities it renewed its work in the
newly-opened municipal Regie-Theater in the autumn of 1918, even before
revolution broke out.

Scene III

INTO THE TWENTIETH CENTURY

The Freie Volksbühne from 1897

The success of the Neue Freie Volksbühne in reconstituting itself so as to be able to resume active life made a great impression on many of those former members of the Freie Volksbühne who had agreed in March 1896 to throw in the sponge. The wounds inflicted by the split had not even yet healed however, and the Freie Volksbühne men could not suggest that the work be continued with one joint organisation. So a committee set about quietly drafting a suitable constitution, though some of the former officers, including Mehring, made it clear that they would not be prepared to resume their posts in a re-founded Freie Volksbühne. On 7 March 1897, a year almost to the day after the formal dissolution of the 'old' Freie Volksbühne, an advertisement appeared in *Vorwärts* for a big public meeting on the subject: 'What is the attitude of the Berlin working classes to founding a Freie Volksbühne association?' The meeting took place on 12 March with Robert Schmidt in the chair. Paul Dupont, the advertised speaker and former vice-chairman, called for the re-establishment of the Freie Volksbühne, putting aside the idea of uniting with the Neue Freie Volksbühne. Adolf Löhr, bringing a forcefully worded message from Bruno Wille, fluently put the case for unity on behalf of the committee of the Neue Freie Volksbühne. After a lively debate the suggestion of a united Volksbühne was rejected, but it was rejected politely, with expressions of regret and the assurance that the reasons were objective, not personal. In spite of this, Wille took the decision badly.

The question must be asked whether the 'new' Freie Volksbühne of 1897 was in fact a direct continuation of the 'old' Freie Volksbühne. Heinz Selo, in his closely argued but highly tendencious thesis of 1930, maintained:

> This investigation proves that the Freie Volksbühne lived and went under with Social Naturalism. It should have been originally the 'literary organ' of the German working class, as the Social Democratic Party was its political organ and the Trades Unions its economic organ. It did not succeed in this. Instead it brought the working class to a taste for theatrical art. For when in 1897 the possibility presented itself to revive the association, it was newly constituted at the pressing wish of many earlier members, now of course in completely altered inner structure. [1]

As Selo's thesis includes nothing after 1896 he brings no evidence to support this last assertion, while his definition of what the Freie Volksbühne *should have been* rests on a very one-sided view of its roots. In whatever sense we take the phrase 'inner structure' it is difficult to see that it was 'completely altered'. The 'aim' was expressed less provocatively with no mention of the topicality and truth of the plays, but most clauses closely resembled the old ones. As to the character of the membership, a census of occupations made at the turn of the century shows that this was still primarily proletarian. [2] The association had the sympathy and trust of the workers. It soon outstripped the Neue Freie Volksbühne (which at this time had only one section, of eight to nine hundred members) and for six or seven years its leadership was never in question. In just over a fortnight one section was full. Steady growth continued until in the season 1907-8 there were over fourteen thousand members in twenty sections.

Although Mehring and Dupont would not stand as chairman and vice-chairman they remained on the committee with other former members and one new, Dr Bruno Borchardt. The members of the executive were new to office, but not to the movement. Dr Conrad Schmidt, the chairman, had been one of the founders in 1890, but in 1891 he had gone to Zürich as a university teacher. Now he had returned to Berlin and was working on *Vorwärts*. For decades to come he was to be a most important personality in the Volksbühne movement. In contrast with Mehring he was meditative rather than pugnacious, judicious rather than rash. His profound and many-sided education enabled him to write play-introductions which were both understandable and full of understanding. His was a lovable personality. He was a man of absolute openness and willingness to serve. He lacked certain qualities required of an active leader, however. Nor was he businesslike or tactically clever. The new vice-chairman, Heinrich Schulz, was a man who had sacrificed his career as a teacher to devote himself absolutely to the service of the Social Democratic Party. The general secretary was Julius Cohn, already on the committee, a man of known qualities, though with dangers hidden in his energy. His assistant Max Buschold, a former painter, was a good subordinate. The most onerous post was still that of treasurer. Being a paid appointment it developed in time into that of general manager. Julius Türk had no intention of becoming an organisation man again and in his place Gustav Winkler was elected. His candidacy was supported by Dupont and by Robert Schmidt: he was treasurer and later manager of the Freie Volksbühne for nearly a generation. Winkler, a stonemason, had been a member since the foundation in 1890 and had become an active one, though without a specific function, after Wille's exodus. He had been a correspondent to *Vorwärts* and assistant secretary in the Berlin Trades Union office. He had led the wage-battles of his fellow stonemasons, even being secretary of an International. Consequently he had been blacklisted within the trade and at the age of thirty-five found it hard to make a living. He was proposed by the stonemasons.

In constitution, working-class membership and socialist leadership, then, the re-founded Freie Volksbühne was the true child of the old one. But Heinz Selo's principal argument for discontinuity relates to the programme: '... the Freie Volksbühne lived and went under with Social Naturalism.' We must examine the programme of the first decade of the 'new' Freie Volksbühne. In the first place, no change in policy was intended. Most members saw the Freie Volksbühne as a member of the working-class movement, but an independent one, neither the supporter of an agit-prop political theatre, nor having a mere average eclectic programme. Plays should be enlightening, educational and such as to tend to liberate the people. The leading figures, of course, realised that every great work of art has a stimulating and educational element, and Conrad Schmidt expressed this in the first issue of the periodical in 1897. Nevertheless, the feelings about ideology were so strong that in the same year the association declined an invitation from Raphael Löwenfeld to participate in honouring Tolstoy's seventieth birthday, because of his belief in suffering and his primitive Christian mysticism. (But three years later, *The Power of Darkness* was included in the programme.)

Conrad Schmidt, more than Mehring, was committed to the Naturalist movement in drama and would have included a high proportion of new naturalistic plays in the programme had these been forthcoming: but they were not. The history of dramatic writing, expressed in the development of the established playwrights and the interests of the younger ones, was determined by many factors other than the desires of the Freie Volksbühne. The lack of these plays was repeatedly lamented in the periodical and in general meetings, and Schmidt had to point out that if an unbroken series of productions was to continue, a broader idea of what were suitable plays was essential. Nevertheless, apart from the paucity of completely new plays and plays still banned by the censor, the programme presented over the next six years, or even over the next decade, does not differ radically in character from the earlier. There were fifty-two productions of sixty-two plays in the next six years; eleven were classics, ten were foreign, and the rest modern German. [3] In the following period (1902-8) seventy-two different plays were presented (a few being one-acters) of which twenty-one were classics, twenty-two by modern foreign authors and twenty-nine by modern German authors. Thus there were many more classics, and the number of works that would not have been found in any ordinary theatre repertoire was extremely small. The repertoire was varied and lively, but not bold. By that time, however, the Freie Volksbühne was competing with the phenomenal growth of the Neue Freie Volksbühne (now collaborating with Reinhardt) and might well be forgiven for popularising its programme.

Even so, the programme was not entirely unadventurous, and certainly not without plays of social and political criticism. In 1902 the Freie Volksbühne presented *The Good Hope* by the Dutch socialist playwright Herman Heijermans; in 1905 followed two more of his plays, both of which had been blocked by the censor: *No. 80* and *Armour*, both works of trenchant social criticism, the one of law and punishment, the other of militarism. As a result the author released to the association his unperformed *Ora et labora* (1906). Tschirikow's *The Jews* (1904) was an exposure of Russian pogroms. But perhaps more significant than these was the Freie Volksbühne's introduction of Shaw to Germany. At the beginning of the century he was virtually unknown there, but by the time the Freie Volksbühne decided to include *Arms and the Man* (1902/3) in its programme, Lindau had already planned to present it at the Deutsches Theater. The Volksbühne production took place first, though not without friction. The *Börsen-Courier* claimed that the Volksbühne performance was an illegal trespass upon Lindau's theatre; it went further and claimed that the performance was not only without Shaw's permission, but against his will. The executive replied that they were totally unaware of Lindau's plans and published a letter from Shaw which said: 'Among all German theatres there is none by which I would rather be produced than by the Freie Volksbühne. [4] Productions of *The Devil's Disciple* (1902/3), *Mrs Warren's Profession* (1903/4) and *Widowers' Houses* (1906/7) followed. Shaw's plays of keen social criticism were closely in harmony with the basic ideals of the Freie Volksbühne, and in the absence of new naturalistic plays the association could hardly have done better than introduce Shaw to its audiences.

If, as is true, the Freie Volksbühne became less experimental in the early years of the new century, 'safer' in its general choice of plays, the reason is not to be sought in a change of intention or aim, but in the sheer size of the growing body. Franz Mehring, who had justified similar policies as early as 1892 on the grounds that it is harder to experiment with large numbers, brought forward the same argument again, out of his own experience, in 1906, when opposing a further expansionist plan within the movement. 'The greater the number of members', he wrote, 'the less can the tendency to experiment exist'. No great human movement, political, ethical, artistic or religious, can retain in its enlarged maturity the purity and intensity of its infancy.

When the Freie Volksbühne was re-founded in March 1897 it was already too late to produce any plays under its own direction in that season. Julius Türk, however, was still presenting Sunday afternoon performances, with the tickets sold through the Freie Volksbühne's own agencies. They were not very good productions. Türk had a shrewd head, but was no Director. The Freie Volksbühne, having no choice, went to his plays, but with little satisfaction. A proposal was put forward to offer Türk the post of play director under Freie Volksbühne management – in this way the association hoped for greater control over him. But he refused. He valued his independence and preferred to negotiate independently with the association. The association responded, but at the same time sounded out other theatres. Several theatres were needed if its members were to be given a satisfactory programme. Türk could offer only one, so the negotiations collapsed. Türk was offended and embittered, and some of the Volksbühne officials became his advocates. The executive remained firm, and eventually the agencies were forbidden to work for Türk. So it came about that Türk, incurably bitten by the theatre bug, and having himself worked for the resurrection of the Freie Volksbühne, now found that its very existence precluded him from any future in Berlin.

In later years need drove him into several different walks of life, those of touring lecturer, of hotelier, of publican; but he always came back to the theatre whenever he saw an opportunity. At one time he worked with Reinhardt, but usually independently, as director of small or medium sized municipal theatres. His theatrical activity took him to Silesia, Saxony, Switzerland and south-west Germany. Sometimes he did well, at others he had to draw on his savings. Inflation after the First World War finally ate up his reserves and he committed suicide, a broken man. He was one who had always meant well, whose aspirations had been fundamentally good. But his actions lacked the guidance of a fine insight, and the movement which he loved might well have been better without his fight against Bruno Wille.

The first theatre manager with whom the Freie Volksbühne made an agreement was its old friend Max Samst, now at the Friedrich-Wilhelmstädtisches Theater. At the same time there was an agreement with Oscar Blumenthal at the Lessing Theater, where the artistic director was Carl Waldow. In the following season the same theatres were used, and the Freie Volksbühne engaged as its own artistic director Adolf Steinert, Hungarian by birth, an eccentric, but a craftsman of the theatre, with imagination and originality. He was to play an important part in the movement for a long time. For the season 1901-2 an additional agreement was concluded with Paul Lindau at the Berliner Theater. In this season each member saw four productions at the Berliner Theater, four at the Lessing Theater (now managed by Fritz Witte-Wild) and two at the Ostend – now called the Carl-Weiss-Theater. This combination of arrangements was far from ideal and it is not altogether surprising that at a general meeting on 25 January 1900 the suggestion was actually voiced that the association ought to build its own theatre. Of course, neither the membership nor the financial reserves were anywhere near adequate and the idea was quite utopian. Any attempt to put it into practice would have been disastrous; but it was a pointer to the future. At the beginning of the new century the association also temporarily lost Steinert who took a post in Barmen (Wuppertal), but he had hardly arrived there when his theatre was burnt down and he returned to Berlin and to his post.

More serious and important were the changes in theatre management that occurred between 1904 and 1906. In 1904 Witte-Wild left the Lessing Theater, and Otto Brahm, ending his historic decade (1894-1904) at the Deutsches Theater, took over from him. The Freie Volksbühne was unable to reach agreement with him, but followed Witte-Wild to the Metropol Theater. At the same time Paul Lindau took over the Deutsches Theater and made a new agreement with the Freie Volksbühne. But early in the 1905-6 season, Lindau went bankrupt and his successor Max Reinhardt, who had already, as we shall see, a relationship with the Neue Freie Volksbühne which placed him under obligations to that body, would not honour Lindau's contract. The Freie Volksbühne was thus driven to various unsatisfactory resorts, including arrangements with the old Ostend – now, under another new management, known as the Bürgerliches-Schauspielhaus. About this time, too, after a brief and unsatisfactory arrangement with Carl Waldow as artistic director, the Freie Volksbühne engaged Steinert (for whom an anticipated post in Cologne had not materialised) as artistic director for the third time.

Through this whole period the Freie Volksbühne avoided performances of plays outside the series which members were committed to see. An exception was two performances of *The Lower Depths*. Otherwise extra performances were all of opera. There were also two or three 'festivals' each year, though the open-air summer event was dropped after 1897. They often took the form of concerts, but also included recitation and lectures. The festivals were a mixture of culture and dancing; one might have a Mozart or Heine evening, followed by a social dance – all for 50 Pfennigs. In the spring of 1905 the festival was a Schiller Festival, celebrating the centenary of the poet's death. Instead of a single evening there were lectures, performances of *Die Räuber* and *Kabale und Liebe* and a performance of Beethoven's Ninth Symphony with the 'Ode to Joy'.

In the 1903-4 season came a decision to hold Cultural Evenings in each of which one composer, author or painter would be celebrated with lectures on and examples of his work: the first was on Beethoven.

Another special activity was the choir. Ernst Zander, a young dentist who had earlier successfully led the choir of the Neue Freie Volksbühne, proposed the idea in September 1903. Soon there was a membership of 150. Discussions arose about financial responsibility and in February 1904 the choir declared itself to be financially and organisationally independent. The original name Volksbühnenchor was changed to Volkschor. Zander wanted it to have a professional conductor, but the members insisted on his continuing, and even though at first he said he was doing it only 'provisionally', he was still its leader in 1930, by which time it was the oldest mixed choir in the Deutscher Arbeitersängerbund.

Throughout this time the periodical *Die Freie Volksbühne* was published. Johann Sassenbach, a well-known trades unionist who ran a press purely to help the workers' movement, published it for the first year, the cost being covered by advertisements. At first the periodical was not much to look at. It was improved in the season 1902-3 with a new cover, showing the back view of a father with his son his knee looking towards a proscenium. It was criticised on the grounds that children were not admitted as members!

It is not easy to believe that the periodical was edited and written on an entirely honorary basis and that, like the organisation as a whole, it had no office. All posts, indeed, were honorary, except that of treasurer, which was poorly paid. Winkler got 150 Marks a month to begin with, which rose by irregular increments to 250 Marks in the early years of the twentieth century: and there was great trouble in 1901 because the resolution that his salary be raised to 225 Marks per month had been proposed by a person not in full membership! That same winter it was decided to get a proper office (even a telephone was suggested) so that Gustav Winkler need not work from his little flat in Rixdorf. But the scheme did not materialise. Just how Winkler worked at home, and at what inconvenience to himself and his family, he has himself vividly described:

> For thirteen years my private flat, the sitting-room and kitchen, served for carrying out the association's business. There could be no question of regular working hours. Only the hours of night interrupted the hours of work. When the regular audit of the accounts took place we had first of all to put my little girl Lisa's cot in the kitchen, so that the auditors could be offered seats. (Lisa was three when I took on the job.) As a part-time job my wife helped me to deliver to the agencies the numerous items of printed matter, and packets of cards and tickets. The leaflets were stowed away with little Lisa in the pram, and so she went, tightly bound in Volksbühne ideas, zigzagging through Berlin to the thirty-six agencies we had established.[5]

Obviously such a body, carrying out such a large-scale operation from so small a base, physically and financially, could not run without frictions or changes. In the spring of 1898, about a year after the new beginning, Schulz, the vice-chairman, left for Erfurt to edit the party paper there, he was replaced by Johannes Gaulke, stonemason and writer. Then Franz Mehring resigned. The immediate cause was differences with the chairman, Conrad Schmidt. Ever since 1892 Mehring had carried on a feud against what he called a 'writers' clique' which was particularly represented by Schönhoff, editor of *Vorwärts*. Schönhoff had taken Wille's side against Türk at the time of the split. An honest man, Schönhoff had reviewed some Freie Volksbühne productions very unfavourably, and in particular he had criticised justly, but sharply, the production and reception of Blumenthal's one-acter, *Abu Seid*. Schmidt himself commented strongly on this in a general meeting and was supported by others, some of whom wanted a complaint to be made to the Press Commission, while Mehring wanted a 'boycott' of the 'clique'. Schmidt, who realised that *Vorwärts* was basically sympathetic to the association, did not want this and would only agree to a retort on the tone of the critique. The committee agreed and Mehring, wounded, resigned. Many regretted his leaving, and with reason. Though one-sided, rough in judgement, obstinate, unjust, lacking in understanding and balance, he had nevertheless done much for the Freie Volksbühne, where, particularly on the political side, he had made a contribution that probably no other man could have made. Benno Maass was co-opted to fill his place and a year later a seventh member was elected to the committee by a general meeting held in April: this was Curt Baake, whose return to office was most valuable.

This clash with the *Vorwärts* critic was the first of several such; another was with Kühl, when the critic actually defended himself at a general meeting in January 1899; another was with his successor Erich Schlaikjer. This time Schmidt's objection was backed by everyone except Maass, and Schlaikjer later took his revenge by giving the name 'Conrad Schmidt' to an unsympathetic character in his play *Des Pastors Rieke*.

The 'critic' problem came to a climax at the beginning of 1902 when Schmidt himself was appointed theatre critic of *Vorwärts*. His opponents said at once (perhaps with some justification) that this was incompatible with his remaining chairman of the Freie Volksbühne. The committee passed, by a bare majority, a resolution of Dupont's to this general effect, with the expected consequence that Schmidt resigned. A stormy general meeting inevitably followed (29 April 1902) in which, as his clinching argument, Cohn suggested that Schmidt had some kind of relationship with the justly hated police chief Merscheidt-Hüllessem! Nothing, of course, could have been further from the truth. But the trick back-fired on its perpetrator and the meeting rallied to the support of Schmidt. Cohn, Dupont, Fraenkel and the auditor Sahm, resigned their posts and ultimately a 'provisional leadership' was set up consisting of Conrad Schmidt himself and two members whose speeches from the floor had swung the meeting round in his favour. Winkler, of course, remained as treasurer. The triumvirate continued for only a matter of days, for at a further general meeting held on 9 May 1902, Schmidt was re-elected to the chairmanship with Baake, his ideal complement, as vice-chairman. The secretary was Dr Hans Davidson, assistant Max Buschold. This was the last major political crisis within the management of the association for many years.

In 1906 Kurt Eisner fell foul of the Social Democratic Party leadership and had to give up the editorship of *Vorwärts*, so that shortly afterwards he left Berlin and had to resign from the Artistic Committee of the Freie Volksbühne – a great loss. He was replaced by Dr John Schikowski. Schikowski was already a leading figure in the Freie Volksbühne Charlottenburg that had come into being in 1905. He was particularly interested in the visual arts and through his preference for abstract painting and sculpture became in later years an enthusiast for modern ballet, so that under his influence the Volksbühne became an important factor in the promotion of this branch of theatre. Schikowski was not only expert in his field, but an original character, uniting Prussian crustiness with dry humour.

The Neue Freie Volksbühne from 1896 to 1908

The decisive year in the history of the Neue Freie Volksbühne – and as it transpired, for the whole movement – was the season 1905-6 when Max Reinhardt went to the Deutsches Theater and the membership of the Neue Freie Volksbühne leapt in one season from six thousand (in seven sections) to ten thousand (in twelve sections). In the following year (1906-7) it overtook the Freie Volksbühne, ending the season with fifteen thousand five hundred members in eighteen sections, and in 1907-8 it had eighteen thousand members in no fewer than twenty-two sections. That is to say, it had to lay on twenty-two actual performances and distribute eighteen thousand theatre tickets each month of the season.

But such success must have been beyond the wildest dreams of its officers in the autumn of 1895, when the problems of censorship had still not been overcome and membership was two hundred at the most. In the summer of 1896 preparations were made for the next season's performances, but although the association had an autumn and winter free of competition (the Freie Volksbühne being non-existent then) this did not greatly help, even the modest goal of two sections not being achieved. In truth the association could not reach the mass of the workers, though its very forcible recruiting leaflet issued at the turn of the year 1896-7 was addressed to them, and though, as censuses of occupations taken in October 1900 and 1902-3 showed, the *proportions* of various workers in membership were much as in the rival body (e.g. the largest single group was that of the joiners) but on a much smaller scale. [6]

The continuation of work in the autumn of 1896 had to be in the form of participation in public performances, as the long negotiations with the police over the new constitution were still in progress, but an arrangement with Brahm enabled the association to book part-houses at the Deutsches Theater. Then, after the new constitution had been passed on 28 November, it was able to present its own, closed performances, and for some years (until

1902) in contrast with the Freie Volksbühne, it took very few productions from existing repertoires.[7] Its own list of productions contained fewer classics than that of the Freie Volksbühne, but only because so many of these were too costly to stage, and the classics chosen were economical ones such as *La Malade Imaginaire, Nathan der Weise* (*Nathan the Wise*), *Maria Magdalene* etc. As a whole the repertoire was considerably more adventurous than that of its larger competitor. For example it included the first German productions of Björnson's *Beyond our Power II* and Büchner's *Dantons Tod,* and world premieres of Björnson's *New System* and *Paul Lange and Tora Parsberg*, as well as six of less lasting worth. The production of *Paul Lange and Tora Parsberg* involved the association in a dispute with the publisher, Alfred Langen, Björnson's son-in-law, who had already given the rights to the Munich Hoftheater. The Neue Freie Volksbühne retorted that its private performances enabled it to play what it liked, and that anyway Langen ought to be thankful that it was so enterprising or he might have waited a long time for a German production of *Beyond our Power II*. This more adventurous programme had to be staged very modestly, with great economy in the settings and casting, though a few well-known names (e.g. Emanuel Reicher) appeared from time to time.

Inevitably such a programme did not attract a large membership. Time showed that it was not simply Wille's failure to win the trust of the workers, but also his uncompromising artistic policy and its far from lavish execution that kept the Neue Freie Volksbühne small during these years, for as soon as this policy was changed, and the association began to include more plays from the programmes of existing theatres, the membership began to increase, until it reached six thousand in 1904-5.

Naturally this development, and the policies that led to it, must be traced back ultimately to the men in charge of the association. Not all were ideally suited to their posts: the first treasurer, Eduard Möller, was no good at detailed 'niggling' work. He kept the money in two cigarette tins; and when his brother-in-law, Siebenmark, the proprietor of a printing works, was imprisoned for his part in the production of the anarchist periodical *Der Sozialist* and Möller took over the works for the time, he paid Neue Freie Volksbühne bills with the firm's money! Naturally that was the end of him as treasurer. His successor, in February 1897, was Adolf Löhr, a type-founder also connected with *Der Sozialist*. In 1899 he became too ill to do the job properly and August Müller, a compositor, undertook to help him unofficially. Müller at once showed that he was a first-class man who wanted no public credit. [8] He soon recognised a problem. Löhr was a *Schlafbursche,* that is a man who rented only a bed, not a room, and was virtually without an address from which to conduct the association's business. So Müller suggested a change.

Heinrich Neft was a man of thirty-one who had been a member of the Neue Freie Volksbühne from its foundation. He had been an Organiser. Though regarded by many people as a wild man he was only apparently superficial. A socialist even in the days of the anti-socialist laws, he had joined the Independent Socialists and had become an anarchist. Having the courage to put his signature to *Der Sozialist* he had been accused of treason and blasphemy, but was eventually acquitted. Originally he had political motives for working with the Neue Freie Volksbühne but it became for him ultimately an end in itself. No doubt the scope it offered for individual initiative suited Neft better than the democratic control of the Freie Volksbühne would have done. In the late summer of 1899 Müller proposed that Neft, who was about to marry Müller's sister, should take over the treasurership; at the same time he assured the sceptics that he himself would be in the background to help. The proposal was accepted. At first Neft leaned on Müller, but he soon became master of the situation. The former wild anarchist became a quiet observer of economic and social struggle. He lived for the organisation which he served, and under him it made great progress. The opposition to him soon came to an end, and a proposal in October 1900 to have Löhr as treasurer again was defeated by ninety-eight votes to fourteen. [9]

Like other Volksbühne officers, Neft worked in his spare time at home until 1902 when the association began to expand and the work became too much. Then the association was able to get him a cigar shop and his wife was able to look after this while he did Volksbühne work. But the shop did not pay too well, and the treasurer's honorarium was increased. Finally, in the spring of 1905, Neft was completely freed of the need to do other work, and a house in the Bremer Strasse was obtained which provided both an office for the association and a new home for the Nefts. In December 1905 as expansion continued, an assistant had to be engaged: the successful candidate was – August Müller.

Predictably, Heinrich Braulich in his Marxist history of the Volksbühne, gives a hostile view of Neft and his achievements. Though, as a plumber he belonged to the working class, Braulich describes him as 'the typical product of the proletarian uprooted from his class' and his position in the Neue Freie Volksbühne as 'a dictatorship lasting thirty years' – Braulich accuses him of having transformed the Volksbühne into 'a gigantic season-ticket institution.'[10]

On the whole, the officers and artistic committee in 1896 constituted a strong group including such men as Gustav Landauer, Fritz Mauthner, Emil Lessing, Max Dreyer (the dramatist) and Dr Ludwig Jacobowski, editor of *Gesellschaft*. Jacobowski soon became chairman and achieved sudden importance in the summer of 1897 when Bruno Wille, on a lecture tour in

Austria, was arrested on accusations of 'disturbing religion and spreading unbelief'. He was released on two thousand Gulden bail but had to remain in Austria until the case was over, which was many months, during which Jacobowski had to carry the whole burden of the association. At the end of it all Wille was sentenced to six days' house arrest. Jacobowski had not really the personality of a leader, and suffered, too, from a speech defect; but he had great gifts. He was a fine, sensitive lyric poet and a serious, creative thinker. He had the courage to publish meaty and substantial extracts from the works of the greatest poets in penny numbers for working-class readers, an enterprise which proves at once his determination to popularise the arts, and his own daring. He had a likeable manner and was a good worker, which compensated for his immaturity and lack of practical sense. He stood by Wille for four years: the artistic activities and particularly the experiments of these years were largely due to him. His retirement was due to eye trouble and he died a few weeks after it, in December 1900.

He was followed by Max Martersteig, who found after a few months that the work demanded too much time and in the summer of 1901 made way for Dr Joseph Ettlinger, whose name first appears in the records in 1896. Ettlinger was the architect of the great expansion. In 1901 he was just over thirty, established as a good translator, novelist and critic. He had made the *Literarisches Echo* a respected periodical. He was not 'brilliant', but was what the association needed – a man of taste and good judgement, possessing both solidity and initiative. He was trustworthy, always eager to help, and had good connections. No trouble or sacrifice was too great for him. A year or so later he became chairman, Wille becoming vice-chairman, as he had done when Jacobowski took over. (Later Wille even became deputy vice-chairman.) Ettlinger remained chairman until 1908. He was a busy man and it was not easy for him to find time for honorary work, but it was characteristic of him that in the season 1906-7 he was making himself available to members for the whole of every alternate Sunday.

Ettlinger considered that his policy was completely in the spirit of Wille's original foundation, and his decision to go over gradually to the use of productions from existing theatres was conceived as an expression of this. He wanted complete political independence, with no one-sidedness in the programme. Of course, the policy had its critics and Ettlinger, answering them in 1906, said,

> What *is* the tendency which, it is claimed, should or could be destroyed? Our whole tendency, the aim of our association is one and only one: to offer elevating and liberating works of art to the working population. [11]

It was thanks to Ettlinger that the Neue Freie Volksbühne in 1903 established a relationship with Reinhardt, a relationship which he cemented by co-opting Reinhardt and his dramaturge Felix Holländer as non-voting 'advisers' to the artistic committee of the association – though both were in fact too much occupied with their own affairs to be of much practical help to the committee. At this time Reinhardt was not yet universally recognised as an outstanding artist, though his productions in the Kleines Theater, especially that of *The Lower Depths*, which was performed five hundred times, had already attracted attention. Therefore Ettlinger must be given the credit for realising that he was the rising star of the theatre to whom the Neue Freie Volksbühne would do well to hitch its still lowly wagon.

The partnership of the Neue Freie Volksbühne and Max Reinhardt has a symbolic quality. Both were in some sense unruly children of Otto Brahm. If the Freie Bühne had not existed, the Freie Volksbühne would probably not have done so, and the naturalistic movement with which Brahm was identified was that with which the Volksbühne originally identified itself. Brahm first saw Reinhardt, then a young, unknown Viennese actor, playing in Salzburg and immediately engaged him for the Deutsches Theater, of which he was then director-designate. From 1894 for nearly nine years, during which he made a high reputation as an actor of old men, Reinhardt worked under Brahm at the Deutsches Theater. Sharing from the start many of Brahm's fundamental leanings, he learned from him indelibly the great principles of unexaggerated truth, ensemble-playing and unconditional respect for the dramatist's text. And though the great eclectic later employed every device and every style that the theatre offered, part of his greatness was that he never wholly lost touch with these roots. Brahm he honoured to the end of his life. So too the association founded by Wille, while it came to express in its play policy the fact that the plain Naturalism practised by Brahm was not the whole of theatrical experience, nevertheless always retained his high conceptions of art and truth.

Not that Reinhardt had ever believed that Brahm's theatre contained all that drama needed or offered. As an impoverished young man he had been a 'Child of the gods' (*Kind der vierten Galerie*) at the Vienna Burgtheater and in the acting of Sonnenthal had experienced something neither known to Brahm nor sympathetic to him. Except for Kainz, Reinhardt said later, Brahm's actors 'lacked the grand manner necessary for the classics, which made those old artists so outstanding'. [12] Even while working under Brahm, Reinhardt, with other like-minded actors, had played in matinées of works that held no interest for Brahm, and founded a cabaret, *Noise and Smoke*. Then, with financial help from one of his colleagues, Louise Dumont, Reinhardt found himself in a position to set up his own management in the Kleines Theater – though Brahm inflicted a fine of 14,000 Marks on him for breach of contract. At first he had only some successes; [13] then came *The Lower Depths* in which Reinhardt played Luka (the last of the young actor's old men) and which was nominally directed by Richard Vallentin, who also played Satin. But it was in this production that Reinhardt first realised his gift of *tuning actors to each other* and awakening in them things they themselves had not dreamed of. This close personal work with actors was probably Reinhardt's greatest gift, too easily lost sight of behind the vast spectacles of his later career. Gerda Redlich, an Austrian actress who trained under Reinhardt in Vienna and made her first stage appearance walking on at Salzburg in *Jedermann* (*Everyman*), and whose architect father was, with Poelzig, responsible for the Grosses Schauspielhaus, has said of him:

> Reinhardt was a very modest, quiet, gentle person. What was typical of him was that when he would sit, he would always sit on his hands, watching what was going on. He would never raise his voice. He did most of his directing by taking actors aside and telling them privately what he wanted to get from them, not in front of the others. It was all gentle and civilised and no showing-off at all, just marvellous.

In reply to the remark that Reinhardt's actual productions were in fact showy, she continued:

> Tremendous, but you see, in England Reinhardt is only known through his *World Theatre* and *Miracle* and that sort of thing, and that – that wasn't his strength: chamber theatre, small detailed, subtle work with actors – and that was his real strength. And he was a fantastic teacher. [14]

The financial success of the Kleines Theater also enabled him to rent a larger theatre, the Neues Theater, and at this point Ettlinger brought about an agreement between him and the Neue Freie Volksbühne. His artistic successes multiplied: this was the year of his newly-furbished *Minna von Barnhelm*. In the next season the association required only three of its own productions to complete its programme, and in 1905 the decision was made to have none. Friedrich Möest, the director, was honourably discharged from his post, and the agreements made with the theatres gave the association not only a say in the programmes, but even some influence over the casting! Then Reinhardt, without giving up the Neues Theater, took over from Lindau the one thousand-seater Deutsches Theater. Because of his existing relationship with the Neue Freie Volksbühne, he refused to honour Lindau's agreement with the Freie Volksbühne, and the Neue Freie Volksbühne immediately booked all Sunday afternoons in the Deutsches Theater. The original intention was that these should replace the performances at the Neues Theater, but the news of the Deutsches Theater agreement brought such a flood of new members that Neft, without consulting his colleagues, went ahead and booked the Neues Theater as well, although thousands of new members would be needed to fill both theatres. The other officers were shocked, but Neft's instinct had led him to act rightly, if rashly; for this was the beginning of the real development of the association. The Neue Freie Volksbühne had gained a monopoly of Reinhardt's Sunday matinees with all the drawing-power this implied. Success breeds success, and the monopoly of the two Reinhardt theatres led to further growth. In the 1905-6 season, the association still went to the Schiller-Theater, and when the limited liability company that managed it got a second theatre, this was used too. In the following season, 1906-7, the Neue Freie Volksbühne was using five theatres: Reinhardt's two, the Schiller-Theater North and Schiller-Theater East, and a new theatre in Charlottenburg, built by the city and rented to the Schiller Theater Company. In 1907-8 a sixth was added.

The change from the policy of mounting its own productions to that of using productions already in other repertoires raised the overall standard of what was presented to members in terms of quality of acting and settings, and the technical resources available. The Schiller-Theater productions were good; but these were put in the shade by Reinhardt's which opened up a new world to the members. They were able to see actors like Reinhardt himself, Kayssler and Agnes Sorma. The real quality of what the association was now offering to its membership can be assessed when we realise that to this period belong most of Reinhardt's great classical productions - his *Minna von Barnhelm*, his *Midsummer Night's Dream* (at first too expensive for the Neue Freie Volksbühne), *The Winter's Tale*, *The Merchant of Venice* and *Twelfth Night*. His *Lower Depths* entered the Volksbühne programme when it transferred from the Kleines Theater to the Neues. Typically, Reinhardt offered variety of plays: Nestroy, Björnson, Courteline, Shaw, Ibsen, Hauptmann, Holz, Anzengruber and Tolstoy were all included. His historic production of Wedekind's *Frühlings Erwachen* (*Spring Awakening*) in his recently opened Kammerspiele in 1906 was put into the Volksbühne programme as an 'extra', the smallness of the theatre (three hundred seats) making it impossible to use it in the regular series.

At the Schiller-Theater members saw some less often performed classics such as Schiller's *Braut von Messina* (*Bride of Messina*) and *Wallensteins Lager* (*Wallenstein's Camp*) with *Piccolomini*, and Hebbel's *Nibelungen, Parts I and II*. At the Lortzing Theater, they saw some operas, including *The Merry Wives of Windsor*, *Zar und Zimmermann* (*Tsar and Carpenter*), *Die Zauberflöte* (*The Magic Flute*) and *Fra Diavolo*. The association's own productions included *The Marriage of Figaro*. Among these productions of its own, along with Gerhart Hauptmann, Björnson, Ibsen and Anzengruber, the association included several world premieres, (for example *Marianne* by Carl Hauptmann, Gerhart's brother) and a remarkable resurrection, *Die Kindesmörderin* (*The Childmurderess*) by Heinrich Leopold Wagner, a *Sturm und Drang* poet. Ettlinger had re-edited and published this play, which had previously been regarded as of literary-historical interest only, but was now given life on the stage.

Giving up its own productions did not mean sacrificing its freedom of choice. Between 1905 and 1908 theatres produced at least eighteen plays at the special request of the association. These included German and foreign classics (Grillparzer, Lessing, Calderón) and many modern plays. Some were revivals of plays that had previously impressed Volksbühne audiences; some were chosen with little regard for the taste of the main body of members (e.g. *The Seagull*). One of these 'Volksbühne' plays, Schmidtbonn's *Mutter Landstrasse* (*Mother Highway*) made such an impression that Reinhardt took it over into his ordinary evening repertoire where it became a 'best seller'.

In this period the Neue Freie Volksbühne was especially active in arranging extra (non-obligatory) performances and special events. In the earlier part of the period the smallness of the association and the need for extra income provided a spur, while in the latter part, the time of great growth, purely social events were left for the voluntary workers to arrange, while the association itself provided a rich programme of concerts and artistic evenings.

The audience of the Neue Freie Volksbühne remained of much the same character as before. Wille, although he felt it his calling to marry art and the people, found it hard to reconcile himself to the audience's limitations and its inability to respond to some of the plays, and he wrote in 1898 that sometimes he felt that the Jacob of art had wooed Rachel only to marry Leah, 'a splendid housewife, and, of course, Rachel's sister ... but often Jacob cannot but sigh over his Leah'. Inappropriate laughter at *The Lower Depths* led the association to issue a pamphlet telling people not to laugh in the wrong place! This rather heavy-handed rebuke led, naturally, to the situation in which people were afraid to laugh at a comedy, and those who did were hushed by their more timid neighbours.

Progress towards Unity 1908–1914

The development of the Neue Freie Volksbühne from 1907 to 1912 was spectacular. It grew from eighteen thousand members (twenty-two sections) in the season 1907-8 to fifty thousand (sixty-three sections) – the population of a small town – in the season 1911-12. This meant the sale and distribution of half a million theatre tickets a year. Ten years before, there had been only two thousand members, one-twenty-fifth of the present size!

By contrast, and, of course actually because of the success of the Neue Freie Volksbühne, the Freie Volksbühne barely expanded during the same period and reached only about eighteen thousand in the 1911-12 and 1912-13 seasons.

Nor was the growth of the Neue Freie Volksbühne merely quantitative. In 1908 the constitution was revised and made a little more democratic, and in the following year Wille became honorary chairman, thus leaving an opening for new blood. In 1910 one of the new 'experts' without voting power on the Artistic Committee was Julius Bab. Bab was the son of the owner of a small woodwork factory who was himself a theatre enthusiast. Even as a grammar school boy, Bab played walk-on parts under Otto Brahm and watched his great Ibsen productions from the gods of the Deutsches Theater. His earliest ambition was to be an actor; in his twenties he also had two plays produced in Stuttgart; but he soon realised that his true calling must involve both his practical abilities and his critical awareness. Nearly every issue of *Die Schaubühne* (founded 1905) in its early years contained an article by him, while he also distinguished himself as a dramaturge and regisseur. He had a deep understanding of the Volksbühne idea and of how it could lead to healthy theatre even in a capitalist society, and the movement also appealed to the pedagogical side of his nature. In 1911 he became a regular member of the committee, and in 1927 he was able to write that he had been active in the Berlin Volksbühne for over half a lifetime, and later in the Federation of Volksbühne Societies also. [15] Had the Volksbühne been a mere cheap-ticket organisation 'he would not have devoted two hours of his life to it'. Nor did he wish for a 'theatre of ideas' in a political sense:

> It is the 'ideas' of the artist which (like those of the pious and wise, in other ways) lead to the irreplaceable moments in which we are blessed again by a feeling of the meaning and purpose of life. That is really the 'idea' for the sake of which I serve the Volksbühne. [16]

Even in 1945, when the Volksbühne had not yet been recreated after its destruction by the Nazis, we find the exiled Bab in New York commending the pre-war Volksbühne as a possible model for certain aspects of an American National Theatre.

In 1911 Dr Josef Ettlinger felt obliged, because of family responsibilities, to leave Berlin and take up a post on the *Frankfurter Zeitung*. To him the association owed its sound financial footing, the relationship with Reinhardt, and the remarkable development of special events. He left with deep regret. 'It is with a very heavy heart that I part from the association to which my love and care have so long been directed.' Sadly enough, Ettlinger fell ill soon after going to Frankfurt and died in February 1912 after a painful illness of nine months. His place was taken for one year by Hans Land, and after that by Georg Springer, who was to prove to be the vital force of the movement for the next few years.

As the administrative work multiplied, the treasurer was renamed the manager, and an additional office helper was taken on (1908). Apart from the periodical, the association published three guides, two to museums, one to an art gallery; but the sales of these were disappointing. In autumn 1911 the association founded a Volksbühne bookshop specialising in quality books.

The period saw many extra performances, several evenings honouring great writers, many concerts (Arthur Schnabel, who always *gave* his services, was a frequent performer), and a whole round of festivals, including balls attended by six to seven thousand people. These more social events, cabarets, horse-displays, Moritat singers and so on, engendered a great sense of unity as well as raising money for what had become the great project of the association – the building of its own theatre. In 1912 an attempt was made to found an experimental theatre club. By the autumn there were only eight hundred members. Four plays were staged, the most successful being Hebbel's *Julia,* [1848] formerly thought to be unstageable. But at the end of one season, partly because of a lack of suitable plays, the scheme ended. [17]

The practical work of the Freie Volksbühne during these years was naturally more modest. There were few 'extra performances' or special events. Even the loose connection between the Freie Volksbühne and the Choir was threatened. The choir had always had a special place in the great combined 'Workers' Choir' (Arbeiter-Sängerchor) which performed for Socialist Party events, for it refused to rehearse propaganda songs and did not wholly avoid spiritual works. Now the choir began to object to its connection with the Workers' Choir. But all was smoothed over in the end and the Freie Volksbühne then extended even more help to the choir.

During the whole of this period the two Volksbühnen were gradually drawing closer together. Even ideologically the differences became less and it would be a mistake from now on to see them as neatly representing the 'artistic' and 'political' approaches to the work, for these arguments went on within as well as between the organisations. By 1910 the leaders of the Neue Freie Volksbühne regarded the problem of the scope of drama with a message (*Tendenzdrama*) within the programme as settled, but still debated the relationship between pure art and entertainment. Ettlinger wrote 'Art strives towards the heights and the depths, entertainment to breadth'. But there was a place for entertainment in the programme.

In the winter of 1910-11 a journalistic debate in the pages of *Vorwärts* and *Neue Zeit* took place between Heinz Sperber (pseudonym of Hermann Heijermans) and Heinrich Ströbel on 'Proletarian and bourgeois art'. This debate was continued within the Freie Volksbühne and led to a clarification of its basic principles. The executive of the Freie Volksbühne gave Heijermans an opportunity to express his views at a general meeting in November 1911. He argued from the basis that art and artists largely depend on the ruling and property-owning classes of their times, and he saw it as a task of the Freie Volksbühne to oppose consciously proletarian art to the dominant 'bourgeois' art. On Baake's advice the talk was not debated, but in issue No. 9 of the periodical that year Friedrich Stampfer replied to Heijermans. He deplored the fact that Heijermans attacked as bourgeois *all* earlier art from the standpoint of an 'adopted class-consciousness'. It was not possible to tell workers that they must not enjoy this or that, because it was 'bourgeois': the worker had the right to enjoy the little culture he had won for himself. He argued that Heijermans must know that art exists by virtue of its own laws, which are not those of national economics or politics. He continued:

> A work that is bourgeois through and through can be a work of art. ... As we now demand from art, that it gives us a picture of real life, we must be thankful to the bourgeois poet who is as bourgeois as he can be.... Ability, not opinion, makes the artist. If he can turn an opinion, a piece of life into artistic form, then he is an artist. Long live 'art with a message' [*Tendenzkunst*] if the message is ours and the art is great art. But the message is not art and can never replace art in any play.

Stampfer criticised earlier revolutionary movements for their artistic intolerance:

> It will be the glory of the revolutionary movement of the working class, that they were the first of their kind *not* to take the road to destruction. With loving care they will carry the cultural wealth of the past over the broad stream that divides today from tomorrow.

But, he said, the working-class did also deserve its own art, and the Freie Volksbühne would open its doors to proletarian art. Heijermans replied in *Vorwärts* that the Freie Volksbühne was on the way to becoming a bourgeois theatre and that Stampfer's exposition was muddled: but he excused himself from answering it on grounds of lack of space. Stampfer replied that the task of the Freie Volksbühne was to open to the proletariat all the treasure chambers in which mankind has locked up its cultural heritage. He could as yet see no signs of real proletarian art able to stand comparison with the great art of the past. Heijermans' final shot in reply was to describe the Freie Volksbühne as 'a consumer association for retailing bourgeois art'. [18]

In June 1911 Heijermans was not re-elected to the committee. Clearly an association which tacitly endorsed Stampfer's opinions was ideologically not far removed from the Neue Freie Volksbühne.

At the same time that this movement towards ideological harmony was taking place, various practical problems were demanding joint thought and sometimes joint action. Among these were a threatened entertainment tax, renewed police hostility and the need for the Volksbühne movement to have its own theatre.

An earlier attempt to impose an Entertainment Tax had been made in 1905, but at that time enterprises such as the Volksbühne Associations would have been excluded. This time there were to be no exclusions and there was a danger that all subscriptions would have to be increased by 10 per cent. Ettlinger approached Conrad Schmidt suggesting joint action. This was agreed but in practice differences soon emerged and the two bodies acted independently. In the event the tax proposals came to nothing.

The police were always suspicious of the Volksbühnen, and made several minor attacks on the associations in 1908 and 1909. A major police attack began, however, on 23 July 1910, when the Police President von Jagow sent a directive to all theatres that had Volksbühne performances saying that in view of the size of these associations and the ease with which they could be joined, the performances could 'no longer be regarded as private and must therefore abide by the laws of public safety and censorship. Von Jagow claimed that he was not really concerned with the censorship issue, only that of safety. This sounded reassuring, but the safety matter could have been dealt with privately, so both associations decided to fight, as the censorship could well hamper their work in the future. This time the Freie Volksbühne took the initiative, but the joint meeting was cool. Eventually each association again acted independently. Dr Heinemann, the Freie Volksbühne lawyer, pursued the matter through legal channels, ending with a legal judgement against the association. Julius Luzynski, the Neue Freie Volksbühne lawyer, met with similar failure.

In the 1912-13 season Rosenov's *Die im Schatten leben* (*Dwellers in the Shadow*), a sincere play about miners, set in the 1880s, was forbidden by the censor although already performed in Frankfurt-am-Main and Mannheim. It was now clear that the police actually did wish to censor the productions of the Volksbühne. Further harassment occurred over choral works in the hall of the Neue Welt. Finally, in 1913, the police refused permission for a Berlin performance of Hauptmann's festival play celebrating the War of Independence of 1813, although this had already been performed at Breslau. Undoubtedly the fight against the censor would have become even sharper had not the outbreak of war intervened.

Even in the 1890s the need for its own theatre had been felt within the Volksbühne movement, but only in the new century did it become a practicable proposition. By the start of the 1905-6 season the membership of the Freie Volksbühne had reached ten thousand and was still rising. To meet the demand, evening performances (an absolute essential if the association were to run its own theatre) were started and were welcomed. In January 1906, therefore, Curt Baake announced to a general meeting the idea of having a Volksbühne theatre as something 'to which we must come sooner or later'. The first step would be to establish a fund built up primarily through small contributions. A start was made by giving the proposed building a name – The Independent Arts Centre (Freies Kunsthaus) – which implied something probably more comprehensive than a simple theatre. But in spite of help from other organisations, a favourable press, enthusiasm in the left-wing press, and solid support from influential people (Alfred Kerr put down 500 Marks), the scheme failed, primarily because of opposition within the Social Democratic Party, led by Mehring. Although the Volksbühne was not formally linked to the party it seemed hopeless to go ahead in face of its opposition. The centrepiece of that opposition was an article by Mehring in *Neue Zeit* published in mid-July. Mehring argued that the scheme showed a lack of 'class instinct' and was not in keeping with the original aims of the movement. He then made a most important point, one based on his own experience as chairman, and one whose truth, or at least partial truth, the whole future of the movement was to demonstrate: 'The greater the number of members, the less can the tendency to experiment exist.' [19] His 'trump card' (the article being addressed to party members) was that the whole scheme was a dispersal and waste of socialist energy – which had been his original objection to the whole movement before he had been persuaded to accept its chairmanship.

Undoubtedly some of his contentions were right; some were arguable; but his conclusion was the result of a somewhat narrow view. In fact, he probably did the movement a service, for had the project been proceeded with it might well have broken an association that lacked the strength and organisation to carry it through. After this abortive effort the Freie Volksbühne lost heart, and it was left to the Neue Freie Volksbühne to take the next initiative.

Before this happened, however, Adolf Steinert, the Freie Volksbühne's artistic director, came forward with a plan for an independent firm with a sleeping partner. The new building would contain a 1,400-seat theatre and a 2,400-seat festival hall. In January 1907 a general meeting gave the plan a cautious welcome. After this – as might have been expected – the scheme began to change, and the terms became much worse for the Freie Volksbühne. In April 1907 a modified scheme was put to a general meeting which sceptically left a decision to the committee. The proposal was changed more and more from its original form, until in the end there was to be no new building at all, merely alterations to the Zentral Theater. By spring 1908 it was clear that the idea had come to nothing.

The Freie Volksbühne's own original plan for building a theatre was naturally discussed also within the Neue Freie Volksbühne, and some members would have welcomed a joint enterprise. But as the rapid growth of the Neue Freie Volksbühne continued, its need for its own theatre became even more acute than that of the Freie Volksbühne. Heinrich Neft was greatly drawn to the idea, Georg Springer became enthusiastic about it, and by the autumn of 1908 agreement had been reached to work towards a building project. The name proposed was The People's Arts Centre (*Volkskunsthaus*). Though the difficulties proved far greater than anyone anticipated, it was this decision, five years before even the foundation stone was laid, that led to eventual success, while to men such as Springer the difficulties were merely a challenge, stimulating greater enthusiasm.

At a general meeting on 29 October 1908 the matter was raised very late under 'any other business' ! Neft gave a factual introduction, Springer made an emotional appeal and a motion was passed, accepting in principle the establishment of a theatre building fund and calling for an extraordinary meeting. This was held on 21 January 1909. Springer, the principal speaker, explained that a building fund would be set up as a separate association. It would be funded by an initial contribution of 10, 000 Marks from the Neue Freie Volksbühne's own account, and afterwards (from 1 September 1909) by means of a 10 Pfennig levy on all entrance subscriptions and ticket sales. This money would not be 'lost' to the contributor, for every ten 10 Pfennig contributions a one-Mark token would be issued, and ten of these on a card would constitute a 'share' eligible for 5 per cent interest. If the project were not under way by 1 October 1912, subscribers would get their money back. It was hoped that some members would also buy additional shares. [20] Springer calculated that the 10 Pfennig levy would bring in 50, 000 Marks in the first year, and hoped it would be doubled by voluntary contributions. He hoped to reach 300, 000 Marks in the second year, when, with the help of a bank loan, work could start on a theatre with an auditorium holding fifteen hundred, two big halls for meetings and concerts, exhibition rooms, restaurant facilities and so on.

In the lively discussion that followed Bruno Wille showed himself to be one of the sceptics: he feared the 'building fund association' might become wholly independent, and he warned against over-optimism, saying that the collection could take twenty years!

Eventually a provisional building commission was elected consisting of Springer, Neft and five others. Public propaganda followed, slides were shown on theatre tabs, special events were arranged to raise further funds, and, of course, the periodical was used. Ettlinger published a leading article urging members to look beyond their individual interests and, of course, supported his views with a quotation from Schiller.[21] Autumn 1911 was the date proposed for the opening of the theatre, but during 1910 it was recognised that this was impossible: by April 1910 only 150, 000 Marks had been raised, and by August only 200, 000 Marks, while the estimated initial capital requirement had risen from 300, 000 Marks to 400, 000 Marks.

Meanwhile Adolf Edgar Licho, chief producer at the Hebbel-Theater, approached Neft with his own ideas about the proposed new theatre, evidently hoping for the post of director. When he understood the financial difficulties he suggested that there was no reason why the association should not in the meantime rent a theatre for its own exclusive use. Shortly after this came an opportunity to rent the Theater in der Köpenicker Strasse – which usually housed visiting companies – from its owner, Professor Ludwig Stein, at a cost of 24,000 Marks per year for three years. It was far from an ideal theatre. Externally it was not unlike an English nonconformist chapel, while the auditorium was decorated in bad 'Jugendstil'; the stage measured only 8 by 9 metres and was technically ill equipped. The news was announced to the members in March 1910 that this would be 'a theatre in which players engaged exclusively for us will act plays exclusively of our choice *only* for members of the Neue Freie Volksbühne'. The theatre was renamed the Neues Volkstheater (New People's Theatre). During the summer alterations were made in the seating, stair-carpeting, stage-equipment and lighting, and on 3 August 1910 it came into use. As the periodical emphasised, for the first time in the history of the German theatre a completely new thing had happened: a permanent theatre, with a permanent ensemble, was playing solely for the members of an association, with the public completely excluded; in other words, a public was creating its own theatre, whereas normally every newly founded theatre had to create its own public.

Ettlinger was formally 'director' to satisfy legal requirements, Licho the artistic director and Neft the business manager. The theatre's finances were kept entirely separate from those of the association, which paid a fixed sum to the theatre for seats and productions and then left it its complete independence. Thus, though the theatre had to toe the line financially it had a great deal of artistic freedom. The programme was arranged in consultation with the artistic committee of the Neue Freie Volksbühne and the executive, but there was no regular interference by Volksbühne administration.

Licho assembled a talented company, giving Jürgen Fehling his first Berlin engagement after his discovery by Licho, Neft and Springer in a touring company. He was a sensitive director with a sense of the dramatic, a good artist with a great future, but not easy to work with. Once in the middle of a season he disappeared for weeks after a quarrel, leaving the whole burden to Neft. This awkwardness of disposition ultimately led to his not even being considered for the post of director of the Volksbühne theatre when this was eventually built. Meanwhile he presented in his first season a repertoire of some character, though not extraordinary, seeking to reflect the work of the younger generation so long as this was 'popular' in a good sense. [22] As a deliberate gesture, the opening production was Ibsen's *Pillars of Society*, the first Freie Volksbühne play of 1890. Plays by Hartleben and others followed, but many practical factors limited the repertoire. Moreover, the majority of the now very large (forty to fifty thousand) membership had not grown up with the association, and as a body lacked the unity of the earlier days (as, indeed, Mehring had prophesied when the Freie Volksbühne had first tried to establish its own theatre), so that a more eclectic programme was necessary. [23]

The movement into theatre management also introduced the element of responsibility towards the employees of the theatre, a further inhibition to reckless experiment. Naturally, the work of the Neues Volkstheater must be seen as complementing the programme derived from other theatres, a programme whose size was only slightly reduced and over which the association could exercise a certain limited influence by proposing plays to theatres. As the Volksbühne could guarantee to fill nearly two dozen houses, these proposals were often accepted. Unfortunately, members justly complained from time to time of unsatisfactory performances, including some in Reinhardt's Deutsches Theater. All too often the actors did not trouble themselves to give their best, or even adequate, performances for Volksbühne audiences, and an almost farcical climax was reached in a performance of Grillparzer's *Medea* in 1910 when huge cuts were made and the rest gabbled, so that the play was over in an hour and a quarter. After members had made complaints to the association and in the press, the Neue Freie Volksbühne sent a strong written complaint to the theatre, and actually refused to pay for the unsatisfactory performance. Reinhardt was away at the time. When he returned he agreed that the complaint had been justified and sent a circular to all members of his company insisting that Volksbühne matinées be played 'with the same artistic seriousness as all others'. Every member of the company had to sign a declaration to this effect, and sanctions for further offences were threatened; but the executive of the Neue Freie Volksbühne remained sceptical – not, it seems, without reason.

Meanwhile progress towards the new building went on. The opening date was postponed to the autumn of 1912, and although the authorities refused to allow a big public lottery in aid of the fund, 400,000 Marks had been collected by October 1911. An alternative plan for completely altering the Neues Volkstheater having been abandoned (its owner being unconvinced by it), the services of Oscar Kaufmann were obtained as architect. He had been responsible for the Hebbel-Theater in the Königgrätzer Strasse as well as other theatres outside Berlin. At the same time a building site was sought and found between the Bülowplatz (now the Luxemburgplatz) and the Linien Strasse. It was a slummy area, but its development, which would be enhanced by the new theatre, was already planned; and it was convenient for working-class areas of the city. The authorities would not sell the plot directly to the Volksbühne, but the development company which was acquiring the whole development area was interested in the theatre scheme and helpful with a mortgage. From now on, Kaufmann worked closely with the building commission. He saw that the means at his disposal would be insufficient for the two concert and meeting halls, and for the exhibition rooms, so these were abandoned. In retrospect one cannot help speculating whether this simple, negative decision, imposed by economic limitations and nothing else, was not a major factor in the whole later history of the Volksbühne, shaping it as a movement firmly based on theatre, with other arts as peripheral interest, rather than as a more widely conceived 'arts association'. The auditorium was to be enlarged from 1,500 to 2,000 seats. Of course, this would pay better, provided it were filled - another factor to influence future policies.

On 23 June 1912 the decision was formally made to buy the land and go ahead. Unfortunately for the Volksbühne, however, the money market had strengthened during the previous months and the Deutsche Bank, partners of the development company, would no longer honour their verbal agreement to provide a mortgage and additional loans. The risk without the bank's help was too great, so yet another year had to be added to the delays while other sources of fluid capital were sought.

The delays gave opportunities for further thought and in September 1912 another decision was reached which although again negative, must have had an enormous hidden effect upon the inner character of the movement in later years. The point at issue was the shape of the auditorium. Many speakers wanted an amphitheatre, modelled on the Schiller-Theater, rather than the proposed stalls and circles. Not only would the amphitheatre ensure a better view of the stage from all seats, but it was also felt to be more 'democratic'. The arguments for retaining the circles were economic, and eventually these won the day. In this way the Volksbühne committed itself, with strange inconsistency, to a form of auditorium reflecting a society divided economically into classes, rather than one, like the Greek, reflecting the unity and equality of all citizens. Erwin Piscator, who referred rudely to 'the pompous building on the Bülowplatz', wrote in 1929: 'It is not without significance for a production how the audience is grouped, whether the auditorium is divided by emphatic circles and boxes or held together by its parts as a unity'. Ironically, economic considerations led the broadly left-wing Volksbühne into building a conservative, 'capitalist' style of theatre.

During 1912-13 intensive money-raising continued, until by summer 1913 three-quarters of a million Marks had been amassed. Then, with the keen support of the Second Bürgermeister, Dr Reicke, himself a writer, the grant of a mortgage for two million Marks at 4½ per cent was passed through all the necessary city bodies. It was 'something extraordinary and unprecedented' that a cultural undertaking should be helped financially on such a scale. 'The way was open.' The building plot was bought a few weeks later, and, thanks to a building society mortgage, the Neue Freie Volksbühne did not even have to take up all the city's offer. Building operations began in June 1913.

Before this, however, a dramatic change had taken place in the relationship between the two Volksbühne organisations. In spite of the considerable public acrimony that accompanied the separately conducted battles over the threatened Entertainment Tax and the censorship issue and the mistrust that still existed, these external struggles had actually brought the two bodies nearer together; the 'hotspurs' of the Freie Volksbühne had been somewhat cooled by the lack of success of the public protests they had urged, and now that both bodies faced the same continuing problems in relation to the police the stage was set for fuller reconciliation. In 1912, Neft approached Winkler about the possible amalgamation of the two, Neft admitting the advantage on his own side of having the support of the Freie Volksbühne in the theatre project. The Freie Volksbühne executive welcomed the suggestion, as it was important to end competition between the two Volksbühne bodies, which benefited no one but the theatre managements. Both associations had reservations about full amalgamation and a solution was found in a cartel in which each organisation would remain independent, while conflict and undercutting would be avoided. The cartel was to be only loosely binding and was to have a small executive; it was to undertake the actual bargaining with theatres, but terms having been arranged, the two associations were to fix their own choice of plays, insofar as these had not already been agreed in common.

The first joint meeting of the leading committees of the two organisations took place on 31 March 1913. It was an almost solemn occasion. Bruno Wille presided, Springer and Schmidt spoke, Landauer gave a talk on the nature and aims of the cartel, and delegates to the new executive were appointed. Although the ordinary members of the two bodies hardly noticed the existence of the cartel, it was actually of vast importance. The Freie Volksbühne decided during the first season of joint working to modify its constitution to be more in line with that of the Neue Freie Volksbühne though without becoming less democratic – no general meeting would have tolerated that.

Six months later (14 September 1913) the foundation stone of the new theatre was laid. Despite the existence of the cartel this was still a venture of the Neue Freie Volksbühne, who issued the invitations. Both Volksbühne organisations, other friendly bodies and the city of Berlin were well represented. Prussia and the Reich sent neither representatives nor apologies! Apart from the invited guests, thousands watched the ceremony from beyond the boundary fence. Contemporary photographs have preserved vivid impressions both of the solemnity of the actual stone-laying and of the excitement and gaiety of the whole occasion, evidently a sunny and breezy day, with the crowded building site, the garlanded poles, the spectators beyond the fence and the rather grim surrounding buildings, heavy blocks of flats and what appears to be a textile mill. The order of events had the typical flavour, or blend of flavours, of the Volksbühne. First, the Typographical Choral Society sang the song 'O Guardian Spirit of all things beautiful, descend!' [24] Then Georg Springer, as chairman of the Neue Freie Volksbühne, himself deeply moved, gave a proud and hopeful introductory address. He was followed by Conrad Schmidt, as chairman of the Freie Volksbühne, John Lehmann, representing the Society of German Dramatists, and Gustav Rickelt on behalf of German actors, who hoped 'this building may become a true temple of our art, in which God's words of the good and beautiful may resound for all who wish to hear them'.

Thus introduced came Bruno Wille to lay the stone, with appropriate rhetoric: 'The ancient world has sunk in ruins, but it has bequeathed us its beauty; the garment of Helen forms a costly inheritance, especially for the Faustian spirit of the German people'. He went on to refer to classical culture as founded upon slavery in contrast with the culture sought by the Volksbühne, founded upon freedom, equality and fraternity. The new theatre was to be a temple dedicated to humanity:

> It is not to be lifeless, a mere building of cold, rigid stone. It should become a cathedral, a forest cathedral, dedicated to Beauty. The singers of the heavens rejoice in its sunny treetops, and at the roots below, couched upon flowers, men hark to the exalted song which Beethoven's Ninth Symphony pours forth in harmony. [25]

And he quoted Schiller's words, by now almost a Volksbühne anthem, which, after Kaufmann, Neft and others had also struck the stone, were then sung by the Typographical Choral Society. An emotional social evening with speeches and poetry followed later in the Brauerei Friedrichshain.

Very soon, in the autumn of 1913, another external threat forced the two Volksbühnen into an even closer association. Reinhardt had plans to transform the Zirkus Schumann, already his 'mass theatre', the 'theatre of a thousand', into a 'theatre of five thousand'. This plan threatened serious competition with the new theatre in the Bülowplatz.

At the same time the District Education Committee of the Social Democratic Party and the Berlin Trade Unions agreed with Reinhardt to take up ninety thousand seats per annum. This was a serious threat to the Volksbühne movement and led to talk of actual re-unification. Complete fusion, however, presented too many difficulties, and on 6 February 1914 the draft of yet another new scheme was accepted by the executive of the cartel.

This was for a Verband (Federation) der Freien Volksbühnen. Its executive was to consist of the executives of the two constituent bodies meeting together. There would be full unification of administration, cash and theatre bookings. Each body was still to recruit its own members, but within agreed limits, to avoid competition, and when one was filled, applicants were to be directed to the other. Subscriptions would be the same in each. Money would be divided proportionately at the end of the financial year; there would be a joint periodical for 1914-15. The whole plan was for a three-year trial period, but renewable. This left the Neue Freie Volksbühne still sole owner of the Bülowplatz theatre. But it was now evident that complete fusion would come sooner or later.

The Federation immediately found it was in a strong position to negotiate with the Social Democratic Party and Trade Union Education Committee, which now gave up its idea of taking seats in Reinhardt's proposed theatre. The Volksbühne offered the committee blocks of seats, at a price 10 Pfennigs higher than the Volksbühne's. Ultimately Reinhardt's plan collapsed.

The Neue Freie Volksbühne was to have three times as many members as the Freie Volksbühne, and both about 20 per cent more than at present. A big propaganda campaign was undertaken, and by July enrolments for the new season had already reached thirty thousand. Then came the outbreak of war, and the question as to whether the Volksbühne could even survive. An executive meeting held the day war was declared decided to go on with the building, but within a few days fourteen out of seventeen fitters and twenty-four out of thirty brick-layers had been taken for war service. There were material delays, too, and lack of transport. The opening was fixed for Christmas Day, and then postponed from that to 30 December.

Apart from the building itself the most important task was to choose a suitable director for it. Licho was not even considered; Neft refused to work any longer with so difficult a person. The number of candidates seriously considered was soon reduced to three. Two were young men - Hermann Sinsheimer from Mannheim, an enthusiast but perhaps too theoretically minded, and Leopold Jessner – a man who had served his time in the theatre from the bottom up, and was destined to become one of the most influential directors of the 1920s but whom Neft thought no businessman; and the third was Emil Lessing, a man in his mid-fifties who had directed for the Neue Freie Volksbühne as early as 1892! His abilities in the theatre and in business were known. He had been Brahm's right-hand man at the Deutsches Theater and later at the Lessing Theater. He was, however, wedded to Naturalism and unlikely to take up any new ways and styles. His candidacy was supported by Bruno Wille and others who had valued his work in the nineties. The conflict between the supporters of the two younger men was extremely bitter, and when Neft declared himself for Lessing, the supporters of both the other two decided that they preferred Lessing to their opponents' candidate. Lessing was therefore chosen, though very few people really thought him the best man.

Lessing could afford to hire no big names, so, aiming at a good ensemble, he engaged a company of thirty men and fifteen women. When, at the outbreak of war, the theatre-opening had to be postponed, the Neues Operetten-Theater in the Schiffsbauerdamm was rented and Lessing had to make his start there in unfavourable circumstances. He produced good, homely fare, no more. In December *Götz von Berlichingen* was rehearsed. Bab wrote a verse prologue to be spoken by Götz's faithful page, Lerse. On 30 December there was a full theatre for the festive occasion, and everyone of importance in the city had been invited. But two days before, disaster had struck. One of the technical features of the stage was a revolve designed by the engineer Knina, 21 metres in diameter, of which half could also be raised and lowered. Two days before the opening performance the lift-system was overloaded, a screw sheared off, and half the revolve fell into the under-stage cavity. Wire ropes used to try to lift it from the depths only broke. As only half the stage area was now available it was impossible to present *Götz* as planned, so the première had to be a less demanding play from the existing repertoire – Björnson's *When the Vineyards are in Blossom*. The opening speech was given by Julius Bab. Georg Springer modestly thought his own Saxon dialect might be bad on such an occasion and wrote an article instead. Bab apologised for the technical trouble and made a speech in which he called the new building 'a memorial to that unconquerable strength of feeling, that strength of idealism for whose sake we love in the true sense our national song "Deutschland, Deutschland über alles" '. He described the building as a means to lead 'the people to art, art to the people'. The play was well received, despite disappointment, and *Götz* was presented a few days later.

Whatever criticism may be made of the Volksbühne Theatre, it was a remarkable achievement. It had cost four and a half million Marks and the shares were in the hands of 14,500 people; mostly small contributors, so that it was genuinely 'owned by the people'. The site, though it covered 3,500 square metres, had not been easy to use and was too narrow to allow an adequate side-stage to be included. There were nearly two thousand seats. The stage, with its great revolve, was 40 metres wide, the cyclorama 26 metres high and the stage tower 42 metres high. An orchestra pit could be sunk for operatic performances, and the lighting was by the Fortuny system. It has been described as a fulfilment of Goethe's dictum of 1817, when he laid down principles for theatre-building: 'The outward form [to be] the result of the inner, practical arrangements, and thus expressing the purpose of the building.' The curve of the cyclorama, answered by the curve of the auditorium back, was repeated externally, and then strengthened by the square corners. Although an amphitheatre had been eschewed, there were no boxes. These were definitely felt to be exclusive and undemocratic. The result, a theatre with circles but entirely without boxes, was, at that time, unique. Although the auditorium was so large, a feeling of vastness was avoided by the use of mahogany cladding throughout the Interior, contrasting with a lighter yellow wood and red curtains in the foyer. The design of the façade was symbolic of the theatre's purpose, and across it was carved the Volksbühne motto: *Die Kunst dem Volke*.

2. The Ostend-Theater in east Berlin where the first performance of the Freie Volksbühne took place on 19 October 1890.

3. Julius Hart (1859–1930), co-founder of the Freie Volksbühne and of the Neue Freie Volksbühne.

4. Wilhelm Bölsche (1861–1939), writer and scientist, co-founder of the Freie Volksbühne.

5. Dr Franz Mehring (1846–1919), political writer and historian, chairman of the Freie Volksbühne 1892–1896.

6.   Erich Hartleben (1864–1905), committee member of the Freie Volksbühne and of the
Artistic Committee of the Neue Freie Volksbühne.

7.   Dr Conrad Schmidt (1863–1932), writer and editor, chairman of the Freie Volksbühne
1897–1918.

8. The lottery for seats at the Neue Freie Volksbühne in about 1900.

9. Foyer of the Volksbühne on the Bülowplatz. The first Volksbühne Conference, at which the Federation of Volksbühne Associations was founded, was held here 23–25 October 1920.

10. Poster from 1892; first issue of the Volksbühne periodical, 1892; membership card
1893–4. Also: Bernhard Kampffmeyer, Fritz Mauthner and Max Halbe.

11. Volksbühne printed material from the years 1892–6.

12.   The hall of the Böhmisches Brauhaus, birthplace of the first German Volksbühne on 29 July and 8 August 1890.

13. The Volksbühne on the Bülowplatz as originally built in 1913–14.

14. Interior of the Volksbühne on the Bülowplatz in its original form.

FIRST INTERMISSION
1914-1918: WAR AND REVOLUTION

The opening of the Theater am Bülowplatz is the 'curtain line' of the first act of the story of the Volksbühne. The second act runs from the end of the war to 1933, when the movement was taken over by the Nazis, while the third act, which is still running, begins with the re-establishment of the Volksbühne after the Nazi defeat. What happened during the First World War may be regarded as an interval between the acts, a sustaining operation simply to keep the movement in being.

With Emil Lessing as director the Volksbühne survived the first winter remarkably well, but at the end of the season the leadership felt that the risk of continuing its own theatrical business in wartime was too great. It was Reinhardt, friend and rival of the Volksbühne, who provided the solution. He offered to take over the theatre for a period of two years – no doubt in part as a substitute, with its two thousand seats, for his own unrealised 'Theatre of 5,000', and in part through good will towards his old colleagues. The former successful co-operation with Reinhardt encouraged the Volksbühne to accept the proposal. Reinhardt took over the theatre rent free, but made half the seats available to the Volksbühne for its members. The Volksbühne was responsible for all costs connected with the house, Reinhardt for all artistic costs. Though the Volksbühne was disappointed that its great aim of operating a theatre and ensemble completely of its own was once again postponed, Reinhardt saved it from hibernation and possible extinction during the hardest years. The membership began to rise again – it had fallen by half in the early months of the war – and in three years had reached fifty thousand. Reinhardt's programme was supplemented by outstanding Sunday morning concerts in the theatre under Leo Kestenberg, and by performances in the Lessing Theater and Deutsches Künstler-Theater.

In the fourth year of the war the Volksbühne decided to revive the old ideal of having its own company in its own theatre. Friedrich Kayssler, an outstanding actor, who also wrote comedies and children's plays, was appointed as director, a post which he held until 1923. In him the Volksbühne obtained the services of one of the most distinguished artists in the German theatre. The new season opened on 4 September 1918 with Immermann's *Merlin*. Written in 1832, this play had never before been performed and the world première gave the new venture a striking send-off. From other points of view the choice was curious. Immermann (1796-1840), director of the Düsseldorf theatre from 1834 to 1837, was a believer in the Prussian State who rejected liberalism and individualism, and though an apologist for the Volksbühne has called the play 'One of the noblest poems of the Germans', [1] it has also been described as 'a Faustian hotchpotch of medieval myth, pantheism, gnosticism and neo-Platonism'. [2] Today, with its sub-Wagnerian, sub-Faustian rhetoric, its Arthurian cast – with Lucifer, Satan, Lohengrin and Klingsor thrown in for good measure – its tedious speeches, ubiquitous cliffs, gorges, dwarfs and snakes, it is almost unreadable; but it could lend itself to spectacular and colourful staging and production, with flames and transformations. Certainly it is, if not in the best sense, 'Germanic'. That the Volksbühne should open with such a play by such an author is an oddity that can perhaps he most charitably accounted for by the distorting influence of a wartime situation.

The first year of Kayssler's directorship was shaken by even fiercer storms than accompanied the opening of the theatre four years before. Even as the season opened the final German military collapse was beginning. Two months later (9 November) came the abdication of the Kaiser, the proclamation of the Republic by Philipp Scheidemann and – two hours later – Karl Liebknecht's rival proclamation of a Russian-style Socialist Republic. The chairman of the Social Democratic Party, Friedrich Ebert, was appointed Reich Chancellor. Overnight the friends and supporters of the Volksbühne movement became the rulers of Germany, while its opponents in high places were driven into opposition or exile, and the Volksbühne itself became allied with the establishment. The following months, however, with the great strikes and street battles, the Spartacist revolt and the short-lived Bavarian Republic, were hard ones for a theatrical enterprise. For days together the theatre had to remain closed. Once it was rumoured that the building itself had been shelled and lay in ruins. Fortunately this was not true, but glancing shots had done a little superficial damage. With the coming into political power of the Social Democrats several leading members of the Volksbühne had to take up important posts in the new government. Gustav Landauer was killed in the revolutionary fighting in Munich. All in all the stage was set for the Volksbühne movement to develop its changed and important role in the new Germany.

ACT II

1918–1933

THE VOLKSBÜHNE IN
THE WEIMAR REPUBLIC

Scene I
BERLIN

To 1923

The dominant figure of the Volksbühne movement during this period, and indeed until his death in 1963, was Siegfried Nestriepke, the 'Grand Old Man of the Volksbühne' as he has been called, without whom the Berlin – and indeed the whole German – Volksbühne movement is unthinkable [1] and to whom Oscar Fritz Schuh referred as 'the expert master-builder of the greatest theatre-audience organisation in the world, to whom not only the German, but the European theatre owes so much gratitude'. [2]

Siegfried Nestriepke was born on 17 December 1885 in Bartenstein, East Prussia. His mother came of an old East Prussian family, but his father, an official surveyor, was Silesian. He went to school from 1891 in Bartenstein Bürgerschule until 1895 when the family moved to Bremen, where Siegfried attended first the Vorschule and then the Gymnasium. He was a clever boy, drawn to literature and poetry, and at the same time, even as a fifteen-year-old, he showed a keen interest in public affairs and contemporary problems, supplementing the study of Horace and Homer with that of modern stories, commentaries and articles which he found in the newspapers and from which he endeavoured to form his own opinions. The struggle of the Boers for national independence kindled his imagination and one of his first published poems was dedicated to General de Wet.

From 1905 to 1910 he studied literature, history and national economy in the Universities of Berlin and Marburg, coming under the influence of such noteworthy teachers as Gustav Schmoller and Adolf Wagner, the so-called 'academic Socialists' (Kathedersozialisten) who sought to give economics an ethical basis and whose preoccupation with ameliorating the effects of class differences anticipated the idea of the Welfare State. But the intensive study of Marx and his analysis of the power of modern capitalism made Nestriepke recognise the inadequacy of the study of merely national economics in the face of the serious problems of the time. At Marburg he was able to become acquainted with the teaching of the great philosopher, Hermann Cohen, without, however, adopting his transcendentalist neo-Kantian philosophy. Under the economist Walter Troeltsch, Nestriepke wrote his first important work on *Trades Union Methods of Agitation* (*Die gewerkschaftlichen Agitationsmethoden*), while the writings and teaching of his literature Professor, Ernst Elster, inspired his choice of doctoral thesis, the Swabian *Sturm und Drang* poet Christian Friedrich Daniel Schubart, who appealed especially to Nestriepke because of his revolt against the tyranny of the absolutist Herzog Carl Eugen von Wurttemberg, which earned him ten years' imprisonment.

At least as important in his personal development as the academic study was Nestriepke's involvement in student politics. He soon attached himself to an independent student movement, the Deutsche Freie Studentenschaft, which strove for the reform of the whole of academic life. Inspired by the 'black-red-gold' ideals of the Wartburg Festival of October 1817, when revolutionary students met to celebrate the death of Luther and the Battle of Leipzig, the movement also wanted to make a breach with the mindless, 'dashing', but actually reactionary Korpsstudententum – members of expensive and exclusive student clubs with great emphasis on the initiation of freshmen, duelling and heavy drinking. This independent student organisation came into conflict during the winter of 1907-8 both with the conservative clubs, who had an overwhelming majority on the allegedly representative student committee, and the university authorities. Nestriepke and others were brought before an academic court and reprimanded: the activities of the independent society were suspended. The twenty-three-year-old Nestriepke, filled with 'righteous indignation' wrote a pamphlet, *The Fight for Freedom in Marburg University (Der Freiheitskampf an der Marburger Universität),* which the Deutsche Freie Studentenshaft published in 1908.

Even as a student he also became involved in German politics. In the 1907 elections he spoke on behalf of Helmuth von Gerlach, the 'enfant terrible' of the Prussian Junkers, and when von Gerlach and others founded the Democratic Union (Demokratische Vereinigung) in 1908 this became Nestriepke's first political home. Two years later he was its party secretary for Rhineland-Westphalia, while pursuing at the same time his chosen profession of political journalist. Within the political field Nestriepke developed a special enthusiasm for Trades Unionism and in 1912-13 he was economic policy secretary to the Federation of Technical-industrial Public Servants and editor of *The Commercial Salaried Employee* (*Der kaufmännische Angestellte*). His progress as a left-wing journalist reached its climax when he was appointed political editor of *Vorwärts,* the central organ of the Social Democratic Party, a post which Philipp Scheidemann himself urged him to accept. From 1915, however, he was able to continue this work only when on leave from war service, until 1917 when he was wounded and returned to civilian life and other journalistic positions. In 1917 he attached himself to the Independent Social Democratic Party, but left it in 1919 as he felt the need for unity in the struggle to build a democratic order, and from 1922 was vice-chairman of the Central Office for the Union of the (two) Socialist Parties, founded by Eduard Bernstein in 1922. Meanwhile he had written a three-volume study of *The Trade Union Movement (Die Gewerkschaftsbewegung)*, which became a standard work, and, as a development of the theoretical part of volume I, a further book, *The Theory of Trades Unionism (Gewerkschaftslehre)*.

Such was the man who immediately after the end of the war came into close association with the Berlin Volksbühne and the movement that was to be his life's work. In temperament and interests he seems to have been ideally suited to the Volksbühne. On the one hand an aggressive social democrat and trades unionist, with both journalistic and organisational experience in politics and trades unions, he was also a genuine scholar and lover of literature with something in him of the schoolmaster, the academic and the author. With astonishing speed he familiarised himself with the nature, history, organisation and problems of the Volksbühne and in 1919 he was elected to the executive committee of the Freie Volksbühne. He made his first important appearance in a general meeting on 8 May 1919, when he delivered an address on the communalisation of the Berlin theatre, coming down heavily on the side of non-commercial but autonomous bodies, rather than nationalisation (the two possible developments of socialism which were being hotly debated in Berlin at this time).

When Nestriepke entered the Volksbühne movement it was, of course, still divided into the two organisations, though the establishment of a good external relationship between them had already led to a steep rise in membership (eighty-two thousand altogether), and they were taking up ten thousand seats in theatres other than their own. Just as he had felt the need for socialist unity, so too Nestriepke became the driving force for the amalgamation of the two Volksbühnen. In an imaginative and disinterested move – which one imagines must have been inspired by Nestriepke – the Neue Freie Volksbühne, on 8 April 1920, revised its constitution so as to bring it completely in line with that of the Freie Volksbühne. A few days later the Freie Volksbühne dissolved itself and a new association, the Volksbühne e. V., [3] subtitled Vereinigte Freie und Neue Freie Volksbühne (United Independent and New Independent Volksbühne) came into being. Thus the Theater am Bülowplatz became the property of the united body. At the first annual general meeting under the new statutes (21 October 1920) Georg Springer, Anton Wagner and Curt Baake (by now an ex-undersecretary of State) were elected as chairmen, and as general secretary Dr Siegfried Nestriepke. At this meeting a decision was taken to publish, in addition to a free newsheet, a periodical for the encouragement of the arts, called *Die Volksbühne*, devoted to serious articles and free from necessary but space-consuming information. Nestriepke became editor and the first number appeared in autumn 1920. A year later this periodical was taken over by the Verband.

Alongside the Theater am Bülowplatz the Volksbühne also managed the Neues Volkstheater in the Köpenicker Strasse where a representative of the society worked alongside the director as adviser and colleague and a programme closely in line with the demands and needs of the Volksbühne was possible. In the winter of 1923-4 the Neues Volkstheater became a subdivision of the Theater am Bülowplatz under Nestriepke's direction. In 1926 this theatre was given up and for one year the Theater am Schiffbauerdamm rented instead. Meanwhile the Volksbühne wanted an opera house where it had some control of the programme and in the spring of 1920 agreement was reached with the State Administration over the Krollschen Oper am Platz der Republik (the Krolloper as it was more simply referred to). The interior of this building, the former Neues Operntheater, was more or less a ruin. The authorities were willing to make over the Krolloper to the Volksbühne for twenty-five years, and to service it with operatic and straight productions, using the Ensemble of the State Theatres, provided the Volksbühne took responsibility for restoring the interior. Mere renovation was inadequate, and Oscar Kaufmann was asked to design a new auditorium. After some hesitation the work was begun in the early summer of 1921 and should have been completed by spring 1922, but there were delays caused by the weather and shortage of materials and soon inflation began to catch up with the money-raising. Despite heroic and sacrificial efforts on the part of the members, the Volksbühne had to give up in the end; all rights in the Krolloper were returned to the State, which completed the work and assumed financial responsibility for the undertaking, nevertheless guaranteeing to the Volksbühne over seven thousand seats per week for twenty-five years at prices within the means of the Volksbühne members. The theatre came into use purely for opera at Christmas 1923, with almost 2,200 seats and what had become one of the largest and most modern of stages.

The period of Kayssler's direction of the Volksbühne theatre from 1918 to 1923 was a highlight in the history of the movement. Kayssler gave the Volksbühne a distinct character, and the theatre exercised great drawing power. The seasons included many world premieres and other noteworthy productions. Outstanding in the first season was Georg Kaiser's *Gas*, which opened on 25 February 1919, just a fortnight after Ebert's election as President of the Republic, and only four days after Kurt Eisner's assassination in Munich. This play, in which the workers in a socialised industry are so seized with greed for profit that eventually their fanatical labours lead to a gas explosion that lays the whole plant in ruins, was both topical and prophetic. The world première had been at the Neues Theater, Frankfurt and the Düsseldorfer Schauspielhaus on 28 November 1918, but it was the Volksbühne production that brought Kaiser the public recognition in Berlin which he had long sought for.

Among the actors in Kayssler's ensemble was Jürgen Fehling, who had been given his first Berlin engagement in the Neues Volkstheater in 1911 and had been playing since 1913 at the Volksbühne in Vienna. Fehling soon had ambitions to direct plays himself, ambitions which were for some time frustrated by Kayssler. Kayssler, as director, was also his own principal actor, and eventually Fehling was given an opportunity to direct Gogol's comedy *Marriage* (March 1919). The production was praised by Herbert Ihering, who as dramaturge in the Vienna Volksbühne already knew Fehling well and saw him as a coming director of comedy rather than of tragedy. Fehling followed *Marriage* with Shakespeare's *Comedy of Errors* (1920), Shaw's *Captain Brassbound's Conversion* (February 1921) and *Der Bauer als Millionär* (*The Peasant as Millionaire*) by the early-nineteenth-century Austrian dramatist, Ferdinand Raimund (May 1921). Between these last two, in April, he produced his first tragedy, Sophocles' *Antigone*. Critics were struck by the production's independence of the example of Reinhardt and the use of music in the choral sections. Herbert Ihering coolly dissected its virtues and shortcomings, but less analytical critics were carried away with enthusiasm.

During the following months Fehling firmly established himself as one of the leading Berlin directors. At the end of September came the first public production of Toller's *Masse-Mensch* (*Masses and Man*), (first performed, privately in Nuremburg, 15 November 1920). One of the greatest and most poetical of all Expressionistic plays, *Masse-Mensch* was written in the prison-fortress of Niederschönenfeld, where Toller was imprisoned for his part in the short-lived Bavarian Republic of 1919:

> It literally broke out of me and was put on paper in two days and
> a half. The two nights, which, owing to my imprisonment, I was
> forced to spend in 'bed' in a dark cell, were abysses of torment ….
> In the mornings shivering with fever, I sat down to write and did not
> stop until my fingers, clammy and trembling, refused to serve me ….
> The laborious and blissful work of pruning and remoulding lasted a
> year. [4]

At the time of the first night, Toller was on hunger strike in the same prison. The play itself deals poetically and expressionistically with the problems of ends and means, the central conflict being between the Nameless One who advocates violence in the cause of the masses, and the Woman (Sonia) who, though deeply involved in the revolution, believes in a non-violent solution:

> If I took but one human life,
> I should betray the Masses.
> Who acts may only sacrifice himself.

Hear me: no man may kill men for a cause.
Unholy every cause that needs to kill. [5]

The critics objected that Fehling made no distinction in the production
between the three 'dream pictures' and the other scenes, but Toller wrote
from prison to Fehling (October 1921), saying:

I want to tell you myself that you have carried out my meaning.
These pictures of 'reality' are not realism, are not local colour;
the protagonists (except for Sonia) are not individual characters.
Such a play can only have a spiritual, never a concrete, reality.

He added later: 'I am surprised at the critics' lack of understanding. Possibly
the play is insufficiently worked out.' [6] Fehling himself has written an
enthusiastic note on the play and its production. He has emphasised that
though Toller is 'a social writer',

this does not mean that his play is political propaganda, for he is a
poet. But his poem, his play, was conceived in the midst of a social
upheaval and inspired by the wrath of a war against social injustice.
Though his battle-cries may at times sound grotesquely, the living
breath of anger and sorrow informs his work and gives his politics
their universal dramatic values.

He concludes.

The whole cast was young, for only the young can adequately
transmit the fiery outpouring of Toller's own enthusiasm. If this
statement seems to hold a latent criticism, I would say that the
author himself desires and need desire no better valuation of his
play. It is a prelude to the poetry of world-revolution, a stormy
morning which may, in happier hours of daylight, be surpassed in
lasting poetic value, but never in the passionate humanity from
which it springs [7]

And Toller himself ended the letter to Fehling:

I need not dwell on the fact that proletarian art must ultimately rest
on universal human interests, must, at its deepest, like life or death,
embrace all human themes. It can only exist where the creative artist
reveals that which is eternally human in the spiritual characteristics
of the working people. [8]

These comments have been quoted at length as exemplifying the Volksbühne
attitude to the relationship of art and politics, and the nature of its continuing
commitment to the socialist cause, and they will be recalled when later the

left-wing criticisms of the Volksbühne are described. They are of immediate importance in the way they reveal the aims and sympathies of Fehling himself. [9]

Later in the same autumn he produced (less successfully) *King Lear,* and ended the extraordinary year's achievement with a remarkable production of the eighteenth-century satirical comedy of Tieck, *Der gestiefelte Kater* (*Puss in Boots*). Later in the same season (March 1922) he set the seal on his rise to eminence with his production of Hauptmann's *Die Ratten* (*The Rats*). This play, having failed when first produced in 1911, had been revived at the Volksbühne in 1916 by Felix Holländer, working under Reinhardt: the success of that production made the critic Siegfried Jacobsohn withdraw his earlier condemnation. But Fehling's production, with Kayssler himself and Helene Fehdmer in the leading parts, lifted the play into another dimension. That production and one of Raimund's *Verschwender* (*The Spendthrift*) were his farewell productions for the Volksbühne. In the autumn of 1922 he went to work as regisseur under Jessner in the Staatstheater.

The Volksbühne's second theatre, the Neues Volkstheater, also made its mark during this same period.

The leadership of the association took over this theatre again in 1921, and after its directors Berisch and Heinz Goldberg had left, Nestriepke took over the direction in addition to his other tasks. He attempted a programme that even Piscator described as 'politically coloured', including plays by Ibsen, Hauptmann and Shaw as well as minor writers. One of his most important acts was the production by Paul Günther, in May 1923, of Ernst Barlach's first play *Der tote Tag* (*The Dead Day*). Apparently the theatre lost money, and for the following season, 1923-4, it was taken over formally as a subsidiary of the Bülowplatz theatre. [10]

Kayssler's years of office included the terrible period of inflation, during which the membership of the Volksbühne actually rose to the largely illusory – figure of 167, 000, failing to about 140, 000 in 1924 and slowly settling to a steady hundred thousand in the later twenties. Also during the Kayssler period the Volksbühne was hit by the two-week strike of actors in 1922, even though the Volksbühne publicly declared that it had no part in the dispute.

Kayssler remained the director of the Volksbühne theatre until the end of the 1922-3 season, when his contract was prematurely ended. Some difficulties had arisen because of his playing leads as well as directing, and when various business and organisational problems were traced back to the arbitrariness of the artistic director, it became more and more difficult for the officers and committees of the association to work with him. With his going the first post-war phase of the Volksbühne's work ended.

The Piscator Affair

Friedrich Kayssler's successor as director of the Bülowplatz theatre was Fritz Holl, up till now principal regisseur of the Württemberg Landestheater in Stuttgart. His term of office was the stormiest in the whole history of the Volksbühne in Berlin, and, primarily because of Piscator, the best known. But, partly because of Piscator's enormous international reputation, partly because he himself published the story from his own point of view as early as 1929 in his book *Das Politische Theater*, and partly because of the hostility of the press to the Volksbühne at that time, Piscator is usually represented, even in books written in recent years, as the 'hero' and Nestriepke as the 'villain' of the piece – and this in spite of the fact that in 1963 the two men worked together again with mutual respect in the new Freie Volksbühne of West Berlin. In this book the events will be seen from the point of view of the Volksbühne, and Piscator's debt to the Volksbühne, as well as the Volksbühne's debt to Piscator, will be examined in addition to the conflicts between them.

When Piscator was invited by Holl to direct a play for the Volksbühne he felt himself ripe for the opportunity to use for the first time the resources of a large, well-equipped modern theatre. His experience in the war, including amateur theatre at the front, had turned him away from 'pure' art ('Art is shit') to politics, and from Social Democracy to Communism. Piscator made his first serious steps at Königsberg in 1919-20 where his company Das Tribunal played Strindberg, Wedekind and Sternheim, using the lesser hall of the town hall as a chamber theatre. Meanwhile in Berlin, Karl-Heinz Martin had founded Die Tribüne – where he produced Toller's *Die Wandlung* (*The Transformation*) – and then the first Proletarian Theatre. [1] Now came the twenty-six-year-old Piscator to Berlin and founded the second Proletarian Theatre which, he said, was distinguished from the Volksbühne – on whose model it wished to create an audience organisation – and also from Martin's Proletarian Theatre, in that the word 'art' was banned, and that the 'plays' were proclamations 'with which we wanted to sieze on contemporary events and act politically'. They acted in halls smelling of stale beer and men's urinals. Once John Heartfield (Helmut Herzfelde) arrived at a *performance* half an hour late with the backcloth he had designed and painted, and insisted on stopping the show to put it up! Except for a few sympathetic professionals, the actors themselves were working people. Six plays were presented in the first year; no bourgeois critics were admitted; the audience was organised exactly on the lines of the Volksbühne and consisted of five to six thousand members recruited largely from the Allgemeine Arbeiter-Union, the Kommunistische Arbeiter-Partel (KAP) and Syndicalists. There was no support from the Kommunistische Partei Deutschlands (KPD) whose organ *Rote Fahne* accepted the traditional distinction between art and propaganda and refused to accept Piscator's theatre as art.

The Proletarian Theatre posed great financial problems and wound up in April 1921. Piscator's next venture was to join with José Rehfisch in acquiring the Zentral Theater. Inflation being rife, they paid three million Marks for it and sold some scrap iron in order to pay! Zickel, the former director, had some Volksbühne bookings and at first these were handed over, but when the Volksbühne realised Piscator's political intentions, it withdrew them: it was his first conflict with the Volksbühne. Indeed the Zentral Theater project was conceived, he says, as an opposition to the Volksbühne, but, in common with the Volksbühne, Piscator could not avoid admitting middle-class members – the number of working-class ones was not enough. [2]

Piscator here directed three highly naturalistic productions – Gorky, *Suburbans*, Rolland, *Le Temps viendra* and Tolstoy, *The Power of Darkness*. Eventually Piscator had to give up the theatre; the year's work there, he says, had enabled him to make great progress into the theatrical life of Berlin, but at great financial loss.

It was at this point that Piscator was invited to direct Alfons Paquet's *Fahnen (Flags)* for the Volksbühne. He himself says it was by chance: 'My invitation came purely by chance, for by chance there was no Director who would have been willing to produce a piece by Alfons Paquet, chosen equally by chance'. [3] It is difficult to accept this view. Piscator had already modelled his audience organisation on the Volksbühne and thought of his Zentral Theater venture as its rival. Further, to him the Volksbühne itself was the historical root of what he called 'political theatre':

> The political theatre, as it has worked out in all my undertakings, is neither a personal 'invention' nor a result of the social regrouping of 1918. Its roots reach back to the end of the last century. At that time forces broke into the intellectual situation of bourgeois society which, consciously, or through their mere existence, altered that situation decisively and to some extent raised it up. These forces came from two directions: from literature and from the proletariat. Where the two intersected a new conception came into being in art – Naturalism – and a new form in the theatre – the Volksbühne. [4]

It is usually said that the invitation came from Holl, but Piscator's widow, Maria Ley-Piscator, writing admittedly long after the events, says. 'Siegfried Nestriepke made the daring step of asking Piscator to direct the forthcoming play at the Volksbühne.' [5] Though the invitation would undoubtedly be extended to Piscator by the artistic director of the theatre, it is interesting that Maria Ley thinks of it as actually originating, like so many bold and imaginative Volksbühne developments, from Nestriepke himself. She may well be right.

Piscator clearly regarded himself as the potential saviour of the Volksbühne. That very movement which he saw as the root of his own political theatre, seemed to him to have been betrayed by the exaltation of art over class struggle. It was, he said, a mere artistic 'Co-op' (Konsumverein), whose only business was to engage the best experts. 'Everything here cooked in butter', he remarked sarcastically and quoted at length a pamphlet by Herbert Ihering, *The Betrayal of the Volksbühne*, which formulated three stages of degeneration- Reinhardt, 'a prodigal genius'; Kayssler, 'a priest of the art of acting; a temple-ward of the theatre; art as a religious service, the stage as a cathedral'; and Holl, 'now formlessness succeeds to formlessness'. Piscator was far too penetrating to charge individual directors with responsibility for the development of the Volksbühne: he blamed the circumstances of the time, particularly the non-emergence of authors and plays:

> Where was the drama? Where were the authors? All forces, all the forces of the drama, production, direction, political leadership, administration and, finally, of the public, united to guarantee the Volksbühne long and undisturbed sleep. [6]

Piscator saw Paquet's play as one of those for which the theatre, and especially the Volksbühne, was waiting, and himself as the appropriate director – because for him, technical and political developments were inextricably bound together. Maria Ley tells us that the surprise invitation produced a crisis of conscience in Piscator, who asked himself how he could work in the theatre which he had condemned for not living up to its own ideals. In spite of his losses at the Zentral Theater, he had not yet come to terms (if he ever did) with the economics of theatrical production. Later, having had his own theatre at the Nollendorfplatz, 'he realised the pressure of the economic battle which was the true reason for Siegfried Nestriepke's sometimes crafty administrative measures'. [7] He decided, however, to accept, hoping to 'turn the tide' at the Volksbühne.

The action of Alfons Paquet's play takes place in Chicago at the time of the unrest among the workers in 1886. [8] Written for a German audience, it concentrates upon the community of German immigrant workers in Chicago, and at one point relates the events to Germany itself by references to Bismarck and the anti-socialist law. The central events of the play are that Cyrus McClure, the capitalist, bribes the Police Captain Shaak to provoke a disturbance at an open-air workers' meeting: he does so. A bomb is thrown and shots are fired. Workers are arrested and accused. One commits suicide in prison and four others are executed. In the final tableau the flags which give the play its name are dipped over the coffins of the martyred workers.

The play is in eighteen scenes, divided into three acts, and is written in a completely factual and naturalistic style without any poetic language or non-naturalistic stage directions. The numerous characters [9] are clearly and simply seen – Fielden, the Englishman, who speaks of the Lancashire Luddites; Parsons, with his Old Testament rhetoric and Indian wife; Governor Ogleby; Lingg in his cell reading his mother's letter and so on. The scenes are similarly plain – the editorial office of the workers' newspaper; Seliger's house with its home-made bombs; McClure's office; a cellar; a court; a citizens' club where a buffalo is being roasted; a prison cell. There is a documentary plainness, too, in the presentation of the sequence of events. No attempt is made to knit a plot, lead up to climaxes or construct shapely acts, and although all the incidents are relevant to the central story, the method is discursive rather than concentrated, narrative rather than dramatic. When the play was printed in 1923, the author subtitled it *A Dramatic Novel* (*Ein dramatischer Roman*), but when Piscator directed it he changed this to *An Epic Drama* (*Ein episches Drama*). [10] It is the first appearance of the phrase which Brecht made famous and upon which he constructed a whole theory of theatre. Alfred Döblin described the play as belonging to a fruitful 'middle ground' (*Zwischengebiet*) between narrative and drama, saying that it was none the worse for that: 'One can not reproach a mule for being neither an ass nor a horse: it is only bad, when it is a bad mule. [11] Leo Lania, writing in the *Wiener Arbeiterzeitung* (2 June 1924) distinguished it from plays, like *Dantons Tod* and *Die Weber* in that the author had renounced all artistic form and limited himself to allowing the bare facts to speak for themselves.

Piscator was delighted at the response of the Volksbühne Ensemble to his ideas, and began to put into operation his distinctive kind of production, later known, as he remarks, as 'epic theatre'. This, he says, briefly consists of a broadening of the treatment, illumination of the background, and the development of the piece beyond the compass of the merely dramatic. 'Out of the play to be seen, grew the teaching material' ('Aus dem Schau-Spiel [sic] entstand das Lehrstück'). He placed projection-screens on both sides of the stage, and, consistently with his aim of presenting the play as clearly and objectively as possible he used these for what he calls 'display texts linking the individual scenes'. Piscator said that as far as he knew this was the first time that slide-projections had been used in this way in the theatre. In fact they had been similarly used four years earlier by the Dadaist, Ywan Goll. Piscator was associated with Dada in 1919, but minimised its artistic influence upon him in his book. [12] The play had a Prologue in verse in which the characters were introduced and the play declared to be a 'puppet show'. Piscator projected photographs of the characters as they were named. [13] At first all went well, but two days before the first night everything began to disintegrate and at the dress rehearsal the invited guests gradually slipped away. At the end Piscator wrote 'Shit' in his notebook and walked slowly upstairs, accidentally overhearing one sentence from a conversation between Holl, Neft and the actor Paul Henckels. 'That's the worst we've had! How could we engage this man! Simply frightful!' To Piscator's honour, he walked straight into the room and declared, 'Gentlemen, I entirely agree with you!' He offered to give up the production; he suggested putting off the opening for a week. The others would not agree. So Piscator went to the actors and proposed that they rehearse, with all properties and effects, from after that evening's performance until the following evening. They agreed! The rehearsal began at 1.00 a.m. and continued until the performance, which had to begin half an hour late. During the performance the applause became more and more stormy, and 'when in the final tableau three great black flags had descended from the flies, a round of applause broke out which almost had something revolutionary in it'. [14]

'A storm of applause answered the storm on the stage. And with justice', were the opening words of Max Osborn's enthusiastic critique in the *Berliner Morgenpost* two days later. Projections, scenery, the use of the revolve, the enthusiasm with which the actors were fired, all were seen as contributing to the whole and silencing any carping criticism of imperfect particulars.

The anonymous critic (Fh ....) of *Vorwärts* welcomed the fact that a writer of note had treated 'the most important problem of the present', and was prepared to forgive the 'dramatic shortcomings' of the play, which he felt were, at least tentatively, compensated for by the light and sound effects and the dramatically moved scenery.

Monty Jacobs, in the *Vossische Zeitung*, was more scathing about the play itself which, he said, owed its place in the Volksbühne to its propaganda value only. 'Paquet's hand trembles uncertainly, but Piscator's fingers work energetically and firmly.' But Piscator is not left blameless. If Paquet shows himself to be his own critic in calling the piece 'a dramatic novel' (and what can that be, asks Jacobs, but an undramatic play?), Piscator reveals a lack of confidence in the play, in his use of projected texts. He uses them like subtitles in the (silent) cinema, so that, when the prisoners are condemned, the words appear CONDEMNED TO DEATH, or when the police commit the outrage – THE POLICE THEMSELVES THROW THE BOMBS (though the author has been objective enough also to show the anarchist domestic bomb factory). 'A director', says Jacobs, 'who thinks such crutches necessary, does not even discreetly hide the lameness of the play ... These superfluous bits of cinema rubbish show that Piscator must make himself strong enough, if he is to help his author's weakness – which the actors, under his direction, already can'.

Soon after this success the Volksbühne and Piscator entered into a contract under which for some years he would direct plays of his own choice in the Volksbühne theatre. He himself admits that, largely because he could not find the kind of plays he wanted, several of the productions were mere journeyman work. His next production in the theatre, in December 1924, was *Under the Caribbean Moon* – Berlin was just 'discovering' O'Neill. It does not seem to have been very successful, though Ihering rather grudgingly admitted it to be the best O'Neill play so far, while at the same time asking when the Volksbühne was going to realise its true vocation. Piscator makes no comment at all in *Das Politische Theater*. The O'Neill was followed at the end of January by *Wer weint um Juckenack?* (*Who Weeps for Juckenack?*), a comedy by Hans José Rehfisch, jurist turned dramatist, who had worked alongside Piscator in the Zentral Theater in 1923. Although this play marks the beginning of Rehfisch's success as a dramatist it was of no more than secondary importance to Piscator - though Ihering, whose hopes for Piscator had been sustained since *Fahnen*, in spite of O'Neill, said that the production was a great credit to the Volksbühne, the greatest since the production of *Fahnen*.

Piscator was much more interested in his next Volksbühne production, Rudolf Leonhard's *Segel am Horizont* (*Sails on the Skyline*). This title was suggested by Georg Kaiser, whose friend and disciple Leonhard was, the original having been *Towarischtsch* (*Comrade*). The germ of the play lay in a report in a Berlin newspaper (7 November 1924) of a Russian ship, *Towarischtsch*, under the command of a woman. In the play itself Angela Alexandrovna Dialtschenskaya, the dead Captain's wife, is elected captain by the crew of sixty. A sexually explosive situation develops, as the men are unable to regard Angela simply as a comrade – she is for them a woman, the one woman among sixty men. They insist that, in order to ease the tension, she must choose one man from among them. She chooses the telegraphist, an intelligent and articulate man, who says, 'No'. She then chooses Kaleb, the illiterate. The tension, so far from easing, becomes worse, and Kaleb is thrown overboard to drown. Angela eventually gains full command of the situation and explains to the crew that her husband had in fact committed suicide because he was jealous of the two sailors Oleg and Morten. The sense of comradeship and duty to the collective gains an uneasy victory.

Piscator liked the play for the way in which an intellectual thesis was developed out of starkly realistic material – sex, murder and violence – though he said that Leonhard had created only a mosaic out of the disparate elements, not, like Kaiser, an entirely new form. Traugott Müller designed a three-dimensional, practicable ship on the revolving stage which 'attained an independent function through which the weakness of the conclusion became dramatically one of the strongest moments of the piece.' [15] Unfortunately Piscator does not explain exactly how this was achieved.

After *Fahnen* the next of his Volksbühne productions which Piscator seems to have regarded as important was another play by Paquet, *Sturmflut* (*Storm*

Flood), though he says he selected it through lack of time while fully aware of its weaknesses. He calls it 'a paraphrase of the Russian Revolution', and summarises it thus:

> The revolution is winning; but money is lacking to carry it through. Granka Umnitsch, its leader, therefore sells Petersburg to an old Jew, who re-sells it to England. Granka and his band withdraw into the forests. There, a battle of love between him and a Swedish woman who goes over to the other side (embodied in the White Guard Sawin). Granka returns secretly to Petersburg, rouses the proletariat and reconquers the city for the revolution. [16]

The weakness of the play lay in the unreality of the symbolism. As one critic wrote: 'Because I am, as I have said, lazy and superficial, frivolous and childish, I require first of figures in drama that they *are* something, before they *signify* something.' [17] Piscator writes similarly:

> Symbol is condensed reality .... But it is not a trademark. It may not become a cliché for reality .... High points of history are themselves symbols in their complete, concrete extent. It is a mistake to drain what is material from such material, [*von solchen Stoffen das Stoffliche abzuziehen*], for through that not a heightening but a disembodiment is achieved. [18]

Thus Piscator, filled, as he says, with the events of the Russian Revolution, with which he was familiar in all their political and social relationships and interrelationships, had to produce a play in which everything 'ran together in confusion, entangled, unclear, pale and half-baked'. [19] Small wonder if, feeling like this about it, Piscator virtually remade the play during the three and a half weeks of rehearsal, 'splitting the piece to its foundations, rebuilding its structure, adding new material, and right up to the opening night demanding further new text from that harassed creature, the author'. [20]

The 'harassed creature' later defended himself in the Preface to the printed edition of the play:

> It is not the history of a revolution; not a description of the life of Lenin; not a representation of Soviet Russia.... it was not a question of a transcript of reality, but of epitomising the driving forces of our time in a few figures, which would rouse the emotions vividly, as reality arouses them. [21]

Meanwhile, what the audiences and critics saw had, as Piscator said, come into being on the stage. It had done so with the author's full co-operation, and to his satisfaction, as Paquet makes clear in a passage omitted from his Preface, which he prints as a Postscript to the play:

Piscator gave me the opportunity of working directly with him and the actors at rehearsal.... The revolutionising effect of this close contact of the dramatist with the essential laws of the theatre working themselves out in a thousand particulars and possibilities, cannot be overvalued. [22]

Apart from the type-characters that Arthur Eloesser found so unconvincing, but which Ihering found to be an exciting, individualised and extended political typology, the most discussed aspect of the production was its use of film sequences. It was this, too, that interested Piscator himself most.

With this production a great step forward was made in working out and refining the film scenes. For the first time it was possible to have whole sections of film specially photographed for the play. [23]

Ihering, who wrote about the production in two successive issues of the *Berliner Börsen-Courier*, devoted much of his second article to the film, giving more details about its use:

Radio news: Revolution in China – on the screen in the background a Chinese mass meeting; speech by Lloyd George – Lloyd George speaks in the film.... Or at the beginning: the stage is the shore, the harbour, the square at Petersburg. The film: ships, sea, inundation. Or at the end: fighting. Or between: motionless background that suddenly becomes alive; contrasts or parallels from other revolutions, or aeroplanes, the stone canyons of the city, forest. [24]

Ihering, who was pleased with the experiment ('The film is no longer ... a trick .... The film is dramatic function') [25] also pointed out that it did not always come off. It was best, he thought, when documentary. Eloesser reached a more negative conclusion. Having remarked that we should murder Piscator if he provided visual aids to poetic passages in Goethe's plays, he continues:

The stage abdicates when it renounces the magic of language, which makes our ear a spiritual eye.
How sweet the moonlight sleeps upon this bank.
If Herr Piscator ... but perhaps we have murdered him already. [26].

Four more productions must be mentioned before that over which the storm broke – appropriately enough *Gewitter über Gottland* (*Storm over Gothland*). Two of these are Piscator's intervening Volksbühne productions, one is his *Die Räuber* at the Staatliches Schauspielhaus, and one Jessner's Piscator-influenced *Hamlet* at the same theatre.

The next Piscator Volksbühne production was Paul Zech's 'scenic ballade', *Das trunkene Schiff* (*The Drunken Ship*). As the title suggests, this is a play about the poet Rimbaud, and is in fact simply Rimbaud's life from his running away from home as a teenager, to his death. Rimbaud is thought of as his own 'bateau ivre' and the scenes of the *Ballade* are named as if the play were a voyage: 'Setting sail', 'First port of call', 'Second port of call', 'Harbour'. Best are the closing scenes and those which show Rimbaud's relationship with Verlaine. Piscator was clearly disappointed that though the play covered an important period in French history it limited itself to the study of individual psychology (though it contains some side-swipes at imperialism), and to compensate, as it were, for this, Piscator substituted for the elaborately naturalistic scenes described in the author's stage directions, projections on three great screens of designs by George Grosz which introduced the social and political environment. He also projected film, not only as illustration, but also, when Rimbaud on his last homeward voyage lies dying of fever, as interpretations of his delirious fantasies.

The other Piscator Volksbühne production in 1926 was Gorky's *The Lower Depths*. Although the play attracted Piscator, he was not satisfied with it as it stood. 'In 1925 [actually 1926] I could no longer think on the scale of one small room with ten unfortunate people, but only on the more extended scale of the slums of a great modern city.' [27] Piscator asked Gorky himself to adapt the play along these lines, but to his disappointment Gorky declined to do so. Piscator therefore fell back upon scenic devices and stage effects. in two places he moved the play in the direction he wished:

> The beginning – the snores and heavy, rattling breath of a mass of
> people, which filled the whole stage space; the awakening of a great
> city, the clang of tram-bells, until the ceiling descended and
> contracted the whole social milieu into the room; and the riot – not
> just a minor rough-house of private characters in the yard, but the
> rebellion of a whole quarter against the police, the uprising of the
> masses. [28]

Meanwhile, in September, Piscator had produced Schiller's *Die Räuber* at the Staatliches Schauspielhaus. Following the example of Brecht's adaptation of Marlowe's *Edward II* [29] and Erich Engel's production of Shakespeare's *Coriolanus*, [30] Piscator set out deliberately to give Schiller's play a modern political significance. It is not relevant here to describe or discuss this famous production in detail. [31] Schiller's play was, as Bab expressed it, stood upon its head, and Spiegelberg – in cutaway coat, dirty brown bowler and Trotsky make-up, became the hero, the true proletarian revolutionary, and Karl Moor reduced to 'a romantic fool'. The production brought into debate the whole question of whether the classics should be thus adapted and in part rewritten in order to give them new life in the twentieth century (the view supported by, for example, Herbert Ihering) or whether the classics must remain themselves and new plays be written to express new ideas: 'A Spiegelberg drama cannot be derived from Schiller, but must be newly written – let us say by Brecht. Or let us turn directly to Piscator's poetic ability and demand something home-made from him.' [32]

The debate was intensified by Jessner's own production in December of *Hamlet*. This, said Bab, did not actually falsify the play as Piscator's production had falsified *Die Räuber* but developed as its main theme the background of court cabal, aristocratic brutality, and stupid convention, that Shakespeare needed for presenting his main themes through Hamlet himself. The play was so directed that it was easy to see actual parallels implied with modern German history: Claudius as Kaiser Wilhelm II; Polonius as Bethmann-Hollweg.

These two productions, coming after Piscator's other work at the Volksbühne and elsewhere, set alight a controversy in literary periodicals and serious newspapers on the politicisation of the theatre – though it also took the form of debates on freedom of thought and the protection of pure art. 'The signs are multiplying. The flags of literary questions are being unfurled.' [33] Left and right began to take to the intellectual barricades. 'Why are we not as active as Piscator?' demanded a speaker at a public meeting of the right-wing National Women's Circle, when the Greater German Theatre Society (Grossdeutsche Theatergemeinschaft) was founded (it achieved only one production); while Herbert Ihering joined Balázs on the left, and called for 'Clear relationships!. Decisions, not mixtures.' Piscator admits that on the right this demand was taken up not only as decisively as on the left but with stronger political insight. Could Piscator, writing in 1929, have by then become aware that he was among those who, through his dipping flags and modern techniques for playing upon mass emotion while claiming only to present sober fact, [34] helped to let out of the bottle the genie who stage-managed the Nuremburg Rallies of the 1930s ?

Nowhere was the conflict felt so keenly as within the Volksbühne itself. While on the one hand the Volksbühne had its contract with Piscator, on the other hand, during the same period it had made 'many concessions to the customs of the Berlin Private Theatres in the "star" system and the shaping of the repertoire'. [35] As Georg Springer's left-wing adversary Arthur Holitscher pointed out:

> After every first night of works of the political opinion that we
> demand, works which demonstrate a proletarian feeling in
> contemporary events, hundreds of letters fly from the membership
> into the office of the Volksbühne, all to the same effect: 'Leave us in
> peace from all these problems – hunger, revolution, class-war, misery,
> corruption, prostitution. We have enough of those at party-meetings,
> in our jobs, at home, in our neighbourhood.' [36]

The magnificent theatre ('catastrophically magnificent', according to Holitscher) demanded a large membership that could not be drawn from one class or one political persuasion, and even had the executive of the Volksbühne wanted its theatre to become a speaking-trumpet for the Communist Party, it would have been economically impossible for it to have done so. But within the Volksbühne the Youth Section strongly supported Piscator and continuously demanded that the Volksbühne 'accept the consequences of taking the road to political drama, so far followed only hesitatingly and unhappily'. [37]

The conflict came to a head in February and March 1927. In the article by Arthur Holitscher already quoted the Volksbühne is accused, along with the whole Social Democratic Party, of betraying the ideals of its founders, and of entering into a 'coalition' with the 'reactionary' Volksbühnenbund. [38] On 14 March the Youth Section unanimously passed a resolution which stated:

> The Volksbühne, whose support is the working class, must express a clear conviction in a lively and consciously purposeful repertoire. The proletarian youth in the Volksbühne refuses to accept the bourgeois interpretation of the neutrality of art. As the theatre is an important instrument in the working class struggle for freedom, the stage must reflect the purpose and life of the proletariat fighting for a new order in the world. [39]

While denying that there was a 'crisis' in the Volksbühne, Georg Springer answered Holitscher in *Weltbühne* on 22 March (the day before the opening of Piscator's next production!):

> The Volksbühne has not the tradition, intention or possibility of equating the word *Volk* in its name with 'radical-socialist working-class'. Of course it grew out of the aim of opening up the arts, in the first instance the theatre, to the workers, and today it still regards it as its principle task to free the way for the proletariat to the good things of art. But the membership of the Volksbühne in Berlin does not consist exclusively of proletarians, and still less in the countryas a whole, and if we wanted to narrow the conception of the *Volk* entitled to an opinion and worthy of help, to radical-socialist convictions, that would be equivalent to blowing up the Volksbühne. [40]

It was into this explosive situation that Piscator deliberately injected his production of Ehm Welk's play *Gewitter über Gottland*. He represents the play as a 'concession' by the executive to the left, a compromise. Herbert Ihering saw it in similar terms, but Piscator must have known better. He himself suggested the play, and says that the executive accepted it because the action took place in the year 1400, 'and so even in my production must still be safe from too dangerous a contemporary significance. The executive had only overlooked one trifle, one sentence. It was on the title-page and said: 'The drama does not only take place in 1400.' [41] From that one sentence Piscator developed the contemporaneity of the theme in a way which could not have been foreseen and was in fact nakedly party-political.

The actual story of the play concerns the struggle between the great trading Hansestadt Hamburg and the Vitalian Federation, a communistic group established on the island of Gottland. Störtebeker, a 'kind of maritime officer of the Baltic provinces' (Ihering) is taken into the service of the leaders of the Vitalians, Michelsen and Asmus Ahlrichs; but his outstanding success in the war at sea makes him independent of them. His revolutionary ideas are primitive and he is personally ambitious. Piscator himself calls him an emotional revolutionary and says that today (1929) he would be a Nazi. He wants to be king, but is eventually handed over to the Hamburgers by Asmus, fanatic of the communist idea. Welk certainly intended his audience to infer the more general, and particularly the contemporary political implications of the play, but Piscator was not content with this. His sympathetic critic Ihering has given an account of the production:

> It begins by illustrating on film the political and religious power, relationships and the social structure of the Middle Ages. An historical sketch.... The characters of the play, Störtebeker and Asmus among them, make their impact on the audience in the film, and by stages change their clothing until Asmus has become Lenin .... Finally, the play begins .... [42]

The result as described in *Der Tag* was:

> There was really absolutely no more question of Art this evening. Politics had devoured it, skin, hair and all. We had unsuspectingly come into a communist election and propaganda meeting, we stood in the midst of the jubilation of a Lenin Celebration. At the end the Soviet star rose shining over the stage. [43]

Small wonder that the leaders of the Volksbühne, themselves social democrats, could not let the matter rest there, specially as *Der Tag* wrote challengingly:

> The leaders of the Volksbühne emphasise again and again that their exertions are purely artistic, beyond and above all politics. So how can they permit this performance? [44]

In reply the executive issued this statement:

> The Executive Committee of the Volksbühne e. V. sees in the nature of the production a misuse of the freedom which the Committee

extend to the persons entrusted with the artistic leadership of the house of the Volksbühne. Ehm Welk's play, whose acceptance was the result not of a certain political aim in it, but of its poetic merits – of course with a full appreciation of the inner relationship of its material to problems of the present day – received in Erwin Piscator's production (whose artistic significance is recognised) a tendencious, political reshaping and extension, for which no sort of inner necessity existed. The Executive Committee of the Volksbühne e. V. confirms expressly that the use of the play as one-sided political propaganda took place without its knowledge and consent, and that this kind of production is in contradiction with the fundamental political neutrality of the Volksbühne, which it is in duty bound to protect. It has already taken steps to guarantee the essential validity of its interpretation of the task of the Volksbühne. [45]

The steps taken were to cut out parts of the films.

In the 'Storm over the Volksbühne' (Piscator's phrase) which now broke out in full force, the issues involved are tangled and confused. On the artistic merits of the production (to which the Volksbühne executive paid tactful tribute in its statement) the critics were at odds, but even Herbert Ihering thought the play monotonous and wished that Piscator had devoted his talents to one more worthy – even another by the same author. So the executive stood on weak ground in asserting that the play had been chosen for its poetic merits. So too, was it on weak ground in maintaining that 'no sort of inner necessity existed' for the political reshaping of the play, and Ehm Welk himself eventually found it necessary to issue his own open letter to the Volksbühne executive, saying that as far as the author's intention was concerned, Piscator was not abusing or distorting his original. But even Ihering wrote with reservations about Piscator's actual success in carrying out his experiments. Paul Fechter, a critic less sympathetic to Piscator's political aims, says that it was shocking. The boredom made him sorry for everyone – the author, director, audience – and himself. The production was mere repetition of earlier Piscator. The Volksbühne was 'gambling with its own existence, with this foolish trickery'. There were a couple of good visual scenes from Traugott Müller, but that wasn't enough for four hours, 'especially when the rest of the scenic machinery continually creaks and gets stuck, and won't work properly....' [46] He accuses the actors of shouting.

> The applause, which likewise seemed to be well produced, was loud. It was, so to speak a failure got up as a success. Piscator and his colleagues were recalled again and again. But I must confess: wild horses wouldn't drag me to another production of that sort. [47]

And Welk, though he accepted the political interpretation and general adaptation, objected strongly to the 'ruin and bungling of the text'. He said that George as Störtebeker, for whole scenes didn't speak a single word of the manuscript, but 'twaddle, trash and nonsense'. It was the artistic success of the undertaking, not Piscator's political slant, that Welk criticised.

It is surely clear that the artistic success and validity of Piscator's production of *Gewitter über Gottland* is, at the least, open to great doubt. [48] It is the political intention that his supporters welcome and praise. It seems extraordinary that commentators still blame the executive of the Volksbühne for resisting the attempt to make the association merely a communist platform. Naturally Piscator was supported by his principals and small part actors – any theatrical director of even mediocre ability generates in his company a personal loyalty that will always support him against 'the management'; how much more a director of Piscator's originality and personality!. Naturally he was supported by an impressive list of writers, and artists, not only of the left, but of liberal persuasion: the sense that 'faceless men' are interfering with artistic freedom always, and healthily, arouses such a reaction.

The supporters on the left called a great public meeting in the Festival Hall of the former Prussian House of Lords (Herrenhaus) (30 March 1927). Arthur Holitscher took the chair, Erwin Kalser spoke for the actors, Victor Blum for the 'supers'; Toller spoke, Jessner, Karl-Heinz Martin, and Piscator himself. It was the end of Piscator's work as a Volksbühne director for over thirty years, but the beginning of a new and fruitful relationship, for in spite of Ihering's rather shrill cries for no compromise the final solution was a compromise, and a valuable one: through the Youth Sections.

The pioneer of the Youth Volksbühne in Berlin was Wilhelm Spohr. Spohr saw performances for children and young people as an influence against 'dirt and trash'. He supported the movement away from 'intellectualism' in education, welcoming such teaching methods as play-readings in class. Writing in 1923 he said that he had first seen *Wilhelm Tell* before an audience of schoolchildren, twenty-five years earlier: 'Poet and performers could wish for no more ideal audience.' His proposals for a Youth Volksbühne were taken up by the Berlin Volksbühne in 1920. For the first year children were reached only through Volksbühne members, but this provided a basis. In the second year the attempt was made to get children committed to a *series* of performances. In the third year some schools and organisations were invited to participate. The performances were all on Saturday afternoons, and personal tickets were exchanged for theatre tickets by the traditional method of lottery. The scheme of linking the Youth Volksbühne to the parent body was not wholly successful and the number of school children grew more and more in proportion to those in youth organisations.

In 1927 the Berlin Volksbühne gave up these school-children's performances to the City of Berlin, and Wilhelm Spohr became Manager of Municipal Children's Plays.

Meanwhile, in 1923, new sections were created *inside* the Berlin Volksbühne for young people not at school – through youth organisations. The sections attended evening performances, and their costs and rights were identical with those of other sections. The core of these sections consisted of young working-class people, recruited through leaflets circulated in youth organisations. The appeal made in the leaflets was a serious one:

> The theatre is of the greatest significance for the continued development of human society. It receives its stimulus – as does art in general – from the tensions and life forces of the time, and if its organism is healthy and its audience ready, it must give the essence of the time artistic form.... The Volksbühne, founded from the working class, wishes to keep the theatre open to the great mass of working people who suffer most profoundly under the needs of the time.... [49]

These sections began with a membership of about a thousand, which more than doubled in a year and by the time of the Piscator 'case' had some four thousand members. They were, as might naturally be expected, the principal supporters of Piscator.

Well before *Gewitter* Piscator had felt the need for his own theatre, where he could pursue his own ideas unfettered, and in the summer of 1926, the scheme was theoretically worked out. The money needed to found the theatre and to give him at least one season in which he could feel independent of the critics he obtained from the actress Tilla Durieux who had approached him after *Die Räuber* with the idea of a close business relationship. She put up 400,000 Marks. [50] Piscator really wanted a 'purpose-built' theatre to express his conceptions, and it was at this time that he and Bauhaus architect Walter Gropius worked out the famous, but 'never realised, designs for the total theatre' – forerunner of many modern flexible theatres. Instead of this he had to be content with the Theater am Nollendorfplatz, with only 1,100 seats, in which Piscator, for his costly productions, required 3,000 to 3,500 Marks per performance. He therefore had to charge what he himself admitted were the 'Kurfürstendamm prices of the Communist theatre'. Many social democrats were sceptical and feared the influence of the KPD (Communist Party). Piscator himself said that the Piscator-Bühne, as the new venture was called, was not party-political but stood nearest in outlook and politics to the KPD. *Pravda* thought the Piscator-Bühne petit-bourgeois rather than proletarian, but said it saw Piscator's problems and supported him.

The Youth Sections of the Volksbühne with the support of other members who favoured Piscator now formed themselves into the Special Sections whose aim was to support the new Piscator-Bühne without breaking with the Volksbühne. A leaflet was issued: 'What do the Special Sections want of the Volksbühne e. V. ?' This leaflet reaffirmed loyalty to the Volksbühne and said that these sections wished to go to the Volksbühne productions but also to ones that did not avoid taking sides or serving as political propaganda. The Special Sections put the Piscator-Bühne in the foreground of their programme. Members were to see three or four productions at the Volksbühne itself, up to two in the Theater am Schiffbauerdamm or Thalia, and five at the Piscator-Bühne. The subscription was to be identical with that of the other sections, 1.50 Marks per performance.

> The largely autonomous leadership of these Special Sections ... came more and more under the dictatorship of extremist forces which drew their ideological weapons from the armoury of the Communist Party and their directives from some very revolutionarily disposed men of letters. The activity of these circles was clearly directed at winning the Volksbühne for the Communist Party. Representatives of left-wing youth organisations of democratic origin ... were forced out of the working committee. [51]

The Volksbühne recognised the Special Sections, which grew very rapidly. By the time the Piscator-Bühne opened they had sixteen thousand members, mostly young. They took up two to three hundred seats a performance at the new theatre, a great help, but not enough to enable Piscator to avoid the easy sneers in left-wing periodicals at the 'bejewelled and frock-coated' audience in his theatre. The compromise (*pace* Ihering) solved the problem on both sides. No doubt the Special Sections were 'the safety-valve for the bolshevik tendencies in the Volksbühne', [52] but the valve worked.

The productions of the Piscator-Bühne, Toller's *Hoppla, wir leben!* (*Whoops! We're alive*), *Rasputin* (with the 'globe stage'), [53], *Schweik* (with the conveyor-belt stage), have been fully described by Piscator and others. They were as artistically adventurous as financially disastrous. Some reminiscences of Gerda Redlich, who played a small part in *Hoppla, wir leben!* as a girl of eighteen, may help, however, to make the image of Piscator more vivid and personal: [54]

> I remember a terrible row between Toller and Piscator. Piscator being extremely quiet and cold – and Toller was a man suffering from consumption, a terribly excitable man – these two men absolutely standing there glaring at each other. We thought they would be fighting any moment, but it didn't come to that! But I cannot tell you what it was about. Toller didn't want all that technical to-do; he

wanted everything very much simpler; that's what it was all about fundamentally. Piscator wouldn't give an inch to anyone.

He had no time for any human touch or any human weakness, or anything like that. It was a bit like a parade ground, like drill, for the small-time actors. Quite different I am sure for Alexander Granach, etc. They would not have taken that. A very hard man on the surface ... oh ... he was obsessed. There was no human feeling at all. I don't ever remember him saying a human word or cracking a joke. I suppose he was tense.

The Piscator affair was, of course, not the whole story of the Berlin Volksbühne during these years. Various changes naturally occurred in the theatres used by the association. A particular enthusiasm of Nestriepke's was the promotion of the 'new' dancing. Matinées in the Bülowplatz theatre brought in as guest artists such dancers as Mary Wigman, Gret Palucca and Harald Kreutzberg. There was also much musical activity, and right through the twenties until 1933 a performance of Beethoven's Ninth Symphony was always given on New Year's Eve in the Bülowplatz theatre. Until 1924 the Volksbühne also worked in conjunction with A. Florath's Sprechchor (Choral speaking group). Then, through Holl's enthusiasm, the Volksbühne established its own, which was very active for the next five years.

The Volksbühne, already weakened by the internal dissensions and external criticisms (even from the right-wing press) arising from the Piscator affair, suffered a further set-back and more adverse publicity when Holl resigned his post at the end of the 1927-28 season. Above all, the economic position of the whole enterprise was precarious, and the first aim had to be to liquidate a deficit and set things on a firm financial basis. Instead, therefore, of a new artistic director being appointed the whole leadership was placed in the hands of Heinrich Neft, who had now been for many years the administrative director. Neft directed in the 1928-29 season an unexceptionable programme, including three notable plays by younger writers: Weisenborn's *U-Boot S.4*, Horvath' s *Bergbahn* (*Mountain Railway*) and Ehm Welk's *Kreuzabnahme* (*Descent from the Cross*) – the very play which Herbert Ihering had suggested as more worthy of Piscator's attentions than *Gewitter über Gottland*. Nevertheless the murderous attacks in the press continued.

As a further attempt to silence the criticisms, the committee appointed at the beginning of the 1929-30 season the brilliant young director Karl-Heinz Martin. He was known as an already experienced theatre director, sound on economies, strong in technicalities and organisation, and one of the most able of the great regisseurs. His leadership had distinction and character and the first season included an impressive opening production of Büchner's *Dantons Tod*, Frank Wedekind's *Frühlings Erwachen* and a memorable world première of Rehfisch and Herzog's *Dreyfus Affair*. But the attacks from the press, especially on the extreme left, continued. Karl-Heinz Martin held the post until 1932; his successor until 1934 was Heinz Hilpert.

Hilpert as a play-director and theatre-leader was always a thorn in the flesh of the Hitler regime. He was clever and skilled enough to continue to achieve social and humanistic relevance in opposition to the anti-humanistic non-culture of the Nazis. During his period at the Volksbühne and subsequently at the Deutsches Theater he made himself unpopular with Goebbels, and even after moving to the Josefstadt Theatre, Vienna, in 1938, he continued to worry the minister. He was a disciple of Otto Brahm, whom he took above all as his example, and when he took over the Volksbühne in 1932 declared his hope that he might follow in Brahm's spirit and pass something of it on to future generations.

On 21 September 1930 Gerhart Hauptmann delivered a speech in honour of the Volksbühne's fortieth year of existence. It was a weighty and moving speech – 'The Volksbühne was young, when I too was young. Many close friends of mine were among its founders' – which concluded by calling upon the Volksbühne to keep its true spirit alive in opposition to all 'fanatical, dogmatic, phenomena of our time'. [55] It is sad to remember that the speaker would later fly the swastika at his home. That swastika was already a strong force in Germany, and when the Nazis came to power in 1933 one of their victims was the Volksbühne. In Berlin, and throughout Germany, party members were forced upon the committees. Many prominent leaders of the movement, including Nestriepke, resigned. For six years the Volksbühne, 'a complete caricature of the former democratic Volksbühne organisation', [56] continued a nominal existence. In 1939 it was dissolved and the Theater am Bülowplatz declared State property.

Scene II

NATIONWIDE GROWTH 1918–1930

Interesting, fascinating and dramatic though it is, the history of the Berlin Volksbühne during the Weimar Republic does not by itself show the importance of the movement in social and theatrical history throughout the country, and indeed, as tends to happen in capital cities, hot-houses as they are for the growth of intense ideological factions, this Berlin history can even convey a distorted picture of the Volksbühne movement taken as a whole. Seen nationally the Volksbühne movement was neither a tool in the hands of left-wing political activists nor a mere artistic soup-kitchen, but a powerful instrument in the cause of cultural democracy.[1]

The concept of a nationwide Volksbühne Organisation went back at least as far as 1892 when Wilhelm Bölsche in a speech to the first General Meeting of the Neue Freie Volksbühne put forward the idea of a *Reichsvolksbühne* with its centre in Berlin and branches in all other big German towns. However, this was, as Niestriepke remarks, Utopian at that time.

In the event, the rebirth of the Volksbühne movement, or rather of its birth as a national phenomenon and as an essential element in the life of the theatre during the whole period of the Weimar Republic until the seizure of power by the Nazis in 1933, emerged from the economic and psychological ruins left by the military collapse of 1918. So favourable to the re-development of the Volksbühne idea were the post-war conditions that to some commentators the remarkable burgeoning of the movement throughout Germany seemed spontaneous, though in fact vision could never have been translated into reality without the dedication and practical activity of a few people – above all, Siegfried Nestriepke.

Noteworthily the constitution and structure of the Volksbühne Federation (Verband der deutschen Volksbühnenvereine) whose founding conference (23-25 October,1920) opened only two days after the first Annual General Meeting of the united Berlin Volksbühne, were so well thought out that during the next decade only very minor modifications were called for. At that first full Volksbühne conference fifteen Volksbühne organisations or committees were represented, while several others, including Munich, were absent. Berlin in its newly united form, and Bielefeld were, as we have seen,the only survivals from the pre-war period.

Annual Conferences to 1922

The Verband held annual conferences at which policies were debated and determined and wider topics were discussed. At the founding conference the Verband's fundamental principles were also established. Every Association in the Federation must "recognise the principle of party-political and religious neutrality and consequently [!] under all circumstances must refuse to adopt a position in conflict with the aims of the socialist movement". A commission was set up to lay down the basic principles for the nationalisation or socialisation of the theatre. At the same time a resolution was passed which read, in part:

> The Federation of German Volksbühne Associations demands in principle that theatre be transferred to public ownership so that the decisive co-operation of organised theatre-lovers may be assured. Until this complete socialisation is fully carried out the Federation demands the widest possible support for the Volksbühne Associations and their efforts, from the State and local authorities. It most decidedly rejects burdening non-profit theatre undertakings with taxes, above all an entertainment tax.

There were noteworthy speeches by distinguished figures such as Julius Bab, and Prof. Leo Kestenberg. Marxist and anti-Marxist views were advanced, but for once, so it is claimed, although starting from different standpoints, the speakers in practice reached the same conclusions in respect of the stance of the Volksbühne and of how its programmes should be planned. Even at this early stage non-theatrical activities in the fields of music, visual art and film were proposed, with a number of voices warning against overvaluing film as an art form.

Some thirty or forty representatives and a number of distinguished guests, including Leopold Jeßner, attended the conference, which ended on 25 October with a public rally of about a thousand people which was addressed by speakers on the general theme of the Volksbühne Movement and the socialisation of the theatre. It was felt to be an auspicious beginning for the newly expanding movement.

In the following October the second annual conference was held, this time at Eisenach, at which fifty delegates represented twenty-four Volksbühne Associations. The movement was evidently growing steadily and healthily. The conference ended with an open-air rally attended by some 700 to 800 people, in the courtyard of the Wartburg which, with its wealth and depth of historical associations, towers above the town, while Julius Bab and others addressed the crowd from the balcony of the castle.

The third conference, in Bielefeld, followed only just over eight months later, June being seen as a better time of year for the conference in relation to the beginning of the theatre-season in the autumn. Again the Federation had grown, and at the same time it faced new and more complex problems. Already, modelled on the Berlin Volksbühne, the *Bühnenvolksbund*, "an alliance for the encouragement of the theatre in a Christian German National spirit" had been founded in 1919 with its head office in Frankfurt-am-Main, and at the beginning of 1922 the Theatre Department of the Prussian Ministry of Culture had set up the Prussian Provincial Theatre (*die Preußische Landesbühne*) as an umbrella organisation designed to promote non-profit-making theatre in co-operation with the two theatre-audience organisations, the Volksbühne and the Bühnenvolksbund. This, as Georg Springer pointed out in his report, gave the theatre-audience organisations new responsibilities and tasks, but in the lively discussion that followed, a Frankfurt delegate, Dr Gebhardt, opposed participation in the Prussian Provincial Theatre unless the Bühnenvolksbund explicitly recognised the Volksbühnen Verband as "a completely neutral organisation". Almost all subsequent speakers opposed this and the proposal was unanimously defeated. Instead, the conference agreed to join the scheme provided this cooperation did not involve changing the character of the Volksbühne or neglecting its special aims and purposes. At the same time the conference expected sustained subsidies for the Volksbühne movement from the state and city authorities. Nor must the Volksbühne members, who were chiefly from the less affluent social strata, be burdened with theatre deficits. This debate continued.

Among minor constitutional changes a new and positive definition was drawn up as to the terms under which an Association could join the Federation:

Associations which "are built upon their members' right of self-determination and while emphasising their party-political and confessional neutrality seek to embrace all circles of the population which strive for a *new community culture.*"

Any false impression that this gathering was in any way isolated from the harsh realities of current events would have been shattered when Kurt Baake from the Chair announced the murder of Walther Rathenau, who had been made Minister for Reparations only four weeks before. Deeply moved, everyone stood up and Baake continued:

"We are not here in a political meeting. But Rathenau's murder is no mere political event. It is the duty of all decent people to defend themselves against intellectual struggles being carried out with instruments of murder."

A prophetic warning indeed!

The Districts and Annual Conferences to 1926

By now the movement had grown so strongly and widely that the need was already felt for local Associations to be grouped, for various practical purposes, into Districts (*Bezirke*), though these had no place in the constitution of the Federation and were not represented as such at the annual conferences. By the end of the decade there were sixteen Districts within the Federation.

The first District to be founded was Thüringia. Here the earliest Volksbühne Association was, with a certain historical appropriateness, in Weimar, where the Director of the National Theatre, Ernst Hardt, brought together governmental, theatrical, and adult-educational interests as well as, most importantly, representatives of blue- and white-collar workers, and civil servant's organisations. Hardt realised that the theatre needed new and wider audiences and that the theatre could raise the quality of life of the workers themselves. As a result of this meeting (13 July 1919) the Freie Volksbühne Weimar was founded on 12 October 1919 on the model of the Berlin Association.

The first performance for the Volksbühne was of Schiller's *Wilhelm Tell* in the National Theatre on the anniversary of the poet's birthday, 10 November 1919. The choice of date and of Schiller's drama of political freedom struck a note in harmony with the aims and future history of the movement. The Weimar Association had over 2,000 members in its first year.

Nine days later a branch of the Weimar Association – which achieved independent status a few months later – was founded at Apolda, some eleven kilometres north-east of Weimar. Performances there had to be given in a not altogether satisfactory hall. Before the end of the year, on 30 December, yet a third Association was founded in the same area at Jena. Its first performance was given in March 1920, the play being Anzengruber's *Der G'wissenswurm*. In a few months this Association, too, had well over 2,000 members.

A year later, December 1920, yet another Volksbühne at Eisenach, some seventy-five kilometres west of Weimar, brought the total membership of this group of four Associations in Central Germany to about 7,000, and on 14 May 1922 a Thüringian Volksbühne Conference was held at Weimar, which decided to form a Thüringia Volksbühne District within the Federation; but in October of the same year the Federation itself established a Central German District Group (*Bezirksgruppe "Mitteldeutschland"*) to which all the Associations in the Free State of Saxony, Brunswick, Anhalt, Thüringia, Hanover Province and Saxony were to belong. However, this was dissolved in June 1923 and on the fifteenth of that month the Thüringia District held its first conference with the newly-founded Rudolfstadt Volksbühne Association in addition to the original four.

Two other Districts were founded in 1922, that of *Hessen, Hessen-Nassau & Saargebiet* and that of *Rhineland*.

The area covered by the former encountered special opportunities, whose causes were often also the basis of special difficulties. Above all, the area had a long tradition of adult education and, since 1907, a highly successful non-profit touring company, *das Rhein-Mainische Verbandstheater* (*Rhine-Main Associate Theatre*). It was also in this part of the country that the fore-runner of the later Volkshochschule movement came into being, and all sections of the population had come into contact with theatre sooner than elsewhere in the country. So this was in no way virgin territory for the Volksbühne movement. On the other hand some of the actual difficulties encountered by the Volksbühne arose because similar but by no means identical forms of organisation already existed, such as popular performances arranged for Trade Unions without there being any sense of obligation upon trade union members to attend them. It is understandable that to local people the Volksbühne seemed unnecessary or even intrusive. Obviously the Volksbühne pioneers had to latch on to the existing situation and rely to a great extent not only on trade and professional unions but also upon organisations of all kinds of tendencies and groupings: the left-wing and liberal political parties and organisations also offered help, and the press, too, was supportive.

Other difficulties were due to the Allied Occupation of parts of the region for many years. (The last Allied troops did not leave the Saar until 12 December 1930.) Political restrictions were combined with the intensity and duration of the economic crisis in this area to create extraordinary difficulties for the Volksbühne. Even so, by 1930 the District comprised 17 Volksbühne Associations with a combined membership of over 22,000.

Of the six Volksbühne Associations that originally formed the District in 1922, four had been founded in the previous year. Ludwigshafen began with only 400 members but seven years later (1928), dissatisfied with the artistic quality of the available touring company, the *Pfälzische Wanderbühne*, it joined with Mannheim in order to benefit from performances of the Mannheim National Theatre: its membership then rose to over 1,000.

In Saarbrücken, with the help of the two audience organisations, the privately-owned theatre was transformed into a non-profit company, with considerable improvements both artistic and economic. There was almost ideal co-operation between political bodies and cultural organisations, though the extremely difficult conditions in the Saar as a whole, and Saarbrücken in particular, made it impossible to maintain the initially high membership.

In Worms, in spite of its religious and other advantages, even the Bühnenvolksbund encountered many problems, while the Volksbühne, depending as it did upon working-class organisations, suffered exceptionally severely on account of tremendous economic difficulties. The town had no resident company in its fine,1000-seater, Festspielhaus but relied solely on visiting companies.

Mainz on the other hand had its own company in a theatre seating 1400. Here, as in many other places, the Volksbühne grew out of an earlier system of performances given solely for trade unions and other organisations, but here, for the first time, the trade unions recognised the rightness of the Volksbühne system whereby members committed themselves in advance, through their subscriptions, to going to performances. A strong Volksbühne of more than 2000 members enabled some modern plays to be subsidised, and objections to the programme by the local bishop were countered by the tireless commitment of the Volksbühne to prevent too strict a censorship.

As we have already seen, the prehistory of the Volksbühne in Frankfurt-am-Main went back thirty years before its founding in 1922, as trade unions had arranged performances for their members at extraordinarily low prices, and ten years before, in 1912, the Director of the Neues Theater had tried to create an organisation on the pattern of the Berlin Volksbühne. This failed partly because it was opposed by the Committee for Popular Lectures, which sold the tickets, and partly because Hellmer, the Director, wanted to limit the Volksbühne to his own privately-run theatre and not to co-operate with the Municipal Theatres.

However, in 1921, serious efforts to establish a Volksbühne were started and the Association was successfully founded early in 1922, on condition that its performances had no adverse effect on the existing Popular Performances. As during the years that followed, interest in public lectures declined, so the Volksbühne grew in strength from 2000 members to almost 10,000 in 1930, and thanks to its taut organisation it became a decisive factor in the theatrical life of the city.

The other Volksbühne founded in this area in 1922 was in Wiesbaden. Again it was the trade unions that supported it initially, but its development was inhibited because during the worst years of the occupation its leading officials were expelled from the region.

The Rhineland District was founded 18th December 1922, six months after the Annual Conference, on the basis of five Volksbühne Associations all founded in 1921 or 1922. As already described, serious but unsuccessful attempts had been made as long ago as 1908 to found a Volksbühne movement in the Rhineland, and now at last were to bear fruit.

Two Volksbühne Associations, Düsseldorf and Wuppertal, were founded in June 1921, both in co-operation with trade unions. The former absorbed an earlier, unsuccessful "Freie Volksbühne" which had hoped to found its own theatre, *Die Szene*, but which, despite being regarded favourably in radical political circles, had failed to gain the support of working-class organisations. Both these Associations were quickly successful, Wuppertal having more than 3000 members by the end of 1921 and Düsseldorf over 10,000 by 1923. The very size of the membership of the latter posed problems and many special performances had to be arranged to supplement the limited number of seats available in the Stadttheater.(The Schauspielhaus was closed at this period.)

Also founded in 1921 were the Associations at Neuß and Aachen. That at Neuß was strongly challenged from the Catholic side and its activities were brought to a standstill by the occupation of the Ruhr in 1923, though later it recovered and by 1930 had about 1000 members against the Bühnenvolksbund's 100+. The Aachen Volksbühne also fell into ruin during the occupation and did not begin to recover until the closing years of the decade.

Most interesting was the development in Cologne where the Volksbühne sprang from the ruins of an actual theatrical enterprise, the Working People's Theatre (*Theater des werktätigen Volkes*) established on the Friesenplatz. At this theatre plays were produced under Johannes Tralow and operas under Fritz Zaun. Its excellent artistic standards quickly gave it a good reputation in the city and it very soon had 10,000 season-ticket holders. Although the high artistic quality offered exceeded all expectation, this sensational start was deceptive in respect of the viability of the enterprise. Inadequate space, inflation, unemployment and difficulties caused by foreign occupation brought the theatre to an abrupt end. Its more modest successor was not a new theatre but a theatre-audience organisation, the *Verein Freie Volksbühne Köln*. Then in 1923 the *Volksbühne G.m.b.H* (Co. Ltd.) was founded in the Metropole Theatre, also a non-profit company. The two worked closely together, the theatre achieving very high standards and an outstanding programme including Shakespeare's *The Tempest*, Hauptmann's *Die Ratten*, and Brecht's *Trommel in der Nacht*. Some productions ran for twenty performances or more. Then this theatre also fell victim to the economic crisis and the membership of the Freie Volksbühne Köln (about 25,000 in 1923) was decimated through the mass unemployment of the worst period of inflation. A theatre ticket could cost 2.7 billion Marks! ! After the collapse in 1924 the Cologne Volksbühne recovered, until by 1930 it had nearly 10,000 members and took up 5000 places per month in the Schauspielhaus and 2600 in the opera.

In the two years following the conference at Bielefeld the movement grew and spread so rapidly that eight new Districts were established. At the 1923 Conference, splendidly housed in the Rococco Hall of the Potsdam Stadtschloß where once Frederick the Great's theatrical performances were held, 52 Volksbühne Associations were represented by 80 delegates. With guests the total attendance was over 100. Altogether by this date there were 88 Associations with a total membership of over 450,000, and by June 1924, when the next annual conference was held at Hildesheim, yet another 40 had come into being. At both these conferences the question opened up in 1922 at Eisenach of collaboration with the Bühnenvolksbund in relation to the Prussian Regional Theatre was in the forefront of debates. At Potsdam a commission was set up whose recommendations were accepted unopposed. These were that although it was incontestable that an audience organisation had the right to a particular world-view (*Weltanschauung*), nevertheless the attempts of the Bühnevolksbund to influence the whole German theatre one-sidedly in the direction of the world-view which it represented, must be decisively opposed. When representatives of the Bühnenvolksbund supported propaganda which was hostile to truthful principles or was damaging to the work of the Freie Volksbühne, this must necessarily be fiercely opposed. But opposing opinions held by audience organisations need not exclude periodical joint representation of common interests in relation to authorities and parliaments.

More positively, the conference instructed the executive committee, in conjunction with local groups, to set out a clear "Programme" stating the politico-cultural stance of the Federation. The wording of this was not finally agreed until 1925 although in 1924 Julius Bab, speaking on *Intellectual Aims of the Volksbühne Movement* made a weighty contribution towards clarification, and a commission of nine was set up to formulate a programme on the basis of Bab's speech.

This long debate over a definitive policy statement was caused by and was an aspect of the persistent attempts of the Communists to turn the Volksbühne into an instrument for promoting their political, revolutionary, aims. This faction objected to what they called the *de-politicisation* of the Volksbühne and saw the 'purely human' values promoted by Nestriepke, Bab and others as being continually abandoned in favour of anti-communism and anti-bolshevism. They said that in order to gain a wide membership the Volksbühne had had to make political and ideological compromises of what they regarded as the worst kind.

At Jena in 1925 two drafts of the policy-statement were presented, one prepared by Nestriepke and Bab on behalf of the commission, the other by Professor Ziegler of Hanover. There was no co-ordinated left-wing opposition to either of these, but a small group, led by Arthur Holitscher who later was to play such a prominent part in the Piscator affair, opposed both drafts and wanted no such programmatic restriction, so that the movement would have greater freedom to adopt decisively combative political positions. Holitscher declared bluntly:

> When I saw the Bab-Nestriepke draft I was sick! There were in it the beginnings of proletarian Will, and on the other hand once more bourgeois ideology ... We must declare ourselves unambiguously as belonging to the proletarian parties and as proceeding from them.

The abolition of the 8-hour day and the fate of political prisoners signify great cultural danger, even for our movement. Our movement must direct itself positively against this danger and support the political parties and their struggle in these matters. That is much more important than fighting here over the wording of a version of a policy statement whose acceptance or rejection is a matter of relative indifference. [2]

Only a few of the delegates supported him and eventually Nestriepke and Bab's draft was accepted with 91 votes while Ziegler's obtained 59.

The Seventh Annual Conferencee, June 1926, was held at Hamburg. The movement had still continued to grow and to flourish, though certain comments on so-called "petty-bourgeois tendencies" showed that attempts were really being made to organise an "Opposition" to the policies so far followed by the Federation; but although Holitscher, as delegate from Berlin, where the Piscator controversy was already alive, adopted a critical tone, appropriate to an "opposition", there was no general impression of a riven and disunited movement. On the whole, however, and despite a series of thoughtful speeches and debates, including an unscheduled discussion of film, which led to the committee's undertaking to investigate seriously the possibility of "Creating a People's Film", the Conference was less happy than earlier ones. The final public rally in the Headquarters was a failure, poorly attended and lacking in unity and force. The big-city venue seemed also to lead to a lack of friendliness and warm atmosphere.

The Spread of the Districts

By now all the sixteen districts established in this decade were in existence, and before looking at the last three annual conferences of the twenties – above all, the historic Magdeburg Conference of 1927 – it will be as well to examine fully the broader development of the movement throughout Germany during this period.

A Volksbühne District was founded in 1923 (19 August) in Lower Silesia (Niederschlesien), an area where the need for the Volksbühne was great and its effects noteworthy. Despite its abundant natural resources Silesia, both Upper and Lower, was a region of wretched social conditions and little cultural cohesion, consequences of its geographical and political situation. Originally containing a mixture of Celtic, Teutonic, Slav, Wendish and Polish tribes, Silesia had been conquered by Bohemia in the tenth century. Bohemia encouraged German immigration into Silesia and it was these German immigrants who built Silesia's civilisation and founded most of its farms and industries. But between the twelfth and eighteenth centuries the province was at various times ruled by Poland, Bohemia and Austria until from 1740 to 1745 Frederick II (the Great) of Prussia won it from Maria Theresa of Austria. It gained more territory in 1815 and became, until the First World War, the largest Province of Prussia, the majority of its population being by now German, with large Polish and Czech minorities. Then by the Treaty of Versailles in 1919 considerable areas were transferred to Poland and Czechoslovakia, even, in part, in defiance of a plebiscite, and these areas included the Teschen (Slask Cieszyfiski) district with rich mineral resources.

Clearly in such a region cultural life was bound to suffer. In particular, theatre as a cultural force was at low ebb, offering the public chiefly operettas, musicals, amateur drama, puppet shows and dialect plays, – a huge, chaotic variety of every kind of light entertainment. Here and there in a few theatres with artistic standards there were those who felt it their task to give the region a cultural face and to try to provide people of all classes with a life-style that in some degree was of the twentieth century.

There were great improvements when the Volksbühne penetrated the area. The first developments were naturally in towns with permanent theatres, which facilitated the work of the Volksbühne. The first District Conference was held in August 1923 when there were already nine Volksbühne Associations and another fourteen preparatory committees in existence.

The movement in Lower Silesia had actually started in Breslau (Wroclaw), where from as early as the summer of 1918 several abortive attempts had been made to set up something of this nature. First, the director of the Breslau United Theatres tried to establish a *Schauspielverein* in which every member would see two plays a month, there being, it was hoped, 20,000 members. The plan was never put into practice. Then, at the end of 1919, Max Scholz, a senior producer, planned to form his own ensemble to put on popular performances in the Hall of the Trade Union Headquarters. The scheme rested on the support of the Education Committee of the Social Democratic Party. But this, too, came to nothing. Finally, in 1921 a highly placed official, Dr Proske, founded a *Theaterkunstgemeinde* (Society for Theatrical Art) intended as an umbrella organisation for like-minded bodies and involving trade unions and professional associations with the object of setting up a *Freie Volksbühne* within the *Theaterkunstgemeinde*, but in spite of strenuous efforts to recruit members the anticipated minimum of 3,000 was not reached, nor in the end was the *Theaterkunstgemeinde* actually formed.

However, in September 1921 Paul Barnay took over the Directorship of the Breslau United Theatres and with his cooperation plans for forming a Volksbühne slowly crystallised and by early 1922 were ready. The preliminary work was led by Barnay and Paul Eggers, current Chairman of the Education Committee of the Breslau Workers. From the very start the head office of the Volksbühne Federation was drawn in. In May 1922 a preparatory committee was formed and a number of major trade union and educational bodies supported a membership drive through the spring and summer, followed by two outstandingly successful recruitment rallies, so that by September a membership of 8,000, more than had been expected, was reached. The formal founding of the Breslau Volksbühne followed on 1 October in the Lobe Theatre. Paul Eggers became Chairman.

During the remaining years of the decade the Breslau Volksbühne became a model not only for its own district but for the whole of Germany, achieving extraordinary success in the face of economic and other difficulties, including unparalleled depression, and its development both internally and in its external effectiveness, continued unbroken. By 1926 it had nearly doubled its original membership and by the 1929-30 season had more than trebled it to 25,000, thus becoming the second largest Association within the German Volksbühne movement. This growth was in contrast with the decline of the Breslau branch of the Bühnenvolksbund whose membership fell from 7,000 to 1,900 during the same period.

The development of good theatre programmes in towns already possessing theatres still left the problem of how to spread the movement to theatreless places. This problem could not have been solved without the help of the Touring Companies. The history of the Volksbühne Touring Companies during this period is told elsewhere in this book, but their peculiar importance in Lower Silesia demands special attention, for it was through them that the 'theatreless province' became the 'Volksbühne Province' par excellence. The first impetus came from the Federation's Touring Company, the East German Provincial Theatre (Ostdeutsches Landestheater). This was founded in 1924 in conjunction with the Province of Brandenburg. Its headquarters were in Berlin and its Artistic Director was Alexander Runge. Its first performance in Lower Silesia was at the little town of Obernigk on 24 October with Lessing's *Nathan der Weise*. At first it toured eight venues in Lower Silesia, but in a few months the number rose to ten. It was obviously too much for this one company alone to meet the demands of both Brandenburg and Silesia. Its tours, however, were the salvation of the theatre in the area and it is small wonder that the demand for its services rose so rapidly that even in the spring of 1925 the possibility of a purely Silesian touring company was being considered. In April, thanks to the co-operation of the Oberbürgermeister of Bunzlau (Wegliniec), Herr Burmann, it was agreed that a Silesian Regional Theatre based on Bunzlau should start up at the beginning of the autumn season.

A generous contract with the Bunzlau municipal authorities guaranteed the company the use of the delightful municipal theatre building, rent-free for twenty years, and as the same municipality also made a cash grant to the local Volksbühne, 60 to 80 performances per season could be given. The first performance under these arrangements was of *Twelfth Night*, 16 September 1925. This was the real start of the phenomenal growth of the Volksbühne in Lower Silesia: not only did existing associations realise that their future was now assured, but other places joined in, so that soon there was an impressive circuit of venues, which by the 1929-30 season had grown to twenty, with several more ready to join.

The change was vividly expressed by a Herr Kickelhahn, a prominent local journalist:

> Oh, we'd seen tragedies by Schiller, by Lessing and Grillparzer, and we'd laughed ourselves to tears. We saw operettas, spectaculars – with not a glimmer of spectacle.... I'd worn my fingers to the bone writing about the poverty of the theatre in the little town [Sagan], the Volksbühne Committee held special evenings to try to get the so-called 'top ten-thousand' interested. But no one was moved. I couldn't blame them. Every half-penny spent on such barn-storming would have been wasted. At last we made contact with the Silesian Regional Theatre. To my genuine surprise I heard from its leading figures something like an artistic programme... But... our mistrust was in no way fully overcome, and ... we thought, "Seeing is believing"(Erst sehen, denn globen). ... *And* the proof was furnished.... Even for superficial theatre-goers, in spite of the limitations of our little stages, the settings were stylish and well thought-out, and even when they could only suggest, they were always appropriate and gave a genuine impression. Then there was the ensemble playing, which made a good impression even on a big-city person like myself, who often enough had had to suffer under the star-system. With the Silesian Regional Theatre day had broken out of the twilight of the barnstormers.

Thus the Volksbühne as a social and artistic movement converted a theatrically barren part of the country into one of the most fruitful.

We now move away north-west to Lower Saxony (Niedersachsen) where Volksbühne Associations were first founded at Celle (1920), Hamelin (1921), Rüstringen (1921) and Hanover (1922). It was the last of these whose development affected the whole province. Its foundation had been preceded by a season during which the leadership of the Volksbühne work was actually in the hands of a Workers' Education Committee, and only after this had been wound up did the Volksbühne become an independent organisation. During that first "provisional" year the membership was a mere 1400 or so, but in the first year of the independent Volksbühne (May 1922 – Spring 1923) it rose to an impressive 27,000, with each member seeing ten productions during the year; and during the worst period of inflation, when the seat prices were still held at 80–90 Pfennigs, the membership rose to 43,000. Afterwards, of course, there was a reaction. Unemployment was high and in addition the Volksbühne found itself in a running battle with the Municipal Theatres, which kept raising the prices charged to the Association, until finally the Volksbilhne went on "strike" until the prices were reduced. These difficulties, and others, reduced the membership to as little as 20,000 by the beginning of the fifth season and finally to 15,000 in the summer of 1928, after which the number appeared to stabilise.

Even during its decline, however, the Association was not inactive. A Speech and Movement Chorus (*Sprech- und Bewegungschor*) was formed, even though there was no one locally able to direct it, and the Director of the Leipzig *Sprechchor*, Otto Zimmermann, had to visit Hanover every week in addition to his own career as a dancer and actor. Also organised were special performances, which increased the Association's prestige in the city, symphony concerts by visiting orchestras, chamber music evenings and dance matinées. A Folk Music School was founded and a sustained effort was made the include films in the Volksbühne programme. The rebuilding of the Deutsches Theater, assisted by a substantial loan from the Volksbühne, broke the Municipal Theatres' monopoly to the Volksbühne's advantage, even though the contracts with the new theatre were not always satisfactory.

Hanover, as the intellectual, economic and political centre of the region, gave its name to a "Regional Group" as early as the autumn of 1923. Temporarily this was part of a Central Germany Regional Group, but by 1928 the rapid multiplication of Associations throughout the area caused the name to be changed to Lower Saxony District, with its own secretariat and no longer dependent on Berlin for its infrastructure.

Of the twenty-three Associations making up the District one of the most significant was Brunswick (Braunschweig). Here, even during the war years and immediately post-war period the People's Reading-Rooms Association, which ran the biggest public library in the Brunswick area, also undertook to provide wide sections of the population with cheap theatre-tickets, while during the period of inflation, trade unions, civil service unions and other cultural bodies got on this band-wagon. But in the post-inflation period they found the resulting competitive situation untenable and, particularly through the initiative of the Educational Alliance of Independent Trade Unions (*das freigewerkschaftliches Bildungskartell*) a Volksbühne organisation was founded in November 1924 with 3,600 members, which grew in three years to 5,600 and by the end of its sixth year enabled 7,350 people per month to go to the theatre.

The original cost of a ticket was only 1.20 Marks for plays, and 1.70 Marks for Opera: members saw five plays and five operas in a season. Even by 1930 the cost of an opera ticket had only risen by 5 Pfennig to 1.75M.

This Volksbühne also diversified its activities. A Youth Theatre was founded in 1927 and later an *Aktuelle Bühne*, presumably to see only significant contemporary plays; special events, a symphony concert and a number of cultural films were also arranged. Most remarkably, in 1924 a news-sheet was started called *The Stage* (*Die Bühne*) which in the next six years gradually developed into a monthly periodical devoted to artistic, cultural and educational matters.

From 1925 onwards the growth of the movement in more rural areas made the touring companies more important, as well as visits by resident companies from larger centres. At one stage the Volksbühne actually decided to work with the Central German Theatre (*Mitteldeutsche Bühne*), based on Wolfenbuttel, even though this was run by the rival Bühnenvolksbund, which at this time, 1926, was making a serious effort to compete with the Volksbühne in almost all towns in the area. But the relationship was short-lived and the divorce complete by the spring of 1927. Before the end of that year the Volksbühne Federation had itself established its own touring company, based at first on Coesfeld. This company, with the somewhat clumsy title *Ostfriesisch-Westfälisches Landestheater*, gave its opening performance, Hauptmann's *Biberpelz*, at Nienburg, where at that time no fewer than 10% of the inhabitants were Volksbühne members.

The success of the Volksbühne in this region, artistically as well as merely numerically, must be seen against its background. This included unauthorised touring companies, normally with very poor artistic standards: in 1930 there were about thirty such companies in the Province of Hanover. Also there were unauthorised visits made to towns without resident companies by *members* of resident companies, a kind of moon-lighting known as *Schwarzspielerei* - 'black' acting. However, the 23 Volksbühne Associations in this region, with a total membership of about 43,000, constituted by 1930 the strongest cultural organisation in Lower Saxony.

Somewhat over 100 miles southwest of Hanover lies the highly industrialised and densely populated area of the Ruhrgebiet. Within this lay in this period about two-thirds of the Volksbühne Associations of the Westphalia Volksbühne District. The social, and therefore the cultural problems of the Ruhrgebiet were as a whole unique in Germany. Rapid industrialisation, stimulated by the great Ruhr coalfield, turned a traditionally agricultural area, not densely populated, into one of the most intensely industrialised areas of Europe. All this happened in the course of a few decades. The new industries attracted workers and their families, with other cultural backgrounds, from other parts of Germany and even from beyond its eastern frontier – people who for generations had lived in close contact with the soil. Now they had to become used to a new homeland and to earning their daily bread in collieries and steel-works. The small villages of the region had over-rapidly developed into big cities which thus lacked all cultural traditions and facilities.

The problems facing local administrations were such that people from cities in Central and Eastern Germany that had grown naturally over the centuries could hardly appreciate. The war had brought civic building to a standstill. After the war the conversion of the arms industry to civilian purposes demanded by the Treaty of Versailles brought its own problems, and when in July 1922 Germany gave notice that she could no longer keep up with the agreed reparations payments, Belgian and French troops, preceded by engineers, foresters and others needed to work the area, occupied parts of the Ruhr in January 1923. During the eleven months of German passive resistance to the occupation, social and cultural problems were obviously intensified. The occupation did not end until 1925. In these conditions arts and theatre took a back place.

In the remaining parts of Wesphalia, not industrialisation but dour peasant conservatism aggravated by widespread alcoholism created equally great difficulties for the development of theatre-culture.

As we have already seen, the oldest Volksbühne Association in this province, and indeed the oldest outside Berlin to survive the First World War was Bielefeld, whose history up to 1930 has already been given. In the early 1920s six more were founded. (Minden 1921; Bochum, Hagen, Münster, Gelsenkirchen and Gladbeck 1922). These flourished during the period of inflation but were decimated during the depression that followed. The Westphalia District was founded in 1923, and the creation of its own Touring Company enabled Associations to be set up in half-a-dozen or so towns which had no resident company. Before this the very existence of Volksbühne Associations had been dependent upon the complex history of the municipal theatres, their resident companies and the varying distribution of plays, operas and operettas in their programming policies.

The fourth District to be founded in 1923 was that of Baden, Pfalz (Baden, Palatinate). Here in the south-west workers' organisations proved to be extremely sympathetic to the Volksbühne movement in comparison with other parts of the country. Class differences here were not so acute as in other areas and even before the war the primarily middle-class liberalism that characterised the region also influenced manual workers, thus producing a closely integrated social organism. A keen desire for culture among working people found its expression in an interest in organisation, thus making the way for the Volksbühne to develop an easy one.

In April 1920 a body calling itself the Karlsruher Theater-Kulturverband (Karlsruhe Association for Theatre Culture) called a Volksbühne Association into being. Membership was, unusually, corporate, not individual, and at the very start trades unions representing blue and white collar workers, as well as civil servants, joined the new Volksbühne Association - altogether 67 organisations representing more than 8,000 persons. (But anyone who could afford the box-office or season-ticket prices was in fact allowed to join.) In the early years the Volksbühne was so successful that the local theatre put on some plays solely for the Volksbühne, who then filled up to eight or even ten performances. During the inflation membership rose to 15,000, only, of course, to fall catastrophically in the depression. From 1924 onwards it slowly recovered, a process greatly helped when in autumn 1928 the theatre administration, in recognition of the cultural significance of the Volksbühne, began to lower the seat-prices charged to the organisation. By 1930 the Karlsruhe Volksbühne had sold no fewer than 700,000 theatre tickets as well as having promoted concerts, lectures, special events and evenings of lighter entertainment, all at low prices. From 1924 a free monthly periodical for members was issued.

The pattern of development at Pforzheim, though on a smaller scale, was similar. Founded in July 1921, primarily dependent upon trades unions organisations, it grew in the year of inflation from 3,000+ to 5,000+ members, then, as elsewhere, fell sharply, eventually to settle down to about 2,000 members after 1926. Unlike Karlsruhe, this body had little help from the local theatre, which concentrated on operettas. To see opera the Volksbühne had to arrange performances in a hall or travel to Karlsruhe; and for plays there were visits from the Badisches Landestheater, also from Karlsruhe. However, this Volksbühne did also manage to issue a newsletter and to arrange concerts and other events on a regular basis, and young people were admitted free to appropriate plays, as were the unemployed.

The city of Mannheim used to put on performances at reduced prices. When these were given up, in the autumn of 1922, it seemed as if there would be nothing for the working-class, who had been the principal supporters of these performances. However, the city once more took the initiative and through the local committee of the Allgemeiner Deutscher Gewerkschaftsbund a Freie Volksbühne was founded, initially but not exclusively for trade unionists. By the end of October 1922, 12,000 potential members had been recruited and the Volksbühne was established the following month: by the end of the first season the membership had almost reached 14,000. By the spring of 1923 the organisation found itself strong enough to influence the theatre's programme and thus get culturally worthwhile productions.

Closed performances, exclusively for members, were first arranged in the 1927-8 season, and only then after a sharp struggle with the Bühnenvolksbund. The Association had reached its lowest ebb in the 1924-5 season, but afterwards grew steadily to 7,000 members in 1930. This extraordinarily successful Association had by 1930 taken up some 621,000 seats in the National theatre as well as promoting a youth group, a movement group and numerous concerts. Visiting ensembles included those of Piscator and Reinhardt, and "Meet the Author" evenings included Toller, Ehm Welk, Zuckmayer, Erich Kästner, Tucholski and Brecht.

For the towns in the District lacking resident companies the need for associated touring companies was soon felt, and eventually this was supplied by two non-profit-making touring companies.

At the same time further Volksbühne Associations were founded within the District, of which perhaps the two most important were in Freiburg and Heidelberg. Freiburg (1924) began its life with a production of *Fidello*. This association so fixed its membership subscription that members out-of-work got their tickets free – some 10,000 between 1924 and 1930!

The Free State of Saxony, formerly a kingdom, was proclaimed a republic in 1918 and its constitution dated from 26 October 1920. Because of unemployment and food shortages, riots among the unemployed in 1923 led in October of that year to the setting-up of a 'Republican Proletariat Government of Saxony' by the Communists and left-wing Socialists with a Dr Zeigner as Premier and communists in key ministries. By using military force the central government forced Zeigner's resignation. Order was re-established by 6 November and the republic continued until 1933 when Hitler abolished its Diet.

Not surprisingly, this naturally rich and highly industrialised region – which, however, had suffered more severely both politically and economically after the war than any other region of Germany – proved fruitful ground for the development of the Volksbühne movement. It became a "Volksbühne Province" of the highest order and by 1930 had no fewer than 41 Volksbühne Associations with a total membership of some 63,000, of whom 20,500 were in Dresden and 16,700 in Chemnitz. The strength of the movement may perhaps be better judged by the example of Nengersdorf, a small town of whose 12,000 inhabitants 2,200 were Volksbühne members. Of these 41 associations eleven were in towns with resident companies while the remaining 30 were dependent upon touring companies which obviously played a special and important role in the Free State of Saxony.

The first, the Saxony Regional Theatre (Sächsische Landesbühne) was set up in 1919 by the political municipalities in order to provide performances in theatreless towns. Each municipality that joined the scheme had to make a contribution proportionate to its population as well as paying a fee for each visit. The Company for its part undertook to give four or five performances on each of two or three visits to each venue during the September to May theatre-season. At first the company's effects trundled from place to place behind a traction-engine, later replaced by a lorry provided by the State. But the plan was financially unsatisfactory. The fee per visit got higher, so that the smaller places could not afford it and dropped out of the circuit, relying instead on visits from the resident companies of larger centres, and spending considerable sums on improving local halls for this purpose. The mountainous region of the Erzgebirge presented particular difficulties in this connection, especially because of transport problems on the mountainous roads. A temporary solution was found in 1925 through the creation of an independent Erzgebirge Volksbühne without official or even Volksbühne Association subsidy, but this proved not to be economically viable and had to go into liquidation after only one season.

In 1926, therefore, a "West-Saxon Regional Theatre", later called the "Saxon Theatre of Culture", was established under the umbrella of the majority of the Saxon Volksbühne Associations, with its base in Auerbach – later in Chemnitz. This was far more successful and in the 1929-30 season, for example, gave altogether 93 performances for 23 Volksbühne Associations, reaching an audience of about 45,000. Although the links between the District and the Company were not legally binding, the moral connection was strong and the District could influence not only the Company's repertoire but its whole business conduct. Even so, to make up the approximately 260 performances per year required by the theatreless towns the 'Saxon Regional Theatre' provided a further 12, while the rest were made up of visits from the permanent companies in the eleven towns having these.

The extraordinary expansion of the Volksbühne movement in Saxony is vividly shown by the following figures:

1920	1	Volksbühne
1921	2	
1922	5	
1923	7	(& some small VBs in the Erzgebirge)
1924	19	
1925	27	– with 28,300 members
1926	30	– with 46,600 members
1927	33	– with 50,270 members
1928	36	– with 55,000 members
1929	39	– with 62,000 members
1930	41	– with 63,000 members

Each of the three largest associations in this region has an interesting history.

Chemnitz Volksbühne arose in 1920 out of the People's Education Committee founded by the local Council of Workers and Soldiers, one of many such that came into existence in the aftermath of the war. Failing to create a theatre of its own it tried to work for one year with Samst, Director of the Thalia Theatre, but inadequate performances and other difficulties soon led instead to a contract with the city, the Association guaranteeing to take up 5,000 seats per week in the municipal theatres. It soon had 22,000 members, many work-forces enrolling *en bloc*, and from 1 September 1920 they were attending seven to nine performances per week, using three theatres. Soon the Association became independent of the People's Education Committee. But during the economic crisis following inflation the membership fell by 50%, climbing again only slowly to 16,700 by the end of the decade. Because of the rational co-operation of the Municipal Theatres with the Volksbühne the former were able to operate virtually free of subsidy. In ten years the Volksbühne had provided an audience of about 2,000,000 for those theatres, – at least 5,000 per week in the Municipal Opera and Playhouse by 1930. Moreover, from January 1924 when the economy had stabilised, until 1930, the Association paid the city a flat rate of 1,538,300 Marks – paying in fact for all seats it had contracted for, whether or not members took them up and in addition giving free seats to the unemployed, of whom there were very many. It also subsidised two Youth Sections by selling them seats under cost price and gave seats to 4,000 students in industry per year.

Apart from this core activity the Association promoted symphony concerts, courses on Gymnastic Dancing for amateurs, innumerable lectures, recitations, chamber-music recitals, Lieder Evenings and *Sprechchor* events. The *Sprechchor* of the Chemnitz Volksbühne was one of the earliest and most active in the whole movement. The Association also sought to raise standards of film by promoting cultural films and opposing sensational rubbish on the screen. Between September 1926 and June 1929 on 92 separate days, 368 films were seen by a total audience of 75,000.

The ground for a Volksbühne in Dresden was prepared in 1921 by a widely diverse group of manual and white-collar workers, civil servants and cultural organisations, and in January of the following year the Association was founded. Initially it was also supported by the Christian Trade Unions but understandably these soon broke away and founded a branch of the Bühnenvolksbund. At first all performances were in the two state theatres, a great attraction which led to a membership of 50,000; but as individual members were offered only two or three performances a year this was not real Volksbühne work. The way out of these difficulties opened up in an unexpected way: a conflict between the management and players at the Albert Theatre led to the secession of most of the actors and other artistic staff, who then formed a co-operative which began to give performances in the fine hall of the Chamber of Commerce (Kaufmännischer Verein) under the name New Theatre, (Neues Theater). The Volksbühne met this artistic co-operative and in the course of time acquired shares in the undertaking. For a time attempts actually to take over the Central Theatre were successful. By the end of the decade the Volksbühne was using two State Theatres and three private theatres, not as a rule for 'closed' performances but instead making block-bookings for public performances. The city also offered Volksbühne members concessions at other performances, and of course the Bühnenvolksbund also took blocks of seats.

After 1924 the Volksbühne arranged concerts by the Dresden Philharmonic Orchestra – 24 in the first year, then falling to 16, but still a considerable achievement. Good films were also promoted and a periodical, *Volk und Kunst* was published, edited by Wolfgang Schumann.

In Leipzig the Volksbühne was not founded until 1926 and even then did not gain a membership proportionate to the size of the city. This was primarily because the same needs had already been met for some years by the Workers' Educational Institute and other smaller associations. Though relations between the Volksbühne and the Institute were cordial and their aims very similar the Volksbühne could not persuade the Institute to transform itself into a Volksbühne Association.

The importance of the Volksbühne movement in this region during the 1920s was forcibly expressed in 1930 by Albert Brodbeck, General Secretary of the Volksbühne Federation:

> The Volksbühne movement has become a powerful cultural factor
> in the Free State of Saxony. All theatres find in the Volksbühne
> Associations a pillar of strength – especially for straight plays.
> Some medium-sized towns with their own theatres in the Free
> State would not be in a position to put on a season of plays but
> for the local Volksbühne. Nowhere else in Germany has the activity
> of the Volksbühne been able to achieve such profound and richly
> rewarding effectiveness as in the broad industrial areas of the Free
> State of Saxony.
>
>   (Brodbeck: *Handbuch* p.298)

In the neighbouring District of Saxony and Anhalt the theatre-scene was completely different. On the one hand the existing theatres were rarely accessible to working-class people, while the so-called educated classes tended to set up organisations promoting mere amusement and diversions. On the other hand the population of Central Germany was exposed to the artistically valueless offerings of an enormous number of tiny touring troupes, often mere family concerns, whose acting was irredeemably ham and presentations hopelessly inadequate. It was no wonder that in reaction to such low standards of professional theatre those whose taste had not already been corrupted set up their own amateur dramatic societies. Their number grew astonishingly until there were towns with hardly more than 15,000 inhabitants which supported not just one but five or even more amateur dramatic societies with the most flowery names imaginable. Nor did either the touring troupes or the amateurs content themselves with performing straight plays but actually ventured to present operettas, musicals and even operas –usually with shocking results!

It is obvious that in this region the Volksbühne would encounter both opportunities and restrictions. In fact its ideas took on comparatively early and some of the oldest associations were to be found here. But because of its fundamental objections to offering its members amateur performances or inartistic work, the Volksbühne found itself in the dilemma of having itself to create an alternative theatre. It is therefore no accident that the first Touring Company of the Volksbühne Federation was established in Central Germany. This was the Regional Theatre of Central Germany (Mitteldeutsches Landestheater). Its establishment in the autumn of 1924 was a catalyst for many other developments, such as the emergence of Volksbühne Associations in many small towns. Later, this company worked closely with the East German Regional Theatre (Ostdeutsches Landestheater) to the extent of exchanging actors and materials, as well as performing in each other's regions, all of which was to the artistic and economic advantage of both companies.

The first Volksbühne in the District, at Halle, had been founded in 1920 with an impressive opening meeting and a membership that soon reached 9,000. The municipality authorised the alterations to the Thalia Theatre which were needed to accommodate regular performances for the Volksbühne, of which the first was a noteworthy production of Goethe's *Iphigenie* in the newly re-designed Thalia auditorium. Even in its first year the Volksbühne was promoting special events and even lectures on fine art, while in the following year the productions in the Thalia Theatre were supplemented by larger works such as Goethe's *Faust* and Operas in the Municipal Theatre, to which the Association transferred its basic programme in 1922. As elsewhere, the membership rocketed during the inflation, reaching 15,000 and requiring all performances to be duplicated and then fell dramatically, finally stabilising at about 6,000, though the economic plight of many older members denied them all playgoing. However, numerous other special events, many of them musical, were arranged and a free periodical issued to members. From the beginning tickets were of one price: a lottery determined in which of three groups of seats one sat.

In Magdeburg, where the Volksbühne was founded in 1922, performances were normally in the Wilhelm Theater where the association took up a total of 600,000 seats in the period 1922-29. Events other than in the theatre were numerous: in the 1929/30 season 50 out of 123 special events took place outside the theatre, and in three months of the same season 32 showings of cultural films had a total audience of 40,000. A monthly periodical was printed in an edition of 30,000/40,000. No wonder that the association's turnover in the 1929/30 season was nearly 300,000M!

In 1924 the founding of the District with a full-time secretariat enabled about twenty more associations and the Regional Touring Theatre to be set up, and by 1930 the District comprised twenty-five associations served by ten permanent theatres and the two co-operating touring companies.

It is hardly surprising that the Province of Brandenburg with Berlin at its heart and the Freie Volksbühne Berlin as an example should have been receptive of the Volksbühne idea, added to which the East German Regional Theatre (Ostdeutsches Landestheater), founded in October 1924, was available to present plays in towns without resident companies. Another touring company, the Mark of Brandenburg Theatre of the Society for Popular Education (Märkische Bühne der Gesellschaft für Volksbildung), one of the oldest of its kind, also promoted through its activities the idea of an adult-educational theatre. So, as soon as the war had ended, the Province, with the help of Berlin, found itself in a favourable position for Volksbühne development.

The oldest and strongest Volksbühne in the Province was that of Potsdam, where well-attended popular performances, arranged jointly by all the trade union organisations, led to its founding with nearly 6,000 members in September 1920; and in the 1921-22 season it was able to plan its own programme of plays.

A company in the old Potsdam Theatre. though municipally subsidised, had an unsatisfactory standard. Eventually, in a bold venture, the local groups of the Volksbühne Federation and the Bühnenvolksbund, supported by the town of Potsdam, took joint control of the theatre. Not only did this ensure the theatre's future but it also gained the Volksbühne a big influx of new members, so that eventually all theatre seats were sold to members of the audience-organisations. Thus the whole theatrical enterprise could express the needs and demands of an organised and culturally aware body of theatregoers. The new company, the Potsdam Playhouse (Potsdamer Schauspielhaus) then limited itself to straight plays, while the Volksbühne provided its members with opera through visits by leading Berlin artistes.

The story was similar in the town of Brandenburg where until 1927 an inadequate private theatrical undertaking could scarecely keep its head above water even with municipal subsidy. Here too, only the co-operative effort of the two major theatre-audience organisations succeeded in establishing the company economically and in raising its artistic standards, dropping operettas from its programme and concentrating on straight plays. Even this arrangement lasted only a couple of years and performances then had to be provided by the non-profit-making touring companies.

More successful was a similar co-operative effort in a small provincial town of Guben, where most of the shares in the new company were held by the municpality and the rest by the two audience-organisations. The result was a theatrical enterprise with standards impressively high in so small a town.

In all, seven towns with Volksbühne Associations had resident companies, while the rest (sixteen of them) were served by the Federation's touring companies. These also achieved very high artistic standards, in no way "provincial". The scale of the touring operation may be judged from these statistics of the 1929-30 season:

East German Regional Theatre	
(Ostdeutsches Landestheater):	230 performances
Art Theatre of the Society for Popular Education	
(Kunstbühne der Gesellschaft für Volksbildung):	79 performances
Brandenburg Theatre	
(Brandenburgische Bühne	
of the Bühnenvolksbund):	48 performances

Just as the example of Berlin in its midst was an important factor in the strong and early development of the Volksbühne movement in the Province of Brandenburg, so too the pioneering example of Hamburg ensured that the extreme north-west of Germany, the 'Northern Marches' (Nordmark) was the area in which, after Berlin, the movement planted its earliest roots.

We have already examined the early Volksbühne developments in Hamburg and Kiel. After the collapse of both these experiments just before the turn of the century nothing was done until after 1914. During the war performances for popular and working-class audiences in both places laid the foundations for re-establishing the Volksbühne movement. In Hamburg what were called "educational performances" were given under directors of the calibre of Leopold Jeßner. Immediately after the war there was debate as to whether Volksbühne work was to follow the Berlin pattern or rely on amateur performances. Happily the former was chosen, the Association was founded on 4 January 1919 and the first closed performance for members only, of Tolstoy's *And the Light Shines in Darkness* was given on 23 March 1919.

A year later the co-operation of some dozen or so other organisations, not only in Hamburg itself but also in Altona finally enabled the Greater Hamburg Volksbühne (Volksbühne Groß-Hamburg) to be set up with Rudolf Roß as Chairman, a position he held throughout the 1920s. Though modelled on Berlin, the Greater Hamburg Association met difficulties not encountered in the capital city, particularly the fact that it never succeeded in acquiring a theatre of its own.

In Kiel it proved more difficult to create a new Volksbühne, but it eventually grew out of performances for armaments workers arranged by the Workers' Education Committee in the final years of the war. From 1918 to 1920 Alberty, the Intendant of the municipal theatres, regularly arranged cheap Sunday-afternoon performances in both the theatres for which he was responsible, and when attendances began to fall off, hoped to build them up again through the creation of a Volksbühne. In May 1920 a meeting of representatives of trade unions, political parties and the Workers'

Education Committee decided to found a Kiel Volksbühne: this began its work in July of that year, but it was adversely affected by inflation, the economic crisis (especially the closing of the ship-building yards) and by various rival organisations which competed for customers wanting cheap theatre seats.

In Lübeck a Volksbühne was founded on 7 December 1921 after a speech by Nestriepke and began steady activity some eight months later, offering its members both opera and straight plays. After reaching a membership of 3,000 during the inflation a decline set in which was checked primarily through the creation of a Youth Section, so that after 1926 the Association began to grow steadily again, while the Youth Section (Jugendbühne) became the largest of its kind in the whole Volksbühne organisation, with a membership in the 1929-30 season of about 2,000.

In Schleswig-Holstein the development of the movement depended almost exclusively on how the problem of theatreless towns could be solved, and this was done in part by visits from the companies in Hamburg, Flensburg, Schleswig and Kiel and in part by touring companies, especially the Niederdeutsche Bühne based at Lübeck and, after 1924, the Nordmark-Landestheater.

The Altona Freie Volksbühne had a particularly striking development from its foundation in 1923. Fruitful co-operation with the municipal theatre led to an astonishingly high number of Volksbühne performances: between 1923 and 1930 no fewer than 1282 events, primarily theatrical performances, with over 800,000 tickets sold. At the same time the Association ran a *Sprechchor*, a library, a 'movement group', musical mornings, dramatisations of *Märchen*, a children's *Sprechchor*, a children's choir, lantern-slide lectures, a chamber orchestra, a Youth Choir, literary mornings and films.

In April 1924 the Nordmark District was established, after which the number of local associations multiplied rapidly, reaching twenty-six by 1930.

We move now from the extreme north-west corner of Germany to the extreme north-east, - to areas which in fact no longer lie within the frontiers of Germany. East Prussia (Ostpreußen) was a detached province of the Prussian Free State(Freistaat Preußen) whose capital was Königsberg (Kaliningrad after 1946). It was a relic of the land held in the Middle Ages by the Teutonic Knights (Deutsche Orden) until their defeat by the Poles and Lithuanians at Tannenburg(Grunwald) on 15 July 1410 reduced their territory to the land around their two great crusading castles Marienburg and Königsberg. After the conquest of the area by the Russians in the Second World War East Prussia lost its identity and was divided between Russia and Poland. That part of East Prussia known as Memelland (Memel Territory), which covered some 1,000 square miles, had been assigned to Lithuania by the Treaty of Versailles, which also, by creating the 'Polish

Corridor' cut off East Prussia together with the Memelland and the city of Danzig from Germany as a whole. No other provision of the Treaty of Versailles had been resented by the Germans as much as this. The poet T.S. Eliot showed keen understanding of this region when a 'character' in *The Waste Land* (1922) says:

Bin gar keine Russin, stamm' aus Litauen, echt deutsch.

The 'Memel Question' rankled deeply with Hitler and the territory was 'liberated' by the Nazis when the Lithuanians, under pressure, signed it away in the small hours of 23 March 1939: Hitler's last 'bloodless conquest'.

"Danzig is German, will always remain German, and will sooner or later become part of Germany, " Hitler told Beck, the Polish Foreign Minister at Berchtesgaden on 5 January 1939. [3] And Danzig was one of the principal pawns in Hitler's diplomatic games leading up to the Nazi invasion of Poland on 1 September 1939. After the Second World War Danzig, as Gdansk, became part of the new Poland.

It was to help these three areas – East Prussia, the Memel Territory and Danzig – that a Volksbühne *Bezirk* (District) was founded in November 1925. This was based on post-war developments, of which the earliest was in Königsberg, where a Volksbühne was founded under trade union leadership in 1920. This at once took over the presentation of straight plays in the Königsberg Municipal Theatre, leaving opera and operettas in private hands: the use of the actual building was shared by these two very different enterprises. Alongside this theatre was the New Playhouse (Neues Schauspielhaus) where Leopold Jeßner's successor, Richard Rosenheim, concentrated on chamber plays or intimate theatre.

The Volksbühne was never successful in gaining adequate membership. Wealthier people patronised the Neues Schauspielhaus. Single price and the traditional lottery for seats were abandoned. After the period of inflation the Volksbühne even tried to take over the operatic work, but still without success. The local association was disowned by the "Verband" so joined the rival Bühnenvolksbund, without, however, improving its position. Finally, the local authorities took over. The Volksbühne was dissolved, straight plays were performed only at the Neues Schauspielhaus, and a recently founded 'Comic Opera' was eventually sacrificed to municipal policy, the Municipal Theatre becoming the local opera house.

Despite the unhappy fate of the first Volksbühne a small group of enthusiasts, collaborating with the Federation (Verband) and with the Director of the Neues Schauspielhaus began in 1923 to set up a new organisation, the *Theatergemeinde*, which took its members to plays at the Neues Schauspielhaus and, while it still existed, to opera at the Komische Oper, as the Municipal Theatre was at that time still being used by the disowned Volksbühne; but by its second season the Theatergemeinde was going to operatic performances at the Municipal Theatre. It soon became the largest theatre-audience organisation in the eastern parts of Germany, with a steady membership of about 10,000, many special events and a concert-going section.

In Danzig a Freie Volksbühne was set up in July 1921 jointly by a group of enthusiasts and the executive committee of the Workers' Educational Association. As the local authorities showed little sympathy for the enterprise a shipyard restaurant had to be adapted for theatrical performances which, ironically enough, were given by the ensemble of the Municipal Theatre whose use was denied to the Freie Volksbühne. Even so, the technical problems of playing in a restaurant hindered the work of the Freie Volksbühne and it was a great boost when in the 1922-23 season access to the Municipal Theatre was gained. An initial membership of 1,000 quickly rose to 2,700, plus a Youth Group of 1,200 consisting of apprentices and school-children from 14 to 20. After this the success of the Freie Volksbühne was assured.

Primarily on the basis of these two organisations, Königsberg and Danzig, a District Secretariat was set up in 1925 by the Volksbühne Federation. Even in the Memel Territory (no longer, since Versailles, legally a part of Germany) the District Secretariat, on the basis of the cultural activities of the Memel trade unions, which for some years had included closed performances for trade union members in the Memel Playhouse, established a Memel Volksbühne organisation, though even in 1930 it had only 600 members.

Nevertheless in the whole of the three-fold area covered by the District Secretariat there were by that date twenty-two local associations, served by six theatres and three non-profit touring companies. These touring companies were extremely important, as they could take performances to the many theatreless towns. The earliest to be founded was the South-east Prussia Touring Theatre based on Allenstein (now Olsztyn) even though the town had no proper theatre. Through the self-sacrificing activity of the writer Max Worgitzbi and with help from the Prussian State the town had by September 1925 a new theatre building which also was an adequate base from which the touring company could cover the whole south-east. In the same autumn the first Volksbühne Association in that area was founded in Allenstein.

However, the South-east Prussia Company made a practice of setting up organisations similar to the Volksbühne in the towns included in their circuit, and as it was the policy of the Volksbühne Federation not to try to start its own associations in towns where something similar already existed, Volksbühne development was limited to towns outside that circuit. This rule could be justifiably broken only if the existing local organisation failed to meet the demands of the theatre or to embrace a broad enough cross-section of the public.

A big change came about when the Federation's own Regional Theatre for East and West Prussia was founded in 1926 and a company from this, the East Prussian Regional Theatre, made several tours in the 1926-27 season. This company was supported by both the principal audience organisations and this to a degree tied the hands of the Volksbühne Federation, so in the 1927-28 season the Volksbühne established its own touring company, through whose visits several more local associations were founded. By 1930 the regional touring company, with a high artistic reputation, was working an eight-month season. The scale and scope of its activity may be judged from the following table of towns visited during one season:

2 towns with over 30,000 inhabitants
3 towns with 15,000–30,000 inhabitants
2 towns with 7,000–15,000 inhabitants
8 towns with 3,000–7,000 inhabitants
9 towns with under 3,000 inhabitants

One would expect that Pomerania would have been the territory most likely to resist the Volksbühne. This coastal strip, much of which is now in Poland, used to constitute the maritime province of Prussia, with a Baltic coastline stretching from Plasnitz in the east to Ahrenshoop in the west. It is primarily agrarian and its population deeply conservative, and strongly prejudiced against the progressive ideology of the Volksbühne, to such a degree that the movement was openly declared to be a cultural threat, *eine kulturelle Bedrohung Hinterpommern*, through its fostering international art! But indeed, Hinterpommern, the most rural part of Pomerania, has always been the butt of jokes in Germany in general. It was greatly to the credit of the East German Regional Theatre that eventually its high artistic achievements won recognition for itself and the movement even here. Nevertheless the District, founded in 1925, contained only seven local organisations by 1930.

Before the Volksbühne came on the scene the whole area, at the end of the First World War, was virtually empty of theatre. In the broad area from Stettin (Szczecin) to Lauenburg, some 300 kilometres by road, there was only one tiny theatrical enterprise. Pre-war commercial theatres in Köslin (Koszalin) and Stargard failed to survive in the post-war period. But between these two towns there was an active, local, non-profit touring theatre run by the Federation of Pomeranian Theatre Associations, to which belonged some thirty local associations. These, however, were extremely small and an average membership of 300 would not be too low an estimate. The area covered was limited and the Volksbühne movement did not try to trespass upon it.

The starting point for the movement in Pomerania was in fact its capital, Stettin, where an association, the Theatergemeinde Stettin, was founded in the autumn of 1921. The season opened with Shakespeare's *Coriolanus* and at the first night the audience joined in singing Schiller's *Ode to Joy*. The growth in membership was remarkable and by the end of the first season there were already three sections. In the second season the members saw six plays and two operas. Noteworthily, from the very beginning the Theatergemeinde arranged its own programme and was not dependent on the theatre's choice of repertoire. The 1923-4 season opened with no fewer than twelve sections. In 1924 Sunday performances, a programme of lectures, and a Concert Section were established. A 'Modern Drama' section in the following season was less successful: only two plays were put on. The association also issued a serious monthly periodical. The District was founded in 1925.

The second strongest Pomeranian association was at the seaside town of Kolberg (Kolobrzeg) where, however, there was some political opposition, and though a plan to set up a rival "German Theatre" did not get beyond a poster campaign it did upset some of the membership. Other local associations had varying degrees of success and there was some organised opposition, particularly in Stralsund.

The other District to be founded in 1925 was that of Württemberg, a region that, seen culturally, could hardly be in greater contrast with Pomerania. It is an area that had given Germany and the world an outstanding series of prominent men and above all of poets. Schiller, Uhland, Mörike and Hauff are but four of the most celebrated. The population as a whole was remarkably interested in intellectual and artistic matters. Nevertheless, at this period the whole of Württemberg contained only three towns with their own theatres. Outside the provincial capital Stuttgart, which possessed two fine state theatre buildings and one privately owned playhouse, only Ulm and Heilbronn had theatres with regular programmes. This paradoxical situation had arisen because Württemberg, despite its culturally rich traditions, had only one large town, Stuttgart, with nearly 400,000 inhabitants. Both Ulm and Heilbronn had fewer than 50,000, while the remaining towns had fewer than 30,000 (most of them fewer than 20,000), too small to sustain their own theatres. The Württembergische Volksbühne, a non-profit touring theatre founded shortly after the end of the war, supplied the needs of all other towns than Stuttgart, Heilbronn and Ulm throughout the 1920s.

Volksbühne associations were founded quite early in all three theatre-towns. In Stuttgart even before the war the "Goethebund" with the active co-operation of the trade unions arranged inexpensive popular performances and these continued through the war until 1920, when the beginnings of inflation brought the Goethebund to an end, and with it these special performances. In the same year the privately owned theatre in this city, the Deutsches Theater, was facing economic collapse, so an "Association for the Promotion of Popular Education" and the Independent Trade Unions created a basis upon which the theatre could continue, supported by a broad, organised mass audience. This 'Volksbühne' enabled the theatre not only to keep open but to maintain high artistic standards: it achieved great things by the simplest means. The Volksbühne gained members by the thousand, mostly from the Independent Trade Unions, and from the start had a single price for tickets with a "Rollsystem" for fairness. But this exciting and initially successful undertaking fell victim to inflation. "A cigarette factory moved into the former temple of the arts"[4] and the audience-organisation with its 8,000 to 10,000 members became homeless. An attempt to move into the State Theatre failed and the Association was on the verge of extinction. But in 1924, with new leadership, a 'new' Stuttgart Volksbühne made a contract with the State Theatre for closed performances, committing the members to eight plays and four operas per year, a new office was set up, a new monthly periodical published, and the membership rose from 5,200 to 11,000 by the 1926-27 season. The demand for seats was so great that the operetta theatre had to change over to straight plays to satisfy the demand for these.

The formation of Volksbühne Associations in Ulm and Heilbronn facilitated the founding of a Württemberg District in 1925, at first with a part-time secretariat, and this in turn led to several more new associations being formed. After 1927 it became impossible to set up any new Volksbühne Associations as most of the towns served by the Touring Theatre formed a *Zweckverband* (*an association of several municipalities for carrying out a specific common interest*). This made the Volksbühne in all these towns superfluous. Even in 1930 all development seemed at a standstill, a situation which Brodbeck, General Secretary of the Federation of German Volksbühne Associations, blamed in part upon a tendency "in Schiller's country" for people to wish to originate their own work and solve their own problems.

With the founding of two more Districts in 1926 this aspect of the movement's growth ended. One of these was Upper Silesia (Oberschlesien), an area where political, economic and cultural tensions had always been severe but had been intensified under the terms of the Treaty of Versailles, by which in 1919 a part of eastern Silesia was ceded to Poland and part of Upper Silesia to Czechoslovakia, – these areas having primarily German populations but large Polish and Czech minorities. Provision was also made in the treaty for certain other districts of Upper Silesia to be allocated according to the result of a plebiscite to be held in the spring of 1921. This plebiscite decided in favour of Germany, but nevertheless some 1241 square miles, with a population of 900,000, including Teschen (Polish: Slask Cieszyfiski) and rich in minerals, was transferred to Poland.

These territorial changes were deeply hurtful to Germans, – and not only to Nazis and other right-wingers, but also to liberal-minded Social

Democrats like Brodbeck, who wrote, with a passion exceptional in his usually very sober *Handbuch* (1930):

> Upper Silesia is bounded on three sides by non-German powers. Since Versailles, whose effects reached even here, the situation has been immensely aggravated... It is not only that the line of the new frontier to the south and south-east of the Province – the most unfortunate and stupid that has ever been anywhere! – keeps lasting tensions permanently alive; not only that the spring and early summer of 1921 have left behind wounds that are still open: *Polish Cultural Propaganda* is seen to be growing rather than diminishing, and one can hardly assert in good conscience that the forces of resistance are comparable with those of the attack. The tragedy of Upper Silesia can be explained through the huge sins of omission in the past. [5]

In Brodbeck's opinion the whole area, neglected throughout the 1920s, was in dire need of cultural nurture, the Polish minorities no less than the German majority. Nor was the German population united in its cultural needs and aims. Owing to the intransigence of the clerical-conservative side and of the working-class-secular side, Upper Silesia was suffering from *Kulturkampf in Permanenz* – as if the cultural battle between Church and State in the 1870s and 1880s was here still being fought. In such an atmosphere the Volksbülhne movement was felt to be "officially" unwelcome and suffered a constant barrage of attack. Any success was almost literally gained by force in a hard struggle.

> (In 1941 Hitler restored the pre-1919 position by dividing Silesia once more into Upper and Lower, with capitals at Kattowitz (Katowice) and Breslau (Wroclaw). Under the Potsdam Agreement, 1945, all of German Silesia east of the Oder was passed to Poland and most of the German population expelled, as were those in the parts of Silesia regained by Czechoslovakia in the same year, a total of nearly 4,000,000 Silesians thus becoming refugees in West Germany.)

It is against this background that the achievements of the Volksbühne movement in Upper Silesia must be understood and appreciated.

A start was made in 1922 when Nestriepke undertook a lecture tour in the summer and autumn. Immediately after this three Freie Volksbühnen were founded in three closely linked towns: Beuthen (Bytom), Gleiwitz (Gliwice) and Hindenburg (Zabrze). In Beuthen there was a privately-run theatre under the Directorship of Hans Knapp, which enjoyed subsidies both from town and state, but whose programme did not satisfy even the most modest cultural demands. In January 1924, for example, there were performances of twenty-six operettas, four comedies, four farces, – and two straight plays! Obviously the Volksbühne suffered in these conditions, especially when the local authority and the theatre-management openly threatened to boycott the organisation.

Gleiwitz had an operetta theatre, but with the help of the Volksbühne in Lower Silesia the operettas were supplemented by straight plays from Brieg and Kattowitz. Hindenberg also had visits from these two companies as well as from Beuthen and Gleiwitz.

In 1924 representatives of all three towns and of both audience organisations, the Volksbühne and the Bühnenvolksbund, formed a joint limited liability company called The Three-Town Theatre, with its office and opera-base in Gleiwitz and its straight-play base in Beuthen. Hubert Reusch was appointed overall Director. Sadly its first year was a fiasco with outgoings of 760,000 Marks and an income of only 310,000 Marks, and the season was cut short in the spring of 1925. The Hindenberg Volksbühne took the initiative in re-organising the whole enterprise, with a new Artistic Director, Eugen Felber from Mannheim, and the Chairman of the Hindenberg Volksbühne as Administrative Director. Under a modified title and with the Mayor of Beuthen as Chairman a fresh start was made on 1 October 1925, only to be threatened by almost immediate collapse. The Artistic and Administrative Directors were sacked and the 1925-26 season completed, though with difficulty. Attempts were continuously made to side-line the audience-organisation, and the 1926-27 season – the last – ended with the loss of 500, 000 Marks, which had to be met by the State and the Municipalities. But in the summer yet another attempt was made to provide theatre for the area in the form of the Upper Silesian Regional Theatre, with its base in Beuthen and Arthur Illing as Director. In a seven-month season, 1927-28, which included, as well as straight plays, operas and operettas with chorus and orchestra, the company gave 444 performances – 63 per month – in five towns!

With subsidies the books were balanced and the enterprise did survive, though in the 1929-30 season it lost 100 performances in Polish Silesia and faced constant difficulties in determining its programme on account of the conflicting ideologies of the region.

The only other towns in this District with their own theatres were Oppeln (Opole), Neiße (Nysa) and Ratibor (Raciborz). In none of these, however, was it easy to develop theatre on Volksbühne lines, though considerable success was achieved from 1923 onwards in Ratibor. A major problem of Upper Silesia was that economically it was virtually impossible for a touring theatre to serve the theatreless towns of the District, though in 1928 the Association for Workers' Education (Bund für Arbeiterbildung) set one up. Its work was, according to Brodbeck, almost heroic. What interest in theatre did exist in these smaller towns was primarily absorbed in a veritable flood of amateur dramatic societies, and these, strangely enough, were generously subsidised by local authorities.

In no part of Germany did the Volksbühne movement encounter so much difficulty as in the Free State of Bavaria. Everything here seemed to conspire against it. In general at that period Bavaria had little manufacturing industry, and vast areas of thinly populated farming country resisted attempts to organise cultural life; naturally such areas were without permanent theatres and virtually without any traditions of theatre-going. There were other peculiarities in the structure of Bavarian society. For example, the southern area, close to the mountains, suffered culturally from the development of tourism, which created a seasonal pattern of life unconducive to continuous cultural activity. Moreover, the remarkable development of amateur drama in Southern Bavaria, not on the whole comparable in quality with the unique Oberammergau festival, was inimical to professional theatre, and it was not easy to raise standards of taste in spite of there being one good touring theatre and local tours from theatre companies. Above all, however, it was the characteristic Bavarian mentality, bringing with it political and ideological consequences, which made Bavaria the most difficult territory not only for the Volksbühne but for almost every liberal cultural activity.

Although the Free State constituted a single District of the Volksbühne Federation, it was in practice thought of in two divisions – north and south. The former was actually serviced by the District Secretariat of Saxony, based in Chemnitz, and the latter from, Munich, where indeed the Bavarian Volksbühne movement had begun as early as 1914. The war had stunted the growth of the Munich Volksbühne and in September 1918 it had to begin to reconstruct itself. It remained the only Volksbühne in Bavaria until 1924 and the only one in Southern Bavaria until 1927.

Even for the Munich Volksbühne life was not easy, as the ideological and religious milieu of the city was far more favourable to the rival Bühnenvolksbund, which possessed in Munich its strongest Association and was constantly in extremely vigorous competition with the Volksbühne. Nevertheless, and in spite of the fact that, unlike the Bühnenvolksbund, it enjoyed little support from the city authorities, the Munich Association maintained a basic membership of around 9,000 throughout the 1920s and joined the Federation in 1925, at which time Georg Mauerer, the city councillor who had originally founded the Association in 1914, undertook the development of the movement in South Bavaria. The task required unstinting devotion and it was not until 1927 that he met with success in three centres: Peißenberg, a small mining town, Penzberg and Weilheim. The two former were dependent on the touring theatre's visiting their general-purpose public halls. In Weilheim the Volksbühne, untypically, entered into competition with a well-established theatre-club, defeated it and took its place. Because of the earlier club's close connection with the local theatre the Volksbühne had difficult relations with the theatre. But the Bavarian Touring Theatre and the Touring Opera of the Bavarian People's Educational Association were both brought to the town.

The last Volksbühne to be established in South Bavaria before 1930 was at Landshut, where the municipal authorities put many difficulties in the way of the thousand-strong body's use of the municipally owned theatre (presenting both straight plays and operettas) and only by painstaking attention to every detail could the organisation continue to exist.

In Northern Bavaria the situation was very different, but no easier. In South Bavaria the relatively strong movement in Munich created a base for such development as there was, but in North Bavaria all attempts to establish a Volksbühne in the largest city, the deeply right-wing Nuremberg, during the 1920s, failed. In 1924 a Volksbühne was founded in Hof, in the extreme north of the area and close to the border with Saxony, which, as we have already seen, was enjoying an extraordinary development as a real "Volksbühne Province". Two years later the Hof Volksbühne joined the Federation. Unfortunately the officers insisted on arranging for members to go to two performances a month, although the District secretariat urged in vain that this be reduced to one. This led to a subscription too high even for many middle-income people to afford and membership fell off. The local theatre was of poor quality and its offerings under a new director inadequate, so that in the autumn of 1928 the Volksbühne was wound up.

In 1925 a Volksbühne founded in Schweinfurt failed to develop, partly because of rivalry between three theatre-audience organisations and partly because local industry was in a constant state of crisis. In the same year the work in Würzburg began well and three Volksbühne groups were set up. There was some loss of membership three years later when the programme of opera was sharply and randomly reduced. A Bamberg Volksbühne was founded in 1926, followed by Fürth at the end of the year and Erlangen early in 1927. The Bamberg company played in Erlangen and also in Schweinfurt, both of which had their own theatres. Fürth was served by the Nuremberg Company. The Fürth authorities gave both that company and the Fürth Volksbühne generous subsidies, which enabled the Volksbühne subscription to be kept low enough to attract many working-class members. Early in 1930 a Volksbühne was founded in Amberg and was served by the Bavarian Touring Theatre. An active audience-organisation, with two sections, in Aschaffenburg preferred to remain independent of the Volksbühne Federation. Several towns had audience-organisations directly associated with the Touring Theatre, but not with the Volksbühne movement. Thus by 1930 there were only six organisations in North Bavaria affiliated to the Federation, with a total membership of a mere 4,200, of which Fürth accounted for 1,700 and Würzburg for 1,000.

It should by now be clear that only the most superficial generalisations can safely be made about this nationwide growth of the Volksbühne movement. On the whole provincial activists were more pragmatically and less ideologically driven than those in the capital Berlin. Where appropriate the Volksbühne would make a common front with the Bühnenvolksbund; elsewhere the two organisations would work in rivalry. Usually trade union organisations helped the development of the Volksbühne but sometimes occupied potential Volksbühne territory. Much depended in larger centres on relationships with resident theatres, whether commercial or municipal, while small, theatreless towns depended on the non-commercial touring theatres or visits from neighbouring resident companies.

The extraordinary spread of the movement soon led to an important structural development within the Federation in addition to the annual conference and the executive committee. This was the Administrative Council (Verwaltungsrat), which consisted originally of the Executive plus representatives of some of the larger associations nominated by the annual conference. In 1925, doubtless in view of the establishment of Districts, the constitution was revised and the Administrative Council thereafter consisted of representatives of the Executive and representatives of the Districts. (In 1930: 26 from the Districts; 7 from the Executive.) The Council met twice a year and was chaired by the Chairman of the Federation. It was in effect a semi-independent 'watchdog' body, advisory rather than executive.

By 1930 there were no fewer than 305 Volksbühne societies, with a total membership of half a million.

Touring Theatres

It has been clear in our examination of the growth of the Volksbühne movement outside Berlin that many provincial Volksbühne Associations were dependent for their performances upon touring companies; indeed by the 1929-30 theatre season more than half the Associations relied completely upon touring companies. Five of these were at that time entirely under the control of the Federation of Volksbühne Associations and others partly, but all were non-profit-making (The German term is *gemeinnützig*, literally "for the benefit of the public"). Although a history of touring theatre in Germany would be out of place here, the importance and significance of these companies can only be appreciated when they are seen in an historical perspective.

Professional touring theatre was first brought to Germany in 1592 by Robert Browne with the first of several companies of "English Comedians" who then, touring Central Europe throughout the seventeenth century, presented repertoires of plays – admittedly often savagely abridged – by Shakespeare and his English contemporaries, acted at first in Plattdeutsch (especially for comic interludes) and later in High German. They were soon joined by German actors who, learning from the brilliant professionalism of the English players, were eventually able to take over the whole enterprise. In this way really professional standards of acting came to be associated with the touring companies, who were sometimes engaged for seasons of varying length by various German princes or sometimes entered into contracts with town authorities. Thus the touring theatre remained the normal type of German professional theatre throughout the stormy and war-torn seventeenth century, and even into the eighteenth century when the actress-manager Karoline Neuber, *die Neuberin* (1697-1760) in alliance, from 1727, with Johann Christoph Gottsched (1700-1766), raised standards yet again and by combining a stateliness derived from French drama with German emotionalism inaugurated a new era in German acting, – still primarily on tour.

Towards the end of the eighteenth century and of course in the nineteenth, the fine theatre buildings that sprang up in larger towns and cities attracted the best actors and companies so that the smaller places, unable to keep a resident company, had to put up with innumerable troupes of barnstormers, often family-run, who made a living as travelling people, providing crude entertainment with no artistic quality. Of course, not all touring companies were as bad as the worst, but by the beginning of the twentieth century adult educational associations began to perceive the need to create touring companies designed to bring back high artistic standards to provincial towns rather than to make a profit, and consequently, almost always, to need subsidising. The earliest actually to come into being was the Rhein-Mainisches Verbandstheater (The Rhine-Main Federal Theatre) created by the Rhein-Mainischer Verband für Volksbildung (The Rhine-Main Federation for Adult Education) in the spring of 1907, followed a few months later by the Märkische Wanderbühne, a joint venture by the Berlin Society for Adult Education and the Berlin Schiller Theatre. The former of these, strengthened in the early 1920s by its fusion with a Hessian non-profit touring theatre, and with additional backing from the Volksbühne Federation was still as late as 1930, under the title Frankfurt Art Theatre for Rhine and Main, the largest and most highly regarded German touring company.

The Märkische Wanderbühne despite various vicissitudes also survived through the 1920s. But it was not until after the First World War that non-profit touring companies really began to multiply and develop. Brodbeck commented in 1930: "What the wealthy pre-war Germany failed to achieve, the new Germany created out of the ruins of a lost war."

The first wave of such companies began in Stuttgart in 1919, followed by Frankfurt, the Rhine Province, the Palatinate and the Saar Region, Bavaria (1921), Saxony (1922) and finally a touring Chamber Opera, based on Berlin.

All these companies shared the common purpose of serving the idea of Theatre for the People. That is to say, they felt themselves responsible for the artistic education of their public, with the corollary that they aimed to build up regular audiences. On average, for a season lasting eight or nine months, such a company needed a subsidy in the region of 45,000 Marks.

These companies, however, could not by themselves cope with the demands of the Volksbühne Associations in towns without resident companies, and moves began to be made to found the Federation's own touring companies. Forerunners of such companies were first formed in 1924. In Zwickau and Eisenach the local Volksbühne Associations tried unsuccessfully to set up their own companies. In Lößnitz an ensemble originally intended only to play that summer in the Open Air Theatre visited other places in the neighbourhood and was kept together for the winter, only to be dissolved in the following spring, as the little Volksbühne Association could not afford to subsidise it. A further attempt to establish a company with broader support only lasted through the 1925-6 winter season. Similar attempts were made in 1924-5 in Schwarzenberg and Neurode.

It was now already clear that any "Volksbühne" touring companies must be provided with a wider base, especially in finance, and in 1924 the Federation took the decision, not an easy one, to form two touring companies of its own. A key factor was a decision of the Prussian Provincial Theatre not to send out companies of its own, but to subsidise companies set up by audience organisations.

This Prussian Provincial Theatre Ltd. (Preußische Landesbühne GmbH) was not, despite its misleading title, a theatre or theatrical company: in fact its nature and structure were often misunderstood even at the time and even by people concerned with theatre. As we have already seen, the 1922 Annual Conference of the Volksbühne Federation only agreed to co-operate with it after a serious discussion concerning relationships with the Bühnenvolksbund which, naturally, was also involved in the scheme.

The Prussian Provincial Theatre was established at the beginning of 1922 by the Theatre Department of the Prussian Ministry of Culture as a non-profit-making limited liability company. Apart from the Prussian Treasury, represented by the Ministry for Science, Art and Education, the central Federations of the two culturally orientated theatre-audience organisations, the Volksbühne and the Bühnenvolksbund, were also incorporated into its structure, which was unique in Germany, no other 'Land' having a comparable body. Governed by a weighty Board of Directors, its actual administration was in the hands of the Chairman of the Board and the Managing Directors of the two cultural organisations.

It existed as an advisory, supportive and subsidising body with responsbility for observing and setting standards in theatrical matters throughout the 'Land' of Prussia. It was concerned with ensuring that theatre-budgeting was sound, and that resources were not wasted. At the same time it was empowered to make grants to cultural theatre. It was to endeavour to raise the standards of the repertoire (for example by discouraging light operettas etc) but without presuming to censor any material on artistic or ideological grounds. It was not to form its own theatre undertakings but to confine its work to advice, mediation and support, including financial support. It was financed by an annual state grant originally of 500,000 Marks, but rising to 1,600,000 Marks by the 1930-31 season. Generous though this may sound, shortage of money was a major restriction on the organisation's activities throughout this period. An additional initiative of the Prussian Provincial Theatre in the late 1920s was to get some municipal theatres to become non-profit limited liability companies with the involvement also of the central Federations of the two main audience organisations.

Obviously the companies which the Volksbühne Federation planned to create could safely anticipate subsidies from the Prussian Provincial Theatre. The first, to tour in the Province of Saxony and Anhalt Free State, was the Central German Provincial Theatre (Mitteldeutsches Landestheater) founded July 1924. This was originally a separate enterprise but was soon taken directly under the control of the Volksbühne Federation to simplify administration. Soon afterwards a second company was formed within the territory of the newly founded company, but it could not stand on its own feet and the two companies were united.

A few months later, in October 1924, a second company, the East German Provincial Theatre (Ostdeutsches Landestheater) was formed whose territory, originally Brandenburg, was later extended to Pomerania. The first season of these two companies was so successful that in 1925 yet a third was created, the Schlesisches Landestheater, to tour Silesia with Bunzlau as its base.

The background to the founding of a fourth company is more complex. The 'rival' audience-organisation, the Bühnenvolksbund, set up a company (Mitteldeutsche Bühne) to tour the Province of Hanover and the area immediately to its west, and this began to supply the needs of a series of Volksbühne Associations in the Province. This led to a request from the local authority that the Volksbühne should seek to influence the running of the company, and for one season, 1926-7, the Volksbühne Federation had two representatives on the Board of Directors, after which the Bühnenvolksbund withdrew from this arrangement leaving the Volksbühne with no choice but to set up its own company in the area, though such a project was fraught with difficulties. Nor was it normal Volksbühne policy to set up a new company where the needs of the audiences were already provided for. After failures to establish the company's base in either Minden or Coesfeld it was eventually based in Emden with the title Ostfriesisch-Westfälisches Landestheater (East Friesian-Westphalian Provincial Theatre). It toured its area in its own bus, which carried the company with its scenery and properties. However, the facilities, especially for rehearsals, at Emden were woefully inadequate and in the 1927-8 season the company's base was moved to Herford and its work from there proceded much more satisfactorily.

In the 1926-7 season a company to tour East Prussia, subsidised by the Prussian Ministry of Culture, and committed to employing unemployed actors from Berlin, was founded jointly by the two theatre-audience organisations, but once more the Bühnenvolksbund soon withdrew with the result that the Volksbühne founded a new company based on Tilsit. The local theatre there agreed to limit its own programme to opera and operetta and to reserve two days a week for straight plays presented by the new Provincial Theatre for East and West Prussia, thus making it possible for the company to tour four productions a month throughout the season.

The question naturally presents itself as to what standard of product these well-motivated companies could achieve in conditions of touring which were, as we shall see, arduous, to say the least. But anyone with experience of small-scale touring companies, such as, for example, The Pilgrim Players (E. Martin Browne), The Adelphi Players (R. H. Ward) or The Compass Players (John Crockett) which toured theatreless towns in Britain during and immediately after the Second World War, knows that simplicity of presentation, so far from being tatty, can achieve fine artistic standards and that dedicated actors under talented directors can rise to considerable heights of performance. Above all it is by the repertoires of such small touring companies that they must be judged, and on this count the Volksbühne's own touring theatres had a remarkable record.

The Central German Provincial Theatre, for example, which presented 29 plays in 346 performances in its first two seasons, included in its programme such classics as *Minna von Barnhelm* (Lessing), *Miss Sarah Sampson* (Lessing), *Urfaust* (Goethe), *Kabal und Liebe* (Schiller), *Gyges und sein Ring* (Hebbel), *Maria Magdalena* (Hebbel), *Des Meeres und der Liebe Wellen* (Grillparzer) and *The Imaginary Invalid* (Molière), also modern classics by Ibsen, Strindberg, Hauptmann, Halbe and Shaw, and plays by contemporaries like Wilhelm von Scholz, Rehfisch and Fulda. It was a programme both sound and adventurous.

The East-German Provincial Theatre presented a similar repertoire, mixing classics and contemporary work. Its first two seasons, with 400 performances and 27 plays, included *Twelfth Night*, *Nathan der Weise* (Lessing), *Medea*, and *The Imaginary Invalid*, as well as Scholz's *Der Wettlauf mit den Schatten*, Hauptmann's *Der Biberpelz*, Shaw's *Widowers' Houses* and Hebbel's *Gyges und sein Ring*.

The Silesian Provincial Theatre actually presented 24 plays in its first season of 183 performances, including 27 performances of Klabund's *Der Kreidekreis* (later to be overshadowed by Brecht's adaptation *Der Kaukasische Kreidekreis*) and 22 performances of Molière's *Tartuffe*. Other plays in the season were Romain Rolland's *Ein Spiel von Tod und Liebe*, Max Halbe's *Der Strom*, Hauptmann's *Elga* and Ibsen's *Rosmersholme*.

Fully to appreciate the achievement of these companies it is essential to know something of the conditions, the restraints and the stresses under which they worked and performed. Even the repertoire had to be within the scope of a company of no more than 12–15 actors, which meant that most plays must need only 8–10 actors or 12–13 at most in order to make life tolerable for the members of the company. Within these and similar restrictions the Volksbühne had total control of the repertoire, which was possible nowhere else, except in the Volksbühne's own theatre in Berlin.

For each touring theatre to cover its region, which could extend as far as 400 kilometres between its most extreme limits, a rational touring plan had to be worked out to avoid the strains and waste of 'wild-cat' touring, and such a plan was usually a circuit, so that each place could be visited in succession at regular intervals with a minimum of travelling. The actual travelling could be by train or by a bus owned by the company. Sometimes the actors would travel by train while the scenery and properties (which often had to include even the front curtain and the lighting equipment) travelled by road. Each method had its pros and cons. Rail travel could be more comfortable, especially when, after November 1929, rules were agreed with the actors' union requiring, for example, the use of First Class (upholstered) carriages for journeys over a certain length, and laying down the conditions under which the actors *must* travel with the scenery (viz. when no more than 1½ hours were needed for setting and striking the set.) Train travelling on the other hand involved so-called 'dead' hours before or after performances when the railway timetable did not synchronise with performance times. Just how exacting touring in this way could be can be seen from the following timetable of a tour of the East German Provincial Theatre, March/April 1930.

(In this case the scenery and properties were taken by road.)

3 Mar.	14.00	dep. Berlin-Charlottenburg
	15.00	arr. Rathenow
	16.00	Dress Rehearsal with Set & Props
	20.00	Performance: RATHENOW, Apollo Theatre.
	(Overnight stay in Rathenow)	
4 Mar.	10.12	dep. Rathenow
	11.13	arr. Berlin-Charlottenburg

	17.57	dep Berlin-Anhalter Station
	19.12	arr. Luckenwalde
	20.00	Performance: LUCKENWALDE, Tivoli
	23.02	dep. Luckenwalde
	23.56	arr. Berlin-Anhalter Station.

5 Mar.
- 17.28 dep. Berlin-Friedrichstraße
- 18.43 arr. Fürstenwalde
- 20.00 Performance: FÜRSTENWALDE, Capitol
- 23.42 dep. Fürstenwalde
- 00.34 arr. Berlin-Schlesischer Station

6 Mar.
- 15.13 dep. Lehrter Station
- 16.50 arr. Wittenberge
- 20.00 Performance: WITTENBERGE, Stadtsaal
- (Overnight stay in Wittenberge)

7 Mar.
- 13.15 dep. Wittenberge (via Neustadt)
- 16.50 arr. Neuruppin
- 20.15 Performance: NEURUPPIN, Schloßgarten
- (Overnight stay in Neuruppin)

8 Mar.
- 09.35 dep. Neuruppin
- 11.17 arr. Stettin Station
- 16.20 dep. Potsdam Station
- 17.13 arr. Brandenburg
- 20.00 Performance: BRANDENBURG, Stadttheater
- 22.35 dep. Brandenburg
- 23.44 arr. Potsdam Station
- (Overnight stay in Potsdam)

9 Mar.
- 16.20 dep. Potsdam Station
- 17.13 arr. Brandenburg
- 20.00 Performance: BRANDENBURG, Stadttheater
- 22.35 dep. Brandenburg
- 23.44 arr. Potsdam Station
- (Overnight stay in Potsdam)

10 Mar.
- 14.28 dep. Görlitzer Station
- 18.08 arr. Sorau
- 20.00 Performance: SORAU, Mothes Lichtspiel
- (Overnight stay in Sorau)

11 Mar. 09.27 dep. Sorau (via Grünberg-Rothenburg)
         13.13 arr. Züllichau
         20.00 Performance: ZÜLLICHAU, Zum Kurfürsten
         (Overnight stay in Züllichau)

12 Mar. 20.00 Performance: ZÜLLICHAU
         (Overnight stay in Züllichau)

13 Mar. 08.12 dep. Züllichau
         12.22 arr. Berlin-Friedrichstraße
         18.05 dep. Stettin Station
         18.48 arr. Eberswalde
         20.00 Performance, EBERSWALDE, Harmonie
         22.55 dep. Eberswalde
         24.00 arr. Stettin Station

14 Mar. 20.00 Performance: WEISSENSEE-BERLIN, Stadthalle

15 Mar. (No Performance. Probably rehearsal)

16 Mar. 14.28 dep. Berlin-Görlitz Station
         16.59 arr. Forst
         20.00 Performance: FORST, Lindengarten
         (Overnight stay in Forst)

17 Mar. 20.00 Performance: FORST
         (Overnight stay in Forst)

18 Mar. 20.00 Performance: FORST
         (Overnight stay in Forst)

19 Mar. 15.03 dep. Forst
         16.49 arr. Finsterwalde
         20.00 Performance: FINSTERWALDE, Victoria Hotel
         23.15 Dep. Finsterwalde
         24.02 arr. Kottbus
         (Overnight stay in Kottbus)

20 Mar. 16.38 dep. Kottbus
         17.02 arr. Spremberg
         20.00 Performance: SPREMBERG, Kobels Konzerthaus
         (Overnight stay in Spremberg)

21 Mar.   20.00   Performance: SPREMBERG
           (Overnight stay in Spremberg)

22 Mar.   07.24   dep. Spremberg
           09.47   arr. Görlitz Station

23 Mar.   08.35   dep. Stettin Station
           14.20   arr. Kolberg
           20.00   Performance: KOLBERG, Stadttheater
           (Overnight stay in Kolberg)

24 Mar.   Performance: KOLBERG
           (Overnight stay in Kolberg)

25 Mar.   13.15   dep. Kolberg
           14.47   arr. Köslin
           20.00   Performance: KÖSLIN, Stadttheater
           (Overnight stay in Köslin)

26 Mar.   13.24   dep. Köslin
           15.17   arr. Lauenburg
           20.00   Performance: LAUENBURG
           (Overnight stay in Lauenburg)

27 Mar.   20.00   Performance: LAUENBURG
           (Overnight stay in Lauenburg)

28 Mar.   14.13   dep. Lauenburg
           18.22   arr. Stargard
           20.00   Performance: STARGARD, Stadttheater
           (Overnight stay in Stargard)

29 Mar.   09.18   dep. Stargard
           11.58   arr. Berlin, Stettin Station

30 Mar.   12.24   dep. Friedrichstraße Station
           14.51   arr. Sommerfeld
           20.15   Performance: SOMMERFELD, Waldschloß
           (Overnight stay in Sommerfeld)

31 Mar.   15.19   dep. Sommerfeld
           15.57   arr. Sorau
           20.00   Performance: SORAU, Mothes Lichtspiele
           (Overnight stay in Sorau)

1 Apr.   09.27   dep. Sorau
          11.33   arr. Grünberg
          20.15   Performance: GRÜNBERG, Konzerthaus
          (Overnight stay in Grünberg)

2 Apr.   20.15   Performance: GRÜNBERG
          (Overnight stay in Grünberg)

3 Apr.   20.15   Performance: GRÜNBERG
          (Overnight stay in Grünberg)

4 Apr.   12.15   dep. Grünberg (via Rottenburg-Guben)
          16.49   arr. Finsterwalde
          20.00   Performance: FINSTERWALDE, Victoria Hotel
          23.15   dep. Finsterwalde
          00.02   arr. Kottbus
          (Overnight stay in Kottbus)

5 Apr.   07.55   dep. Kottbus
          09.47   arr. Berlin, Görlitz Station
          16.20   dep. Potsdam Station
          17.13   arr. Brandenburg
          20.00   Performance: BRANDENBURG, Stadttheater
          22.55   dep. Brandenburg
          23.44   arr. Potsdam Station

(NOTES: The company was based in Berlin, but members had to sleep away from home 26 nights out of 32. Train travel was 2nd Class (un-upholstered!).

Two plays were presented during this tour, *Hokuspokus* until 21 March, and Klabund's *XYZ* from 23 March.

Hokuspokus was evidently rehearsed before the tour began and was dress-rehearsed at 4.00 p.m. on the same day that it opened at 8.00 p.m.

XYZ must have been rehearsed on tour, wherever and whenever rehearsals could be fitted in and was no doubt dress-rehearsed on the 'free' day, 22 March.)

Finally, the economics of the companies and the degree of subsidy they required may be illustrated by the example of one year in the work of the Provincial Theatre for East and West Prussia, whose outgoings for the year, 107,149 RM (Reichsmarks) brought in an earned income of 64,400 RM, leaving 42,749 RM (39% of total income) to be met by subsidy.

A Typical Budget
Provincial Theatre for East & West Prussia

A. Expenditure

(Monthly)

Salaries

7 Male,5 Female (Average salary 250 RM)	3,000 RM	
Dramaturge (proportion)	100 RM	
Prompter	175 RM	
Theatre Manager	240 RM	
2 unskilled workers	240 RM	
Design	75 RM	
Artistic Direction	600 RM	
Administrative Direction	550 RM	
Office Staff	150 RM	
Stand-ins	200 RM	5,330 RM
Car 2000 Km at 0.90 RM per km.	1,800 RM	

Expenses

15 persons @ 8 RM for 23 days	2,760 RM	
2 persons at 12 RM for 18 days	432 RM	
Rent	300 RM	
Royalties	500 RM	
Costumes, Wigs, Properties	420 RM	
Setting, Lighting	570 RM	
Welfare Charges	300 RM	
Advertising, Halls	120 RM	
Travel	100 RM	
Scripts	35 RM	
Payments to Agents	90 RM	
Sundries	107 RM	7,534 RM
		12,864 RM

(Annual)

Season:

7½ Months @ 12,864 RM per mth	96,480 RM	
½ Month (pre-tour rehearsal)	2,489 RM	
4½ Months Direction (1150 RM)		
Office(150 RM), Rent(300 RM)	7,200 RM	
Company members' journeys (return)	480 RM	
Direction's business journeys	500 RM	
	107,149 RM	

B. Income

(Monthly)

1 Performance @ 450 RM	450	RM
2 Performances @ 400 RM	800	RM
4 Performances @ 350 RM	1,400	RM
4 Performances @ 375 RM	1,500	RM
5 Performances @ 330 RM	1,650	RM
5 Performances @ 300 RM	1,500	RM
3 Performances @ 250 RM	750	RM
	8,050	RM

(Total)

8 Months @ 8,050 RM	64,400	RM
Subsidy	42,749	RM
	107,149	RM

The Magdeburg Conference, 1927

Of the ten annual conferences held from 1920 to 1929 the most momentous was the eighth, held at Magdeburg in June 1927. By now the development of the movement in the interwar years was effectively complete: the sixteen districts had been founded and the pattern of touring companies established. The Volksbühne movement was riding high on the crest of a wave. Over 400 delegates and guests from all over Germany attended this conference. A brilliant exhibition was open throughout and participants had the opportunity of seeing exemplary productions of Shakespeare's *A Midsummer Night's Dream* and Strindberg's *A Dream Play,* by the ensemble of the Berlin Volksbühne in the Magdeburg Municipal Theatre. A performance by the combined Chemnitz and Berlin Volksbühne Speech and Movement Choirs, accompanied by the Magdeburg City Orchestra, dedicated to the idea of a new genre of Community Art, made an exceptionally deep impression. But the high spot of the artistic offerings was the first performance of Bruno Schönlank's choral work *Der gespaltene Mensch* (*The Divided Man*) by the Berlin Volksbühne. At the final rally 4000 people filled the newly built Town Hall to hear inspirational speeches by leading Volksbühne figures and items by a Magdeburg choir. Finally, the following resolution, proposed by Baake on behalf of the executive committee, was passed unanimously with acclamation:

> The Federation of German Volksbühne Associations sees its task as
> striving to bring together free, sovereign art and the free, sovereign
> people. Unlike all organisations which subordinate artistic
> experience to denominational or political points of view, it
> emphasises afresh its intention to serve the whole population.

The significance of this apparently innocuous resolution lies in the debate which had preceded it, a debate which had threatened to split the whole movement, although, as Brodbeck noted three years later, the attack from the so-called 'opposition', which had begun even at the Hamburg conference in the previous year, really concerned, at least initially, the Berlin Volksbühne rather than the leadership of the Federation. This 'opposition' was itself complex and fundamentally lacking in unity.

By its very nature the Volksbühne from its foundation had contained the seeds of possible dissension. There always had been those who emphasised the artistic mission of the movement and those who emphasised the political, and, personalities apart, it was this division that led to the secession of the founder, Bruno Wille, from the Freie Volksbühne after the stormy Sans Souci meeting of 4 October 1892 and to the founding of the Neue Freie Volksbühne less than a fortnight later. After the re-unification in 1920 the inner conflicts took another form. No longer was the Volksbühne, as an organisation with strong links with the SPD, in constant conflict with the State, for the dominant party in the Weimar Republic was the Social Democratic. On the other hand the now-ruling Majority Social Democratic Party was already seen, after the suppression and murder of leading Spartacists and the overthrow of the short-lived Munich Soviet Republic, as being a 'New Right' to be opposed by a whole spectrum of socialists from the Independent Social Democratic Party to the heir of the Spartacist movement, the Communist Party (KPD). The 'political' aspect of the 'opposition' was led by Communists – though these were variously motivated. About 1926 a policy of entryism was advocated within the KPD. In the KPD journal *Die rote Fahne* for 3 July 1926 Alexander Abusch contributed an article on *The 7th Volksbühne Conference and the Work Force*, in which he wrote:

> The 7th Volksbühne Conference which was held at the beginning of last week in Hamburg, is worth the attention of class-conscious workers. The reason for this is not the fact that the programmes of the Volksbühne as it exists today have a certain ideological content which is an expression of the proletarian class struggle, but that an organisation exists with over 600,000 members who consist predominantly of proletarians, an organisation whose daily work it is to influence these members through the theatre: THAT makes it necessary to adopt a stance in relation to the question of the Volksbühne movement as it shows itself NOW at this 7th Volksbühne Conference.[6]

This is a clear invitation to members of the KPD to ensure that the influence of the Volksbühne is a Communist one. Abusch takes for granted that the day to day objective of the Volksbühne is to *influence* its members. This is the purely political view of the Volksbühne, which believes that

> the history of the Volksbühne is a chapter in the history of German Social Democracy.[7]

Whatever element of truth there is in this statement, the history of the Volksbühne is primarily a chapter in the history of the German Theatre. And while most of the 'opposition' took the former view, wanting to see the movement as a propaganda instrument for the Communist Party, the Volksbühne leadership, and indeed the vast majority of the membership throughout the country, as represented at both the 7th and 8th annual conferences, took the latter view.

But there was also an important theatrical, artistic, element in the 'opposition', an element that possessed its own identity although it was also exploited by the Communists of the political 'opposition'. This artistic dispute arose, of course, from what we have called the 'Piscator Affair', which we have already examined in its Berlin dimension.

By June 23-26, 1927, when the Magdeburg Conference was held, the rift between the Volksbühne and Piscator was complete and Piscator's own Piscator-Bühne was set to open on 3 September with his version of Ernst Toller's *Hoppla, wir leben!*. But the Volksbühne management knew that the Piscator matter would be used at the conference to spearhead the 'opposition' and therefore chose their principal speakers with care.

Kurt Baake from the chair challenged from the very start those who wanted a narrowly politicised Volksbühne:

> Fundamentally we are all really of the same opinion: we want to
> build bridges between Art and Life: we want to make art alive and
> life artistic ... We make only one common demand: we all want 'new
> art', but it should be 'art' and not a substitute based on political
> slogans. We want contemporary drama (*Zeitdrama*) but not news-
> paper and pamphleteering theatre (*Zeitungs-und Flugblättertheater*).
> We consider that to be unworthy of the masses. [8]

This "typically bourgeois conception of art" (Schwerd) was of course anathema to the politicisers.

Both establishment and opposition agreed that the speech by Professor S. Marck of Breslau on *Kulturwillen der Massen* (*The Desire of the Masses for Culture*) was a significant and masterly achievement, though the two sides obviously interpreted it differently. Brodbeck praised Marck's historical analysis of the cultural needs of the masses and the possibilities of their being realised, emphasising that the whole speech was both intellectual and rhetorical. But it was also possible to emphasise, as Schwerd does in his account of the speech, that Marck said in effect that the masses can only become bearers of cultural values if they are class-conscious and that adult education consists in supporting the masses in their *Kulturkampf*– by which he meant "the whole economic struggle of the modern proletariat" [9]

Evidently to counterbalance Marck, the second principal speaker was Julius Bab. In his lecture on *Theatre and Politics* Bab emphasised that all spheres of life are subordinate to a unity, the "very source of life" (*Urgrund des Lebendigen*). For him the function of politics was "to order the outward spheres of life" while art was committed to an "inner order" through which "human feelings are heightened through the power of rhythm".[10] Later in discussion Marck claimed that his own contribution was "socialist" and that of Bab "liberal". These speeches, representing as they did two 'poles' of Volksbühne thinking were well planned to open up the debate that followed. It was not possible to claim that the "class" aspect had been suppressed or marginalised by the Volksbühne leadership, though Brodbeck, for the establishment, thought that Marck had by implication rejected the call for propaganda theatre, and Schwerd expresses regret that Marck's considerations remained purely theoretical and did not lead to demands for changes in Volksbühne policy.

Surprisingly the figure chosen as 'spokesman for the opposition' was not a delegate to the conference, though he was held in high regard in the movement: Ernst Toller. Toller's part in this conference and indeed in the whole controversy is of the greatest interest and cuts right across the theoretical lines of debate both political and artistic.

Converted to pacifism by his front-line experiences in the war and to a non-communist socialism tending to anarchism by Kurt Eisner and Gustav Landauer, ousted by the hard-line communists from his brief leadership of the Munich Soviet Republic, imprisoned for five years for his part in that Republic, Toller had emerged from prison on 15 July 1924 as the leading left-wing dramatist of his generation. During his imprisonment his play *Die Wandlung* had been directed by Karl-Heinz Martin at the "Tribüne", *Masse Mensch* by Jürgen Fehling at the Berlin Volksbühne; *Die Rache des verhöhnten Liebhabers* at the Freie Volksbühne, Jena; *Die Maschinenstürmer* by Karl-Heinz Martin at Reinhardt's *Großes Schauspielhaus*, and *Hinkemann* several times. He had also written scenarios for several of the Leipzig *Massenfestspiele*, (1920: *Spartakus*; 1922: *Der arme Konrad*), big, spectacular open-air pageant-like performances. After his release Toller went through a period of re-adjustment to the outer world and through his wide-ranging lecture tours became a world figure. In 1926 he was once more working on a new play and by 1927 was actively collaborating with Piscator on what was to become *Hoppla, wir leben!* At first Toller evidently found this collaboration with a director of great talent stimulating and exciting, and at the time of the Magdeburg Conference was deeply involved in it. But by the time the production was being rehearsed conflicts between author and director developed; by October he had restored his original ending and three years later could write:

> I regret now that, prejudiced by a contemporary fashion, I destroyed the structure of the original work in favour of the structure of the production ... today I prefer that a director extracts too little from a work than that he puts too much into it.[11]

But at the time of the conference Toller was still carried away by his enthusiasms for Piscator's theatrical innovations, which he saw as being censored by 'faceless men' at the head of the Volksbühne. In fact Toller had been waging a running battle with the Volksbühne since 1925 on account of Heinrich Neft's procrastinations in producing *Die Wandlung*, even though a contract had been signed. Neft's rather unconvincing arguments as to why he kept postponing a production were that "the piece had too strong a propaganda message", "the piece is too radical".

Neft is "bound to be afraid that he would frighten away the Volksbühne membership with the production". Toller's anger is understandable and in fact the play was never produced at the Berlin Volksbühne and the matter became subject of a lawsuit. This was another factor which certainly influenced Toller's stance *vis-à-vis* Piscator and the Volksbühne. He had already, along with over forty other public figures, signed a statement of solidarity with Piscator addressed to the management of the Volksbühne. The list of signatories is drawn from a wide spectrum of progressive opinion and in itself proves that though the KPD wanted to exploit the Piscator Affair for political ends, many on the non-Marxist Left were prepared to champion the Director's artistic freedom. All these things contribute to our understanding as to how and why Toller, who despite his own rhetoric actually had much in common with the liberal socialism of Bab, came not simply to ally himself with his old opponents, the Communists, but even to become the spokesman of the Communist-driven Volksbühne 'opposition'.

On 30 March 1927 as one of the principal speakers at the *Herrenhaus* meeting of Piscator and his supporters, Toller, in an address on *Drama – Idee – Message*, declared:

> Drama means conflict, means we must be radical if we are to be anything at all ... The Volksbühne has no face, no character, has not the courage to make itself disliked.

> (*Berliner Volkszeitung*)

He then, tactlessly, went on to refer to his personal conflict which, as the *Berliner Volkszeitung* remarked, was 'unnecessary'.

So we come to his important contribution to the 8th Volksbühne Conference. [V. Appendix E]

Baake invited Toller to speak "as a guest", and he was greeted with applause. After saying that the basic relationships that drama attempts to embody are timeless in their tragic tensions, Toller went on to say that historically the struggles in society take the form of class struggles which in turn must be given dramatic form. This did not mean 'the cult of the proletariat', nor was all the good to be portrayed on one side and all the evil on the other. He thought that Bab's ideas could equally well have been put forward by the rival, right-wing Bühnenvolksbund. Soon he was accused from the floor of making a party-political speech. Denying this, he tried to move to the 'Piscator Case', but Chairman Baake said he could do no more than touch upon it. In doing this Toller reminded the audience that many voices, not only those of socialists, had been raised in protest when the Volksbühne Board of Directors intervened over Piscator's production of a play, (it was Ehm Welk's *Gewitter über Gottland*, but Toller had no need here to name the play) when it had already been put on.

– It may be asked why Piscator's production of *Gewitter über Gottland* caused such conflict when his earlier productions of contemporary, left-wing plays, Paquet's *Fahnen* and *Sturmflut*, had not done so, even though he 'virtually remade' the latter during rehearsal. The answer would seem to be that in directing Welk's play Piscator turned it into blatant Communist propaganda.

> He wanted to establish a direct connection between what happened
> in 1400 and what happened in Russia in 1917, in Germany in 1918
> and in China in 1927. [12]
>   Playing the part of Asmus, the 15th Century rebel, Alexander
> Granach appeared not only made up as Lenin, but credibly imitated
> him in facial expression, gesture, tone of voice and in movement.[13]

But the criticisms of the production were also artistic, Schwerd suggests that the reason that this production in particular caused the decisive conflict between Piscator and the Volksbühne was that in this production "the technical aids caused the dramatic text to retreat far into the background." [14]

And it was these 'aids' which carried the contemporary political message:

> The propaganda effect especially of the films, which were
> masterpieces of symbolic meaning, cannot be overestimated. [15]

Toller quoted Alfred Kerr, who suggested that Piscator had done his job too well, and although Toller himself argued politically it is clear that his most strongly felt conviction was that of the need for *artistic* freedom.

Toller argued that not all plays are appropriate for Volksbühne production, even if they are works of art – a play in honour of Frederick the Great, for example – and he criticised Bab for publishing an anthology of patriotic war poems. He reminded the Volksbühne leaders of their own youth and their youthful revolutionary enthusiasms and urged them not to alienate contemporary youth, represented by the Youth Sections, as they had already alienated Piscator.

Toller's speech, as Brodbeck admitted, was 'not undiplomatic', but the vast majority of the delegates stood behind the official speakers. One cannot but wonder to what extent some delegates realised how much Marck's speech had in common with the 'opposition'. Indeed, the 'opposition' within the Volksbühne now took on a different form, and when at the Mainz Conference next year Ehm Welk read a *Manifesto of the Opposition* it roused no noteworthy disharmony in the general unanimity of opinion.

Press and Publications

No history of the expansion of the Volksbühne movement in the 1920s would be complete without some account of its publication programme which, after modest beginnings, and always subordinate to the basic aims of the movement, made a significant contribution to the literature of theatre during that period.

At first, only periodicals intended primarily, though not exclusively, for internal consumption were published. In September 1920 appeared the first number of *Die Volksbühne* (full title: *Die Volksbühne: Zeitschrift für soziale Kunstpflege*) produced by the Berlin Volksbühne but immediately taken over by the Federation when that was founded only a month later. It was a serious and weighty journal appearing at first bimonthly and then quarterly, with 40 to 80 pages edited by Siegfried Nestriepke, now General Secretary of the Federation. All problems of direct or indirect interest to the movement could be discussed in its pages and contributions from all branches of intellectual and cultural life gave it a noteworthy character. There were extracts, too, from dramas and poems. The second half was a topical survey of theatre and of the Volksbühne movement itself. After five years it was decided that the now widespread movement would be more effectively served by a periodical which could appear more frequently; so in December 1925 the heavy quarterly appeared for the last time and on 1 January 1926 *Die Volksbühne* appeared as a twice-monthly newspaper of six to eight pages [18–24 wide columns] edited by Hans v. Zwehl. Useful to the movement though this was it proved not to be economically viable, and although Kurt Baake took up the editorship in July 1927 it had to cease publication in March 1928, giving way on 1 April to a revival of the weightier format, this time, however, appearing monthly with 48 pages. The first two issues were still edited by Baake and the next five by Nestriepke, who at this time was asking to be relieved of his part in the Federation; so from November the editorship passed to Brodbeck, soon to be Nestriepke's successor.

The Federation also published a duplicated, free, press-handout issued at irregular intervals, circular letters to all associated Volksbühnen at 6-8 week intervals, and the programmes of the Touring Companies. More important than the circular letters were the *Dramaturgische Blätter*, edited by Julius Bab with assistance from others, to help associations to choose their play-programmes. They appeared every 4–6 weeks and contained summaries and critiques of some 20–25 new plays, not forgetting the classics. At this period about 300 new plays were produced each year in Germany and – perhaps surprisingly – about three times that number published. The *Dramaturgische Blätter* with their careful critical selections thus had a great influence not only on the Volksbühne Associations but also on theatre directors, who found them of value in deciding their repertoires.

In the early years a section of *Die Volksbühne* was made available to individual associations unable to produce their own periodicals, but this ceased to be necessary as more and more associations did produce their own. Many of these local periodicals came out monthly, some at longer or shorter intervals. They were issued free to members and contained introductions to plays, and also, if space allowed, general articles as well as local information. Some were substantial periodicals of 20 or even 30 pages; most, of course, were smaller.

By 1924 the need for the movement to have its own publishing house and sales agency in order to publish and distribute good material at non-commercial rates led to the founding, as a limited liability company, of a Volksbühne publishing and distributing house, *Die Volksbühnen-Verlags-und Vertriebs G.m.b.H.* During the following six years the house published 15 brochures by Nestriepke and others, the proceedings of all the Federation's Annual Conferences and a series of five books under the general title *People and Art* (*Volk und Kunst*):

Modern Theatre Business (Nestriepke)
Modern Drama (Rudolf Kayser)
Working-Class Poetry (Julius Bab)
Modern Dance (John Schikowski)
The Theatre in Revolutionary Russia (Arthur Holitscher).

The most ambitious publishing venture was that of the *Volksbühne Classics* – standard works sold at 3 Marks (and later at 2.50 Marks) per volume. They were well edited with introductions and notes. Thirty-two volumes were published, covering the works of nine major poets and dramatists. By Autumn 1930, 70,000 volumes had been sold.

The other arm of the limited company was a play-distributing agency which looked for young authors, especially those with something 'special' to offer. About half the manuscripts read were rejected at once. Eventually 2% to 4% could be considered, and it was a year's work to find eight to ten plays. These were not printed, but duplicated, the object being to get professional productions for them. Altogether 55 plays were distributed in this way and many times 10, 000 Marks passed to authors, whose names, among many less well known, included Oedön Horvath, Lunacharsky, Karl Heinz Martin (a version of Shakespeare's *Julius Caesar*), Alan Monkhouse (a translation from English) and Ehm Welk. Some of the more successful were later published in book form. Also published were Bruno Schönlank's two great *Sprechchöre : Ein Frühlingsmysterium* (*A Spring Mystery Play*) and *Der gespaltene Mensch* (*The Divided Person*). The *Sprechchor* was one of the principal performance-forms of German working-class culture, but artistically worthwhile texts were few and far between, hence the particular importance of these two publications.

The End of the Decade

From the perspective of the 1990s it is difficult to understand the relaxed complacency which preceded the depression of 1929 and the meteoric rise to power of the Nazis from then until 1933. In the 1928 elections the Nazi party polled only 810,000 out of the 31,000,000 votes cast and had only 108,000 actual party members, so perhaps it is understandable that after. Hitler's release from prison in 1924 Dr Heinrich Held, Prime Minister of Bavaria, had believed that "The wild beast is checked" [16]. There was certainly no visible shadow over the Volksbühne Annual Conference held at Mainz in the summer of 1928. This was opened with an official dinner and concluded with a steamboat trip on the Rhine, complete with flood-lighting of the bridges! Delegates had for the first time seen the production of a play actually published by the Volksbühne, Lunarcharsky's *Der befreite Don Quichotte* (*Don Quixote Liberated*)[1922] at the Mainz Municipal Theatre. Lunarcharsky [1875-1933] was at that time People's Commissar for Enlightenment in the USSR. Before the revolution he had studied philosophy in Zürich and his plays are regarded as rather bookish in inspiration. In this play he "portrays the tragic comedy of 'The Knight of the Sorrowful Countenance'. The breath of our own times pervades the historical milieu."

Also for the first time at an Annual Conference the leader of a large trade union movement, Siegfried Aufhäuser, formally assured the representatives of the German Volksbühne that both blue- and white-collar workers needed the Volksbühne movement and that this trade union federation was ready to do all in its power to spread the Volksbühne idea.

Although the executive had asked speakers to concentrate on practical issues Wolfgang Schumann read a paper which not only broke out of this framework but also propounded a series of considerations and theses which were bound to be displeasing, in that he disparaged the theatre itself! In the discussion that followed his ideas were unanimously rejected, but even Friedel's paper on *Detailed Organisational Work* did not entirely wipe out the effect of Schumann's speech.

Thoughtful, eloquent speeches' on *Volksbühne, the State and Local Government* (Bürgermeister Dr Burmann) and on *Volksbühne, the Press and Criticism* (Robert Brener) were followed by a so-called *Manifesto of the Opposition* presented by Ehm Welk, but this was in fact now so closely in harmony with the majority opinion that little discord was felt, and it was evident that the internal conflicts that had troubled the movement for several years had now been resolved.

The final conference of the decade was held in a similarly optimistic mood in the Free City of Danzig – then, of course, part of Germany – on the theme *Problems and Recovery of the German Theatre*. The theatre was indeed passing through a crisis, not least an economic one, which the Volksbühne inevitable shared, though it had survived the depression with 285 federated associations.

In 1928 Nestriepke had asked to be relieved of his post as General Manager in order to concentrate on his work with the Berlin Volksbühne. Instead of accepting his resignation immediately the conference had sent him on holiday and had given him a Deputy, Albert Brodbeck, who now, in 1929, finally took over from him. In his last speech as General Manager of the Federation (he remained a member of the Executive) Nestriepke gave a wide-ranging and penetrating survey of the current situation and its problems. He tackled unsentimentally the most serious problems concerning the way in which theatres were staffed and set these in the centre of a comprehensive, knowledgeable and stimulating view of theatre organisation and economics. Inevitably he touched upon many sore points and went on the offensive against what he called – probably with justification – the 'anarchy' of the theatre. In no way did he limit himself to a merely academic discussion of vital theatrical matters. His conclusions deserved to be widely heeded, wrote Brodbeck, who was, after all inheriting the problems.

Other speakers were equally positive and practical. The tenth conference heard that the Volksbühne idea was being taken up in other countries, and it ended on a high note with music, a production and inspiring speeches in the Danzig Municipal Theatre.

'It was not just an aesthetic pleasure, it was a revelation, a ceremony in the truest sense of the word.

The movement seemed to be set for a future of continuing success and development in the next decade, but this was not to be.

15. Exterior and interior views of the Neues Volkstheater in Köpenickerstrasse.

16.   *Das trunkene Schiff (The Drunken Ship)* by Paul Zech. World première at the Volksbühne on the Bülowplatz, 1925. Directed by Erwin Piscator, with projected scenery by George Grosz.

17.   Final scene from *Sturmflut (Storm Flood)* by Alfons Paquet, directed by Erwin Piscator. World première at the Volksbühne on the Bülowplatz in 1925.

18.   Fritz Holl (1883–1942), director of the Volksbühne on the Bülowplatz 1923–1928.

19.   Dr Dr h.c. Siegfried Nestriepke (1885–1963), one of the most important figures in the history of the Volksbühne movement.

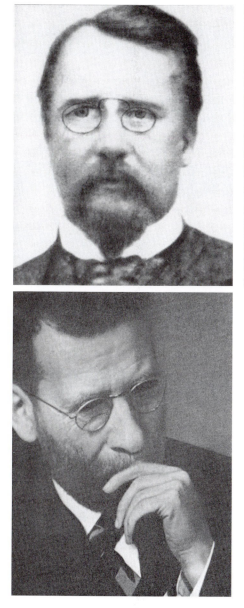

20. Curt Baake (1864–1938) full face.

21. Gustav Landauer (1870–1919) in profile.

22. Julius Bab (1880–1955).

23.   Exterior of the Volksbühne on the Luxemburgplatz. Photo: Cecil Davies

24.   View of the stage from the auditorium (in use for a Communist Youth ceremony) at the Volksbühne on the Luxemburgplatz. Photo: Cecil Davies

THE NAZIS: 'NIGHT OVER GERMANY'

By 1930 the Volksbühne was a nationwide movement with a membership of half a million in over three hundred local societies: It was 'the greatest cultural organisation in Germany'. Like the inflation of 1923, the economic crisis of 1931-32 gave it, at least in some cities, a temporary illusion of even greater strength. Theatres which had closed their doors to Volksbühne bookings now welcomed them to fill their emptying seats. But the economic crisis also provided the last push needed to bring the National Socialists into power. Rudolf Ross, since 1928 Bürgermeister of Hamburg, warned the members of Hamburg Volksbühne in October 1932 that the forces of reaction were on the march:

> Just as the nation's impulses of feeling and will were stifled before
> the development of the *Storm and Stress* period at the time of Goethe
> and Schiller, a growing reaction might also now subjugate everything
> of potential greatness in dramatic art to an intellectual and spiritual
> autarky. That could mean a reverse from which we might not recover
> again for generations. [1]

That was October 1932. At noon on 30 January 1933, President Hindenburg entrusted the chancellorship to Adolf Hitler, and on 5 March the Nazis won the elections with 288 seats. Almost at once the policy of political co-ordination (*Gleichschaltung*) was applied to the arts as well as to all other aspects of German life. A single theatre audience organisation, The German Stage (Deutsche Bühne) was created, of which all existing organisations must become part.

Volksbühne leaders saw all too clearly what was coming and attempted to rouse the membership to some degree of resistance. For example the executive of the Hamburg Volksbühne issued an appeal to its members in April 1933:

> While the Volksbühne has existed, its business has been to open the
> German Theatre to *all* our fellow-countrymen – especially the less
> well-off working population – who desire the arts, *without regard
> for the party or beliefs* of the individual member ... We work ... in the
> spirit of the *key sentences* of the *Jena Volksbühne Policy Statement*.

'The Volksbühne ... *rejects every subordination to political or sectarian points of view, of its struggle towards expression in artistic form.*'
   We have never been subject to a party, and we wish also in future to serve only art, especially *German* art, *free from all party ties.* [2]

Within a few weeks of this brave declaration the Hamburg Volksbühne (like all others) was absorbed by the Deutsche Bühne, which took over the administration and assets. Members attempted some resistance, as this passage from a report from the delegates of the Deutsche Bühne on a members' meeting on 18 May 1933 shows:

> ... To the question asked from the floor of the meeting, on what grounds the political co-ordination had taken place, Herr Pohlmann answered by referring to the fact that the only theatre audience organisation recognised on the government side was the Deutsche Bühne. Therefore the transfer of the Volksbühne to the Deutsche Bühne was necessary. The meeting took an extraordinarily rowdy course, stirred up by provocateurs, so that objective agreement was impossible. The chairman repeatedly threatened to close the meeting if order was not restored. When, in spite of this, objective discussion became impossible, Herr Pohlmann closed the meeting. [3]

What happened in Hamburg typifies what happened all over Germany and, of course, not only to the Volksbühne but to its Christian counterpart, the Bühnenvolksbund. Nor were the Nazis content with destroying the present, and, as they believed, the future existence of the Volksbühne movement; they sought also to annihilate its past by consigning its records, in the manner of the men of *1984*, to the Memory Hole – they destroyed, in fact, the archives of the Federation and of most of the Volksbühne societies. [4]

   In Berlin the effect of the economic crisis. had been more serious in its effects on the movement, because here the Volksbühne itself was involved in the management of a great theatre. Even from 1924 houses had suffered badly because of unemployment, and when after the crash of 1929 the number of unemployed rose to six million the theatre's deficit became really serious. Measures were taken to rationalise the business and reduce the deficit, and Nestriepke believed that eventually the theatre on the Bülowplatz would have overcome its own economic crisis.

   When the Nazis came to power the Volksbühne leadership in Berlin was evidently divided between those who would admit compromise with them and those who would not, and when the association expressed its position on 11 May 1933 in terms of compromise, Nestriepke resigned, leaving Curt Baake, as chairman, in control. Under pressure from the legal adviser Rudolf Pahl, Baake called a general meeting on 19 December 1933, without preliminary members' meetings or the election of delegates. Opening the meeting, he said,

> We believed we must dispense with convening members' meetings and with new elections of delegates. The principle of strict, responsible leadership has everywhere taken the place of the electoral system. That must apply to us too. [5]

Although the Federation of Volksbühne Societies had been subsumed under the Deutsche Bühne, the Berlin Volksbühne, because it owned a theatre, was allowed to retain a nominal independence. Low membership and financial difficulties, however, compelled the Volksbühne leadership to play even further into the Nazis' hands if the association was to avoid dissolution – a course that many would have thought more honourable. In the season 1933-34 the membership was down to nineteen thousand, while forty thousand was the minimum needed for economic viability, and of the required income of 700,000 RM there was a shortfall of at least 400,000 RM.

The Volksbühne leadership went to the Ministry of Popular Enlightenment and Propaganda, negotiated with Laubinger, leader of the new National Chamber of Theatre, [6] and Schlösser, National Dramaturge, and got a subvention of 440,000 RM. As the association was now in effect directly financed by the Nazi government, Goebbels' ministry could hope soon to replace its leadership with ministry nominees. During 1934 and 1935 the constitution was changed so that the chairman now nominated the executive and other important officers. In August 1935 the executive dissolved itself and invited a Nazi cultural official (*Reichskulturamtsleiter*), Moraller, from the National Chamber of Culture, to be leader of the association (*Vereinsführer*). He took up his post in September 1935 and formed a Nazi executive. Curt Baake received a letter of thanks from Moraller for his past contribution to the Volksbdhne, and a pension of 300 RM. [7]

In the season 1935-36 the Volksbühne theatres (on the Bülowplatz and Nollendorfplatz) had a deficit of over 1,400,000 RM. This was covered by government subsidy, and theatre seats were filled with Sturm Abteilung men, soldiers, police, schools and military police. Graf Solms, the theatre director, was replaced by Eugen Klöpfer, and the constitution was again revised so that he became in practice head of the whole Volksbühne organisation in Berlin. Only two more steps were needed to complete the Nazi victory. In 1937 the old executive, who were still legal owners of the Theatre on the Bülowplatz, were induced or compelled to make over to the State the theatre and the land on which it stood. A year later (May 1938) the theatre firm was wound up. The Volksbühne as an audience organisation still existed. In October, Moraller's hand-picked executive again chose him as leader, and on 1 March 1939 the Berlin Volksbühne was wound up.

Although the Volksbühne, after nearly fifty years of activity, had ceased to exist, the theatre that had for so long been associated with it was still standing, and Klöpfer took advantage of its great name and its association with that Volksbühne tradition. He brought in actors and authors with strong Volksbühne associations and international reputations such as Heinrich George and Gerhart Hauptmann. The latter became in effect the in-house author of a 'Volksbühne' that had actually lost its meaning, but he gave the theatre and its new leadership the successful productions it wanted. For his seventy-fifth birthday on 15 November 1937 *Rose Bernd* was produced, and in October 1938 *Kollege Crampton* was an economic as well as an artistic success. On 6 April 1940 *Die versunkene Glocke* was performed in the author's presence, in January 1942 Karl-Heinz Martin directed *Winterballade*, and in December of that year Hauptmann attended a performance of his *Florian Geyer*, a fact that Klöpfer was happy to report to the Nazi National Dramaturge, Schlösser.

Even if the eighty-year old dramatist had inner reservations concerning his association with the Nazi cultural policy he was not the man to challenge Klöpfer and his backers openly. Klöpfer, of course, fully understood how much his theatre, and through it the Nazi party stood to gain by association with this world-famous name.

Braulich's summary of this period is not unjust:

> During these years the political line of Goebbels' Ministry emerged clearly in the repertoire and production policy of the theatre of the old Volksbühne. The Intendant, responsible only to the Ministry, supported an apparently non-political programme in which a classical repertoire was interspersed with trivial pieces and even Nazi-political ones. His having the best actors, known to the public through film, and at the same time a varied change of plays, guaranteed the theatre an audience which was average in quality and adequate financially. Big names were integrated into the programme even when it was probably less and less agreeable to a poet like Hauptmann to be wheeled out as a showpiece in the Nazi Theatre. The bourgeois, lower-middle-class and working-class audience found in this theatre relaxation and "experiences" which helped them to forget that they were playing no part in the political affairs of the state. The theatre and its drama, even when it presented plays by socially critical authors from the past was politically defused and no longer had the least intention of exercising a progressive influence on its audience. [8]

After his resignation in 1933, Nestriepke became a freelance writer until his exclusion from the National Chamber of Literature. After a long period of unemployment he became, in 1935, Secretary to the Board of Directors of

Fritz Staar's cinema business in Berlin and Potsdam. Later he became deputy manager of the business. 'And it is only natural,' he wrote in 1956, 'that with my hope for a speedy collapse of the Nazi regime I also always united the other hope – that a new Volksbühne would carry on the work of the organisation which had been destroyed.' [9]

The Volksbühne theatre on the Bülowplatz was severely damaged in an air-raid in 1943. Its ruins remained as a symbol both of past achievement and of future hopes.

ACT III
THE VOLKSBÜHNE SINCE 1945

Scene I
IN BERLIN AND EAST GERMANY

New Beginnings. The Volksbühne Re-founded

At the end of the war the German theatrical scene was one empty waste; nearly all theatre buildings had been destroyed, the companies were scattered and many leading figures had emigrated. The ruined theatres stood amid ruined cities, Berlin among them. Yet in cities without traffic, window-panes or domestic services the Germans gave theatre, music and the arts priority over many other pressing claims on scarce resources. Carl Ebert, who toured Germany on behalf of the Allied Control Commission, found there a burning thirst for culture – hundreds of people standing for two and a half hours on a cold winter Sunday afternoon in the shell-damaged auditorium of Frankfurt University to listen to Bach's *Art of Fugue*, others trembling with cold in the ruined stock-exchange to hear a piano recital, when the only available electric heater was needed to save the pianist's fingers from stiffening. Friedrich Luft has written an unforgettable account of crossing Berlin for the opening of the Deutsches Theater. He crossed a canal hand-over-hand on the remains of two pipes, was nearly beaten up by looters, was rowed across the Spree in a leaking boat, and on the way home was waylaid by thieves, robbed and knocked unconscious.

> I didn't get home that night. I slept in the Zoo. It was next day before my family saw me again and they had already almost written me off and imagined me perhaps on the way to Siberia. Theatre-going was dangerous. [1]

In the context of such national enthusiasm for theatre and the arts the veterans of the pre-1933 Volksbühne associations all over Germany found fruitful ground for re-establishing the movement, and even before the end of 1945 the Volksbühne was being reborn throughout the country. Once more we shall centre the story in Berlin, for although this city's situation was unique, the special problems there serve to highlight those of an occupied and politically sundered country.

On 2 May 1945 the Russians entered Berlin. Less than three weeks later (20 May) Siegfried Nestriepke sent a memorandum to the Municipal Council, 'The reorganisation of the Berlin system of theatres', in which,

189

among other things, he proposed a Volksbühne type of organisation. Bruno Henschel, an old Volksbühne colleague of Nestriepke's and later head of the East Berlin publishing house of Henschel, showed the memorandum to the Soviet Central Command. [2] Two days later a car with two Russian officers called at Nestriepke's flat to take him and Henschel to meet the City Commandant, Colonel-General Bersarin, to discuss the memorandum. Unfortunately Nestriepke was not at home and could not be found: the Russian officers had to return without carrying out their mission. So the next day Henschel and Nestriepke walked (they had no car and of course there was no public transport) from Wilmersdorf to Friedrichsfelde, but no one at the Soviet headquarters had even heard of the memorandum, and the two men had to return wearily home. On 2 June Nestriepke sent a letter to Bersarin: there was no reply. 'I mention this *Intermezzo*', comments Nestriepke, 'only as an indication of the way the Soviet Central Command functioned at that time.'

After four weeks' delay Nestriepke was invited to exchange views with Otto Winzer, Communist *Stadtrat* (city councillor – but in effect Minister) for education. Winzer wanted to see a revival of the Volksbuhne, and a small commission was formed to which Nestriepke presented a detailed memorandum; but it all came to nothing, in spite of Winzer's support, because the occupation authorities were opposed to the formation of another mass organisation. Resigning himself to indefinite delay, Nestriepke took on responsibility for theatre within the Central Administration for Education and worked with Boleslaw Barlog for the reopening of the Schlosspark Theater. He also aroused the interest of the leadership of the Kulturbund (Kulturbund für die demokratische Erneuerung Deutschlands) through whom he was to give two broadcasts on Berlin Radio advocating his ideas, but at the last minute (in January 1946) these were forbidden by the Soviet censor.

This was the beginning of Nestriepke's protracted struggle with the Soviet authorities and with German Communists. His next opponent was the independent German Trades Union Federation (FDGB) which thought a Volksbühne unnecessary, as tickets could be distributed through trade unions. Another important rival was Karl-Heinz Martin, one-time director of the Bülowplatz theatre. Karl-Heinz Martin was not a *party* Communist, and he enjoyed the support both of the Russians and of the Americans. He opened the former Prater Theater in north Berlin under the name *Volksbühne*, 'as a contribution to the Volksbühne idea', as he expressed it. Nestriepke wrote that the Volksbühne was *essentially* based on an audience organisation, though a theatre might follow. His comment was probably never published.

Meanwhile Volksbühne developments were taking place both in East and West Germany, though those in the West, notably at Hamburg and Hanover, were not reported in the Berlin press. In the Soviet Zone, in spite of the official opinion of *Tribüne*, the organ of the Communist-dominated FDGB, a number of Volksbühne associations were founded in the second half of 1946. In most of these individual membership (as advocated by Nestriepke) was possible, but corporate membership (of trade unions, etc.) was the norm. The associations were usually founded jointly by the trade unions and the Kulturbund. They did actually get people into the theatres and even reached the stage of forming *Land* Federations: a *Land* Federation for Sachsen-Anhalt was founded on 1 August 1946. These Soviet Zone Volksbühne associations were not politically independent, however, and acted as organs for the SED (Sozialistische Einheitspartei Deutschlands), effectively the Communist Party.

Frustrated in direct achievement of their aims, Nestriepke and his friends now diverted all their energies into politics. New elections for the City Parliament were imminent, and in fact in October 1946 the Social Democratic Party (SPD) defeated the SED. This appeared to open the way for founding a Volksbühne on traditional lines. At the same time Nestriepke's Volksbühne colleagues proposed him as *Stadtrat für Volksbildung* (Berlin Minister of Education) and he was appointed to this important and influential post. Within a few weeks he had worked out the sketch for a new organisation, shown it to a circle of friends and written invitations to appropriate bodies to form a very broadly based founding committee, which was to include trade unions and the SED as well as other organisations and parties. The invitations were ready for posting when the Communists took action. Evidently they had wind of Nestriepke's plans and wished to forestall them. Nestriepke himself, knowing that his predecessor, Otto Winzer, had ensured that most employees in the education department were reliable party members, believed that his desk drawers had been rifled in his absence. The newspaper *Tägliche Rundschau*, the official organ of Russian policy, published a 'Call for the founding of a Volksbühne' in Berlin over thirty influential signatures including those of Barlog and Karl-Heinz Martin. Many of the signatories were non-Communists who probably did not appreciate the implications of their action. The 'Call' in itself was one to which any former supporter of the Volksbühne might have subscribed, and ended with the hope of making real the slogan carved over the doors of the old Volksbühne theatre: Art for the People. Nestriepke has pointed out the irony of the fact that when the Communist Administration actually undertook the restoration of the Bülowplatz theatre, this inscription was deliberately chiselled off!

Nestriepke promptly posted off his own invitations and wrote to the papers himself, as if the call of the thirty signatories were support for his own plans. His founding committee met on 20 December 1946. The rival scheme led to no more than a meeting of trade union officials who put forward the idea of a People's Cultural Circle. This scheme was published

on the same day as the second meeting of Nestriepke's committee, but the
FDGB representatives, Fugger and Baum (Communists) and Pickert (SPD)
made no reference to it. This was on 8 January 1947. On the founding
committee compromises between the various views seemed possible; but
Fugger and his supporters apparently went straight to the Soviet authority
who then cut the ground from under Nestriepke's feet by publishing in all
Berlin newspapers (15 January 1947) the fact that a licence to re-form the
Volksbühne and rebuild its theatre had been issued to Karl-Heinz Martin,
Heinz W. Litten and Alfred Lindemann. Of these only Martin had played
any important part in the pre-Nazi Volksbühne. Nestriepke, who was
informed of the licence by word of mouth *after* the press release, strongly
attacked the Soviet move in an anonymous article in the *Sozialdemokrat* and
in an 'interview' (he wrote it himself) in the *Telegraf.*

A period of complex negotiations and in-fighting followed which
involved the three licensees (themselves often not in agreement), the FDGB,
represented by Fugger, and the Soviet authorities, represented by Major
Dymschitz, the influential and devious head of the Cultural Department.
In the midst of this the situation was again modified, and the attitude of
Lindemann, spokesman of the Licensees, considerably softened, by the
formation of a Committee of Allied Theatre Officers: the officials of the
western powers had been kept informed of events by Nestriepke and
warned of the danger of Communist domination. By the end of February a
draft constitution for the new association had been agreed. The committee
was to consist of two representatives of the city administration, two of the
Youth Department, four of the FDGB, two of Trade Union 17 (which included
theatre workers), the three licensees, and representatives of the four political
parties in proportion to their strength in the city assembly. A letter, over the
signatures of the licensees was sent to the Committee of Allied Theatre
Officers; Paul Eggers (chairman of Breslau Volksbühne before 1933) was
proposed as general manager, and the names of the proposed appointees
were collected. An attempt by the Soviet authorities to exclude Nestriepke
and Fritz Barthelmann was unsuccessful.

The reply from the cultural committee of the Allies came at the very end
of March: the whole proposed committee structure was rejected, as it was
claimed that the political parties would have too much power. Instead, the
Allied Theatre Officers were to nominate all the committee, which was to
consist of four representatives of each section of Berlin, plus the three
licensees. Nestriepke, who thought it 'grotesque' that the committee for so
utterly German an organisation should be nominated by the occupying
powers, was nevertheless relieved that the Communists would be in a
permanent minority.

A long delay followed, with no list of nominations from the Allies.
Lindemann and his two colleagues were already impatient, and even at the

beginning of March had announced that a production by Karl-HeinzMartin of Hauptmann's *Die Weber* in the Kastanienallee theatre would be the opening Volksbühne production. The première was on 24 April. [3]

An anonymous critique appeared in *Die Volksbühne*, a new monthly published by Henschel:

> In accordance with the Director's [viz. Karl-Heinz Martin] wish the ensemble was not a seething mass of rebels in revolt, but a ghostly procession of beaten individuals. The Chorus was, so to speak, dissolved into single voices. The speakers were like the creations of a Käthe Kollwitz. Their manner of speaking and acting lay upon the hearts of the audience like a nightmare. Even in the dramatic climaxes of the action the minor key of this production predominated, as for example the scene in Dreißiger's house, in which the outraged people carried out the looting almost like a ceremony in which windows were smashed without the clinking sound of broken glass ... less a drama, more a tragedy. Timeless symbolism, freed from historical reminiscence, stronger than mere agitation, having a broad effect directed towards the future. A beginning not without weaknesses. But a beginning. [4]

There was still no Volksbühne. Lindemann made a speech regretting the delay and threatening to go ahead without the committee. This so provoked Nestriepke that he decided to use a very dirty weapon against Lindemann. He had uncovered a black spot in Lindemann's past, and he wrote an article in the *Telegraf* in early May asking whether, as Siegfried Nestriepke and Fritz Barthelmann were apparently not good enough for the Soviet military administration they realised that one of their own representatives (he didn't give the name, but knew it would be easy to guess!) had a criminal record. Even though the Allied Command then opened an investigation, Nestriepke's trick partly misfired, and Lindemann was retained when the constitution of the committee was announced. He later held various offices in the Eastern-sector Volksbühne. On 22 May the list of names for the committee was received from the allies. There were twenty names, four from each sector, the three licensees and Nestriepke *ex officio*. While it included on the Russian nomination Fugger and Herbert Ihering, the Western nominations included such figures as Professor Dr Joachim Tiburtius, Erich Otto and Hilde Körber. Tiburtius and Hilde Körbe, with Dr Karl Forster, were Christian Democrats, and six of the others, including Nestriepke, Social Democrats. Understandably the list did not please the Communists. Fugger told the press the committee was abortive and lacked popular and youth support. 'But', says Nestriepke, 'the Allied Command had spoken.' It had taken a full two years to achieve, but the Berlin Volksbühne could at last be re-established. The new committee met first on

18 June 1947 (Nestriepke not being present) and before it met again Nestriepke's own position was changed.

Since the SPD had gained control in the October 1946 elections the Russians had made great use of the device of 'investigating' elected officials, apparently in order to disrupt the administrative machinery.

Active in this was Major-General Kotikov, former adviser to Colonel General Kuznetsov, and very clever at conference techniques. As we have seen, the Education Department had been thoroughly filled with Communists, and now they held every key position in education except that of Head of Education, Nestriepke's post. Kotikov therefore wanted to get rid of Nestriepke and replace him with Wildangel, the deputy head, a reliable Communist. At this time Nestriepke was only one of about a dozen elected officials whom Kotikov had under attack, and at this stage he would probably have been content if the responsible American officer, Brigadier General Frank Howley (United States Army) had been prepared to reprimand him for alleged violation of Kommandatura orders. This Howley was not prepared to do, as it was simply not true, though Howley himself evidently underestimated Nestriepke's calibre, for he says of him: 'he was not a particularly smart politician and was in fact a good example of the absent-minded professor....' [5] Into this situation – indeed, when Kotikov was about ready to drop the Nestriepke issue – came a new and brash American general who thought he knew better than his colleagues. At his first Kommandatura meeting, ignoring the briefing his colleagues had given him, he played into Kotikov's hands.

> 'I'm used to the Germans,' he blustered, 'I know them from the last war. They'll twist us and take advantage of us whenever they can. I propose we remove this man from office'.'
>
> If a thunderbolt had landed on the conference table, the effect could not have been more devastating. That an American official should recommend removal of an elected official, without trial, stunned me [i.e. Frank Howley].
>
> When I was able to speak, I leaned over and whispered to the Commandant,
>
> 'My God, General, now we're really in hot water ... the whole educational system of Berlin now goes into the hands of the Communists. [6]

News of the blunder spread, American journalists demanded a press conference and the new commandant was 'sacrificed to the press'. [7] But Howley's fear that Wildangel would be appointed to replace Nestriepke was not fulfilled, and in fact his elected successor, Walter May, proved himself a friend and ally of Nestriepke and his aims. As for Nestriepke himself, he was not sorry to be relieved of his public office, as he now had more time and energy to devote to the Volksbühne.

For two months the new four-sector committee struggled for progress, while Lindemann pursued plans of his own, and on 19 August the press announced that Lindemann and Litten were to found a Volksbühne for the Soviet Sector only. (Karl-Heinz Martin was not involved: he was asked by the Americans to become Intendant of the Hebbel-Theater, where he remained until his death in December 1947.) No legal action against Lindemann was possible, and there was relief that the work in the three Western sectors could now proceed unhindered. Berlin was at that time undivided, and Nestriepke has described the split in the Volksbühne committee as a symbol of what was to come. A new committee was formed by co-opting new members to the rump of the old, but because there was no precedent for treating with the three western Occupying Powers as a group, three separate, but virtually identical, Volksbühne associations had to be formed, one for each sector, with arrangements for some kind of co-ordinating committee for practical purposes. Moreover, the name *Volksbühne* having been pre-empted by Lindemann, the Western groups reverted to the original title of 1890, *Freie Volksbühne* (now commonly known by its initials, *FVB*). For financial aid sympathetic newspapers were approached and 25,000 Marks raised.

Paul Eggers, the proposed manager, had gone to work for Lindemann, perhaps not so much from conviction as through his daughter's influence and because he was anxious to work without further delay. He did valuable work for a year and a half in the Eastern-sector Volksbühne but was always suspect to the party, and was later given the job of 'overseeing' the rebuilding of the Volksbühne theatre, but with no power. In his place the FVB appointed Bruno Braunsdorf, a learned printer who had left his business and had been in the English military administration. His assistant, Hubert Geilgens, had ten years' experience in the Berlin Volksbühne. An office (which was used till 1953) was found in Wilmersdorf, and by mid-October over a hundred ticket-agencies were established. State subsidy was essential and Walter May put through the necessary recommendations. At first only seats in municipal theatres were to be subsidised, but shortly afterwards private theatres were included. Although theoretically the city was still undivided, the Western groups of Volksbühne associations were refused the use of municipal theatres in the Soviet Sector. Membership, of course, would be drawn from the whole city. Because the Western municipal theatres were in a strong economic position it was not easy to negotiate for seats in them, while on the other hand not all the private theatres were thought to be artistically adequate. The search for a Volksbühne's own theatre continued – even a transportable aluminium theatre was investigated at Hanover, but found unsuitable.

The opening public meeting was held on 12 October 1947 in the Titania-Palast, Stegiltz, with Carl Zuckmayer as principal speaker. Julius Bab sent a message and the press response was good – though ironical in the East. Five days later Walter May made an unsuccessful attempt to bring East and West together, but Lindemann would not accept Nestriepke's presence and the meeting failed. Meanwhile, *Ordner* were found – many of them veterans of pre-1933 days – a periodical began to appear, several special events took place, and on 15 December 1947 the first 'regular' performance: *Aida* at the Municipal Opera. During that month the Soviet Theatre Officer made an attempt to heal the split in the movement, but once more Nestriepke himself was the stumbling block – the Russians would not accept a joint committee while he remained. The Western group entered 1948 with twenty-two thousand members which grew to thirty-five thousand soon after the first annual general meeting on 23 February at which members sat and voted in three sectoral groups, to satisfy the forms.

Although membership rose to fifty thousand by June, the first season of the new association was a hard one. The monetary reform of June meant that two currencies were circulating in Berlin and all financial questions, especially those of subsidy, had to be discussed in relation to these. On 24 July the USSR stopped road and rail traffic between Berlin and the West and all the hardships of the blockade began. Although tempered by the Berlin airlift this continued until September 1949. The demand for seats rose in the early part of the year and performances were seen in no fewer than ten different theatres, while throughout the summer the Volksbühne was granted the Rehberge open-air theatre rent-free on condition of putting on worthwhile shows. Having failed to create a company of its own the Volksbühne drew upon the theatres with which it already had contacts. Twenty performances of opera and forty of plays were seen by some seventy thousand people though not always heard, as the theatre lies near the Tegel airfield and the constant aircraft noise from the airlift often made the dialogue inaudible. These open-air performances were seen only as a makeshift and a whole series of ideas was mooted for a Volksbühne theatre. Among these was the rebuilding of the Schiller-Theater, which would have needed two and a half million Marks, as well as virtually unobtainable building materials. At one point a 'somewhat shadowy personality' was given 80,000 Marks to bring timber from East Berlin. He thereupon disappeared 'into the forests of the east'. He never brought the wood, though some months later he repaid the money. The Schiller-Theater remained in ruins.

The problems of the second working year (1948–49) were no less. The blockade and airlift continued, with unemployment running at some 350,000. East-West tensions increased with demonstrations outside the City Hall (which was in the East Sector) culminating in a mob attack upon it on

6 September 1948. On 30 November a separate administration for East Berlin was set up, the city was divided and the Iron Curtain came down. The two-currency problem persisted into the spring of 1949. On the other hand the elections in the West, immediately after the city was split, gave the Social Democrats an absolute majority. Walter May continued in charge of education and Ernst Reuter became Chief Bürgermeister. The loss of its East Berlin income was a serious blow to the organisation and had to be compensated for by increased subsidy from the West. The railway strike in the early summer of 1949 also prevented people from going to the theatre and the Freie Volksbühne had to pay for empty, unpaid-for seats. But for the Freie Volksbühne, theatres would often have played to empty houses at this time. Also, despite the Iron Curtain, the Freie Volksbühne was an important link between East and West, for East Berliners came West to its performances (there was no Berlin wall until 1961) and thus Western culture went East. The authorities, thanks to Walter May's sympathy, made several concessions to the Freie Volksbühne. All seats, including those occupied by East Berliners, were to be subsidised in West Marks and the 'closed' performances were to be ended, thus relieving the Freie Volksbühne of the necessity of filling every seat.

During this season the continued search for a theatre of the Freie Volksbühne's own met at last with success, and in January 1949 an agreement was signed to take over the Theater am Kurfürstendamm on 1 September in the same year.

The Volksbühne in the Soviet Zone and in the German Democratic Republic

The original Volksbühne theatre lay in East Berlin on the Bülowplatz, re-christened the Karl-Liebknecht-Platz, now the Luxemburgplatz. Early in 1947 the licensees attempted to rebuild it with voluntary Sunday labour, helped by a lottery – but neither the labour nor the lottery materialised. Nor was there much help from the Russians. But the clearing of the site began in April and May. The architect Friedrich Demmer undertook plans: the third circle was to be done away with, there was to be a new style of forestage, and two side stages. But the scheme would have cost millions and months went by without anything being done. In 1948 the Russian command cut through the problem: the city was to provide the money and labour, and report progress monthly. Ironically, in 1949, the Berlin Commission for Claims on Property declared the Freie Volksbühne to be the legal inheritor of the building, though this was only theoretical. Legally this view was confirmed in 1954, the year in which the theatre reopened.

The restored building still had shortcomings in its sightlines and acoustics, and was too large. In 1972 it was closed for half a year for major alterations.

These included the removal of the first circle. The stalls were then given a much steeper rake, thus bringing the theatre rather nearer to the amphitheatre style that some had favoured even when it was being designed before 1914. Although the 'cold magnificence' of the decor was not entirely done away with, the auditorium now gave an impression of being smaller and sight lines and acoustics were improved. Externally, the Volksbühne on the Luxemburgplatz now looks simpler and plainer than it did when built. Apart from the erasure of the motto, *Die Kunst dem Volke*, the statuary over the entrances has gone, while the flat roofs of the wings of the facade give the building a feeling of great width at the expense of height.

In mid-May 1947 a congress of East Zone Volksbühne associations led to the founding of a Federation of German Volksbühnen. Invitations were in fact sent to the re-founded Western associations, but no delegates went. Several 'Western' people were co-opted to the Praesidium, but all the speeches were given by Communists. Karl-Heinz Martin was elected chairman.

Within a day or two of Lindemann and Litten's announcement (19 August 1947) that they were founding a Volksbühne in the Soviet Sector only, they issued a hastily written appeal for members, with over 140 signatures. A week later the FDGB decided to encourage membership of this Soviet Sector Volksbühne, while the SPD specifically warned its members not to join, but to wait for the Western Volksbühne. A plan already conceived by Lindemann for taking over the Colosseum theatre fell through and seats had to be taken in the municipal theatres. An opening meeting was held in the Deutsches Theater on 21 September with Wolfgang Langhoff (theatre intendant), Herbert Ihering and Paul Eggers as speakers. Walter May represented the city. By November preparations could be made for performances. In March the Volksbühne presented the first of its own productions (*Der Zimmerherr* (*The Gentleman Lodger*) by Hermann Mostar) in the Oberschöneweide Accumulator Works, but by July it was settled for the season in the Prater Theater in the Kastanienallee where Karl-Heinz Martin had run his so-called Volksbühne from May 1946 to August 1947. In September 1950 the company moved to the Theater am Schiffbauerdamm where it remained until 1954, when the old Volksbühne theatre was reopened and Brecht's Berliner Ensemble took over the Schiffbauerdamm theatre - though by this time the Volksbühne as an audience organisation had ceased to exist in the Soviet Zone.

In the two years following the founding of the East German Federation of Volksbühnen in 1947 the growth in membership in East Germany as a whole was enormous, and in August 1949 the executive of the Federation, supported by the SED, reorganised itself as a central, combined German Volksbühne. The East Berlin Volksbühne, by far the strongest in East

Germany, still retained some independence until the following year. In November 1949 the SED issued guide-lines which were endorsed by the Federation in January 1950. These made the Volksbühne in future especially responsible for 'the political, cultural and intellectual care of the working-class theatre public'. But it was not – in East German opinion – in a position to fulfil these new demands, because in effect it was too independent. So in 1953, apparently at the instigation of the cultural conference of the FDGB, a delegate conference of the German Volksbühne decided to bring the whole movement to an end in East Germany. This was done, and at the end of the 1952/53 season the East German Volksbühne ceased to exist. Its work was in some sense continued by factory groups and collectives, and its name persisted as the name of the Theatre on the Bülowplatz – Volksbühne.

Although the Theatre on the Luxemburgplatz was no longer associated with a Volksbühne Organisation it retained its name and with the name something of its traditions. Significant is the play chosen as the opening production, 21 April 1954, Schiller's *William Tell*. It was directed by Fritz Wisten. A few weeks earlier Wisten had been mentioned, together with two other directors, by Walter Ulbricht, as having achieved 'socialist realism': "German art in the GDR has overcome decadence and formalism devoid of ideas" ('ideenlose Formspielerei') (IV. Parteitag der SED zum Theater). But Wisten was no mere party hack, and during the comparative freedom of the immediate post-war period, 1945-1949, he had developed a character-istic personal style.

By the time the Volksbühne Theatre reopened, the second 'official' period of GDR history, from the founding of the State (7.10.49) to the building of the Berlin Wall (August 1961) had run nearly halfway through its course, and artistic freedom was already far more limited.

In 1959 the Cultural Section of SED (Communist Party) at the so-called 'Bitterfeld Conference', mounted what was in effect an attack on the whole movement, primarily of younger dramatists and directors who, since 1955/6 and largely inspired by Brecht and the avantgarde theatre of the twenties, had worked towards an alternative theatre, socialist, indeed, but concerned to bring out, without idealisation, the inner conflicts and contradictions of the socialist state.

Though couched in terms of taking 'theatre to the people' by theatre-artists actually going into factories and work-places in order to experience for themselves the humanisation of the new, socialist persons, the Party's demands actually constituted an attack on some of the brightest and most original dramatists and directors of the time. There was nothing new in the idea of going into factories, performing in factories and conducting discussions with the workers. Brecht's Berliner Ensemble had done it, and Heiner and Inge Müller, without any prompting from the authorities, had taken their plays to the 'Brown Coal' workers, but the apparently positive initiative was in fact an assault on individual authors. Heinar Kipphardt was especially attacked. He was alleged to have a false conception of artistic quality and to have turned Materialism and Dialectic into mere empty bourgeois clichés. Authors were accused of seeking out contradictions for their own sake, rather than trying to resolve them.

The building of the Berlin Wall in August 1961 had profound effects upon the arts and upon theatre in particular. Some artists moved west, one of the most distinguished being the Director Peter Palitzsch. Others welcomed the change, embraced the opportunity to appeal only to the GDR audience without reference to the west, and welcomed the freedom from 'damaging effects' which the open frontier had brought and the greater peace in which theatre people could now work. Later, in 1990, H. Bentzien wrote in *Theater der Zeit*:

> The determining factor in the time after the building of the Wall was that artists believed that they now had, without interference from the West, the chance to show what can be made out of this country. That was generally agreed.

These hopes were soon shattered. Within weeks, for example, Heiner Müller's *Die Umsiedlerin* was banned, its author turned out of the Writers' Union and 32 other people punished in various ways.

In April 1964, at the Second Bitterfeld Conference, Walter Ulbricht declared that the Party must lead and steer all processes: there was no autonomy for art. To achieve this required strict leadership and control to be built up. In this increasingly oppressive climate the Volksbühne as a theatre pursued what can only be described as an adventurous policy. In 1965 it put on plays by Kurt Bartel (*Terra Incognita*) and Peter Hacks (*Moritz Tassow*), the latter directed by Benno Besson. Attacks on these, and on Müller's *Der Bau*, soon followed. They were accused of being part of an organised tendency to scepticism. Besson sturdily defended the qualities of theatre in the GDR and the growing reputation of that theatre abroad. But the Volksbühne was soon in trouble again. 'Unsound political attitudes' found among its personnel were traced back to the leadership. Müller was told to re-work the text of *Der Bau*. Meanwhile the Volksbühne's programme included Max Frisch's *Andorra*, and one of Dario Fo's plays. Then in August 1969 Benno Besson was appointed Artistic Director.He brought a reputation going back to 1950, both as an adapter of classics and as a Director. His productions had included Molière's *Don Juan*, Farquhar's *Drums and Trumpets*, the premières of Brecht's *The Good Person of Sezuan*, *Mann ist Mann*, and *St Joan of the Stockyards*, the world première of Peter Hacks' version of Aristophanes' *Peace*, Shakespeare's *Two Gentlemen of Verona*, & Peter Hacks'

Moritz Tassow (at the Volksbühne). As co-directors he had Manfred Karge, Matthias Langhoff and Fritz Marquardt. It was the beginning of a fruitful and important epoch in Volksbühne history.

Besson's opening production at the Volksbühne (29.9.'69) was Gerhard Winterlich's *Horizonte* (*Horizons*) arranged by Heiner Müller. He had already co-operated in a production of this play at the Schwedt Oil-processing-plant in June of the previous year as part of the Tenth 'Arbeiterfestspielen', but with the intention of adapting it for the professional theatre in celebration of the 20th Anniversary of the GDR in 1969. In the Volksbühne production he was primarily interested in parallels between this play and *A Midsummer Night's Dream* – problems of identity, its loss, recovery, confusion and disguise. At the same time he saw in its structure a concept in the field of cybernetics which enabled him to fulfil official demands to use the theme of 'Scientific-technical revolution'.

Three months later (12.12.'69) Ostrovsky's *The Forest* opened under the direction of Karge and Langhoff. The play rivals *The Storm* to be considered Ostrovsky's masterpiece. This production emphasised the theme of the relationship between artist and society and showed the insecurity and ultimate fossilisation of the latter. The joint directors acknowledged a profound debt to Meyerhold's experiments in the twenties, saying that their production would have been unthinkable without his pioneering work. This was the first time that a relationship with Meyerhold had been acknowledged in a GDR production.

In December 1970 Besson directed Molière's *Le Médecin malgré lui* in a strongly musical production, clearly intended primarily as entertainment, and in February 1971 Karge and Langhoff directed Schiller's *Die Räuber* in a highly controversial production aimed at a young audience. During the run the directors conducted discussions in senior schools. The *Räuber* controversy rumbled on in the pages of *Theater der Zeit* into March 1972.

During 1971 the Volksbühne endeavoured to establish an 'artificial theatrical language' between stage and audience. This was done with the help of masks, historical archetypes, and clowning (in Heiner & Inge Müller's *Weiberkomödie*) and by drawing on the tradition of the *Commedia dell-arte* in Besson's production of Carlo Gozzi's *King Stag*. Carlo Gozzi (1720–1806) is chiefly remembered for his opposition to Goldoni's reforms and for his attempt to revive the *Commedia dell-arte*. Besson aimed in this production to revive that old dispute and make a contemporary contribution to it, thus at the same time trying to establish for the Volksbühne a theatrical language distinguished by strong conventionalisation.

In October a Karge/Langhoff production of *Othello* had Othello (Rolf Ludwig) in a black leather mask 'like a grotesque exotic bird' among the Senators 'wrapped in severe black cloaks'. Katharina Thalbach played

Desdemona with a piping voice 'as a spoiled child of aristocracy'. The production 'did not show the story of a great love, but the destruction of a man who, through jealousy dragged his nearest to death with him.' (Quotations from *Theater Heute* Dec. 1972).

In May 1973 Besson introduced a wholly original idea into the Volksbühne Theatre. He called it SPEKTAKEL. On entering the foyer-space you found yourself watching an introductory piece lasting about twenty minutes and adapted from an old French farce, such as *The Fart* or *The Flying Doctor*. You then had a choice of three plays: André Müller's *The Last Paradise*, performed on the main stage, but behind the safety curtain; Emil Rosenow's *Kater Lampe*, performed in the auditorium in front of the safety curtain; or Arne Leonhardt's contemporary play *Der Abiturmann*, performed in the Middle Foyer of the Dress Circle. These all ran for ten consecutive nights although such *en-suite* performances were unheard-of in Germany outside the commercial *boulevarde* theatre. The "Spektakel" was immensely popular, though Manfred Nössig, Principal Editor of *Theater der Zeit*, questioned whether it bore any real relationship to the need to raise the quality of the art of the socialist theatre. Although described by Christoph Hein, who was involved as an author, as a BOCKWURSTFEST (A Sausage Festival), that did not worry him. It was, he said, something completely NEW. Besson himself explained that this was not 'theatre' but 'really a friendly invitation', devised as prelude to a further, very demanding programme, consisting of three classics from three European countries, excluding Germany: Shakespeare's *As You Like it*; Racine's *Britannicus*; and Gozzi's *The Beautiful Little Green Bird*. This 'European Wedding' was the most demanding, though not the most successful, of the Volksbühne's projects.

So successful was the concept that a second Spektakel was presented in September 1974, this time offering a choice of twelve plays, eight of which were world-premières, one a first production in the GDR, one a collage from works by GDR dramatists, and one an ancient love-story. It was seen as a splendid demonstration of East German dramatic writing and theatre.

The idea was taken up again in March 1976 by the Schwerin Theatre under the title *Entdeckungen* (Discoveries). The programme, again played, as at the Volksbühne, in various parts of the theatre, included, *inter alia*, a Ballet, a play by a working-class woman, and an Athol Fugard.

Productions at the Volksbühne during these three years included an important production of *The Wild Duck* (Dir. Karge & Langhoff) and the world première of Heiner Müller's *Die Schlacht* (by the same two directors). In February 1976 Besson and Langhoff spent twelve days with blue- and white-collar workers at the Nationalised Firm SECURA, working on Brecht's *The Exception and the Rule*. It was a noteworthy operation by any standards. Workers came from several firms, including electric light bulb manufacturers, and escalator and lift manufacturers. Sixty workers were given a fortnight's leave to take part in the seminar.

In May Fritz Marquardt directed Heiner Müller's *Die Umsiedlerin oder Das Leben auf dem Lande,* under the title *Die Bauern.* The play had been published the previous year and was the first of Müller's plays to be published in the GDR.

It must be understood that the *Schauspiel* department of the publishers Henschel enjoyed a monopoly in play-publication. As there was no alternative to Henschel's, authors of plays they rejected had to send their scripts to the theatres directly. The theatre would then enquire from Henschel why the play had been turned town, and if the grounds were political, obviously the play was not produced. Two attempts were made to set up an independent publishing house for plays, one in 1975, which failed, and one at the end of 1988, not very long before German re-unification, when authors and theatres were venturing to rebel and to produce plays published by the independent house, the *Kollegium* as it was called.

Despite all restrictions there had been something of a thaw in relationships between artists and the state especially in the atmosphere of a new cultural policy that seemed to be promised when Honecker succeeded to power on the death of Ulbricht. The hopes that had been aroused were shattered in November 1976 when the writer and performer Wolf Biermann was deprived of his citizenship.

Wolf Biermann was born in November 1936 in Hamburg into a deeply committed Communist family. He was the only son of Emma and Dagobert Biermann. His mother was evidently a woman of character, who rescued her 6½ year old son from the great air-raids on Hamburg in the summer of 1943. His father, arrested earlier as a Communist, died that year as a Jew in Auschwitz. After the war Wolf joined the Young Pioneers, and in 1953, as an idealistic sixteen-year-old, he moved into the GDR, and two years later began to read Political Economy at the Berlin Humboldt University. From 1957-59 he worked as an Assistant in Brecht's Berliner Ensemble, but then, and until 1963, resumed his studies, this time in Philosophy and Mathematics. In 1960 he began to write and compose, and even attempted to set up a Student and Workers' Theatre, which, however, was closed even before it opened. In 1962 he gave his first public performance, but in June 1963 was banned from performing. However, in 1964 he was performing in an East Berlin Cabaret, *Die Distel,* and even toured in the Federal Republic. His contact with Hanns Eisler had led him virtually to create his own profession, that of *Liedermacher,* that is, a poet-composer who performs his own works. The principal influences upon him as a poet were Brecht and Heine. His songs, widely enjoyed through his own performances of them, were sometimes openly critical of what was still his chosen homeland. The tension can be felt in his poem *Berlin*:

Ich kann nicht weg mehr von dir gehn
Im Westen steht die Mauer
Im Osten meine Freunde stehn
Der Nordwind ist ein rauher.

(*Die Drahtharfe*.1967.p.50)

More than once he was forbidden to perform or publish, but in 1976 he was permitted to embark upon a concert tour in the Federal Republic, organised by IG Metall. He later came to regard this as a trick, for after a concert in Cologne (13.11.1976) he was expatriated and deprived of his citizenship of the GDR.

The expatriation of Biermann aroused a storm of protest and was in fact a watershed in the history of the relations of the State and the Arts in the GDR. About a hundred authors, theatre people and other artists, including Heiner Müller and Volker Braun supported the protest, which primarily expressed itself in an open letter: this, however, was published only in western media. Immediately afterwards Thomas Brasch, who had already suffered a prison sentence on account of his protest against the invasion of Czechoslovakia by Warsaw Pact countries in 1968, and Katherina Thalbach, who had played important roles in the Berliner Ensemble and at the Volksbühne, were forced to leave the country, while many of those who remained adopted an increasingly critical attitude to the official line. The 'thaw' was ended before it had properly begun.

In 1977 Benno Besson the Intendant, and two fellow-directors, Manfred Karge and Matthias Langhoff left the Volksbühne and in the spring of 1978 Benno was succeeded as intendant by Fritz Rödel, who had been chief Dramaturg at the Maxim Gorki theatre.

That the Volksbühne evidently retained something of a special relationship with the dramatist Heiner Müller through the period that followed is one of the clearest indications of an independent stance by the theatre. In September 1980 his play *Der Bau,* which had aroused such controversy in 1965, was at last produced by Fritz Marquardt at the Volksbühne. There had been two pre-view performances in June, after which Marquardt took part in a discussion with two students of *Theaterwissenschaft* at the Berlin Humboldt-University. They raised the question, among others, of the value of producing, so long after it was written, a play that aimed at political immediacy. What in it was originally intended to be tragic could easily become merely comic.

Nevertheless, in November, only two months later, Müller himself, in co-operation with Ginka Tscholakowa, directed another of his own plays, *Der Auftrag. Erinnerungen an eine Revolution,* at the Volksbühne, and in the following year the Volksbühne arranged colloquia on the work of Müller and in this connection presented the whole of this theatre's Müller repertoire.

One of the ways in which dramatists during the seventies and eighties contrived to make contemporary political statements or ask awkward contemporary political questions without incurring the wrath of the authorities was through adaptations or carefully slanted productions of Classical plays - the ancient Greeks – or of Germany's own national literature. This policy was described in 1991 by the Director Wolfgang Engel:

> The citizens of the GDR had learnt how to live together with two languages, or rather to speak in one language and to think in another. You could describe that in a negative sense as the language of slaves, which it plainly was. In this manner an understanding could be created among like-minded people, which did not rub people up the wrong way. To uncover the power-structures of the GDR through an old play, or to describe using that device, the damage to the individual caused by those power-structures, was a distinguished task of the theatre right up to the end of the GDR: in this way the theatre created kind of mirror-image.

(W. Engel: *Eine Art von indirektem Spiegel.1991*)

In September 1982 Müller and Tschokalowa directed *Macbeth* at the Volksbühne: Shakespeare is seen as part of Germany's 'national' repertoire. The production was badly reviewed in *Neues Deutschland* and *Junge Welt*. It was attacked for 'fatalism','dissonance',and as a 'celebration of a Black Mass'; it was 'unshakespearean'; at best it was an attempt to present the world as pluralistic, a waxwork variety of irreconcilable existences. It was singled out in October for harsh criticism at a cultural conference of the *Freie Deutsche Jugend*. Hartmut König, Cultural Secretary of the Central Council of the FDJ, having declared that not everything 'modern' or 'avantgarde' can be regarded as belonging to the socialist world of ideas, went on to attack Müller's *Macbeth* ('that embarrassing effort at the Volksbühne') by quoting the *Neues Deutschland* review. He declared that in this production, not only historical perpective but even belief in humanity was lost.

The production was not taken off, however, and the attacks gave it publicity leading to a big increase in audiences. On the other hand the Volksbühne did not make any new productions of texts by Müller until 1987 when the theatre put on a *Berlin-Spektakel* to celebrate the 750th anniversary of the foundation of the city, when his *Preußische Spiele* and scenes from *Leben Gundlings* were put on.

In the previous year(1986) Müller had been honoured by the State: he was awarded the National Prize of the GDR. But it seems likely that this award was 'tactical', a move in the direction of 'if you can't beat 'em, join 'em'. Müller, bridled to some degree by the award, was less dangerous, even with his crowd of admirers and imitators, than a young anarchic firebrand who was now making his presence felt: Frank Castorf, later, much later, to become Intendant of the Volksbühne.

Castorf came into prominence in the early eighties as Principal Director in Anklam and as a Director in Karl-Marx-Stadt (Chemnitz) and Halle. In Anklam, July 1983, his was the third production in the GDR of Heiner Müller's *Der Auftrag*. The Communist Party (SED) tolerated Castorf's early experiments. In these he aimed to release the emotional content of classical pieces and communicate it to the present day through association. This "Attack on the emotions of the audience, stamped as they were by convention" (Castorf 1989) was of an entirely different character from the fundamentally affirmative productions thought out by intellectuals like Heiner Müller and Volker Braun.

Castorf's theatrical work during the eighties was not simply a form of political opposition because he expressed through allusion what was otherwise censored and treated as taboo. The political explosiveness of his productions lay in his conveying a feeling of really being alive, which had died out in the GDR. His anarchic and complex productions united protest with pleasure.

Some of his productions during this period were at the Volksbühne, notably Paul Zech's 'Rimbaud' play *Das trunkene Schiff*, which Piscator had produced there in 1926.

Soon after *die Wende*, he was appointed Intendant of the Volksbühne Theatre.

The Theater am Kurfürstendamm

Meanwhile in West Berlin in 1949 a special limited liability company was formed to run the Theater am Kurfürstendamm, so that the Berlin Freie Volksbühne's finances as a whole should not be put at risk. This theatre had been constructed in 1923 by adapting the Exhibition Hall of Berlin Independent Secession, the architect responsible being Oskar Kaufmann. This rather overdecorated theatre was burnt out towards the end of the Second World War and rebuilt in the autumn of 1947 with a very insignificant exterior, but an interior at once dignified and comfortable, though with only 736 seats. Nestriepke became Intendant and, after a number of more distinguished men had declined the post, the artistic direction was entrusted to Rudolf Hammacher, who had made a name for himself under Hilpert at the Deutsches Theater.

Aiming at ensemble rather than star acting, Hammacher engaged his whole company of twenty for a year. But he overestimated their abilities and it became necessary, as far as the limited finances permitted, to engage guest artists to play leads. It was obviously rash to open with *Hamlet*. The company was not equal to it and Vasa Hochmann's Slavonic accent did not help the title-role. The critics did not like the production, though the public did. The season that followed was mixed, the most disastrous failure being a play favoured by Nestriepke because of its side-swipes at East European dictatorships.[8] Two of the most successful were directed by Ernst Karchow, who was appointed artistic director for the following season.

Karchow, described as 'noble, distinguished, modest and extremely cultivated', had been for years an actor of high repute in the Bülowplatz theatre before 1933. Since then he had worked as deputy to Reinhardt in Vienna, and after that at the Bremen Kammerspiel. He was a man who knew his own mind, and disagreements over the choice of the very first play provided an opportunity for the independence of the artistic director and the status of the advisory committee to be settled. From September 1950 until the end of the 1952–53 season Karchow not only made some noteworthy productions himself (especially Hauptmnann's *Fuhrmann Henschel* (*Drayman Henschel*) with Walter Bechmann and Maria Becker) and acted in others very successfully, but also brought in some very distinguished guest directors, above all, Oscar Fritz Schuh, who, although he already had an international reputation, had not before directed in Berlin. Karchow changed Hammacher's 'ensemble' policy. He engaged about six actors on long contracts and the rest for single shows. This enabled him to get better leading actors more economically, though the Freie Volksbühne executive had doubts, and the actors' trade union protested. His one-year contract was extended, but in February 1952 he had a stroke while directing Zuckmayer's version of Hauptmann's *Herbert Engelmann*. Otto Kurth of Hamburg took over the production which earned forty-two curtain calls on its first night. Another unfortunate incident during this season was the letting of the theatre to the city for a visit of Werner Krauss with Ibsen's *John Gabriel Borkman*. Krauss had played *Jew Süss* and though he had publicly repented of his Nazi associations the visit gave rise to demonstrations and even to fighting in the auditorium, which ended when the stage-hands came in front of the curtain, took the law into their own hands and ejected the trouble-makers.

Karchow continued as director in the next season, but by November (1952) it was plain that ill health would force him to retire soon and that a successor must be sought. Nestriepke approached Oscar Fritz Schuh and before long had contracted him for two years from October 1953. Karchow retired at the end of the 1952-53 season and was dead by October.

Schuh's five seasons at the Kurfürstendamm were brilliant. Born in Munich in 1904, Schuh gained a reputation in the 1930s as director of the Hamburg State Opera. In 1940 he moved to the Vienna Opera whose tours gave him a foreign reputation. After 1945 he recreated the Salzburg Festival. His guest production of Pirandello's *Six Characters* for the Freie Volksbühne in October 1951 was a major theatrical event. He had plenty of opportunity in Berlin to express his ideas – about which he was very articulate. He did not wish the Kurfürstendamm theatre to be merely an 'all-round' theatre, but to have a special artistic character of its own, serving quality and intellectual progress. Not fearing experiment, he did not wish to be 'avant-garde at any price': nor did he take progress for granted. While regarding a good ensemble as a necessary basis, he did not want contracts to go on for ever. In direction he called for clearsightedness, cutting through emotional factors and showing the reality of the dramatic creation and making its intellectual background clear. 'The work of art should not pester and importune the listener, but persuade and convince.' He was able to put many of his ideas into practice, and though he could not have a complete ensemble he drew on a regular pool of actors, eliminating those who did not fit in and inviting over again those who did. He was wholly devoted to his work. What he continued to do in Vienna and Salzburg took second place, but cast reflected glory on the Freie Volksbühne. Unlike many great directors, he kept economic realities in mind and though he might explode when asked to retrench, he invariably did so. After two years his status was raised so that he and Nestriepke were equal directors. Among the productions he directed, Chekhov's *The Seagull*, Strindberg's *A Dream Play* and O'Neill's *A Touch of the Poet* were outstanding. The company visited Wiesbaden twice, Recklinghausen and London once, and undertook two tours of West Germany.

When his contract was renewed for the 1955-56 season Schuh stipulated that a second theatre should be made available to him in the foreseeable future, as he was not fully extending his talents in the one small theatre. The Freie Volksbühne itself, with a waiting list of many thousands for membership, could also have welcomed a second theatre – if subsidy were available. Nestriepke tried in vain to rent a second theatre; he then got plans for a new theatre of seven hundred seats, and finally in 1958 drew up a scheme for a large new theatre which would entirely replace that on the Kurfürstendamm and be economic to run. Such a scheme was likely to obtain credit and to materialise, but Schuh felt unable to wait longer – he was in his mid-fifties – and accepted the post of Intendant for the municipal theatres at Cologne. He departed on good terms with the Freie Volksbühne, but his going was a terrible loss.

At this time too, Nestriepke, now well over seventy, decided he must give up his post as director. His place was taken by Hermann Ludwig. Originally an actor, he had ten years' experience with the Volksbühne and experience as an Intendant. In Schuh's place came Leonard Steckel, an actor and director of great experience who had had his first job under Nestriepke at the Neues Volkstheater. He had, however, never had charge of a theatre.

Nor was his temperament compatible with that of Ludwig, and he remained only a year.

His successor, Rudolf Noelte, also failed to co-operate with Ludwig, who resigned for the sake of the theatre, to be succeeded by Walter Papproth, for many years deputy Intendant and administrative director of the Municipal Opera. But Noelte could not work with him either, resigned, then withdrew his resignation. But the leadership of the Volksbühne decided that they could not sacrifice yet another experienced administrator to this less experienced man, and sacked him. Very unpleasant conflict followed, culminating in legal action, which brought a great deal of unwelcome public interest in its train. Learning from this bitter experience, the Volksühne abandoned the 'two-headed' leadership of the theatre and appointed one man as director, Günter Skopnik, who had held a high position in the Frankfurt theatres. He remained for two years, when he left for a better-paid post in Kassel. By then the opening of a new Freie Volksbühne theatre was less than a year away.

Opposition and Difficulties

Throughout this period the greater part of the West Berlin press was extraordinarily hostile to the Freie Volksbühne, and especially to its theatre. The company was referred to as 'democratically licensed barnstormers'. Friedrich Luft, implacable enemy of the Volksbühne, said that the Kurfürstendamm theatre 'had done the reputation of Berlin gross injury with improper assistance from the taxpayer'. Of course the East Berlin press was consistently hostile.

Any excuse seemed to serve to attack the Volksbühne. In February 1952 Frank Lothar directed at the Tribüne the world première of a play by Tettenborn, *Perspektiven* (*Perspectives*), whose subject was the persecution of the Church in an unidentified Communist State. The production clearly identified the State as East Germany. The Freie Volksbühne executive thought it misrepresented East Germany and feared for its East Berlin members if they were seen by spies at the play. It was therefore not included in the 'obligatory' list, but optional tickets were made available, and the play offered as an alternative. This action was seen by the press as prejudice against young writers and against Christianity.

In 1950 there came an extraordinary attack on the Volksbühne in the form of a footnote to the city's subsidy recommendation for the next season. This footnote derived from a document which the Allied Kommandatura had sent to the city authorities on 4 April 1950. It (i) expressed the concern of the Allies for the development of the cultural life of Berlin; (ii) proposed a special committee of all interested circles, on the cultural situation; and

(iii) made a series of specific proposals, one of which was: 'to close down the uneconomic Theater am Kurfürstendamm as one of the undertakings controlled by the Freie Volksühne and to limit the activity of the Freie Volksbühne to supporting other theatres by providing them with audience (that is, to become a mere ticket-agency). The Theater am Kurfürstendamm would then be turned into a concert hall. Apart from its lack of factual knowledge, the impertinence of this brought angry responses even from newspapers normally opposed to the Freie Volksbühne:

> The Allied Command informed the city authorities by letter that they were very concerned for the development of culture in Berlin. That is charming of the Berlin Allied Command. We don't know whether the letter began, 'Hello, Boys, make a bit more Culture!' It's possible we're a clumsy people politically and are open to good teaching in this area. But they had better leave concern over our cultural development to us'. [9]

The Freie Volksbühne executive also reacted strongly, pointing out that its theatre was more soundly based financially than any other in Berlin.

A public meeting with a thousand present was held at the end of April at which support for the FVB and its theatre was evident, and the cultural committees of both main parties (SPD and Christian Democratic Union) favoured the FVB Theatre. Consequently the city parliament unanimously threw out the footnote (20 June 1950). Even so it was not until after October 1950 that the threat of subsidy-withdrawal was finally removed – and all this happened at the time when Schuh had already firmly established the theatre's artistic standard and reputation'.

The FVB was not without internal difficulties. During the 1952-53 season the association had to leave its rented offices, and after using an unsatisfactory alternative decided to build its own. The new building was completed by December 1954 at a cost of 230,000 DM, without grant aid or mortgage.

During the seasons 1952-53, 1953-54 constitutional disputes led to a general meeting on 26 May 1954 at which the executive committee resigned in a body – only to be asked to continue in charge until another general meeting could be held. The crisis concerned the relationship between the executive and the administrative council. A solution was worked out and a new arrangement was accepted in November 1954.

The last serious blow to the FVB during the period of the Theater am Kurfürstendamm was the closing of the Brandenburg Gate and the sealing off of the border between East and West Berlin on 13 August 1961, followed by the building of the Berlin wall a few days later. The last cultural links between East and West were broken. The twenty-five thousand East Berlin members of the FVB were immediately out off, as were the equal number who came from East Berlin as ordinary box-office theatre audience. At the time no one could believe that the closure could last long, and on 15 August (that is, *before* the wall was built) the FVB executive broadcast a message on the West Berlin radio to the East Berlin members urging them to be faithful to the FVB and not to be shaken in their relationship with the cultural life of the West. The East Berlin members were promised that their membership rights could be taken up again as soon as the 'infamous closure' was ended.

The New Theatre and the Return of Piscator

When Oscar Fritz Schuh pressed for a second theatre, Nestriepke not only approached the architect Fritz Bornemann to draw up plans for a new seven hundred-seat theatre, but also opened a building fund. It soon became clear that this second small theatre would be uneconomic both to build and to run, so the aim was changed to that of building a single new theatre with 1,000 to 1,200 seats – the Theater am Kurfürstendamm to be given up. Bornemann estimated the cost of this at nine million DM. The scheme was approved by the city planning authorities, a credit of four and a half million DM was obtained from Bonn, the Berlin Senate and House of Representatives agreed to a bank credit of three million DM, help was given by friendly organisations, especially trade unions and the West German Volksbühnen, money was made available from the Berlin lottery, and, of course, the members themselves helped by contributing to the loan fund. Despite the inevitable delays, the scheme moved forward. A fine open site in the city centre was bought for 788,000 DM and the foundation stone laid on 6 October 1960. From this moment progress was steady and rapid. The topping-out ceremony took place on 15 December 1962 and the theatre was opened according to schedule on 1 May 1963. Bornemann had almost kept within his estimate of nine million DM, and even with the cost of the site and of financing the project the total cost was little over ten million DM.

The theatre, as conceived by Bornemann, is an integral part of the park-like open space on which it stands. The foyers and box-office hall are fully glazed so that except in the actual auditorium one is conscious of being in close relationship with external nature – for the surroundings of the theatre are fully planted and rich in trees. The spacious uncluttered auditorium seats 1047 and the stage is wide, deep and fully equipped – though the architect was also fully aware of the danger that modern technology can as easily come between the play and its audience as help to project it. The theatre, which houses excellent workshops and wardrobes, occupies only a small fraction of its triangular site, the rest of which is taken up partly by car parks – some on two levels – and partly by parkland. Though he gave careful consideration to the claims of an open-space theatre, Bornemann eventually designed a traditional, but flexible theatre, with proscenium stage

21 metres broad and 20 metres deep, with a 15 metre revolve, and side- and rear-stages with wagons.

Such a theatre called for an artistic director worthy of it. In October 1961 Erwin Piscator directed Arthur Miller's *Death of a Salesman* at the Theater am Kurfürstendamm, and when Günter Skopnik moved to Kassel in 1962, Piscator succeeded him. In 1932 Piscator had gone to the USSR to make films, in 1936 he was in Paris and from 1938 to 1951 in New York where he founded the Dramatic Workshop. Since 1952 he had directed many productions in Germany, including some in West Berlin. His return to the Volksbühne, especially at this time, ready to direct the still unfinished new theatre, was an event of special significance.

> ... for Siegfried Nestriepke's friends it was an unforgettable experience, how these two self-assertive men, who in the twenties had disagreed vehemently over ends and means in the Volksbühne, met again for new work in common. [10]

Some say that when he returned to the FVB, Piscator was still trying to fight battles of the twenties over again. Indeed, he had little sympathy with much that was typical of European theatre in the late fifties and early sixties: 'What is called avant-gardism today is bourgeois decadence. It is Waiting for Godot, it is the so-called Nothing, Emptiness, *Angst.*' [11] But in what was lasting in his outlook, his belief in 'understanding, humanism, humanity, greatness of thought', [12] he still had much to offer.

> This man, who is committed to the eternal rights of man, was always a moralist, a zealot, as Savonarola was, for the theatre to him is not aesthetic self-indulgence, but a tribunal of the times. [13]

What is perhaps the fairest assessment of his post-war contribution to the Volksbühne was made by Dr Günter Schulz on 24 June 1966, less than three months after Piscator's death. Piscator should have been the principal speaker at the twenty-second Volksbühnen conference at Dortmund with the subject 'Zeittheater – Theater unserer Zeit' (a neat title that may be less neatly translated as 'Theatre of contemporary problems – the theatre of our time'). In his place Dr Schulz (assistant general secretary of the Federation of Volksbühne Associations) spoke on the same subject. After describing Piscator's idea of Zeittheater about 1930, when he called for a 'teaching theatre' and 'the education of the audience even against its will', Schulz added,

> We know, that Piscator too gave up this standpoint later. [14]
> When Piscator came home from exile he had experienced, if only from a distance, the second world war, the even more extensive extermination of people, the effect of atomic horror. He came back not as an altered man but rather as a man transformed, whom things

as they had been no longer satisfied and could no longer satisfy. He had outgrown the ideological propaganda-theatre, the theatre of party-political outlook. He himself defined the position he had reached, thus:

'For me the Political is nothing other than it was for Aristotle, who defined man as a political animal, that is to say, a creature that is capable of community, in need of community and able to create community, and that lives in a *Polis*, that is, in a place in which communal functions and interests are ordered on a communal basis. Political art, political theatre, is in this sense an art, a theatre art that chooses as its subject what pertains to the community, or to use a modern word, to society, that demands social attitudes and calls forth social reactions.'

In the face of humanity threatened in its existence by the means of mass destruction, an ideology for changing this situation no longer sufficed for Piscator. So, from the theatre of political *Weltanschauung* he arrived at a theatre which he still called 'political', but which I, to avoid error, with a distinction that is perhaps rather pretentious but justified by the broadening of the material, may call 'human-political' [*Menschheitspolitisches*] theatre. This theatre, too, is with him consistently not an exclusively teaching theatre, even though, now as before, it naturally aims at teaching and changing ... 'Perhaps we don't want a teaching-theatre, but we certainly want a seeking-theatre ...' [15]

The first three productions of the 1962–63 season were the last in the Theater am Kurfürstendamm: all were directed by Piscator, who, by a happy coincidence was immediately called upon to present a representative work of Gerhart Hauptmann for the celebration of the centenary of his birth. He chose the *Atrides Tetralogy*. The name of the author of *Die Weber* evoked memories of the *Blütezeit* of the Volksbühne in the 1890s, while Piscator's production reaffirmed both his independence as a director and his concerned preoccupation with contemporary problems. Regarding Hauptmann's work as a fundamental criticism of the situation in the Third Reich, but with contemporary allusions disguised as mythical material, Piscator accentuated what had relevance to Nazi Germany and added statistics, recorded speeches and film to underscore what he claimed to be the author's original intention. The production was better received internationally than by the Berlin press.

His second production was of a recent play, Anouilh's *La Grotte* (1961); but it was his third – the last to open in the rented theatre – which made theatrical history. *Der Stellvertreter* (The Representative) of Rolf Hochhuth. Luft characteristically remarks that Piscator had the good fortune to get into his hands, in Rolf Hochhuth's provocative play about the Papacy, *Der Stellvertreter*, a politically explosive drama with which to demonstrate anew his conception of primarily political theatre. [16]

The suggestion of mere good fortune is unfair. When first appointed to the FVB Piscator had noted in his diary: 'I must find plays – the like of which have never existed before – hard, difficult plays, saturated with reality. Back to the style of the twenties.' [17] The right play rarely meets the right director by mere good fortune. It is not surprising that Hochhuth should have chosen Piscator, newly appointed to his important post, as the director to whom to submit his script. It was what Piscator was looking for:

> an epic play, epic-scientific, epic-documentary, a play for the epic, 'political' theatre for which I have fought for thirty years; a 'total' play for a 'total' theatre ... the fate of an individual (treated) comprehensively enough to be symbolic, exemplary in the original meaning of the word, 'representative' for the generality [18]

It was, however, as Dr Schulz has pointed out, a play 'that was by no means ready for the stage'. Schulz went on: 'As is well known, Piscator gave the play its stage-worthiness, which he distilled out of a written mass of dramatic discussion.' [19] Having done this, he was able to present the text without injecting extraneous material or using very unconventional forms of staging. Reporting on the production to the twenty-first Volksbühne conference in Augsburg in 1964, Günther Abendroth of Berlin said, '*The Representative* testified how even today art can arouse and change humanity.' [20] The play, of course, moved into the new theatre, and Abendroth goes on: 'The inauguration of the Freie Volksbühne Theatre discovered its true importance in a world-wide rebirth of the "moral institution" [21] (referring of course to Schiller's concept of the theatre as moral institution). '*The Representative*', said Schulz, 'showed completely how for Piscator the problem and not the *form* stood fundamentally at the centre.' [22] While on the one hand that problem, the substance of the play, aroused fierce controversy throughout Germany and even beyond, its style fathered a whole generation of 'documentary' drama. Piscator's own contribution to the genre as a director consisted of the FVB productions of Heinar Kipphardt's *In der Sache J. Robert Oppenheimer* (*The Case of J. Robert Oppenheimer*) (first Berlin production: it was not produced at the Berliner Ensemble until the following year), Peter Weiss's *Die Ermittlung* (*The Investigation*) (world premiere) and Hans Hellmut Kirst's *Aufstand der Offiziere* (*Officers' Uprising*). It would do Piscator an injustice to equate his conception of political theatre with the documentary drama to which it contributed. As Schulz says in his lecture:

Piscator's political theatre has really nothing to do with documentary theatre in itself, that is talked of so much and which is often taken for the world theatre movement which I may call 'human-political' .... Piscator never thought that merely quoting documents and no more was art, or could replace the artistic effect of the theatre upon the audience.... Nevertheless he held firmly to the documentary as a starting-point. [23]

The Investigation, that almost unbearable 'Oratorio', carried the documentary method to its extremest limits. Piscator appreciated the utterly stark simplicity of it, and though he had assembled photographs and films to illustrate the words, he did not finally use any of them.

Piscator explained that for him this 'Oratorio' was, so to speak, the 'Third Testament'. In his own words: Here the theatre re-enters the realm of religious ritual, which it had left. It turns back from the regions of the purely aesthetic and of beautiful appearance, and becomes the ritual exorcism of an incomprehensible fate, the most moving and meaningless Passion in world history. What is here aimed at as a cultural experience is no longer fear of the gods, but man's fear of himself. [24]

The *Aufstand* was Piscator's last production. He was already mortally ill when it opened at the FVB Theatre on 2 March 1966, less than a month before his death on 30 March. The subject of the play was the attempt by senior officers including Klaus von Stauffenberg on 20 July 1944 to assassinate Hitler. Schulz said of this production:

He [Piscator] had pressed the theme of 20 July – the *Officers' Uprising* – almost violently upon an author [Kirst] who was a brilliant novelist but, as this play shows, quite obviously not a dramatist ...
   In this play, where the material or the shaping of the material would not carry the theatrical work, Piscator once more used the Global Stage, projection, film and simultaneous setting, as a retreat from a development which we, who knew him, thought after *The Investigation* to be almost settled ... [25]

Such a development however, depended on dramatists emerging capable of writing plays of the quality of *The Investigation*, and, Schulz commented, less was done to develop young writers in Germany than in some other countries.

The new theatre on the Schaperstrasse opened on 1 May 1963 with a new production, the last to enter the season's repertoire, an adaptation of Romain Rolland's *Robespierre* – one of Piscator's many experiments in drawing on non-theatrical material for the stage. The narrative form held much that Piscator wanted for his 'epic' drama, and he had already produced stage versions of *War and Peace*, Sartre's *Iron in the Soul* and two American novels. [26]

Surveying Piscator's work from 1962 to 1966 – a period which included, in 1965, the seventy-fifth anniversary of the founding of the Volksbühne – Günter Schulz inevitably recalled Bruno Wille's original manifesto and his aim for a theatre concerned with 'great contemporary questions': 'it' (the Volksbühne) 'committed itself at the start to a theatre of great contemporary questions ... Erwin Piscator ... has opened again to the Volksbühne the way to its first sources ... [27] To take that way the Volksbühne must heed the admonition of Alfred Kerr: 'Occupied with the Arts? Yes, even to my heart's blood, but art was always only an excuse for a better, juster human order.' [28]

After Piscator's death his deputy, Dr Peter Stoltzenburg, became provisional Intendant until a successor was appointed. This was Hansjörg Utzerath, director of the Düsseldorf Kammerspiele, who took up his post, after a transitional period, at the beginning of the 1967–68 season. Forward plans that still bore Piscator's stamp – for example, Hochhuth' s new play *Soldaten* (*Soldiers*) – had gradually to be adapted to new personalities and situations. During the following years it is surprising how frequently it is reported that the reaction of the public and the critics differed sharply from each other.

Two of Piscator's aims had been to establish a permanent ensemble and with this to present plays in 'true' repertoire. But for financial reasons he had not achieved either. The idea was revived during the 1968–69 season, and the 1969–70 season opened with a small permanent ensemble playing in true repertoire – not *en suite* repertoire. The further problem of balancing avant garde experiments against more popular plays was in part solved during the 1967–68 season by introducing a contrasting and more adventurous programme of late-night shows. The first of these was Peter Zadek's production of Edward Bond's *Saved*.

The greatest loss suffered by the Berlin FVB, and indeed by the whole movement during this period was the death of Siegfried Nestriepke. Barely had he brought his life's work to a fitting climax with the opening of the new FVB Theatre than he himself died on 5 December 1963, shortly before his seventy-eighth birthday. A month later, on 12 January 1964 a memorial meeting to the 'Grand Old Man' of the Volksbühne was held in the theatre. Richard Voigt, former Minister for Cultural Affairs and Chairman of the Federation of Volksbühne Societies presided, and Walther G. Oschilewski made a memorial speech, later printed and published. 'His printed speech ought always to be for us a little book whose leaves we turn over to remind ourselves of our friend Siegfried Nestriepke.' [29]

After the blow of losing twenty-five thousand East Berlin members at a stroke in 1961 the FVB rapidly recovered and by 1964 and 1965 had reached its highest post-war membership – about a hundred and twenty thousand. It was realised that this could not be maintained. Many of the newer members did not become permanent, and the turnover of membership each year was numbered in many thousands. By 1967–68 membership had fallen to a hundred thousand and by 1969-70 to 83,000. [30] This drop was in part parallel with the so-called 'theatre crisis' that was developing in Germany by 1970, but it may also have reflected public taste. Other less seriously intentioned theatre clubs were springing up and some people moved to these because they found the FVB programme too heavy. [31]

Not until the 1969–70 season was a serious attempt made to meet the more varying demands of the modern public by offering a choice of programmes. in that season however, prospective members were able to choose between five programmes. (i) 'The established selection', (ii) 'Thoughtfulness', (iii) 'Topical questions', (iv) 'Relaxation' and (v) 'Own choice'. [32]

During the season 1952–53 the FVB Berlin had investigated the occupations and status of its members. Seventy-five thousand copies of a questionnaire were issued of which thirty-two thousand two hundred were completed. Of these 67.1 per cent were from West Berlin addresses and 32.9 per cent from East Berlin – about the same proportion as the membership as a whole. Out of thirty-two thousand respondents, nineteen thousand were in professions but of these only two thousand in positions of financial comfort and security. A high figure for pensioners corresponded with the situation in Berlin. The figure for manual workers was very low (2,757 : 8.6 per cent of the respondents; 14.3 per cent of respondents with jobs). [33] The obvious contrast with the Volksbühne of the 1890s is at least in part a reflection of the contrast between society in the 1890a and the 1950s.

> The Volksbühne has nevertheless remained true to its principles in so far as it still always regards as its urgent task to make theatre-going possible for the worst placed class of the population. But before 1933 this was the working class, after 1945 – along with certain groups of the working class – it was especially the middle and lower salaried classes. [34]

A decade after its opening the new Volksbühne theatre began to present serious problems. With the membership of the FVB falling towards fifty thousand it was too large, and the circle was no longer used. The general public turned against it. Its traditional design inhibited experiment, and its back-stage facilities proved inadequate.With scarcity of good new German plays, young writers could get their work produced in State theatres, and the FVB lost an important function. It even abandoned repertoire for *en suite* playing.

West and East Berlin until 1995

The theatre entered the 1980s under the direction of Prof. Kurt Hübner, whose existing contract as Intendant had in 1979 been extended for a further five years. Its financial situation was still difficult and in 1982 was only saved by help from the Berlin Senate and a long-term loan from the Volksbühne Association. At one point things were so bad that the CDU section in the Berlin parliament even suggested that the operation be moved to the smaller, poorly situated and dilapidated Hebbel Theatre. After widespread opposition from the theatre, the Volksbühne members, the public and some of the press, the absurdity of the scheme became manifest and it sank without trace. An architect's imaginative plan to reconstruct the interior of the Schaperstraße Theatre on flexible lines fell through on grounds of cost.

In spite of the constant threats of closure, the theatre during the Hübner era achieved much artistically, one of its greatest successes being, Enzenberger's version of Molière's *Misanthrope* at the beginning of 1980. This was followed in March 1980 by Schulte-Michel's extraordinary production of Peter Weiss' *The Investigation* in which the audience and actors were united upon the stage. This led not only to a great demand for tickets but also to public discussions almost every evening. This production initiated the celebrations marking the Volksbühne's 90th Birthday. There was also a foyer exhibition, *Julius Bab and the Volksbühne*, set up in collaboration of the Berlin Academy of Arts, a special commemorative publication, a lecture by the Senator for Culture, Dr Sauberzweig, and a reunion of Gerhart-Hauptmann prize-winners. The season also included Zadek's production of *The Importance of Being Earnest* that was sold out for its whole run, Lessing's *Emilia Galotti*, and a new play by Hochhuth.

1981 opened with a controversial production by Klaus-Michael Grüber of Pirandello's *Six Characters in Search of an Author*. An unpopular visiting production from Munich of *The Magic Flute* was withdrawn and replaced by a low-budget production of *Look Back in Anger*, in order to save money for the next major production, *The Taming of the Shrew*, directed by Zadek. This was praised by most of the press and was a box-office success, though the Volksbühne membership was divided over it. An unsatisfactory production of *Tartuffe* ended the year in a precarious financial situation, so that in 1982 some major productions which had been planned had to be replaced by visiting companies.

Nevertheless the 150th Anniversary of the death of Goethe was celebrated by a memorable, if controversial, production of *Faust* by Klaus-Michael Grüber, which the periodical *Theater heute* named as 'the production of the year'. Later, Rudolf Noelte directed Ferdinand Bruckner's *Elizabeth of England* which was panned by the critics, so that the box-office takings were poor even though the Volksbühne membership applauded the production. The losses incurred by *Tartuffe* and *Elizabeth of England* led to the serious financial crisis already mentioned. The year's work was saved by a visit of the Vienna Schauspielhaus with *Piaf.*

On the whole 1983 saw more success. In the spring a grant from a public lottery enabled the booking-hall to be adapted so that, with due regard for security, in-house productions and those of visiting groups could be presented there. The year began with a consistently successful production by Kurt Hübner of Thomas Bernhard's *Über allen Gipfeln ist Ruh,* and though Roberto Ciulli's production of Peter Weiss' last play *Der neue Prozess* was less successful, Zadek's production of Ibsen's *The Master Builder* by a visiting company from Munich was more than booked out. The twentieth anniversary of the opening of the theatre was celebrated this year. In the autumn a visit from Stuttgart State Theatre with *Who's Afraid of Virginia Woolf?* met with success, as did a play *Bekannte Gesichter – gemischte Gefühle.* Between these came a controversial in-house production of *A Comedy of Errors.* To close the year Hübner chose *Charley's Aunt* hoping to please the audience and do good business – in both of which aims he failed. According to Dr Günter Schulz, Chairman of the Berlin Freie Volksbühne, the hostile critiques kept the public away and the English 'understatement-humour' did not appeal to the Berlin audience.

The policies and problems of the Berlin Freie Volksbühne and its theatre on the Schaperstraße reverberated in the wider Volksbühne movement. In his report as General Manager of the Federation at Essen in June 1984 Dr Jürgen-Dieter Waidelich implied serious criticism of the policy of that theatre, now the only Volksbühne theatre, since the Theater am Turm(TAT) in Frankfurt had become a municipal undertaking which played virtually no part in the activity of the Volksbühne. Waidelich suggested that the obligatory two visits per year to the Freie Volksbühne Theatre by Berlin members could well have been halved during the previous five years. Although the approximately 50,000 filled seats this brought to the theatre contributed its very backbone, the fact remained that whenever a production in this, the Volksbühne's own theatre, failed to please, resignations followed. The fall in membership must be checked or the Volksbühne would become a mere ticket-agency, – a fate which, he said, had already overtaken the rival Bund der Theatergemeinde.

> Our pioneers did not want to lease and let out theatre seats: they wanted to create democratic opportunities for disseminating culture in a democratic society. [35]

He argued that the cultural avant-garde was often socially reactionary, while the Volksbühne must be one of the forces of social progress.

Defending his own report on the Berlin theatre Günter Schulz argued that on the whole the record of the theatre, in spite of financial ups and downs, had been good over recent years and that the *Charley's Aunt* disaster had not been the result of a poor production – which it was not – but of hostile critiques in the press, and he went on to maintain that hostile critiques, but not favourable ones, exercised too strong an influence over Berlin audiences, and that Hübner's task as Intendant was a perpetual tight-rope act.

Waidelich, however, would not let the matter drop. The choice of *Charley's Aunt* betrayed a failure to understand the aims and significance of the Volksbühne past and present.

> Our members in Berlin gave the answer in that they responded to this project by taking up only 36% of the seats. There are plenty of works of dramatic literature which are more important and gain a better response from the public than such a farce, and on top of that, in such a questionable production. [36]

The democracy of the FVB became a liability in an age that values efficiency more highly, and the traditional lottery for tickets was not liked, when other organisations sent tickets through the post.

After the death of Nestriepke, Günther Abenroth became the dominant figure, first in the Freie Volksbühne Berlin and later, after the retirement of Gerard Schmid, in the Federation, earning himself even in his lifetime the title *Mister Volksbühne*. He was born in Berlin in 1920 and in his youthful theatre-going had opportunities of seeing Gründgens, Heinrich George, Käthe Dorsch and others of that tumultuous period. He left school in 1939 and trained as a laboratory technician: indeed, throughout his life his cool scientific mode of thought balanced his passionate enthusiasms in the fields of theatre and politics. He was called up, but in 1944 was sent to a concentration camp because he was partly Jewish. He survived, but his experience determined that the foundation-stone of his politics always remained *Never again Fascism*! He regarded capitalism as the cause of Fascism but could not accept the Soviet alternative and in 1946 joined the SPD, the Social Democratic Party of Germany where Willy Brandt exercised an important influence upon him. Inspired by Werner Stein's readings of Tennessee Williams and Thornton Wilder he joined the newly revived Volksbühne but gave up his membership to concentrate on his scientific studies, which, however, he soon also abandoned to take up a post as chemist in the Bio-chemical Research Institute in Berlin-Schöneberg. Meanwhile his critical outspokenness led to his rapid progress in politics. He rejoined the Volksbühne in 1957; by 1960 he was on its executive committee and in 1961 was chosen to succeed Nestriepke as chairman of the Berlin Freie Volksbühne – just when the building of the Berlin Wall deprived the association of its nearly 25,000 East Berlin members, though ironically this opened the door for the 20,000 West Berliners on the waiting-list to join.

The most important decision of his first year in office was to get Piscator back as Volksbühne Intendant - a decision of the executive which was not unanimous. When subsequently Piscator was from time to time caught in the cross-fire of internal Volksbühne politics, Abendroth always defended his policies. For example, when a demand came for the programme to contain more classics and at the same time more 'relaxation and entertainment' Abendroth's reaction recorded in the executive minutes was that 'You could not say that the classics do not show us problems. The German classics were not soft and could not be presented softly. Political theatre which served to broaden our field of vision was the first task of the Volksbühne. Piscator was liberal-minded and cosmopolitan, so naturally he would be judged according to the political position of those who judged him. Of course, Piscator had remained on the Left. He was proud of that, and so was Abendroth.' [37]

A convinced democrat in politics, Abendroth believed that although art could thrive only in a democratic society, questions of art had to be decided authoritatively and not by majority decisions. He therefore never interfered in the province of theatre leaders and he remained true to his principles throughout his three decades as chairman of the Freie Volksbühne Berlin. In 1970 he was elected to the chairmanship of the Volksbühne Federation.

He was keenly aware that the Volksbühne movement's traditions and principles were increasingly threatened by consumerism, but also believed in the mission of the Volksbühne to combat this:

Our members may often have to come to us as [mere] consumers.
Our aim must always be to win them as mature citizens participating in cultural life and conciously co-operating in shaping it. [38]

Whether Abendroth, as chairman of a great audience-organisation, was always right to take the side of artistic directors in a theatre so heavily subsidised that these directors could all too often ride roughshod over public taste and win critical acclaim for productions which played to almost empty houses, is another matter. When we come to consider the problems faced by the Volksbühne in the 1980s, this question will arise again. Certain it is that under his chairmanship the membership of the Freie Volksbühne Berlin fell from 123,000 to about 16,000, and even though other factors were undoubtedly involved it cannot be denied that the Bund der Theatergemeinden actually experienced a revival in Berlin during the same period.

From the building of the Wall in 1961 until its demolition in 1989 Berlin was in effect culturally two cities. Indeed, long before the era of the Wall, the theatre had, according to Günther Rühle [39] become the instrument of

mutually hostile political systems, as we have already seen even in
Nestriepke's post-war struggles with the occupying powers, east and west.

One result of the division of Berlin was that theatrical provision, heavily
subsidised on both sides of the Wall, was duplicated, so that when in 1989
the city was re-unified and the newly re-united Germany had to face the
cost, especially to the former West Germany, the Bonn government
drastically cut its subventions to Berlin theatres so that many had to close,
or reduce their programmes severely. The Freie Volksbühne Theatre on the
Schaperstraße was affected in 1992 and became a 'musical' theatre. Even
the Schiller Theatre, the Schloßpark Theatre and the Schiller Theatre
Workshop were forced to close in 1993, thus depriving the Volksbühne of
approximately 28,000 seats in straight-play theatres. By then many smaller
theatres had already been forced out of existence. From 1 July 1994 the
Berlin Senate abolished the so-called 'seat-subsidy' – a proportion of the
cost of every theatre-ticket sold through an audience-organisation. It had
thus been an indirect grant to the theatre itself. Its abolition meant that the
non-profit theatre-audience organisations had to negotiate ticket prices with
each theatre individually, so that these organisations became almost
indistinguishable from season-ticket agencies.

> The cultural policy of the Senate has forced the non-profit-making
> audience-organisations almost to the point of insignificance ... The
> closing of so many large and small theatres in so short a time ... has
> changed the theatrical landscape of Berlin. A quantitative shift from
> plays to musicals can be seen.

> Thus Ruth Freydank, Chairman of the Freie Volksbühne Berlin, in
> September 1994. [40]

The social aim and claim of the Volksbühne movement to offer the
economically less well off access to the theatre at a price within their means
and thus gain for them a cultural life, largely fell by the wayside and a
growing proportion of the membership belonged to the lower and middle
strata of the educated classes. Politically motivated educational aims became
more and more irrelevant. Socio-political motivation to join an audience-
organisation was lost. Membership fell to 16,000 at the end of 1993 and
further to about 12,500 by the end of 1994. The four active Berlin audience-
organisations (the Freie Volksbühne, Theatergemeinde, Theatre Club and
Theatre Ring) maintained between them a fairly constant membership of
about 100,000 consisting of people who valued the opportunity of visiting
the theatre on a regular basis but who probably cared little about the
differing ideological roots of those organisations.

The re-unification opened the doors of the 'western' theatres to the
'Ossies', as well as those of the 'east' to the 'Wessies', and the Freie

Volksbühne operated throughout the whole of Berlin, having united in 1990 with the 'Neue Freie Volksbühne' which was re-founded in the former East Berlin immediately after re-unification. But there was no dramatic increase in Volksbühne membership. In some respects the East Berliners suffered after the change (die Wende), especially economically through the breakdowns of businesses and institutions, and these breakdowns were linked with the cultural lives of those affected, some having to find new equipment and some suffering redundancy and early retirement. Theatre tickets in the former East Berlin had been extremely cheap and heavily subsidised, but in the unified city the 'eastern' theatres lost their subsidies along with those of the west, so that just when the East Berliners saw the doors open to apparently unlimited consumerism, theatre ticket prices became drastically more expensive. Moreover, their initial curiosity satisfied, many East Berlin theatre-goers found West Berlin, with its high proportion of light, boulevard theatre, artistically inferior to that to which they were accustomed and simply did not feel 'at home' in it, while on the contrary theatre-goers from the west found, after some initial hesitation, that the East Berlin theatre was easily accessible to them.

The Volksbühne Theatre on the Rosa-Luxemburg Platz – nominally a 'Volksbühne' Theatre throughout the history of the German Democratic Republic – suffered various set-backs immediately after re-unification. During the uncertainties of the first months the acting director, Annegret Hahn, with Winifred Wagner, courageously dragged the theatre through the 1990-91 season, which she herself called "das Jahr der Flops". These 'flops' included a characteristic production by Frank Castorf of Schiller's *Robbers*. It was in this production that he had Karl Moor's gang sing the famous *Moorsoldatenlied* written by an unknown prisoner, in a concentration camp and set to music by another. The words of the refrain,

Wir sind die Moorsoldaten
(We are the soldiers of the bog)

in this context involved a rather awful pun on 'Moor': bog or marsh; Karl Moor.

When Castorf later was accused of introducing inappropriate jokes into serious plays and was told not to make jokes about Auschwitz, he was able to reply that he had already done just that! [41]

In April 1991 at the end of this unsuccessful season, a group of 'experts' including Ivan Nagel, a prominent spokesman of the Berlin Senate, proposed a plan for the future of the theatre: it was to be the place where a "young, avant-garde company" could prove its worth. Nagel gave the theatre and the company two years to become world-famous or close down. As Intendant the Senate chose the candidate also wanted by the company –

Frank Castorf. Castorf regarded the two-year challenge as giving him great freedom in choosing his company and staff. The Senate allowed for 22 redundances.

The choice of Castorf was bold – some might say 'rash'. He was born in 1951 into a family of small business people. His father dealt in iron-ware, chiefly metal blinds and the like. The business had been founded by Frank's grand-father in 1889 and the shop remained a private concern even in the GDR, though not without difficulties. Frank, as the son of a 'private capitalist' was often passed over at school in favour of workers' children, in spite of his good examination results. By the age of ten, he says, he was a convinced anti-communist. He is proud of his father's independence of spirit.

> I've learnt one thing from my parents' petty-bourgeois training in survival: that one can survive as a person in very different political systems, without being destroyed or adapting oneself. My father was never a member of the SED [East German Communist Party]; my grandfather was never a member of the Nazi Party. [42]

Castorf became politically conspicuous when he co-directed Karl Grünberg's *Golden fließt der Stahl* in Brandenburg in a totally unsocialistic manner, so that by the time he became a director in Anklam, far in the provincial north, he was already under surveillance by the Stasi.

Through his intimate friendship with Gabriele Gysi, four years his senior, he had gained contact with the East Berlin Volksbühne where she was engaged as an actress. Her father was Minister of Culture under Ulbricht, while her brother Gregor, a lawyer, defended dissidents, including Castorf, in the Courts.Through his connections with this family Castorf became 'a big political case'.

Castorf is extremely articulate and he was able in many interviews and articles to make his aims and policies clear. His treatment of the author's text, be it Shakespeare's or a contemporary's is cavalier: "Faithfulness to the original is not the most important thing".(Werktreue ist nicht das Wichtigste). Dramatic literature for him is the occasion to express what he sees in the outside world. Thus his Volksbühne productions were from the first governed by that theatre's position in the east of a 're-unified' Berlin still culturally divided after almost half a century of political division; by his own background as an unhappy dissident in the GDR; by the needs of the young in this situation, and by the traditions of the Volksbühne itself, especially as exemplified in the 'Piscator' period of the 1920s. He understood that the Volksbühne movement from its very beginnings had a two-fold tradition, cultural and political. For him the expression of the contemporary political and social scene through theatre was what was most important.

In seeking an audience he soon found his constituency in the youth of East Berlin. His seats were very cheap (5DM), his outrageous productions 'fun', and his theatre soon became 'the thing'. It did not trouble him, for example, when Skinheads rioted and broke windows during a performance of *Clockwork Orange*; on the other hand he was pleased when the homeless came to *King Lear* - and came again. *King Lear* was his opening production in 1992. This production, like others of his was a 'potpourri of fragments of the play, jokes, commentaries and "alienation" effects'. Castorf wanted to express the theme of a collapsing empire, whether of 'Mr' Lear or 'Mr' Honecker was not important. Even admirers of his work, however, have had to admit that his writing is weaker than his scenic devices, and though his strength was to have made the theatre once more a forum for the problems of contemporary society, the danger, as seen even at the end of his first session, was that this kind of theatre could soon degenerate into a mindless mixture of tricks and mere show-business. Much of what was presented was described as 'mind-blowing', but much was formless and there was little 'poetry' in it.

However, his five productions that comprised the first season – *King Lear*, Arnolt Bronnen's *Rheinische Rebellen* (1924), Johann Berg's *Fremde in der Nacht*, Anthony Burgess's *A Clockwork Orange*, and a 'version' of Euripides' *Alcestis* – did give the theatre the world-wide, or at least European-wide, fame (or notoriety) that Nagel had demanded; and anyway Castorf was happy that his productions should either be loved or hated, with no middle way.

In place of the interlinked circles of the 'western' Volksbühne Castorf adopted a new logo, a roughly drawn wheel with legs developed from a medieval gipsy graffito associated with the thieve's cant of the 'travelling people' which he had already adapted for his 1990 *Robbers* production in order to direct attention to sub-cultures and alternative art forms. It quickly became a synonym for rebellious theatre.

Castorf's theatre was the first to be awarded the newly-founded Friedrich-Luft Prize, and in 1994 the Kortner Prize went to Castorf. No one pretended that Castorf's young ensemble was polished. The Theatre was described as the liveliest in Germany, not the best, nor the most successful. The 'kids' felt at home there and came in droves. Nor were the productions in the main auditorium everything, but rock-concerts, discussions and other activities took place in the Red Salon, and even in the foyer.

A danger, similar to that suffered in Brecht's theatre, lay in the fact that Castorf's team were also his disciples, artists of talent who had not yet escaped from the shadow of the 'master'. He was said to need competition in his own theatre, and as well as the young rowdies, a further public was needed which was not afraid of radicalism but knew how to distinguish firecrackers from art, between good intentions and real quality.

When Castorf's company visited London in July 1995 with *Murx*, an evening put together by Christoph Marthaler, it had clearly lost neither vitality and contemporary relevance, nor its rough edges.

We must recall that the theatre on the Rosa-Luxemburg Platz had been declared state property by the National Socialist Government in 1939 and was therefore still state-owned in 1989. After re-unification, the Freie Volksbühne Berlin, its original owner, put in a formal "Application for Restitution" to have the theatre returned, even though the FVB was in no position actually to run its own theatrical undertaking there. In the relationship between the FVB and the theatre under Castorf's direction the fact that the former was nominally owner of the theatre was virtually ignored by the latter and there was no special relationship between the two bodies, simply that which existed between the FVB and other Berlin theatres. Thus while as theoretical owner of one of Berlin's finest theatres the FVB might be considered rich it had in fact no money, as its Chairperson Ruth Freydank pointed out to the General Meeting of the Association on 23 September 1994.

Despite the membership's apparent lack of interest in the ideologies and social and artistic aims of the audience organisations, the constitution of the Freie Volksbühne, 1992 edition, made its aims very clear, the first being that the association had as its purpose to arouse in its members understanding of artistic achievements and to increase their receptivity and discrimination in relation to them. In the second clause it was emphasised that although this independent association was open to all artistic movements and works of social significance, it gave preference to works whose content was of contemporary significance and was socially critical.

It seemed clear by the mid-nineties that if the association did not succeed in once more activating its basic principle of promoting theatre with politico-cultural content it would sooner or later become so uninteresting and unimportant that its demise would pass unnoticed. The question was whether the Volksbühne, bearing in mind new developments in society, but conscious of its original aims, could, at a time when the state seemed to be in retreat in many aspects of education, so achieve its basic task as to educate a theatre public which in future would be drawn from all classes of society. The theatres themselves had, it seemed, forgotten to feel responsible to their wider potential audience, so that if the Volksbühne failed in its aim, theatre was in danger of once more becoming the preserve of the wealthy and highly educated. On the other hand, if the Berlin Freie Volksbühne, having a strong capital base in the land and theatre which it owned on the Schaperstraße and its claim on the theatre on the Luxemburg Platz, used its economic independence to regain its original cultural and social character, it might send an effective signal through the whole Volksbühne movement.

It is to that wider movement, primarily as embodied in the Federation of German Volksbühne Associations (from which the Berlin Freie Volksbühne had withdrawn in 1990) that we must now turn.

25. Professor Oscar Fritz Schuh, director of the Theatre on the Kurfürstendamm
1953–1958.

26. Professor Erwin Piscator, adminstrator of the Freie Volksbühne Berlin.

27. The new theatre of the Berlin Freie Volksbühne in Schaperstrasse, Wilmersdorf, west Berlin, in 1963.

28. Exterior and interior views of the new theatre built in west Berlin in 1961–3.

29. World première of *In der Sache J. Robert Oppenheimer (The J. Robert Oppenheimer Case)* by Heinar Kipphardt, directed by Erwin Piscator, 1964.

30. *Trauer muss Elektra tragen (Mourning Becomes Electra)* by Eugene O'Neill, directed by Oscar Fritz Schuh, 1955–6.

Scene II

THE LATER HISTORY
OF THE VOLKSBÜHNE FEDERATION

Until 1972

The rebirth of the Volksbühne societies in West Germany from 1945 was generally easier than in Berlin and the East, as there was no conflict with Communist Party ideas. The refounded societies kept in touch and the Federation was re-established in May 1948 in Hamburg with Nestriepke as chairman. In 1951 it moved its headquarters to Berlin, being the first major national organisation to do so. A policy statement in 1954 re-expressed in contemporary terms the principles enunciated in 1890 and 1925. By 1955 there were seventy-five affiliated societies with three hundred and fifty thousand members, 26 per cent of whom were in Berlin. But after reaching the maximum growth in 1963 the movement steadily declined both in membership and in the number of affilliated societies.

A doctoral thesis of the mid-sixties on the taste of smaller Volksbühne societies [1] showed that within the context of the general levelling of class differences after the Second World War, the Volksbühne had remained true to its original principles in serving the most financially under-privileged sections of the public – now low-salaried white-collar workers; that members tended to be better educated than the average citizen; that the percentage of working-class people in the Volksbühne was higher than among theatre-goers as a whole; and that the Volksbühne helped those in the socially weakest positions to go to the theatre. The thesis also proved that the Volksbühne flourished best in predominantly Evangelical, rather than in predominantly Catholic towns; that in some centres (for example, some university towns) over half the members were under thirty, though in others the figure was only 10 per cent; that the taste of a group of theatre-goers was open to be influenced, though the process was slow; that societies with a 'lighter' programme gained most membership, and that class did affect taste. Though not startling, the findings answer both the hostile critics outside the movement and the starry-eyed within it.

Hamburg Volksbühne, the largest outside Berlin, celebrated its fiftieth birthday in 1969 and in the early 1970s introduced a Volksbühnen-Pass, which offered a free choice of plays and dates at reduced prices in ten theatres. The idea of such a pass had originated in Frankfurt and was the brainchild of Conny Reinhold, a distinguished political cabarettist who, until his untimely death in 1974 at the age of forty-three, was manager of the Frankfurt Volksbühne. This was part of a unique organisation, the Frankfurt Federation for Popular Education, whose post-war development was the work of Carl Tesch (1902-1970). For almost twenty years he was director of the organisation, which comprised a Folk High School, the Volksbühne, and the famous Theater-am-Turm (TAT), all housed in the massive Volksbildungsheim, a few yards from the ancient Eschenheimer tower.[2]

In 1972 the Volksbühne Federation adopted a new emblem or 'logo'. To the eye this new symbol – still in use in 1999 – expressed unity in diversity, movement with stability, organisation without stagnation. Its interlinked rings of concentric circles were a fitting symbol for the Volksbühne of the period, a community that felt itself to be standing between past and future.

After 1972

Despite the optimism embodied in the interlinked rings of concentric circles of the logo adopted by the Volksbühne Federation in 1972, the later history of that Federation, and of the movement as a whole, has been one of decline and of disintegration. During the decade of the seventies these tendencies were not obvious, but during the eighties the movement literally tore itself apart. Even during the seventies it had difficulties in responding positively to the profound economic and social changes taking place in society. No longer a working-class association, the Volksbühne tended to use the new slogan *Theater für alle* (*Theatre for everyone*) rather than the traditional *Die Kunst dem Volke* (*Art for the People*). The increasingly prosperous membership, now consisting chiefly of petty bourgeoisie, the middle classes and social climbers, was on the one hand not in the least interested in the original aims and ideals of the movement, and on the other was becoming more interested in the services the organisation could provide than in single-

This map shows both clearly and vividly how strong the movement still was in West Germany in the 1970s.

priced tickets. Most associations replaced the lottery for tickets with a 'rolling' system (*Rollsystem*), and in some cases allowed members a choice of play instead of laying down a rigid programme. In what proved to be a disastrous experiment Hanover Volksbühne in the early seventies tried to computerise its bookings at a time when this was uncommon and expensive (though computerisation was successful in Hamburg). Berlin had its control of play-choice policy constrained by a legal judgement which compelled it not to omit any theatre from the choice offered to members, thus also making it impossible to omit any which it would have preferred not to arrange for its members on artistic or qualitative grounds. [3]

By the early eighties it was evident that the whole movement was in danger of losing its way, and at the 28th Conference, held 16-17 June 1984 in Essen a Volksbühnenerklärung (*Volksbühne Statement*) prepared by a small Commission was presented in an attempt to provide a temporary policy statement until 1990, when it was hoped that a Centenary Policy Statement would be prepared. Ten years later, in 1994, Dieter Hadamczik, a member of the Commission, described what they had attempted:

> At that time we worked really hard to formulate the current validity of the old theses. Naturally we started from the assumption of the freedom of art, of tolerance and of equality of opportunity, which in the mid-eighties were not yet as explosive topics as today, but – to take one example – which for the first time included the thought of addressing ourselves to people, among others, who have come to us from other countries. They ought to be protected from being uprooted culturally and at the same time should gain access to what their new homeland had to offer culturally. [4]

(Apparently the Commission was referring to the so-called 'Guest Workers', mostly Turkish, who were rapidly becoming an underclass, alienated from society as a whole.)

The Statement also mentioned the new part played by the international nature of theatre and the national impact of the audience-organisations in relation to democratic forces – that is, to make the financing of culture a legally enforcible duty. The Volksbühne must work against the tendency for division of labour and new technologies to stifle creativity. In the field of adult education the Statement emphasised debate on social developments, the dangers which threaten human existence, and problems encountered by people when they meet modern literary forms.

From his standpoint in 1994 Hadamczik saw the Essen Conference as marking the start of

> the end of the common umbrella organisation of the Volksbühne Associations, a Federation founded in 1920, which still [1994] exists, but from which the Associations and 'Land' Federations with the

largest membership have to a large extent withdrawn. There are economic and personal grounds for this, as well as the content of plays. I think that looking back today we can already say that it was not by chance that these developments ran in parallel with theatrical developments in general and with the increasing lack of meaningful content in theatre programmes in the mid-eighties. [5]

But to return to the actual Conference: after customary formalities and the unanimous acceptance of the Statement, Günther Abendroth spoke from the Chair. He drew attention to the significance of the date: it was the eve of 17th June, a date which recalled the hubris of the German people and the misery of a divided nation. Even the imminent European elections could not raise hopes for the future in face of the senseless subsidies for over-production, the haggling over national contributions and above all the 12 million unemployed, whose fate seemed to play only the smallest part in European debates. He looked back at the situation only four years before, when the Conference had devoted itself to the theme *Theatre in the Leisured Society*, behind which stood the optimistic conviction that increasing prosperity would bring increasing leisure-time, as futurologists towards the end of the 1960s had prognosticated, while today (in 1984) the 'leisure time' of the unemployed had become almost unbearable. Although the Volksbühne now worked for all classes of society – *Theater für alle* – it would cease to be itself if it wanted to operate without the less well-off. Television, being cheap and at home, was now a serious rival to the theatre, but the 'goggle-box' could never replace theatre.

He referred to the Volksbühne catastrophe in Hanover where, in addition to internal conflicts, the State and Municipal Theatres had effectively robbed the Volksbühne of members through setting up their own season-ticket organisation, and to the withdrawal of Düsseldorf and Cologne Volksbühne Associations from their 'Land' Federation. The financial situation of the Federation's periodical *Bühne und Parkett* (*Stage and Stalls*) had been stabilised, but its future was uncertain. [In fact it was forced to cease publication on economic grounds in 1988].

At this Conference Abendroth gave up his position on the Federation's Executive which he had held for twenty-two years. In 1970 he had, though not without misgivings, become the Federation's Chairman in succession to the outstanding figures of August Kirch, Siegfried Nestriepke and Richard Voigt. His task had been made possible largely by the General Manager Gerhard Schmid. That great gentleman, who was ready day and night to serve the movement, who knew the Federation like the palm of his hand, a steadfast colleague, (without whose help and encouragement, incidentally, this book could not have been written) had in 1980 resigned his salaried post and become the Federation's Honorary Treasurer.

Born in 1915, Schmid became a member of the Bielefeld Volksbühne in 1948, after his return from being a prisoner of war. Here he soon became a member of the Executive Committee. In 1953 he was appointed by the Federation as District Manager for North-West Germany, where he remained for about a year and a half until in 1955 the Federation's Administrative Council appointed him Business Manager. After 1980, in addition to his honorary work as treasurer and as a member of the Executive Committee, he was Honorary Manager of the Bavarian 'Land' Federation, and furthermore the so-called General Secretary (he didn't use the adjective 'general') of IATO, the International Working Group of Theatre Audience Organisations. [6] He lived latterly in Augsburg and finally in Switzerland. He had been succeeded as General Manager of the Federation by Jürgen-Dieter Waidelich.

Waidelich had already a distinguished career as a practising man of the theatre with a strong academic background. Born in 1931, he studied Theatre, German Philology, Folklore and Journalism. After an academic post in the University of Munich he moved to dramaturgy and play-direction, becoming Intendant first of the Württemburg State Theatre and then of the Bremerhaven Municipal Theatre. Other honorary positions soon followed: membership of the German UNESCO Commission and of the North German *Theatertreffen*; he became spokesman for the Performing Arts Section of the German Cultural Council in Bonn (from 1982). In 1983 he was elected Chairman of the North-Rhine-Wesphalia Federation of Volksbuhne Associations.

He had already tabled his full, factual report as General Manager and was thus free to express more personal comments in his speech – as we have already seen in his clash with Schulz on the question of the Freie Volksbühne Theatre in Berlin. In his tabled report Waidelich referred to the disappointment in 1952-53 that a Pan-German Volksbühne Federation was a lost dream. Subsequently, in his opinion, television and "directors' Theatre" had led to the public's "voting with its feet", so that if the late seventies and early eighties were compared with the 'golden sixties' the German theatre had suffered an average yearly loss of about three million bookings. Likewise, of the thirty-six years since the post-Nazi refounding of the Federation in 1948, the first eighteen had seen a consistent rise in membership and the latter eighteen a consistent fall, the high point in 1963 actually coinciding with the year of Nestriepke's death.

Summing up the current position Waidelich concluded:

> We can remain aware historically that we grew out of workers' education. But to insist on this and thus to cut off openings in the new areas of society would be equivalent to self-destruction.[7]

Unlike Abendroth, he still had hopes of a post-industrial leisured society and, ironically citing the notorious Nazi slogan of the concentration camps, *Arbeit macht frei*, he declared that the future would teach that Culture helps Freedom, and that it would be the task of the Volksbühne to convey that message into the Third Millenium.

At this period Volksbühne Conferences, originally held annually from 1920 until the movement's dissolution by the Nazis in 1933, and then after the refounding in 1948 every two years until 1972, were now held every four years with 'Politico-Cultural Congresses' interspersed. It was decided at this 1984 Conference to add to the next Politico-Cultural Congress, planned for 1986 in Frankfurt, an Extraordinary Conference on the Constitution.

The primary object of the Extraordinary Conference was to be to frame and approve a new Constitution. It is often when political, religious or artistic movements seem to be losing impetus and direction that they start to re-examine their structures in the hope that changing the shape of the mechanism will provide the fuel to generate new power – a hope that is frequently a vain one. The disruptive forces that were to damage the movement in the late eighties with, perhaps ultimately fatal consequences, were not yet fully in the open, though the personal and ideological rifts, particularly between Abendroth and Waidelich, could already be perceived.

In his Introduction to the published documentation of the 1986 Frankfurt Conference Waidelich was still able to typify the occasion as a *New Beginning* (*Neues Beginnen*), echoing the title of Nestriepke's book on the post-war refounding of the Berlin Freie Volksbühne. Whether this was an over-optimistic view may be judged from a closer examination of the conference itself and of the subsequent history of the Federation.

From the start it was felt that if agreement was to be reached at all it would be in one day, though two days had been assigned, and that it would be important that the constitution was in harmony with the current structure of the Federal Republic - namely, that the 'Land' Federations should be given more power. But the preparatory commission had put forward alternative structures and there was pressure, especially from Abendroth and the Berlin Freie Volksbühne, that both should be discussed. From the beginning even procedural matters, such as the order of the agenda aroused quite prickly arguments. A steering committee of three was then elected unanimously, and its spokesman, Richter, from Aschaffenburg, admitted at once the difficulties ahead. Waidelich was appointed to take the minutes and changes in the order of the agenda were eventually approved. After further procedural matters, Dr Milow of Stuttgart Volksbühne put forward the Commission's proposals and their constitutional problems, the principal issue being whether the Federation should have two constituent organs, the Conference and the Executive Committee, or three: Conference, a Federal Council, and the Executive Committee.

Milow's introduction was immediately challenged by Abendroth, who argued at somewhat tedious length for means of reducing costs by cutting down the numbers of committee members and meetings: but it was evident that behind the arguments lay a power-struggle, and indeed the next speaker, Dr Gisela Schwarze from Münster, said bluntly:

Constitutions are only significant when situations of conflict arise. [8]

Her own plea was for greater democracy within the movement, and this was apparently the core of the detailed constitutional debate which followed and which fills over thirty closely typed pages in the published report! Even just before the vote was taken there was an argument as to who had the right to vote. A ballot had been demanded, and after a further squall on the wording of the motion it was ultimately agreed that a voting card must be used that offered:

"A" (the Commission's proposal) or "B" (the Berlin proposal). Even then a dispute followed as to whether this was an actual change in the consititution, demanding a 75% majority, or merely a change of direction, needing only a simple majority. The ballot was taken, but after a much needed fifteen minute interval it was alleged that the number of votes did not correspond with the number qualified to vote and that the vote must be taken again! This was done, the final result being:

A.	54 votes	(33.8%)
B.	105 votes	(65.6%)
Abstentions.	1	(0.6%)

The Berlin proposal was thus carried. But the voting did not end the debate, and the meeting insisted on discussing and voting on the Berlin motion paragraph by paragraph, which led to further petty criticism over minor details of words and phrases. In the end "Any other business" had to be abandoned. The detailed voting did result in the required 75% for the new constitution, and Högener, the chairman, brought the procedings to a not altogether happy close. He was sure that delegates would understand why his enthusiasm for the outcome of the voting was "somewhat restrained". He was, he said, allowed a concluding comment, and he thought this important.

The Volksbühne Conference has today delivered a veto which is directed as strongly as possible against members of the Executive. That can be seen clearly from the result of the votes. Therefore I will call a meeting of the Executive in the not too distant future, and then the Executive must clarify its own situation. I see that as essential, and it must be done. [9]

Waidelich's 'new beginning' already looked more like the beginning of the end.

At the Essen Conference in 1984 Karl-Friedrich Meinert had been appointed acting Chairman and in the autumn of 1986 became Chairman. He hoped to extricate the movement from the difficulties in which it found itself, but the task proved even harder than he had anticipated. As a pragmatist rather than an ideologue he had set himself a few modestly practical aims and had worked hard with his committees to achieve them, but in the deteriorating financial situation he was forced to announce in his opening address at Bremen in 1988 two drastic economies: the closure of the Berlin office of the Federation, and the demise of the periodical *Bühne und Parkett* on 31 December 1988. He also announced in unspecific terms a plan to achieve economies by a concentration of power at the head of the organisation. What that plan was might have been guessed by the less well informed through a special motion proposed at the very beginning of the conference by Günther Abendroth on behalf of the Berlin Freie Volksbühne to the effect that the positions of Federal Chairman (honorary) and Federal Business Manager (employee) should remain separate and be occupied by two different people. The motion was noted and added to the agenda in the appropriate place. The reason for its being introduced soon emerged.

Dr Waidelich who, like the chairman, said he was hoping that the meeting could be harmonious and that the hatchet could be buried, began his report with some autobiographical comments leading up to his having been selected as General Manager ten years before, in 1978, taking up the post in 1980. He gave a full account of membership and financial matters, strongly defending his own stewardship but advancing detailed arguments in favour of the proposed retrenchments, showing how great the savings would be. He was highly critical of some of Chairman Högener's decisions two years before and claimed that only his own initiatives had prevented the Federation from reaching 1988 with a deficit of some ten thousand Marks. This, he said, was where dual-control led, and this was what Berlin wished to perpetuate. He had therefore agreed to an idea and proposal of the retiring Chairman, Meinert, and the request of many friends from various 'Land' Federations, and was putting up for the position of Executive Chairman, – that is, for him to be at one and the same time Chairman and principal officer, the very situation the Berlin motion wished to ban. He claimed to be acting in the interests of the Federation and its future and for these ends he was ready to sacrifice the time and extra work that the honorary post would demand. Moreover, by his renouncing any salary until the next regular conference the Federation could be financially secure into the mid-nineties without raising the contributions of individual associations. At his age, 57, he would be prepared to continue working in an honorary capacity for a maximum of four years, thus clearing the way for a successor. The so-called 'Berlin' solution of dual-control would cost a great deal more and be less efficient. After paying tribute to Gerhard Schmid as treasurer and Meinert as chairman he brought his surprising speech to a close.

Despite Waidelich's policies the Federation had lost 21.6% – over one fifth – of its membership between 1984 and 1988 and was now virtually without capital. Abendroth thought that much of the loss was due to the move from Berlin to Essen, while Hadamczik (himself a former editor of *Bühne und Parkett*) questioned whether the movement could sustain its public relations without a periodical, and in this he was supported by Dr Pforte of Berlin, though Schimdt of Bremen pointed out that with a circulation of a mere 1700 the periodical could not really be effective with the general public.

By the end of the day's sitting the dispute had clearly developed into one between Waidelich and Berlin. Dr Schwarze of Münster considered that Waidelich was being made a scapegoat. The Berlin delegates reacted strongly to her speech and Abendroth, after accusing her of deliberately stirring up strife in a manner unprecedented in the movement, reminded the conference that the Federation Executive, at its meeting on 19 March in Hamburg, had, with two abstentions, agreed to keep the two offices separate and had recommended support for Professsor Doll as candidate for the Chair. As Business Manager, Waidelich ought to have supported this policy, and the purpose of the Berlin special motion was to prevent this decision from being 'ironed away'. Even though Pforte insisted that the Berlin motion was not a personal attack on Waidelich but was intended to strengthen his Managerial position the session ended with a further appeal from Meinert for opponents and delegates to endeavour next day to express their differences more objectively and to avoid personal attacks.

Further pleas from the Chair did not prevent the opening of the next morning's session from being stormy, with constant interruptions. The first debate, often bitter and violent, concerned the Berlin Special Motion and when not simply angry and personal turned primarily on the principle advocated by Montesquieu of the separation of legislative, executive and judicial powers. Supporters of the Berlin motion argued passionately that if Waidelich held the two major positions in question this principle would be violated. A certain Frau Siepmann-Böhmer from Worms, evidently a lawyer by training, delivered a long lecture on this theme, to which Waidelich replied brilliantly and with considerable irony. Agreeing with Montesquieu's principles, and with some sharpness informing the lady that he had not expected to be instructed by her in his understanding of civics, he argued forcefully that in this case the legislative was the Volksbühne

Conference itself and that the Federal Executive Committee (which, of course, included the Chairman) together with the General Manager constituted the Executive; and he drew parallels from other organisations. He had announced his candidature some three weeks ago at a 'Land' Federation Conference in Baden-Württemburg. He had been nominated by the Federal Chairman at the same time that Berlin had nominated Professor Doll. He claimed that Schulz, at the very meeting to which he, Schulz, had brought Doll's nomination, had said to him: "If we in Berlin had known that Waidelich, our fellow member in Berlin, could possibly be a candidate and be proposed, then we could perhaps have considered the matter differently". But Waidelich claimed that later he found in the Berlin Executive Committee Minutes of a fortnight earlier, a minute saying that if Waidelich put up, they would propose Doll. Dr Schulz immediately replied that to the best of his knowledge this account of what happened was not correct.

After an almost farcical interlude in which a non-member called Koschare from Frankfurt was prevented from speaking, Franz-Heinz Köhler from Coblenz questioned Doll's standing in the meeting, and this having been established the vote on the Berlin motion was taken by ballot. The motion was lost by 67 votes to 62, with no abstentions. It was thus now possible to proceed with the election of the Federal Chairman, preceded by the election speeches of the two candidates.

Doll, who had arrived late the previous afternoon in the middle of Waidelich's opening address, explained that he was suffering from severe lumbago and had come with great effort by car from a hospital near the Czech border. His *curriculum vitae* which followed was impressive. Born 1925, a member of no political party, he had been engaged as dramaturge in a number of distinguished theatres from 1947 to 1961. Between 1962 and 1972 he had been Intendant first in Heidelberg and then in Brunswick, and then for thirteen years until 1985 Intendant in the State Theatre in Stuttgart. During this time he had worked in the fields of opera and ballet and had made 44 foreign visits in the west and east, and had indeed travelled the world as a man of the theatre. He had studied literature and theatre history in the University of Frankfurt and held an honorary University Chair in Baden-Württemburg. In recent years he had published seven books on theatre, literature and art, and up to 1991 was bringing out four more. [10] Throughout his theatrical career he had worked closely with many of the outstanding figures of the Volksbühne movement, including Nestriepke, and above all with his old friend Gerhard Schmid. The Berlin Freie Volksbühne would have liked him to succeed Piscator twenty years before as Director of the Berlin Volksbühne, and the final shortlist had consisted only of himself and Utzerath, the latter being the successful candidate. It was at this time that he first got to know Abendroth with whom he had subsequently co-operated. At Stuttgart, in the face of strong opposition, he had freed the Volksbühne from its so-called 'Monday Ghetto', so that its members could come throughout the week. He was a member of the Volksbühne in Hof, and for the past three years had directed the Luisenburg-Festspiele, which the Hof Volksbühne had visited for several decades. His case appeared strong but was not perhaps strengthenedby his admission that he was standing for the Chair because he was strongly opposed to the union of the two offices, chairman and Manager, in one person. He added an implied personal criticism of Waidelich, though without naming him:

> The lust for power, ladies and gentlemen, is a very human phenomenon. And history has shown us how seductive power can be. [11]

The chairman of the session, Tschirner, promptly interrupted him, but after a storm of interruptions from the floor he was eventually allowed to continue and even to repeat and enlarge upon his comment on power and his oblique attack on Waidelich, claiming that even apart from the constitutional question, the concentration of so much power in one person would be such that even a most determined person would not be able to resist it without damaging his own personality. Doll pointed out that at his time of life he did not need the Chairmanship to forward his career or feed his vanity. He hated conflict, believing that intelligence ought to transcend conflict. He had been greatly distressed by the conflicts of the previous day and the manner in which the arguments had been conducted. If elected he asked to be trusted as a person and to be free from domestic squabbles. Addressing Waidelich directly, he said that if Waidelich was elected he would accept the democratic decision and wish him well, and that he trusted that Waidelich would respond similarly if the vote went the other way.

Waidelich, in his final speech as candidate welcomed the fact of any election, and also welcomed (politically correctly!) the number of women who had contributed to the discussion. He thought the Volksbühne in the next few years offered neither 'Power' nor anything to feed 'Vanity', but only unremitting work. The subscriptions from local Associations to the Federation could not be increased any further and so he re-affirmed his willingness to work unpaid for three or four years to get over this crisis, after which he hoped a younger person could take over the salaried post. He was anxious to organise the 1990 Centenary Celebrations in Berlin, after which he was prepared to help a successor to take over. Unlike Doll, he was a party member (he had no need to add 'of the SPD') and had been an active Trade Unionist for over thirty years.

The speeches were over, but questions directed to either of the candidates were invited. Herr Hoffmann of Witten asked Doll how long in fact he had been a member of Hof Volksbühne, to which Doll replied quite simply:

Four weeks. It was a tactically clever question but it led to nothing and a few minutes later the vote was taken. Doll gained 65 votes, Waidelich 61. There was one abstention and two invalid voting papers. Thus Doll was elected, Waidelich retained his salaried post and the subsequent elections and reports of working parties were less dramatic.

From this point it becomes more difficult to reconstruct the history of the Federation in detail. Somewhat absurdly the published minutes of this Bremen Conference are incomplete because the audio-tape ran out before the end! Further, in April 1994 a burst water-pipe destroyed the records of the Federation which had been stored – for safety! – in the cellar of the office in Essen.

Although elected, Dr Doll evidently did not take up his position in the Chair but withdrew his candidacy, having, it seems, suffered personal verbal attacks by delegates. He returned to his profession as Intendant, helping out several theatres as interim director. He was at the Frankfurt Playhouse in the season 1990/91, at the Opera House in the same city 1991/2, at the Brunswick State Theatre 1992/3 and in 1994 at Basel.

When the Federation held its Extraordinary General Meeting in the following year (1989) on 30 September in Hanau, Karl-Friedrich Meinert was again in the Chair and Waidelich still General Manager. The circumstances of this conference illustrate vividly the strange state of partial disintegration in which the movement now found itself. The host Association, Hanau, had resigned from the Federation on 23 August – only a week before! – on the grounds that the Hamburg Volksbühne Association had also resigned only a few days earlier: yet Meinert was also chairman of the Hamburg Association. After the constitutional debates in 1986 Gerd Högener (Düsseldorf) and Dr Milow (Stuttgart) had both resigned their positions leaving Meinert as Chairman. His hopes of successfully establishing a new Executive in 1988 and of leading the Federation out of its dire situation had, of course, been in vain.

Up until then the Hamburg Volksbühne had hoped to host the next regular Conference in 1992, after Berlin had hosted the Politico-Cultural Congress of 1990 at which the centenary of the movement would be celebrated. But things turned out differently when the Bremen Conference dispersed without having elected a competent Executive, so that the old Executive had to be asked to take up its duties again on 14 January 1989, Meinert also having to resume his position as Chairman, which he had given up at the 1988 Conference. In fact, for many months, the whole burden fell upon Waidelich's shoulders.

The Hanau Conference of September 1989 was in effect continued in a further Extraordinary Delegate Conference held in Lüneberg on 18 November 1989 where a motion from the Schleswig-Holstein 'Land' Federation that the Federal Executive should be dissolved was passed by

50 votes to 30, with one abstention, but as there was not a quorum for constitutionally winding up the Federation the motion was nevertheless lost. That such a motion should be proposed and even receive a majority vote gives a clear indication that the future of the Federation was becoming more and more uncertain: Meinert, still acting Chairman, evidently wanted to relinquish his post. Two new candidates were proposed. Both declined to stand, but each agreed to support the other if elected. After a break, one of the candidates, Axel Wolters of Gelsenkirchen, agreed to stand and was elected in the first ballot by an absolute majority. Later a further motion to alter the constitution was withdrawn after a short debate.

The 1990 Centenary Celebrations of the Berlin Freie Volksbühne were naturally held in Berlin, and in that same year the Berlin Freie Volksbühne withdrew from the Federation. A commemorative book, *Freie Volksbühne Berlin 1890 bis 1990*, edited by Dietger Pforte was published, and Waidelich delivered an introductory speech of greeting. Its main theme was the economic situation of contemporary theatre. Whether theatre should be valued culturally or merely as economic property was a question that would take on a European dimension in the European Community after 1992. Apart from subsidised and purely commercial theatre he commented on the development of sponsored theatre. This was different again from support by wealthy patrons, as commercial sponsors were driven by the profit-motive. The Iron Curtain and the Berlin Wall now being things of the past, Waidelich emphasised the strength of theatre – so long as it had conformed to the State – in the former German Democratic Republic. Even there, in Kottbus, a private theatre had just opened. Was the salvation of the theatre to be found in private theatres? Was touring theatre to be the commercial theatre of the future? All these unanswered questions lay open for discussion.

The first General Meeting of the Federation (another "Extraordinary" one) in the last decade of the twentieth century was held in Gelsenkirchen on 27 & 28 April 1991 with Axel Wolters in the chair, with Meinert present now as a guest from the Hamburg Volksbühne, and as guest speaker Jochen Poß, SPD spokesman on financial politics in the Federal Parliament. Inevitably the speech and discussion turned on problems of money and taxation.

Waidelich had ceased to be General Manager in the middle of 1990 and the office had been run by Frau Erika Müller-Scheffler, with voluntary help from members of the executive. Waidelich's report to this 1991 meeting was anything but cheerful. *Bühne und Parkett* had latterly lost the Federation 80,000 DM a year, – a sum which would never be recovered. He himself was now an "Elder Statesman" of the movement and as deeply committed to it as ever. But small-minded pettiness and everlasting constitutional debate [*Kleingeistiges Krämertum und ewig währende Satzungsdebatten*] had led to his resignation. At present only about 40 Volksbühne Associations were members of the Federation, with a total membership of about 100,000. In 1923 in Berlin alone there had been 167,000 members. Now there were fewer than 20,000.

From 1991 to 1994 the Federation met regularly and took important decisions in connection with keeping non-profit Associations free of taxation, thus assuring these Associations of their basic income. In a consultative capacity it had exercised its influence on decisions of politico-cultural importance. Through cultural congresses and symposia the Federation had sought to establish closer relations with the Volksbühne on the Rosa-Luxemburg-Platz. But the Intendant at that time. Dr Rödel, was later dismissed, and the split between the Berlin Freie Volksbühne and the Federation meant that the relationships were 'frozen'. The Federation tried also to found new Volksbühne Associations in the former East Germany, and immediately after reunification not inconsiderable sums were made available to associations such as those at Nordhausen and Wittenburg. The money was accepted, but there was no other response worth mentioning. On the other hand very many western Volksbühne Associations organised cultural trips to cultural 'strongholds' such as Dresden, Weimar and others. But even in 1994 it did not seem possible to rely on firm relationships with those on the former German Democratic Republic side.

Then on 14 September Professor Waidelich died after a short but severe illness, at the age of 63. Tributes to him immediately appeared in the newspapers. In Essen he was remembered as Intendant of the Essen Theatre from 1974 to 1978 and as its historian. [12] Since 1990 he had also held a Chair as Director of the Institute for Theatre, Film and Television Studies in the University of Bochum. One of the obituaries referred to the fact that as General Manager of the Federation of German Volksbühne Associations "he had had to share the experience of the 'slow disintegration' of this audience organisation."[13]

It seemed once more as if the Volksbühne Federation had reached the end of the road, and winding-up was again seriously considered.However, the Federation (Bund), now subtitling itself *Föderativer Zusammenschluß von Kulturgemeinschaften*, (*Federal Amalgamation of Cultural Groups*) through a 'Committee of Spokespersons' elected Franz-Heinz Köhler as its Chairman in succession to Axel Wolters, Manager of the Theatergemeinde at Gelsenkirchen, 'a Volksbühne Association which had already withdrawn from the Federation,' whose term of office ran to 1994. Köhler's appointment provided, as the press-release said, a foundation for the continuation of the work of the Volksbühne Associations.

Köhler actually regarded himself as successor to Waidelich, thus showing that he intended to be an active and not just a nominal Chairman. He hoped it might be possible for him to lead the Federation into a more hopeful future, but feared this might not be possible in view of the lack of community feeling in those Volksbühne Associations which still existed in the western part of the enlarged Federal Republic. But when he was elected it was basically clear that the only task remaining to him might be to give the Federation an honourable burial. There were by now only 19 Volksbühne Associations within the Federation [14] with about 18,000 members in all. Outside the Federation there were probably about 55, but accurate figures were difficult to obtain. The scale of the catastrophic decline in the number of federated associations may be seen by the fact that in 1993 the Federation still listed 78 associations as probably being in membership, if only nominally. A research circular addressed to these 78 in 1994 drew replies from only 19, of whom only 6 were on Köhler's list of Federation members. So of that list of 19 (Köhler's) 13 were not even interested enough to reply.

(Köhler himself sent out a circular (20 December 1994) to all Associations within the Volksbühne Federation, to which the response was so poor that he sent a second circular dated 7 April 1995.)

Interestingly enough, almost all the non-federated Associations that did respond to the research circular declared themselves true to the traditional principles of the movement. Only one, Tübingen, now regarded itself as a mere season-ticket agency. Almost all the rest had a single-price ticket/subscription and all but two achieved overall fairness through the *Rollsystem*. These two, Kiel and Lübeck, used the original lottery system of allocating tickets. Together with Flensburg and Rendsburg these four had formed the Schleswig-Holstein 'Land' Working-Group, which proudly regarded itself as rich in Volksbühne tradition. All the Associations that responded, whether or not in the Federation, were non-proft societies with 'e.V.' status and free of tax. Few had been noticeably affected by German reunification, though Bielefeld's subsidy from the town had fallen because of the town's legal contribution to the fund for German unity. Duisberg found cultural trips to the east had become easier, and Northeim was now able to include three East German towns (Nordhausen, Heiligenstadt and Meiningen) in its programme. This Association had also helped materially and with advice in the re-founding of the, Nordhausen Volksbühne. Some were hopeful as to the future, some not. Stuttgart, a large and strong Association, admitted to no longer sharing the Volksbühne positions in all respects. Some Associations had left the Federation because of the internal squabbles. Others said it now offered them little, especially since the death of Waidelich. The Federation was said only to exist on paper [Bremen], to be useless unless reformed, and to be inefficient. This broadly was the situation into which Köhler entered.

He had for some years been on the Federation's Executive Committee and since 1983 had been Chairman of the Coblenz Volksbühne Association. He described himself as an Ur-Koblenzer (typical of Coblenz), a city which had never had any proletariat worth mentioning – a fact he thought important in the Volksbühne context. At 60 he had recently retired from a high post in the local government of his native town. It was Waidelich who had persuaded him to lead the Coblenz Volksbühne since 1983. Through his involvement in various investigations into theatrical affairs he had been a member of the Cultural Committee of the German Congress of Municipal Authorities from 1971 until his retirement, and editor of the Theatre Statistics of the German Theatre Association from 1975 to 1988.

Though rightly cautious as to the future of the Volksbühne movement he actually saw in the current shortage of public funds and the fierce competition for all sorts of public funding an opportunity for the Volksbühne to attract subsidy by demonstrating that a general need existed in the population for the art of the theatre. He realised, however, that unless the Associations that had seceded were won back, the Federation had little hope of survival. He warned members of Associations not to 'kid themselves': the situation was dreadful partly through internal events, partly through external – shortage of cash coupled with rising theatre prices; the multiplicity of cultural alternatives to theatre; and, above all, the growing exclusiveness of 'Directors' Theatre', which currently was penetrating into almost every provincial theatre. Directors' theatre offered to audiences drawn from ordinary people and the middle classes (audiences which must be in the front line of Volksbühne concern) unintelligible theatrical methods expressing the Narcissism of directors and intendants, who thus totally failed to carry out their real cultural task. This rift between 'directors' theatre' and ordinary theatre audiences was Köhler's principal concern. Over-subsidy in the former West, which even reached 86.7% of the total income of theatres, had enabled intendants and directors virtually to ignore their audiences; but present financial stringency was changing that, and thanks above all, in Köhler's opinion, to the broad connections of Professor Waidelich, who had sat on a wide range of committees, the Volksbühne as representative of the audience had not passed wholly into oblivion. Many prominent figures in the Federation, for fear of being thought unfashionable had allowed themselves to become mere dogsbodies of the intendants and directors so that by their own policies they had silenced the voice of the movement and decimated the membership.

In the power-struggles of the 1980s Köhler had been on the side of Waidelich. Abendroth, as we know, had normally placed himself firmly 'on the side of art,' but Köhler recalled how in 1981, when Abendroth was President of the Federation, he and Jakob Baumann, then President of the *Bund der Theatergemeinden*, had published an Open Letter in which they declared that artistic freedom would be endangered if the present tendency of the theatre to ignore the audience were to persist. When attacked for this in the press by a number of prominent directors and intendants, Abendroth and Baumann immediately knuckled under, which in the former's case was wholly consistent with his usual stance. In Köhler's opinion, as in Waidelich's, this policy was the cause of the disastrous fall in membership of the Berlin Freie Volksbühne under Abendroth's leadership. He had been elected to represent the audience, not the artists, and, wrote Köhler, the Volksbühne must in future be the lone voice of the audience, for the press and almost all cultural politicians were on the other side.

Köhler was, of course, not wholly isolated in the world of theatre. The doyen (along with Dr Doll) of German-Speaking Theatre, Hellmuth Matiasek, in an interview given to *Die deutsche Bühne* in February 1995, mounted an authoritative attack on 'Directors' Theatre' in terms which Köhler, in his second circular (7.4.'95) wholeheartedly endorsed.

Köhler concluded his circular:

Final Quotation.
The critic Moritz Rinke, *Tagesspiegel*, 17.12.'94:

People here think: either the theatre is good and empty, or bad and full. No one in theatre comes to the idea that even the stupid audience would recognise and accept really good, passionate theatre. No one believes the stupid audience to be capable of anything.

I certainly don't consider the situation to be quite so hopeless! [15]

Meanwhile a move was afoot to bring together the Volksbühne Associations which had withdrawn from the *Bund*. A body calling itself the *Interessengemeinschaft deutscher Volksbühnen* (*Interest-group of German Volksbühnen*) arranged a conference at Hof in Bavaria primarily for these associations. This was to take place from 29 September to 1 October 1995 and nine outstanding speakers from the world of German theatre had agreed to speak. The theme was *Trends in Theatre 1995 - their causes and their effects on the public.* [16] However, after two enrolments from members of the *Bund* had been withdrawn only seven remained and the conference had to be cancelled. Not surprisingly one of its organisers, Dr Dieter Hadamczik, a veteran of the Volksbühne in earlier times, privately expressed the opinion that one might confidently forget to write the future history of the Volksbühne Federation.

On the other hand, only a few days before the date of the abortive conference in Hof a Volksbühne Seminar arranged by the *Bund* in collaboration with the Volksbühne Federation of North Rhine-Westphalia in Olpe (22-24 September 1995) on the general Theme, *The End of Advanced Civilisation? or: When are our Opera Houses closing?* was so well attended that the venue could not contain all the participants. Principal speakers at this successful event were: Franz-Heinz Köhler as the Federation's chairman; his Deputy, Franz Irsfeld; Bernd Fülle, Administrative Director of the theatres of the city of Köln, and Michael Söndermann of the Centre for Cultural Research, Bonn. [17]

Six months later (15 March 1996) a one-day conference for the Secretaries of Volksbühne Associations held in Köln was felt to be successful, though only ten Associations were represented by sixteen participants, and this was followed in September (9–13) by a four-day seminar on *Politico-cultural Perspectives of the Publicly Subsidised Theatre in Germany.* But the biennial General Meeting required by the constitution had to be postponed until the Spring.

To add to the problems of the Federation, it lost its office premises in Essen. These had been shared with another cultural organisation which accepted an invitation of the Federal Ministry of the Interior to move to the *House of Culture* in Bonn. In the event, the offered office space in Bonn proved unsuitable and the Essen office had to be given up at the end of June. This also meant that Frau Müller-Scheffler, who had run the office for many years, had to be given her notice. In the face of this emergency all administration had to be reduced to a minimum and the work that remained carried out in the private houses of the Chairman and his Deputy. In reporting this, Herr Köhler added:

> Finally, there remain among the members of Volksbühne Committees very few idealists and people who feel that they owe a duty to an idea that goes beyond their own parish pump. [18]

At a Committee meeting on 26 August 1996 Köhler, who had been Chairman since 1994, announced that he wished definitely to resign at the end of November, remarking:

> In the present situation of the Federation Hamlet's monologue may be cited:
>
> *To be or not to be, that is the question.* [19]

Wolfgang Meisen, of Duisburg, took on the duties that Köhler had conscientiously carried out, and was officially elected Chairman in January 1997. He took the post on with something of a heavy heart as 'a thankless task in a difficult time', He had accepted only because he and Franz Irsfeld, the Deputy Chairman 'could not bring themseves to wind up an association so rich in traditions.' But he saw that unless more Volksbühne Associations joined the Federation it would no longer be sensible to carry on into future years.

EPILOGUE

After its idealistic beginnings, its *Blütezeit* between the wars and its encouraging *Neues Beginnen* (in Nestriepke's optimistic phrase) the story of the final years of the Volksbühne movement can only be told, echoing Edward Gibbon, as the History of its Decline and Fall, and just as the Roman Empire did not disintegrate only because of internal strife and the personalities of individual Emperors, so too, the fate of the Volksbühne was determined not only by internal factors, important though these were, but also by broader currents of modern German history.

The Volksbühne had, as Irsfeld said (24.11.96), slept through the transformations of society from the workers' educational associations of pre-war years to the rebuilding of Germany and the reshaping of its cultural life in the time after the Second World War. The Volksbühne was fragmented and therefore weak and ineffective, and this was because the Volksbühne Associations had turned their backs on the Federation and thus had relinquished their power. There was now no choice but to call in the receivers or develop a new and fundamental concept of the movement. Other organisations had done this and the Volksbühne must follow suit. (Irsfeld no doubt had the continued success of the Theatergemeinde in mind.) [1]

With the development of universal education the principal potential Volksbühne membership, namely, a highly intelligent section of a proletariat desiring education both for its own sake and as a means towards political power, had disappeared. The attempt to counter this situation with the new slogan *Theater für alle* (*Theatre for all*) was doomed to fail, as the new, petty-bourgeois audiences had other expectations. In addition, the old, nineteenth century proletariat had to some extent been replaced by foreign *Gastarbeiter* not primarily interested in German culture, though as we have seen, the *Volksbühnenerklärung* prepared in 1984 did recognise that the Guest-Workers needed both to be protected from being uprooted culturally and yet be given access to the culture of their new homeland.

Apart from these broader social factors the decline in membership of the Volksbühne was also part of the general decline in theatre-attendance. As Waidelich pointed out in 1984 theatre-bookings had by then declined by an average yearly loss of three million. This decline had many causes. Although it has become a cliché to mention television in this connection it is clear that its influence on theatre-bookings goes far beyond mere ease of accessibility at home. It has also affected the kind of play people wish to see, and the compulsive effects of soap-opera are not to be underestimated. With television, play-watching becomes a private entertainment for the individual, or at most the family, and the need to participate in a communal reaction to what happens on stage is gradually lost, or is transferred to sport – though even there the mass-reactions on the terraces can be shared by the home-viewer.

Television offers naturalism in its most extreme form. Actors do not even have to project themselves or their voices into an auditorium and as mankind tends to be naturally lazy this becomes the easiest kind of 'theatre' to watch. Directors, actors and designers, on the other hand, value conventions and stylisation of one sort of another which create art-forms that make bigger intellectual and imaginative demands upon the audience. It is the tension between the artistry on stage and the demands of the audience who put 'bums on seats' that results in acceptable theatre – and occasionally great theatre.

If theatre Directors are so heavily subsidised that it becomes unnecessary for them to attract audiences, this tension is lost and self-indulgent Directors, preferring the praise of the critics, or even mere notoriety, to the honest satisfaction of filling the theatre and communicating with an audience, will present productions that satisfy their egos and empty the theatre. This is what has happened in post-war Germany. In Frankfurt/Main in 1995, for example, the subsidy for plays amounted to 317, -DM for every member of the audience, and for opera, 668,-DM. These figures speak for themselves. It is perhaps no coincidence that two years later the Frankfurt Volksbühne had to wind up, fifty years after its post-war re-foundation. It still had three thousand members, who now would be contacted directly by the municipal theatres. The *Frankfurter Rundschau* deeply regretted the passing of one of the 'most active associations for popular education ... in Germany ... Thus the past is wound up and nothing in sight for the future.' This 'Directors' Theatre' question was vividly posed within the Volksbühne in the contrast between the views and policies of Abendroth and Waidelich.

In recent years unemployment has been another factor in the decline of the Volksbühne. Though in its beginnings the ticket prices were within reach of all but the most poverty stricken, the increasingly high prices charged by the theatres themselves have made it impossible to keep even Volksbühne tickets within reach of the unemployed.

The surviving practical idealists such as Köhler and Meisen did their best to keep the Federation as a Discussion Platform where all the associations could exchange views; and they were determined at the same time to keep such discussion "far from the cut-throat constitutional discussions of former years" (Meisen). Köhler also hoped that "perhaps the final years of the Volksbühne Movement could run their course honourably and without internal discord."

That the final cause of the disastrous collapse of the movement as a national body was in fact the suicidal feuding between members of the leadership cannot be denied, but that feuding would not have occurred had not the movement already been weakened by loss of membership and uncertainty of purpose, and both these, the loss and the uncertainties, were caused by changes in society outside the Volksbühne's control.

It must be honestly admitted that the Volksbühne Movement, or its fragmentary and dying body, belongs to another age, an age in which it was possible, without pomposity or hypocrisy to inscribe on the façade of a great theatre in the heart of a mighty European capital, the motto of the Freie Volksbühne:

DIE KUNST DEM VOLKE [2]

NOTES

For abbreviation of titles in Notes see 'Principal Sources'

PROLOGUE

1   *H,* pp. 11–12.
2   *S,* p. 185 [See Appendix B]
3   Schlieper, p. 198.
4   Two years later, in 1871, six months after the establishment of the German empire, Bismarck was to begin his *Kulturkampf* against the supra-national pretensions of the Catholic Church.
5   Taylor, pp. 129–30.
6   *F,* p. 64.
7   Cf. Sartre's use of a classical subject in *Les Mouches.*
8   *S,* p. 18.
9   1845–1909.
10 Even some months after the founding of the Freie Volksbühne in August 1890, came the Association for Popular Entertainment, (Verein für Volksunterhaltung) whose chief aim was to try to prevent Social Democracy from monopolising theatrical movements. It planned to give seven performances in its first year, including two plays by Schiller and two by Charlotte Birch-Pfeiffer (1800–1868), a popular purveyor of other people' s goods – e.g. her play *Die Waise von Lowood* (*Jane Eyre*). The admission charge was to be 40 Pfennigs and the deficit covered by wealthy patrons. This never came to life.
11 *S,* p. 2 6.
12 Osborne, p. 2.
13 *Frankfurter Zeitung,* 10 May 1904.
14 *Neue Rundschau* (1913), p. 328.
15 *Frankfurter Zeitung,* 12 January 1887.
16 Conrad Schmidt, editor of the *Berliner Volkstribüne.*

ACT I/Scene I   The first decade

1   *Deutsche Illustrierte Zeitung,* 13 June 1885.
2   *Freie Bühne für modernes Leben,* Jahrgang 1, Heft 3.
3   Some sources omit Stockhausen and mention others.
4   Schley.
5   *Die Nation,* 26 October 1889 (in Brahm, pp. 298–9).
6   Schley, p. 52.

7   Brahm, p. 299.
8   He did not hurl them on to the stage (see Schley, p. 46 and note 134).
9   Schley, p. 46.
10 *Die Gesellschaft*, Jahrgang 1893, Heft 2.
11 All these citations from *S*, p. 185 ff.
12 *Die Kunst dem Volke*, Nr 6, quoted in *G*, p. 11.
13 Cf. his reference in the 'Appeal' to 'the cheap seats'.
14 *G*, p. 17.
15 See Appendix C.
16 The ultimate exclusion of the first two may have been on account of their large casts.
17 *G*, p. 18.
18 *S*, p. 106.
19 Türk, quoted in *S*, p. 106.
20 *G*, pp. 46–7.
21 Franz Mehring. *Die Volksbühne*. 1892/3. Heft 7. pp 3–7.
22 *Neue Freie Volksbühne*, 18. Spieljahr, Heft 2, 1907/08.
23 O.E. Hartleben in *Vorwärts* v. 10.2.1891.
24 Namely: *Vor Sonnenaufgang, Doppelselbstmord, Thérèse Raquin, Ghosts*.
25 *G*, p. 45.
26 *G*, p. 34.
27 Bernhard von Richthofen (1836–1895) was a relative of Frieda, wife of D. H. Lawrence. His comment on the theatrical developments of this time was: 'Die ganze Richtung passt uns nicht!' (see Robert Lucas, *Frieda Lawrence*, English translation, 1973, p. 19).
28 *F*, p. 39.
29 *S, passim.*
30 *G*, p. 68.
31 List of artistic experts: Bruno Wille, Wilhelm Bölsche, Julius Hart, O.E. Hartleben, the two Kampffmeyers, Fritz Mauthner, Leopold Schönhoff, Carl Wildberger (all of the 'old guard'); Gustav Landauer, Dr Albert Dresdner (historian), Adalbart von Hanstein (poet), Maximilian Harden (publisher of *Zukunft*), Wilhelm Hegeler (short-story writer), Max Marschalk (musicologist), Wilhelm von Polenz (a 'lord of the manor' turned novelist), Ernst von Wollzogen (a clever conversationalist), Victor Holländer (orchestral conductor), Emil Lessing (theatre director) (*G*, pp. 69–70). Nestriepke says there were twenty, but gives only these nineteen names.
32 Mehring, p. 291.
33 *S*, p. 73.
34 For example: Ibsen, *The Master Builder*; Hauptmann, *Hanneles Himmelfahrt* (*Hannele's Assumption*).

35   Mehring's socialist activities continued unabated after his leaving the Volksbühne. At the start of the First World War he was a member of the Opposition and later was one of the founders of the Spartakusbund. He died on 29 January 1919, physically broken through the harsh conditions so-called 'protective custody'.

36   1892–93: two sections (2,400 members).
      1893–94: five sections (5,000-6,000 members).
      1894: six sections (6,600 members).
      October 1894: seven sections (7,600 members).
      April 1895: eight sections (7,600 members).

37   See Appendix D.

38   This, however, could also have been due to the fact that the proposal involved having evening performances as well as those on Sunday afternoons. The idea was to have been presented to an extraordinary general meeting, but because of police action this never happened.

39   *Bildungsschwindel*. Said in 1892 by party secretary Auer in relation to the Frele Volksbühne and the Arbeiterbildungsschule.

40   The Freie Bühne was revived for single plays in 1893, 1895, 1897, 1898, 1899 and 1901. In November 1909 it was resurrected for the last time to present a memorial performance of *Vor Sonnenaufgang*.

41   In a letter of 1 August 1893 (see Osborne, p. 131, note 1).

42   Schwab-Felisch, p. 195.

43   *Ibid.*

44   Fritz Mauthner in *Magazin für Literatur*. 60. Jg. Nr 16, 18.4.1891.

45   *Berliner Zeitung*. 26.5.'91

46   Wille (quoted in *G*, p. 119).

47   List given in *G*, pp. 122–3.

48   *G*, p. 111.

49   Other places where attempts were made to found Volksbühne associations even as early as this were Cologne, Frankfurt am Main and Leipzig. Interested persons in Vienna, Zürich and even Milan were in contact with the Berlin leaders.

50   *G*, p. 133.

51   This is clearly the view of Heinz Selo.

ACT I /Scene III   Into the twentieth century

1   *S*, p. 78.
2   See Appendix D.
3   Lists in *G*, pp. 179–81 and 229–31.
4   *G*, p. 234.
5   *G*, p. 170.
6   See Appendix D.

7   List in G, pp.207–9.
8   In 1898 he volunteered to write one thousand addresses every month in order to enable the periodical to be sent by post at a cheap rate.
9   Löhr became worse in health and died in April 1902.
10   Heinrich Braulich *Die Volksbühne*. Berlin 1976. p. 85.
11   *G*, p. 263.
12   Melchinger, p. 8.
13   Particularly in plays by Strindberg, Wilde and Wedekind at the Kleines Theater.
14   Tape-recorded interview with the author, 10 May 1974.
15   Julius Bab, *Volksbühne*. In *Literarische Welt*, Berlin, Heft 26 (30 June 1927), p. 6. Reprinted in Bab/Bergholz, p. 305.
16   Bab/Bergholz, p. 307.
17   The four plays were: *Walter Volk* (Federow); *Das Urteil des Salomo* (Else Torge); *Feindliche Seelen* (Loyson); *Julia* (Hebbel).
18   These quotations from *G*, 289–91.
19   *G*, p. 246.
20   Later it was decided that the interest on single shares (10 Marks) would be added to the capital, but that interest on blocks of five shares would be payable yearly on 1 October. All share capital was ultimately to be repayable, either after two years from the opening of the theatre (with six months' notice), or gradually, through amortisation; also if the holder were ill, unemployed, no longer living in Greater Berlin, or deceased.
21   'Immer strebe zum Ganzen! Und kannst du selber kein Ganzes werden, als dienendes Glied schliess an ein Ganzes dich an!' (*G*, p. 342)
22   Lists in *G*, pp. 327–8, 387–9.
23   Season 1910/11. Plays produced in the Neues Volkstheater: *Pillars of Society* (Ibsen); *Erziehung zur Ehe* (O.E. Hartleben); *Ysbrand* (F. van Eeden); *Der G'wissenswurm* (Anzengruber); A Tolstoy Memorial Celebration; *Die Schmetterlingsschlacht* (Sudermann); *Hanneles Himmelfahrt* (Hauptmann); *Kater Lampe* (E. Rosenow); *Der Vielgeprüfte* (W. Meyer-Förster).
24   'O Schutzgeist alles Schönen, steig hernieder.'
25   *G*, p. 353.

FIRST INTERMISSION   War and revolution

1   *H*, p. 349.
2   L. Löb in *Penguin Companion to Literature*, vol. 2, p. 390.

ACT II / Scene I Berlin 1. To 1923

1 Oschilewski, p. 51.
2 *Ibid.*
3 'eingetragener Verein': a 'registered society', for legal purposes.
4 'The author to the producer, October 1921', translated by Vera Mendel in *Masses and Man*, Nonesuch Press, 1923, pp. ix-x.
5 Translated by Vera Mendel (see note 4).
6 *Masses and Man*, pp. ix and x.
7 Jürgen Fehling, 'Note on the production of *Masses and Man*', translated by Vera Mendel, pp. 57–8.
8 *Masses and Man*, p. x.
9 See Cecil Davies: *The Plays of Ernst Toller*, for a fuller account of this.
10 According to Piscator – not a reliable witness in this matter – the executive bore Nestriepke a grudge on account of this for a long time.

ACT II / Scene I Berlin 2. The Piscator affair

1 Even this, alleges Rühle, was 'because the Volksbühne had remained spiritually untouched by the revolution and had not found the way back to the social commitment of its origins,' (Rühle, p. 198).
2 Piscator's theatre supported the actors' strike, and the actors' union authorised the theatre to play; then Gorter, the actual concessionaire, dismissed the company; but Piscator re-engaged them half an hour later.
3 *PT*, p. 60.
4 *PT*, p. 40.
5 Maria Ley-Piscator, p. 72.
6 *PT*, p. 60.
7 Maria Ley-Piscator, p. 74.
8 Piscator says 1880, but this is typical of the slips in *Das politische Theater*.
9 Fifty-six actors are needed.
10 Oddly enough, Piscator does not claim credit for this, but gives it to the author: 'The author has expressed the events in an objective manner and without poetic pretensions, in a kind of scenic illustration. Not for nothing does the piece bear the sub-title: *An Epic Drama*' (*PT*, p. 61).
11 Quoted in *PT*, p. 62.
12 *I*, p. 17.
13 Innes says that Plscator 'experimented with a formal prologue in *Flags*, in which the play was declared to be a puppet show' (*I*, p. 105).
14 *PT*, p. 63.
15 *PT*, p. 85.

16   *PT*, p. 78. Piscator misnames Umnitsch 'Umeltet' and Sawin 'Ssarin'.
      He is obviously writing from memory.
17   Arthur Eloesser in *Das blaue Heft*, 15 March 1926. In Rühle, p. 694.
18   *PT*, p. 79.
19   *PT*, p. 81.
20   *PT*, p. 82.
21   Paquet, *Sturmflut*. Volksbühne Verlag, Berlin, 1926, p. 7.
22   *Sturmflut*, p. 110.
23   *PT*, p. 80.
24   Rühle, p. 693.
25   Rühle, p. 692.
26   Rühle, p. 695.
27   *PT*, p. 84.
28   *Ibid.*
29   Staatliches Schauspielhaus, 4 December 1924, directed, by Jürgen
      Fehling – his only close contact with Brecht. They disagreed strongly
      over the production (see Hanser, p. 36).
30   Company of the Deutsches Theater in the Lessing Theater, 27 February
      1925. Brecht regarded this as a decisive attempt at epic Theatre (see
      Hanser, p. 37).
31   See *PT* pp. 88 ff.; Rühle, pp. 721 ff.; Bab/Bergholz, pp. 163 ff.
32   Bernhard Diebold in *Tod der Klassiker*. Quoted in *PT*, p. 91.
33   Bela Balázs. Quoted in *PT*, p. 95.
34   'The strongest propaganda that can be devised arises simply out of
      objective, unretouched, raw reality' (*PT*, p. 80).
35   *H*, p. 359.
36   Quoted in *PT*, p. 99.
37   *PT*, p. 97.
38   Holitscher must mean the Bühnenvolksbund, the 'Christian
      Volksbühne' founded in 1919 (see Appendix F).
39   *PT*, p. 97–8.
40   *PT*, p. 100.
41   *PT*, pp. 100–1.
42   In Rühle, p. 785.
43   *PT*, pp. 101–2.
44   *PT*, p. 103.
45   *Ibid.*
46   *Rühle*, p. 788.
47   *Rühle*, p. 789
48   'Owing to lack of time, neither Herr Welk, nor Herr Holl, the director,
      nor I myself, saw a finished dress rehearsal, with the result that the
      night before, I disclaimed responsibility' (!) (*PT*, p. 109).
49   *H*, pp. 134–5.

50 See also Tilla Durieux' own account of this: 'In 1927 1 saw a production of Schiller' s *The Robbers* in the Staatstheater and thereby became acquainted with a – for me – new man: Erwin Piscator. His manner of production pleased me so much that I sought his personal acquaintance. He told me his plans, which so enthralled me that I determined to provide him with the money for a theatre. I gave him 400, 000 gold marks and he rented the Theater am Nollendorfplatz, one of the largest in Berlin. It was opened on 3 September 1927 with *Hoppla, wir leben!* by Ernst Toller. I played a role in the following production, that of the Czarina in the play *Rasputin*. Piscator's talent is indisputable. He was the first to follow Max Reinhardt in new ways of staging. He tried to combine film and live theatre, and achieved thereby astonishing results. And when in the epic satire, *The Adventures of the Good Soldier Schwejk*, he had Pallenberg marching on the 'treadmill', and landscapes and artificial people passed him by, it gave an effect that was new and enthralling.... But these contrivances cost so much money that it could not be covered by the box-office receipts from the audiences that streamed in in great numbers. After a brief existence the theatre had to close'. (Durieux, pp. 317–18.)

51 Oschliewski, p. 36.

52 *Kreuz-Zeitung*, 14 July 1927.

53 Piscator admitted some truth In Alfred Kerr's description of this as a creepy-crawly tortoise of grey tent-cloth'.

54 Tape-recorded interview with the author, 10 May 1974.

55 Quoted in Oschilewski, p. 58.

56 Oschilewski, p. 39.

ACT II / Scene II: Nationwide Growth

1 Unless otherwise stated the source for factual information on the Volksbühne movement in this section is H.

2 Braulich p. 138

3 Shirer p. 457

4 H. p. 323. Eine Zigarettenfabrik zog in den einstigen Kunsttempel ein.

5 H. p. 262.

6 Quoted by A. Schwerd *Zwischen Sozialdemokratie und Kommunismus*. p. 81.

7 Ibid. p. 2.

8 Der 8. Volksbühnentag: Magdeburg 1927. pp. 46–47.

9 Ibid. p. 90.

10 Ibid. p. 102.

11 Toller *Gesammelte Werke*. 1. p. 146.

12　　Schwerd op. cit. p. 94.
13　　Ibid. p. 96.
14　　Ibid. p. 97.
15　　Ibid.
16　　Shirer p. 168.

SECOND INTERMISSION　　The Nazis

1　　*Chronik*, p. 28.
2　　*Chronik*, p. 29.
3　　*Chronik*, p. 30.
4　　Bochow, pp. 17–18.
5　　*Protokolle der Hauptversammlung vom 19.12.33*. In: *Volksbühne e. V. (2),
　　　Materialien des Berliner Stadtarchivs*. Quoted in Braulich.
6　　'Seven sub-chambers were established to guide and control every
　　　sphere of cultural life: the Reich chambers of fine arts, music, the
　　　theatre, literature, the press, radio and the film. All persons engaged
　　　in these fields were obligated to join their respective chambers, whose
　　　decisions and directives had the validity of law. Among other powers,
　　　the chambers could expel - or refuse to accept – members for "political
　　　unreliability", which meant that those who were even lukewarm about
　　　National Socialism could be, and usually were, excluded from
　　　practicing [sic] their profession or art and thus deprived of a
　　　livelihood'. (Shirer, pp. 241–2.)
7　　Neft, who had been pensioned in 1932, continued under the Nazis to
　　　receive a pension of 700 RM.
8　　Braulich, p. 170f.
9　　*NB*, p. 13.

ACT III / Scene I

1　　Luft, p. 10.
2　　Only the Russians occupied Berlin at this time. The American and
　　　British troops moved into their appointed sectors of the city on 4 July
　　　1945; the first session of the Allied Kommandatura was on 11 July
　　　1945. The French troops occupied their sector on 12 August 1945. (*In
　　　Brief*, p. 33.)
3　　This date is given by Nestriepke and confirmed in the official *25 Jahre
　　　Theater in Berlin. Theaterpremieren 1945–1970*. Braulich wrongly states
　　　'28th April'.
4　　*Am Anfang die 'Weber'*. In *Die Volksbühne*. Henschel 1947, 1. Jg. Heft 1.
　　　S. 13.

5 Howley, p. 141.
6 Howley, p. 142.
7 Howley, p. 143.
8 *Ist die Welt nicht schön?* by Alec Dyer, the pen-name of a German living in London.
9 From the weekly periodical, *sie*. Quoted in *NB*, p. 126.
10 Oschilewski, p. 50.
11 Piscator, extempore speech to the Volksbühne conference in Kassel, 1962. Quoted in Oschilewski, p. 59.
12 Oschilewski, p. 60.
13 Oschilewski, p. 50.
14 22. Volksbühnentag, p. 22.
15 22. Volksbühnentag, pp. 29–30.
16 Luft, p. 7.
17 Quoted in *I*, p. 175.
18 Piscator's introduction to the *rororo* edition of the play.
19 22. Volksbühnentag, p. 31.
20 21. Volksbühnentag, p. 117.
21 Ibid.
22 22. Volksbühnentag, p. 31.
23 22. Volksbühnentag, p. 33.
24 22. Volksbühnentag, p. 32.
25 22. Volksbühnentag, p. 34.
26 Piscator's other FVB Productions include: *The Merchant of Venice*, *Androcles and the Lion*, *Fuhrmann Henschel* (Hauptmann). Other productions during his directorship include: Osborne, *Luther* (Peter Zadek), Arden, *Workhouse Donkey* (Ulrich Erfurth), Walser, *Überlebensgross Herr Krott* (The larger than life Mr Krott) (Peter Palitzch), Sartre, *Nekrassov* (Robert Freytag).
27 22. Volksbühnentag, p. 40.
28 Ibid.
29 Richard Voigt (*21. Volksbühnentag*, p. 65).
30 23. Volksbühnentag, p. 102 and 24. Volksbühnentag, p. 142.
31 22. Volksbühnentag, p. 110.
32 24. Volksbühnentag, p. 133–4.
33 See Appendix B.
34 Bochow, p. 76.
35 28th Volksbühnentag. Essen 1984. p. 26.
36 Ibid. p. 37.
37 *Freie Volksbühne Berlin* 1890–1990. p. 238.
38 Ibid. p. 239.
39 Ibid. p. 258.

40   Rechenschaftsbericht der Vorsitzenden, Ruth Freydank für 1993 anläßlich der Hauptversammlung der Freien Volksbühne e.V. Berlin am 23.9.1994.

41   In an interview with the weekly periodical *Freitag* (4.6.93). The *Moorsoldatenlied* had already been used (seriously) in Ernst Toller's last play, *Pastor Hall*.

42   Quoted by Helmut Schödel in an article, *Das trunkene Schiff.* Periodical and date not known.

ACT III / Scene II

1   Bochow. See List of Sources.

2   During the 1970s the TAT suffered vicissitudes. An unsuccessful attempt at a collective directorship was followed by the appointment of Rainer-Werner Fassbinder as director in 1974. His brief period of office was stormy, though some productions, notably his *Uncle Vanya,* were outstanding. He resigned without notice in June 1975. In December 1976 the city took over the TAT and Frankfurt Volksbühne as a municipal limited company, the former becoming a Children's and Youth Theatre.

3   Dieter Hadamczik, *Neue Formen des Volksbühnenverbundes werden zu finden sein.* In *MY Feuilleton* 22.10.'94, in *MY Theater-Korrespondenz* 8. 22.10.'94. Spielzeit 1994/5.45.Jahrgang. Publ. by Mykenae Verlag Rossberg KG, Ahastraße 9. D-64285 Darmstadt.

4   Ibid.

5   Ibid.

6   28. Volksbühnentag, Essen '84. Eine Dokumentation des nichtöffentlichen Teils. p. 92.

7   Ibid. p. 113.

8   Außerordentlicher Volksbühnentag, Frankfurt '86. Eine Dokumentation des volksbühneninternen Teils. p. 25.

9   Ibid. p. 80.

10   30. Volksbühnentag Bremen '88, 10-12 Juni. Schriften-Reihe Bd 23(b). p. 46.

11   Ibid. p. 48.

12   Waidelich, *Essen spielt Theater.* (Econ Verlag)

13   WAZ 17.9.'94

14   Bergisches Land, Bielefeld, Castrop-Rauxel, Hagen, Hamm, Kaiserslautern, Köln, Koblenz, Leverkusen, Lüneburg, Memmingen, Minden, Mülheim/Ruhr, Oberhausen, Pforzheim, Solingen, Uelzen, Velbert, Trier. (Information from Köhler, 13.4.1995)

15   Franz-Heinz Köhler: 2. *Rundschreiben des am 30.10.1994 gewählten*

Sprechergremiums des Bundes deutscher Volksbühnen e.V. Essen.7.4.1995. pp. 7–8.

16 Theatertendenzen 1995 – ihre Ursachen und ihre Wirkungen auf das Publikum. (From the published announcement of the conference.)

17 From the published invitation to the Seminar. Further information supplied by Köhler.

18 Viertes Rundschreiben des Sprechergremiums 1994/96 des Bundes deutscher Volksbühnen e.V. an die örtlichen Volksbühnenvereine. 4.6.'96

19 Protokoll der offenen Vorstandssitzung des Bundes deutscher Volksbühnen am 24 November 1996 in Köln.

EPILOGUE.

1 v. Note 19 above.

2 December 1998:
The Federation still exists, even though few Associations still belong to it. Its activities are limited to an Annual Seminar in Bad Münstereifel. [The 1998 Seminar was held 23–27 November on the theme **Theatre, where are you going? From public funding to privatisation.** It was addressed by Wolfgang Meisen (Chairman of the Federation) and five other distinguished speakers: Dr Bernd Meyer (Köln), Linda Reisch (Frankfurt/Main), Prof. Dr Heinz Lukas-Kindermann (Trier), Carmen Emigholz (Bremen), Dr Kay Carius (Hamburg) and Dr Helmut Mörchen (Bad Münstereifel).] The individual associations are still active, many celebrating or about to celebrate the 50th or 75th Anniversaries of their foundation. Nearly all the larger Associations arrange Theatre- and Art Trips for their members. This is the so-called "Second Leg". Members are thus offered a wider service which also generates income for the association. Thus the Volksbühne Movement still exists although the Volksbühne Federation has only a modest existence.

Information from Wolfgang Meisen
October 1998

The *Deutsches Bühnenjahrbuch 1998* lists 75 locally based Theatre Audience Organisations which "work according to Volksbühne principles" but the majority of these are independent of the Federation.

PRINCIPAL SOURCES

The abbreviations by which works are referred to in the Notes and Appendices are given in parentheses.

Books and dissertations

BAB, Julius: *Über den Tag hinaus: kritische Betrachtungen*, ed. H. Bergholz.Veröffentlichungen der deutschen Akademie für Sprache und Dichtung, Darmstadt. Verlag Lambert Schneider, Heidelberg/Darmstadt, 1960. (*Bab/Bergholz*)

BIERMANN, Wolf: *Die Drahtharfe*. Verlag Klaus Wagenbach. Berlin 1965.

BOCHOW, Peter: 'Der Geschmack des Volksbühnen-publikums'. Inaugural-Dissertation, Freie Universität Berlin. Berlin, 1965. (*Bochow*)

BRAHM, Otto: *Kritiken und Essays*. Klassiker der Kritik. Artemis Verlag. Zürich and Stuttgart, 1964. (*Brahm*)

BRAULICH, Heinrich: *Die Volksbühne. Theater und Politik in der deutschen Volksbühnen-bewegung*. Henschel, Berlin 1976.

BRODBECK, Albert. *Handbuch der deutschen Volksbühnenbewegung*. Berlin, 1930. (*H*)

Chronik der Hamburger Volksbühne. Hamburger Volksbühne e. V. , 1969. (*Chronik*)

DAVIES, Cecil: *The Plays of Ernst Toller: A Revaluation*. Harwood Academic Publishers, 1996.

DURIEUX, Tilla. *Meine ersten neunzig Jahre*. Herbig. Munich-Berlin, 1971. (*Durieux*)

EBERT, Carl: 'Theatre as necessity of Life', in *Unsere Theaterneubauten nach 1945*. German Section, International Theatre Institute, Berlin, n.d. (unpaginated). (*Ebert*)

FELDENS, Franz: *75 Jahre Städtische Bühnen Essen*. Rheinisch-Westfälische Verlagsgesellschaft, Essen, 1967. (*Feldens*)

Handbuch des Bühnenvolksbundes, Wille und Werk. Berlin, 1928.

HANSER, *Brecht-Chronik*. Carl Hanser Verlag, Munich, 1971. (*Hanser*)

HASCHE/SCHÖLLING/FIEBACH: *Theater in der DDR*. Henschel, Berlin 1994.

HENZE, Herbert: 'Otto Brahm und das Deutsche Theater in Berlin'. Inaugural-Dissertation, Erlangen, 1930. (*Henze*)

HIRSCH, Helmut: *Viel Kultur für wenig Geld? Entwicklungen und Verwicklungen der Volksbühne*. ECON Verlag, Düdsseldorf-Wien.

HOWLEY, Frank: *Berlin Command*. G.P. Putnam & Sons, New York, 1950. (*Howley*)

IHERING, Herbert: *Von Reinhardt bis Brecht. Eine Auswahl der Theaterkritiken 1909–32.* Edited with an Introduction by E. Badenhausen. Rowohlt, 1967.

In Brief. Berlin. Presse- und Informationsamt des Landes Berlin, 1972. (*In Brief*)

INNES, C.D.: *Erwin Piscator's Political Theatre.* Cambridge University Press, 1962. (*I*)

JOHANN, Ernst and JUNKER, Jörg: *German cultural history of the last hundred years.* Nymphenburger Verlagshandlung, Munich, 1970. (*Johann/Junker*)

KNILLI, Friedrich and MÜNCHOW, Ursula: *Frühes Deutsches Arbeitertheater 1847–1918 (a Documentation).* Carl Hauser Verlag, Munich, 1970. (*F*)

LEONHARD, Rudolf: *Ausgewählte Werke: Segel am Horizont, Dramen und Hörspiele.* Verlag der Nation, Berlin, 1963.

LEY-PISCATOR, Maria: *The Piscator Experiment.* J.H. Heinemann Inc., New York, 1967. (*Maria Ley-Piscator*)

LUCAS, Robert: *Frieda Lawrence.* Translat. by G. Skelton. Secker & Warburg, London, 1973. (*Lucas*)

LUFT, Friedrich: *25 Jahre Theater in Berlin. Vorwort* by Luft. Heinz Spitzing Verlag, Berlin, 1972. (*Luft*)

MEHRING, Franz: *Beitrage zur Literaturgeschichte.* Berlin, 1948. (*Mehring*)

MELCHINGER: *Max Reinhardt.* Friedrich Verlag, Hannover, 1968. (*Melchinger*)

MENDEL, Vera (translator). Ernst Toller: *Masses and Man.* Nonesuch Press, 1923.

MITTENZWEI, Werner: *Theater in der Zeitenwende.* Henschel Verlag, Berlin, 1972.

NESTRIEPKE, Siegfried: *Geschichte der Volksbühne Berlin. 1. Teil: 1890 bis 1914.* Volksbühnen-Verlags- und Vertriebs-G.m.b.H., Berlin, 1930. (*G*)

NESTRIEPKE, Siegfried: *Neues Beginnen. Die Geschichte der Freien Volksbühne Berlin 1946 bis 1955.* arani Verlags- G.m.b.H., Berlin-Grunewald, 1956. (*NB*)

OSBORNE, John: *The Naturalist Drama In Germany.* Manchester University Press, 1971. (*Osborne*)

OSCHILEWSKI, W.G.: *Freie Volksbühne Berlin.* Stapp Verlag, Berlin, 1965. (*Oschilewski*)

– *Zehn Jahre Theater am Kurfürstendamm.* arani Verlags-G.m.b.H., Berlin-Grunewald, 1960.

PAQUET, Alfons: *Fahnen.* In: *Deutsche Revolutionsdramen.* Herausgegeben und eingeleitet von Reinhold Grimm und Jost Hermand. Suhrkamp Verlag., n. d.

– *Sturmflut.* Volksbühnen-Verlags-und Vertriebs-G.m.b.H., 1926.

PFÜTZNER, Klaus: *Schriften zur Theaterwissenschaft*, vols. 1 and 4. Herausgegeben von der Theaterhochschule, 'Hans Otto', Leipzig. Henschel-verlag, Berlin.

PISCATOR, Erwin: *Das Politische Theater*. Rowohlt Verlag, 1963, (*PT*)

REUTER, Rudolf: *Christen vor der Bühne*. Theater-Rundschau-Verlag, Bonn, 1968.

RÜHLE, Günther: *Theater für die Republik 1917-1933 im Spiegel der Kritik*. Fischer, 1967. (*Rühle*)

SCHLEY, Gernot: *Die Freie Bühne in Berlin*. Berlin, 1967. (*Schley*)

SCHLIEPER, Inge: *Wurzeln der Democratie in der deutschen Geschichte*. Siegler & Co., Bonn, 1967. (*Schlieper*)

SCHWAB-FELISCH, H.: *Gerhart Hauptmann: Die Weber. Dichtung und Wirklichkeit*. Ullstein. Frankfurt am Main-Berlin, 1969. (*Schwab-Felisch*)

SELO, Heinz: 'Die "Freie Volksbühne in Berlin". Geschichte ihrer Entstehung und ihrer Entwicklung bis zur Auflösung im Jahre 1896'. Doctoral Dissertation, Erlangen. Berlin, 1930. (*S*)

SHIRER, W.L.: *The Rise and Fall of the Third Reich*. Secker and Warburg, London, 1973. (*Shirer*)

TAYLOR, A.J.P.: *The Course of German History*. Hamish Hamilton, London, 1945. (*Taylor*)

TOLLER, Ernst. *Gesammeslte Werke*. Ed. Spalek and Frühwald. Hanser, Munich, 1978.

TOLLER, Ernst: *Hoppla, wir leben!* Reprinted in Günther Rühle: *Zeit und Theater. Von der Republik zur Diktatur. 1925-33*. Band II. Propyläen Verlag, Berlin.

ZECH, Paul: *Das trunkene Schiff, eine szenische Ballade*. Schauspiel-Verlag, Leipzig., n. d, (1924).

Some important articles, brochures and proceedings

BRANDT, Willy: 'Theater als Politicum', *Theater Rundschau*, 18. Jahrgang (November 1972).

BRAULICH, Heinrich. 'Der Verrat an der Volksbühnenbewegung – Von den Anfängen bis zur Übergabe der Berliner Volksbühne an den Hitlerfaschismus (1890–1939)', *Wissenschaftliche Zeitschrift der Humboldt-Universität zu Berlin. Gesellschafts—und Sprachwissenschaftliche Reihe*, Jahrgang XVIII (1969), Heft 1, pp. 37–52.

DAVIES, Cecil W.: 'Educating a theatre audience. The German Volksbühne' *Studies in Adult Education*, vol. 3. David & Charles, 1971.

– 'The Volksbühne – a descriptive chronology', *Theatre Quarterly*, vol. II, No. 5. (1972), pp. 57–64.

– 'Theatre seat prices in the Federal Republic of Germany', Appendix V of the *Report of the Committee of Enquiry into Seat Prices*. Arts Council of Great Britain, 1973.

NESTRIEPKE, Siegfried: 'Volksbühnen und Theater-Austellung', *Die Viertewand*, vol. 7 (1927), pp. 2–4.

– Der Weg zur Volksbühne, Berlin, 1948.
– 'Vom Bülowplatz zur Bundesalle', *Freie Volksbühne zur Eröffnung, Berlin, 30 April 1963*. FVB, Berlin, 1963.
OSCHILEWSKI, W.G.: 'Mehring, ein Pionier der VB', *VB Spiegel* (March 1971).
– 'Ein grosser Moralist unserer Zeit [on Mehring]', *VB Spiegel,* (June 1971).
– *Siegfried Nestriepke zum Gedenken.* arani Verlag, Berlin-Grunewald, 1964.
PAUL, Anton A.: 'Die Meinungen des Volksbühnen-Publikums', *Bühne und Parkett,* (September/October 1973), p. 26.
PISCATOR, Erwin: 'Volksbühne heute', *Freie Volksbühne zur Eröffnung, Berlin, 30 April 1963*. FVB, Berlin, 1963.
Schriften des Verbandes der deutschen Volksbühnen-Vereine e. V.: Heft 11, *Der 21. Volksbühnentag* (Augsburg, 1964); Heft 12, *Der 22. Volksbühnentag* (Dortmund, 1966); Heft 13, *Der 23. Volksbühnentag* (Saarbrücken, 1968); Heft 14, *Der 24. Volksbühnentag* (Düsseldorf, 1970).
Schriftenreihe des Bundes der Theatergermeinden e. V.: Heft 6, *Düsseldorfer Theatergespräche '71*: 'Theater wozu – Theater wohin?'; Heft 7, *Mainzer Theatergespräche '73*: 'Politik und Theater. Theater und Fernsehen.'
SCHULZ, Günter: 'Die Volksbühne und ihre Forderungen an das Theater', *VB Spiegel* (October 1970), p. 1.

APPENDIX A

'DURCH'
THE TEN THESES

The independent literary association of poets, writers and friends of literature, which meets under the name and slogan *Durch* (*Through*), has no binding constitution whatever; but the literary opinions which are current in this circle are expressed in the following clauses, which at the same time represent the character of all modern literature.

1) All the signs are that contemporary German literature has reached a turning-point in its development, from which the prospect of a peculiarly significant era is opening up.

2) Just as all literature ought to illuminate the spirit of contemporary life through art, so it is the task of modern poets to give poetic form to all significant and would-be significant forces of present-day life, both in their positive and negative aspects, and to break new ground as pioneers and prophets of the future. Accordingly, social, national, religio-philosophical and literary struggles are specific, principal elements in contemporary writing, without its tendenciously subordinating itself to the service of parties and ephemeral movements.

3) In its nature and content our literature should be modern; it is born out of a world-view which is gaining ground every day despite all opposition, and which is the result of German idealist philosophy, of science, which is triumphantly unveiling the secrets of nature, and of technical cultural activities which are arousing every power, transforming material, and bridging over all rifts. This world-view is humane in the purest sense of the word, and proves its validity first and foremost by re-shaping human society, as it impinges on our times from various angles.

4) By careful attention to the inter-relations between all branches of world literature German literature must aspire to a character in keeping with the spirit of the German people.

5) Modern literature should portray man truly and mercilessly with his flesh and blood and passions, without overstepping in the process the self-imposed limits of a work of art, but rather to heighten the aesthetic effect through its magnificent truth to nature.

6) Our highest artistic ideal is no longer the Ancient but the Modern.

7) With such principles it is necessary to fight against outmoded imitation of the classics, against stylistic vanity and blue-stocking dilletantism.

8) It is equally necessary for modern literature to take note of endeavours aimed at decisive, healthy reform of the prevailing condition of literature, as of the urge to bring about a revolution in literature in favour of modern artistic principles.

9) Literary criticism seems to be an important and essential weapon in preparing for a new flowering of literature. To clear away from criticism uncalled-for, uncomprehending, ill-disposed elements and to build up mature criticism is as vital as artistic production itself, as the principal task of a modern literary movement.

10) At a time like the present in which every new kind of poetry, filled with its own peculiar spirit, comes up against a closely packed phalanx, it is necessary that all minds that are striving in the same direction, far from cliques or even mere academicism, should join in the common struggle.

APPENDIX B

Bruno Wille: *Appeal for the Founding of an Independent People's Theatre. (Berliner Volksblatt. 23.3.1890)*

The theatre ought to be a source of high artistic gratification, of moral uplift and a powerful stimulus to thinking about the great topics of the day. It is, however, for the most part degraded to the level of insipid drawing-room chatter and light fiction, trashy novels, the circus and comic papers. The stage is simply subordinated to capitalism, and the taste of the masses has been corrupted in all classes of society predominantly through certain economic conditions.

Meanwhile, under the influence of honestly striving creative writers, journalists and orators, some of our people have freed themselves from this corruption. Indeed, authors like Tolstoy and Dostoevsky, Zola, Ibsen and Kielland, as well as several German 'Realists' have found a sounding-board in the working people of Berlin.

This section of the population which has been converted to good taste needs not only to read the plays of their choice but also to see them performed. But public performances of plays in which a revolutionary spirit lives, are frustrated either by capitalism, for which they do not prove to be good box-office, or because of police censorship. These obstacles do not exist for a closed society. It is therefore possible for the 'Independent Theatre Society' to arrange the production of plays having the tendencies referred to. But seeing that membership of the 'Independent Theatre' is denied to the proletariat on economic grounds, it seems to me that it is appropriate to found an 'Independent People's Theatre'. The undersigned imagines this Independent People's Theatre somewhat as follows: The Society consists of a leading group and of its members. The leaders choose the plays to be performed as well as the performers. Through a quarterly subscription the members buy the appropriate theatre seat for three performances. A performance takes place each month, on a Sunday. The subscriptions aim only to cover the theatre rental and fees for the actors. They will be worked out as low as possible. It is hoped that the cheap seats can be purchased for 1.50M a quarter (that is, for three performances!).

All who would like to join such an 'Independent People's Theatre' are asked to send the undersigned on a postcard (which of course can include a number of names,),

1. Their name and address
2. The quarterly subscription they believe they could manage.

These details do not commit anyone but aim only to determine roughly upon how many members the founders of the Independent People's Theatre can reckon and thus how low the subscriptions can be calculated. If sufficient addresses arrive an undertaking is assured that can contribute something to the intellectual and spiritual improvement of the population. The result of this appeal, as well as more precise proposals, should be published soon.

Dr Bruno Wille

From: Heinz Selo: *Die "Freie Volksbühne" in Berlin. Inaugural-Dissertation, University of Erlangen*, 1930. pp 185–186

APPENDIX C

THE ARTICLES OF ASSOCIATION OF THE FREIE VOLKSBÜHNE

From S, pp. 187 ff. Reprinted from Berliner Volksblatt, 10 August 1890

1 The Freie Volksbühne Association sets itself the task of bringing before the people poetry in its modern sense, and particularly to present, read in public and explain through lectures up-to-date works executed with truthfulness.

2 Membership is acquired by payment of the registration fee (11). It lapses automatically if the minimum contribution (11 & 12) is unpaid by the 7th of any one month.

3 An Ordinary General Meeting is held every April and August.

4 Notice of each General Meeting and its agenda is given at least four days in advance through an insertion in a workers' daily newspaper published in Berlin and to be decided by the Executive, and by street posters on the day of the meeting.

5 The August General Meeting elects the Chairman, Treasurer and Secretary, the six ordinary committee members, the Organisers and the three Auditors.

6 The form of election is decided by the meeting before each election.

7 The Chairman, Treasurer and Secretary together constitute the Executive.

8 The Executive manages the business of the Association, represents it publicly, is authorised to conclude binding agreements, enter into engagements, acquire and dispose of property on behalf of the Association. It is responsible for choosing and appointing an artistic director [*Regisseur*], it selects the actors, readers and lecturers. If the Association's means permit, it is empowered to engage a permanent acting company. If the number of elected organisers is inadequate, it may nominate organisers to make up the full number.

9 The Committee consists of the three members of the Executive and six ordinary members [5]. It has the right of co-option to fill vacancies caused by individual resignations during the working year. If, however, the number of the Committee falls at any time to four, or the Executive is reduced to one, a General Meeting must be called within fourteen days for supplementary elections.

10 The Executive decides the plays to be produced, the subject of lectures and readings, and decides in all questions, what is authoritative for the literary character of the Association.

11   The size of the registration fee and the regular monthly contributions
      is decided by self-assessment, but the registration fee must amount to
      at least 1 Mark and the contribution for the months October to March
      inclusive to at least 50 Pfennigs per month, for the remainder of the
      year at least 25 Pfennigs per month.

12   The Executive is empowered, if the expenses are covered, to decide
      that the contributions for the months of March and September remain
      unlevied, and if the normal income does not suffice to cover the
      expenses, to levy supplements to the contributions of up to 10 Pfennigs
      per month.

13   The Treasurer sets up collection offices in all parts of the city according
      to need, whose occupiers receive the contributions and registrations
      of members. The membership card is issued on payment of the
      registration fee. It bears on the first page the name, status and
      permanent address of the member and is valid for the named member
      only. The monthly contributions can be paid at any chosen collection
      office. The receipt is given by sticking a voucher to the value of the
      contribution paid on the appropriate monthly column on the card.
      Only a member who can prove by producing his card that he has paid
      the statutory contributions has the right to attend performances and
      general meetings.

14   The Treasurer administers the property of the Association. He is bound
      and empowered to deposit amounts of over 300 Marks in a place of
      safety. For drawing deposited money a cheque is required signed by
      all three members of the Executive. The Treasurer must present a
      statement of accounts to each ordinary general meeting.

15   The auditors are empowered to inspect the account books jointly at
      any time, and are required to do this at least once a quarter.

16   In each month from October to March at least one performance takes
      place for each member.

17   If necessary the membership is divided into sections by the Executive.
      The performances for each section are the same.

18   Seats are allocated at performances by the organisers by means of a
      lottery.

19   The organisers choose a chairman and two committee members from
      among their number. These put the tickets in the urns and decide
      which seats are to be excluded from the lottery when the number of
      seats available is greater than the number of members who should
      obtain seats at the performance.

20   The lottery must be prepared in time for members to be able to draw
      their tickets one hour before the beginning of the performance at latest.

21   Each member who has produced his card at the theatre entrance, goes
      to the lottery tables on which urns with the duplicate tickets stand

and draws from the urn a ticket on which the name and number of the seat is indicated. Each urn is superintended by one organiser.

22 The Association's working year runs from 1 September to 31 August.

23 Resolutions concerning alterations to the statutes or winding up the association must be delivered to the Executive at least fourteen days before the particular general meeting at which they are to be debated.

24 A two-thirds majority of those present is required to alter the statutes or wind up the Association.

25 In the event of the Association's being wound up the assets in hand are to be disposed of according to the decision of the last general meeting.

[For the many modifications made to these articles in the early years, see *S*, pp. 187 ff.]

APPENDIX D

Membership statistics of the Freie Volksbühne. 1893–94 (From G. p. 89)

Total membership: 6,312
Men: 3,272
Women: 3,040

Occupations	Men	Wives
Carpenters	448	144
Not certain	269	79
Locksmiths	217	66
Shop assistants	204	29
Stonemasons	193	58
Painters	154	46
Bookbinders	144	34
Shopkeepers	134	42
Compositors	124	33
Tailors	121	–
Beltmakers	113	28
Mechanics	102	28
Printers	94	24
Lathe operators [*Dreher*]	88	28
Tinkers	95	34
Upholsterers	76	27
Woodturners [*Drechsler*]	71	24
Shoemakers	76	11
Lithographers	64	26
Engravers	63	19
Moulders	63	19
Domestic servants	57	17
Saddlers	50	15
Civil servants and teachers	27	9
Engineers and technicians	22	8
Draughtsmen	10	3
Manufacturers	9	4
Drivers	6	3
Editors	5	2
Students	10	–

Women in employment
Tailoresses		290
Unskilled female workers		246
Female shop assistants		67
Women teachers		4

Occupation unknown	259	1,132

Membership statistics of the Freie Volksbühne at the turn of the century (From G. p. 156).

4,921 members, male and female, gave their occupations.

Men
Joiners	357
'Workers'	252
In commerce [*Kaufleute*]	238
Printers	230
Tailors	142
Stonemasons	122
Mechanics	110
Machine-minders	110
Turners	102
Belt-makers	96
Bookbinders	86
Tinsmiths	78
Painters	77
Paperhangers	70
Builders	63
Moulders	62
Wood-turners	60
Leatherworkers, etc.	58
Civil servants	20
Writers	14
Private means	12
Doctors	6

Women
'Women workers'	405
Needlewomen	276
Tailoresses	270
Saleswomen	74
Bookkeepers	41
Dressmakers	30
Ironers	25

The Neue Freie Volksbühne: Census of occupations. October 1900 (From G. p. 193)

548 men answered the questionnaire and a few hundred women. Details of women's answers are not available.

Cabinet makers	55
Printers	41
'In trade'	38
Fitters	30
Tailors	24
Mechanics	20
Shoemakers	18
Turners	15

The Neue Freie Volksbühne: Census of occupations. Winter 1902–03 (From G. p. 251)

1, 022 answered the questionnaire.

Men

Cabinetmakers	98
Printers	69
Retail trade	51
Fitters	39
Tailors	33
'Workers'	31
Turners	24
Glass-workers	24
Upholsterers	23
Builders	22
Shoemakers	22
Painters	21
Bookbinders, etc.	20
Writers	6
Manufacturers	3
Editors	2
Dairy owner	1
Engineer	1

<u>Women</u>

Tailoresses	53
Sempstresses	35
Female workers	27
Shop assistants	26

(and others in smaller numbers)

Membership statistics of the Freie Volksbühne Berlin, 1952–53.

75,000 copies of questionnaire issued.

32,000 completed: 67.1 per cent from West Berlin;
    32.9 per cent from East Berlin.

<u>A.</u>

Professions	17,998	55.9%
Out of work	1,417	4.4%
Pensioners	5,087	15.8%
Housewives, daughters, school children, students without income	7,695	23.9%

<u>B.</u>

Occupations of the 19,415 who gave a profession (whether or not in work):

Self-employed	2,019	10.4%
Helping in family business	116	0.6%
Commercial and administrative employees in leading positions	466	2.4%
Commercial and administrative employees *not* in leading positions	8,524	43.9%
Other salaried employees	5,534	28.5%
Manual workers	2,757	14.2%

<u>C.</u>

Category *Self-employed* (2,019) included:

Lawyers, economic advisers, doctors, dentists, chemists	434
Others: cabinet makers, tailors, electricians, hairdressers, agents and masseurs, etc., approximately	300

That is, out of 2,019, there were about seven hundred with secure positions and incomes.

D.

Category *Other salaried employees* (5,534) included:

Magistrates, State lawyers, salaried doctors and dentists,
   high school and Oberschule teachers, engineers, architects   652

Others: technicians, foremen, elementary school teachers,
   librarians, nurses, kindergarten teachers, etc., approximately   250

That is, out of 5,534, there were about nine hundred with
above average incomes.

E.

Self-employed with secure positions and income   700
Salaried employees with secure positions and income   900
Commercial and administrative employees in leading positions   466

Approximate total of those with secure positions and income   2,000

Age-groups and occupations of new members of FVB. 1965–6
Total number of new members asked: approximately one thousand

A. Occupations (%)

Occupation	%
Salaried employees	35.0
Housewives	21.4
No information	18.4
Craftsmen and manual workers	15.0
Academics	4.0
School-children and apprentices	3.0
Pensioners and those of private means	3.0
Own business	0.3

B. Comparison of these with population of West Berlin as a whole (%)
   (Figures available in four categories only)

	New members	Population
Salaried employees	64.0	34.0
Manual workers	28.0	51.0
School / Apprentices	7.5	5.0
Self-employed	0.6	10.0

C. Ages of new members compared with whole population of
   West Berlin (%)

Year of birth	New members	Population
1880-1899	4.0	23.0
1900-1919	21.0	37.0
1920-1939	51.0	27.0
1940-1949	24.0	13.0

i.e. 75% members under 45 years of age,
   against 40% in West Berlin as a whole.

Reasons for resignations from FVB (results of two enquiries) %

	1962	1965
Dissatisfaction	28.0	33.0
Age or Illness	25.0	26.0
Professional or family reasons	15.0	15.0
Change of address	15.0	13.0
Financial reasons	4.0	3.0
Other reasons	–	0.9

APPENDIX E

TOLLER'S MAGDEBURG SPEECH

(Julius Bab spoke on *Theatre and Politics*, "in order to defend the idea of the sovereignty of art as the basis of a genuine Volksbühne". Toller answered him.)

Chairman Baake: Herr Ernst Toller wishes to speak now. He is our guest. Of course he may speak now.

Ernst Toller (greeted with applause): If I criticise the Volksbühne today, as it appears to us in reality in the Conference which we see going on around us here, I do that out of a sense of mental and spiritual responsibility. I make this criticism out of the strongest consideration for the cause of the Volksbühne and with the most severe *in*considerateness – for the sake of the idea of the Volksbühne.(Applause from a part of the assembly.)

I have gained the impression here as if the Volksbühne were in the year of its foundation and had not 31 years of practical work behind it.(*Voices:* Now, now!); thus a clarification of decisive matters must already have been achieved. Here, problems were touched upon, so vague, so woolly, that I ask myself – where is the foundation of what is being said here? The question of the neutrality of art was touched upon.

Drama attempts to embody the relationships between person and person, the relationship of the person to society, the relationships of classes and sections. Certainly also relationships are given form in drama which are "timeless", the relationship of man and society to the universe, to nature – relationships which express themselves through the predominance of cosmic powers over the will-power of society and individuals. These relationships are 'timeless' in their tragic tensions.

We know that historically the struggles in society take place in the form of class-struggles. Anyone who has recognised that cannot avoid approving of giving these class-struggles dramatic form also.(*Calls:* right, obviously, Bab has done that too!) Oh, not at all.! Giving form to class-struggles is not 'The Cult of the Proletariat' in inverted commas. And incidentally it must also be said that what was always denounced here as 'The Cult of the Proletariat', plays a quite minimal role in Russia. In the first year [viz., after the Russian Revolution *CWD*] great experiments were undertaken with the cult of the Proletariat, but up till now these experiments have not in the main found the artistic expression which they aspired to. (Cries of 'Aha!'

and laughter.) I'll answer this 'Aha!' Has the cult of the proletariat any existence anyway or has it not? It does exist in so far as the cult of the Proletariat is more than art and less than art. Less than art, because the cult of the Proletariat generates a party- political, tactical claim centrally. More than art because the cult of the proletariat operates directly, spurs people on directly to take certain actions on that very day.

Portraying class-struggles does not mean a dramatic form in which all the good is on the one side and all the evil on the other. What is crucial is not individual morality, but whether one idea is greater than the other. It is a matter of the struggle of ideas. We socialists say, our idea is the greater, and we must express this idea artistically.

The ideas of which Bab spoke here, the idea of 'undivided life', the idea that the theatre ought to lead us back once more 'to the fountainhead of life', these are demands which could equally well be put forward at a conference of the Bühnenvolksbund or even at a German Nationalist Theatre Conference. (Agreement and disagreement.)

It is a matter of the *Way*. We, who believe in the socialist way, we know that this way cannot know any woolliness, any lack of clarity, any liberal 'Utopias' of political freedom without social freedom. This way must be unambiguous. For us this way is the way of socialism. And socialism is struggle. Yesterday Professor Marck said: "The bourgeoisie came to power, through property and education." Is that so? *No!* The bourgeoisie nowhere came to power through property and education but through struggle. It was thus in England and in France. When the bourgeoisie did not fight, it got the proletarian storm-troops to march, in order to come to power itself, as we have experienced in Germany.(*A Shout:* You're making a party political speech!) I'm making a speech in the spirit of the original idea of the Volksbühne. (Applause in one part of the assembly; lively shouts in opposition: Completely wrong, no idea!) If you think that I have no idea, you can prove me wrong; I am trying to prove the correctness of what *I* say, through my work, my life and my writings. *Do it in **your** way!*

Art must certainly also know how to contemplate that ultimate thing in us, which I like to call the Peace of the Universe; yet our art must be before everything an art of struggle, not an art of woolly, beautiful intentions. For beauty is the goal and not the beginning. And the people [Volk] is not the beginning but the goal. We still have not a People; a People will exist when there are no longer any classes. Whilst art goes along with the way of socialism it is one of the means of creating a people.

Here begins the Volksbühne Case, not the Piscator Case which public opinion has stirred up. I hope you will allow me to say a few words about the Piscator Case, not for the sake of Piscator as a person, but because Piscator has manifested himself as the exponent of an idea ..

Chairman Baake: I would ask you please not to proceed with this discussion, the prerequisites are totally lacking here to pass judgement; we shall only become involved in interminable discussion. But you can stick to generalities —

Toller: I only wish to touch upon the case.

Chairman Baake: You can do that, but I ask you not to proceed with a further discussion; I would not permit it.

Toller (continuing): I shall only touch upon the case. The Berlin Volksbühne regards itself as the liveliest theatre in the Association.(Partial opposition). You dispute that? What mistrust in the Berlin Volksbühne!

In the Piscator case the Volksbühne's board of directors believed it might undertake an intervention in the artistic structure when the play had already been put on. You know that this intervention was disapproved of – not only by us, the crucial socialists. People objected to the intervention even in the press of the right and centre – for example, in *Germania*. (Shout of protest.) A voice which was important to you, the voice of a man who had for many years been influential in artistic life and whose voice undoubtedly has great weight namely Alfred Kerr (laughter) . . . Kerr wrote thus:

"... The 'political propaganda' in Piscator's production was not at all 'one-sided' (as '1848', for example hardly signifies 'Bolshevism') but it showed in the film with indisputable justice the painfully and slowly advancing earthly development from slave-state, to People's State. Is that forbidden? Long live the strong, courageous German Republic!

"There is a proverb that the Volksbühne can take to heart in view of a play-director as rare and distinguished as Piscator; it runs: "The bridegroom complains that the bride is too beautiful". Here the proverb must have a rider:" And he is not afraid of disowning his own bride afterwards.

Poor Bridegroom!" "

Unfortunately the Volksbühne has lost Piscator; he is to open his own theatre and will show there what he can do. (*Interruption:* Hope so!) That is extraordinarily regrettable for the Volksbühne anyhow. Now Piscator has turned to the Volksbühne and proposed to it that it forms an artistic community with his theatre; the Volksbuhne would send to his theatre the members who have an interest in it. He has already declared himself ready to undertake further productions in the Volksbühne, he has proposed an exchange of artistic forces, so that the financial burden is not too great: everything has been rejected. Piscator has been offered only the sales of guest tickets, which is undertaken for every other theatre! (*Interruptions.*)

All of you who are turning against me now with laughter and interruptions, all of you, who jeer at us today, fight us, and indeed persecute us (*Cries of 'Oho!'*) – is it not persecution when the editor of the association's periodical *The Volksbühne*, which had accepted a few scenes from a revolutionary poet, may only publish some of the scenes if another dramatist is printed at the same time, so as to appear as if the Volksbühne were disclaiming its solidarity with the poet, and the crucial point not – because the scene was 'indecent'?

Just recall how you fought as young people! Where are the fify Youth Delegates who were supposed to be here? Where are they? Not once has the Berlin Volksbühne Youth Section got the delegate it wanted, although three thousand young people there were united. (*Interruption:* We simply vote democratically!) This treatment of youth is very dangerous; it is a bad sign. It is also symptomatic that a journal in which youth found expression may not be continued on the same lines as up to now and that the editor has been removed.

The Volksbühne, as it actually is today, has lost its way, for the way is clarity and conviction. (*Interruption:* We don't want class war!) Poor heckler, you don't want class war. We can't *want* class war – it is there; we're blind if we will not see it. I consider Herr Bab the most dangerous ideologue in the Volksbühne; he is a spiritual danger for the Volksbühne.(*Disturbance*). An example: Bab said, "Art is free, there is no need to enquire about the monarchic or republican convictions of a work of art." But the creator, who stands behind a work of art, does not stand nowhere, in heavy mist. The artist stands living behind the work; in him a totality of impressions, philosophies of life, ways of looking at things, and insights, is at work: this totality finds expression in his artistic work, and we call this totality "fundamental conviction": if we fostered what Bab has set out as an artistic demand, the Volksbühne might indeed as well prefer a Frederick-the-Great play, a fascist play or a pop drama, only because it has artistic form. (*An interruption:* Of course if it *is* art!) Is that the idea of the Volksbühne? (*Voices:* Yes.) Then I pity the Volksbühne, that things have gone so far with it.

The creative artist's basic convictions become obvious in his work. It does not depend upon whether a work of art states that the Second or the Third International is the real one: "Cult of the Proletariat" can do that. It depends on the revolutionary atmosphere which lives in the work, which spurs on the worker sitting in the theatre, which clarifies for him what he dimly feels, and gives his feelings intellectual expression. Not *every* play should be performed by us – that would be a failure to appreciate the Volksbühne idea. When the person who interrupted me says we would produce a Frederick-the-Great Play or a pop play that comes to us, if it is a work of art, I say, No! We ought not – and I believe that I am in agreement with the board of directors in this and that it would firmly refuse to allow such a play to be performed in the Berlin Volksbühne. Just understand: Education alone achieves absolutely nothing. Did bourgeois education, with its pure opinions, prevent the World War? Did all his education prevent

Herr Bab from publishing an anthology of patriotic war-poems? Education without conviction isn't worth a thing!

If you want to turn back to the original idea of the Volksbühne, you must begin with what is alive, with *our* times. Only someone who gets through the present will reach what we call 'beyond time', 'timeless'. Only by completely penetrating the present time can we arrive at a true valuation of the work of former times. When our friend Bach from Vienna says that present-day working class youth does not value the theatre as the older generation did, because the theatre, as we see it today, cannot express youth's desire for culture – that is true. Youth does not value the theatre because today it offers for the most part woolliness and false beauty. (*Interruption:* We've been waiting for years for a work in keeping with the times!) You've seen many experiments in contemporary drama, and the Volksbühne members have listened to these experiments with whole-hearted attention.

The theatre is governed by the rules and nature of theatre (*die Theatralik*). Herr Bab has described this in terms of Wilhelmine politics. (*Interruption:* That's not art at all!) Certainly not, that's what I'm really talking about. There is a distinction between party politics and artistic policy. Party politics put forward practical demands for the struggles of the day; artistic policy only knows absolute, unconditional demands, but *absolute through a conviction,* **not** *absolute through* **no** *conviction.* (Applause from part of the assembly.)

When Bab says the workers reject politics in art, and that they don't want to be pushed up against the actuality which they see around them every day, I must affirm that Herr Bab is not pushed up against any actuality. The workers who see their life in artistic form in the theatre are very strongly attracted to such theatre. Ask the Viennese, let them tell you how the workers identified with what they saw and how they felt: "It is *you* that speaks and acts here." [Toller uses '*du*' in this sentence to emphasise the personal intimacy of the statement.] This political act has nothing to do with a political party's leading articles, nothing to do with slogans – it has to do with the great demand of the socialist idea. Theatre cannot create community: community is the prerequisite of theatre.

We have community of the socialist idea; it may be problematic today, it may be fragile, but is is there; we foretell its growth, it will blossom out in socialist society. Collectivism does not signify repression, but the full development both of the individual and of the community.

The great artist was always the mouthpiece of the effective idea of the times, of the struggling community of the times.

Think again: discover once more the way to the workers!

Do not believe that the workers organised in trade unions are on your side today. No, even the trade union leaders are discontented with the Volksbühne in Berlin and in the whole country.

Find the way to what is alive, to revolutionary youth; give them the chance to express themselves artistically; don't drive youth away as you have driven Piscator away, for then you are driving youth away from *all* theatre.

In your youth – we never forget it, and we remain thankful to you for it – you were fighters, you who founded this organisation and have led it to greatness. Were you not thankful at that time for everyone who joined up with you and helped you?

If you do not help us we are compelled to go our own way. Then one day we must declare: *We* are the bearers of the Volksbühne idea, *you* are *not!* Decide, decide today! (Stormy outburst. Applause from one part of the assembly. Expression of opposition from the great majority.)

APPENDIX F

THE CHRISTIAN 'VOLKSBÜHNE' MOVEMENT

1 Der Bühnenvolksbund (The National Theatre Union)

Following the tendency in the early years of the twentieth century known as the re-encounter of culture and Church (*Wiederbegegnung von Kultur und Kirche*) a journalist, Wilhelm Karl Gerst, founded in 1916 in Hildesheim a broadly based Union for the promotion of German Theatrical Culture (Verband zur Förderung deutscher Theaterkultur), united under the motto 'Cultural theatre instead of showbusiness' (Kulturtheater statt Geschäftstheaters). This soon saw the Berlin Volksbühne as its organisational model, and at a conference held in Frankfurt am Main in April 1919 the Bühnenvolksbund was founded with Gerst as general secretary and a head office in Frankfurt (later moved to Berlin). It described itself as 'an alliance for the encouragement of the theatre in a Christian German National spirit'. Closely modelled on the Volksbühne and with an impressive list of publications to its credit, the Bühnenvolksbund, starting from the Christian-National rather than the Socialist-International position, achieved work comparable with that of its prototype and rival, until Nazi measures in 1933 brought it to an end.

2 Der Bund der Theatergemeinden (Union of Theatre Societies)

After 1949 organisations formerly associated with the Bühnenvolksbund began to revive, especially in the Augsburg–Munich and Cologne–Düsseldorf areas. In February 1951, chiefly through the initiative of Max Hohenester and Karl Fürst, both of Augsburg, a conference held in Frankfurt decided unanimously to found a successor to the Bühnenvolksbund: Der Bund der Theatergemeinden. A steering committee was set up under the chairmanship of Dr Rudolf Reuter, a library director of Cologne, who later became the 'Grand Old Man' of the movement, and whose professional and voluntary interests were bound up with literature, theatre and adult education. Though not the first chairman (that was Hohenester until his death in 1956), he became vice-chairman in 1954, succeeding to the chair in 1956, a position he held for seventeen years, resigning at the 21st Annual Conference at Mainz in 1973.

Conflict with the Volksbühne came quickly. Dr Benecke, Managing Director of the Deutscher Bühnenverein, welcomed the formation of a Christian theatre audience organisation. Nestriepke replied in an open letter: the formation of such an organisation was mistaken; 'Christian' audience organisations could only exist to draw attention to, or produce, works of their own persuasion. In response, Dr Reuter pointed out the historical roots of his movement and its independence from party or confessional ties; he suggested that the two organisations had many common aims and ought to co-operate, but that the new body could make contacts inaccessible to the Volksbühne.

The themes of the annual conferences express a wide spectrum of interest in the theatre. The monthly periodical, *Theater Rundshau*, published since 1955 carries serious reviews and articles. Information sheets, brochures and booklets are also published.

Since 1955, the Bund, its headquarters now in Bonn, has been affiliated to the International Theatre Institute, and its general manager, Dr Welzel, was vice-president of the German section of the ITI from 1964 to 1971. It was strongly represented at the international meetings of IATO where, as elsewhere, a friendly relationship with the Volksbühne was well established.

By 1975 the Bund had a membership of about 140,000 persons in thirty local societies with about three hundred 'feeder' groups. On the whole this 'Christian' organisation flourishes best where the 'Social Democratic' one has less success. The following is a list of the largest affiliated bodies of the Bund der Theatergemeinden (1971) with the Volksbühne figures (1969) in those places for comparison:

Place	Theatergemeinde (1971)	Volksbühne (1969)
Munich	50,000	1,650*
Berlin	17, 000	83,780
Düsseldorf	13,000	13,500
Cologne	13,000	10,000
Bonn	11,500	2,790
Augsburg	5,000	2,275
Würzburg (including Youth Organisation)	4,600	716
Wiesbaden	2,800	639
Münster	2,500	833
Mönchengladbach	2,000	–
Wuppertal	2,000	11,750
Bamberg	1,250	347
Frankfurt	1,000	18,232
Totals (thirteen places)	127,650	146,566
Total (omitting Berlin)	110,650	62,786
Total (omitting Berlin and Munich)	60,650	61,136

*There was also a larger 'breakaway' Volksbühne in Munich, whose constitution excluded it from the Federation.

The growth of the movement continued steadily:

1979:	approx. 150,000 members
	34 local societies
	approx. 400 so-called 'feeder' groups.
	This number remained constant into the mid-1990s.
1981:	approx. 158,000 members
	35 local societies
1983:	approx. 162,000 members
	37 local societies
1985:	162,338 members
	35 local societies
1987:	171,704 members
	37 local societies
1989:	178,425 members
	45 local societies
1991:	179,277 members
	45 local societies
1993:	178,977 members
	53 local societies

These local societies were grouped in State Associations. There were six of these in 1979 and their number had grown to ten by 1993. With the re-unification of Germany new societies were founded in Leipzig, Dresden, Stendal, Kottbus and Eisenach, and in 1993 the biennial conference was able to be held in Leipzig in association with the 300th anniversary of the Leipzig Opera.

Throughout this period the conferences had each had a more or less controversial theme. At Trier in 1979 (Theme: Theater über die Grenzen) Dr Klaus Rohr argued that the internationality of theatre, lost in the 18th and 19th centuries, must now be recovered.

In 1981 at Aachen the theme was 'Theatre as Provocation'. Two years later in Darmstadt opera and music-theatre were discussed, and in 1985 the importance of language and speech in drama. The next two conferences looked at more general contemporary questions, but in 1991 a more controversial theme was again chosen: the adaptation, and especially the translation, of operas. Is faithfulness to the original a chimera? Inevitably the theme of the 1993 Leipzig conference was the relationship of culture and politics, and the President of the Federation, Friedrich v. Rekulé, concluded his keynote speech on the politico-cultural situation in Germany:

> The process of German Unity must be seen as an intellectual and spiritual challenge. Consideration must be directed towards a further growth in culture, not the contrary.

And he quoted Gero Hammer:

> The German Theatrical Landscape is part of the essential character of our people, - including structural changes, of course.

As early as the mid-1950s the need to attract the young to the theatre had been felt in Bonn, and at the beginning of the 1960s 'Junge Theatergemeinden' were founded also in Köln and Würzburg. Others soon followed and in 1981 the 'Bundesarbeitsgemeinschaft (BAG)' of the 'Junge Theatergemeinden (JTG)' held its first conference. By 1991 this was celebrating its tenth birthday.('Youth' was defined as 'under 27'.)

In addition to its periodical *Theater Rundschau*, still flourishing in the mid-1990s, the Bund der Theatergemeinden published between the late 1950s and early 1990s a series of some forty or more booklets on subjects as various as *Theatre in Schools*, *The Religious Element in Twentieth Century Opera*, and *Common Problems concerning Children in Children's Plays*, and an even larger series of booklets on individual plays including Webster's *The White Devil*, Synge's *Deirdre of the Sorrows*, Stoppard's *Night and Day*, as well as many by modern, and even contemporary German playwrights.

From 1984 onwards the Bund awarded a series of prizes for dramatists:

1. Dietrich Feldhausen (b.1941): *Kartoffelschalen*.
2. a. Ria Endres(b.1946): *Acht Weltmeister*
   b. Klaus Hoggenmüller (b.1954):*Wendels Heimat*
3. a. Tilman Hanckel: *IV B 4 (Das Eichmann-Experiment)*
   b. Ingrid Hentschel & Torsten Hänel: *CA IRA! es war einmal eine Revolution.*

(Hanckel withdrew his play from the proposed production and Torsten Enders' *Kowatz*, a runner-up, was produced instead.)

At the end of 1993 Dr Gotthard Welzel who had served the Bund as General Manager for several decades, had to retire because of his health. In him the Theatergemeinde movement lost the services of a great man, though apparently his family continued to be involved, as Dieter, Jürgen and Manfred Welzel were active in the Youth Organisation: Jürgen was its vice-chairman in 1991.

GENERAL INDEX

Note:
ä, ö, ü are indexed as a, o, u
The Definite Article is usually ignored in the alphabetical arrangement.
Orthographic variations (e.g. ss / ß) follow the sources cited.

INDEX OF NAMES

Other titles in the Contemporary Theatre Studies series:

This book is part of a series. The publisher will accept continuation orders which may be cancelled at any time and which provide for automatic billing and shipping of each title in the series upon publication. Please write for details.